WORKING ACROSS CULTURES

Working Across Cultures

John Hooker

STANFORD BUSINESS BOOKS

AN IMPRINT OF STANFORD UNIVERSITY PRESS

STANFORD, CALIFORNIA 2003

Stanford University Press
Stanford, California

© 2003 by John Hooker. All rights reserved.

Printed in the United States of America on acid-free, archival-quality paper

Library of Congress Cataloging-in-Publication Data

Hooker, John, 1949-
  Working across cultures / John Hooker.
    p. cm.
  Includes bibliographical references and index.
  ISBN 0-8047-4807-1 (alk. paper)
    1. Intercultural communication. 2. Cross-cultural orientation.
3. Multiculturalism. 4. Social values–Cross-cultural studies. 5. Business ethics.
6. International business enterprises–Social
aspects. I. Title.
HM1211.H66 2004
306–dc21

                                             2003007573

Designed by Rob Ehle.
Typeset by Interactive Composition Corporation in 10/12.5 Sabon.

Original Printing 2003

Last figure below indicates year of this printing:
12 11 10 09 08 07 06 05 04 03

Special discounts for bulk quantities of Stanford Business Books are available
to corporations, professional associations, and other organizations. For details
and discount information, contact the special sales department of Stanford
University Press. Tel: (650) 736-1783, Fax: (650) 736-1784

In memory of
Ken MacLeod, editor extraordinaire

The idea of a single civilization for everyone, implicit in the cult of progress and technique, impoverishes and mutilates us. Every view of the world that becomes extinct, every culture that disappears, diminishes a possibility of life.

Octavio Paz, 1967, quoted by Jamake Highwater in *The Primal Mind: Vision and Reality in Indian America* (Meridian Books, 1982: p. viii).

Table of Contents

Acknowledgments

A number of people have helped me explore world cultures. They include Sira Allende Alonzo, Kim Allan Andersen, Gautam Appa, İlker Baybars, Ömer Benli, Alexander Bockmayr, Uma and Vijay Chandru, Eleanor and Jim Crossley, Anna and Hero David, Boyé Lafayette De Mente, Ali Doğramacı, Erdal Erel, Sergio Fuentes Maya, Giorgio Gallo, Gu Huifang, A. M. Gumbo, John Kurewa, Li Xiangdong, Liu Yingming, Ken McKennon, Bruce McKern, Olukunle Iyanda, Maria Auxilio Osorio, Giacomo Patrizi, Clarence Da Gama Pinto, Franz Josef Radermacher, Jesús Sandoval, Lourdes Sandoval Solís, Dr. David Schwartzman, Bruno Simeone, Søren Tind, M. Vidyasagar, H. Paul Williams, Xu Chen, Yan Hong, Yang Jirui, Ye Naiyi, and Zhu Benshen. My apologies to those I omitted, and my thanks to all for their patience when I learned my cultural lessons the hard way: through blunders and faux pas. I also owe thanks to my agent Georges Borchardt and to the highly professional staff at Stanford University Press.

I make special mention of my editor Ken MacLeod, a man of wide-ranging interests and insight. Ken believed in this book and offered unwavering support, along with gentle and wise suggestions for improvement. He will not see the book in print, from an earthly perspective at any rate, since he passed away unexpectedly during its production.

1 *The Cultural Iceberg*

A bishop from the United States stood before a congregation of African women in Mutare, Zimbabwe. Sermons run long in Zimbabwe, and he honored the custom. About an hour into his homily, he began to discuss the conflict between the Tutsis and Hutus in Rwanda. Refugees from the civil war fled their homes so quickly that they had to leave everything behind. The bishop told about their desperate need for the basics of life, such as food and clothing.

At this point many of the women in the congregation began to disrobe. They brought their garments to the front of the auditorium and piled them before the pulpit. A bystander explained to the startled bishop that they were donating their clothes to the refugees. Did he not say that they needed clothing? The following day, the bishop noticed that several women were wearing large plastic bags. They had given away their only piece of clothing.

Someone told me this story shortly before I arrived in Mutare to take a teaching job. Knowing what I now know about the Shona people of the region, I do not doubt its accuracy for an instant. This kind of generosity is part of the culture.

We Westerners find Shona generosity bewildering because our culture is universalist. Most of us want to believe that everyone is basically like us. Naturally there are surface differences in language, cuisine, and customs, but any other differences are explained by the level of development. Other peoples are simply less advanced. The problem is that the Shona do not fit into this scheme. It is difficult to put their largesse on the same level as cuisine or custom, because this level of selflessness is scarcely conceivable in the West. Yet it is even less reasonable to attribute saintly behavior to a lack of development. I suggest a third possibility: the Shona operate on a radically different worldview than we do, one we cannot grasp unless we suspend some of our deepest assumptions about society and human nature.

We Westerners must change the way we think about other cultures. We must become aware of how our universalism narrows our perspective. In many ways it connects us with others, because it sustains our interest in the world and inspires us to give assistance and, perhaps all too often, advice. But this same universalism blocks our comprehension of what these cultures are all about, because we cannot acknowledge how fundamentally different they are.

The old analogy of the iceberg says it well. Culture lies primarily under the surface, beneath conscious awareness. This means that the most important cultural differences are invisible. It took me years to realize this, but when I did, my eyes began to open. I began to see different peoples as facing the same basic life problems but finding radically different solutions, solutions that challenge my deepest assumptions but that nonetheless have a logic of their own. Paradoxically, now that I recognize how different other peoples are, I am in a position to relate to them authentically and live and work among them successfully.

The purpose of this book is to help prepare Western professionals for the otherness of other cultures. It is written for the growing number of business people, negotiators, social workers, lawyers, physicians, military personnel—and, of course, clergy—who work on the international scene or in multicultural settings. It draws on the insights of cultural anthropology to understand culture as a fascinating subject in its own right, but it simultaneously infers practical lessons. The two are in fact inseparable, because it is through everyday experience that we learn how culture works.

The Western Mind-Set

Western culture is so called because it originated in the western part of the Eurasian land mass. It might be defined as the dominant culture of Europe and its ethnic offspring, including Australia, Canada, New Zealand, and the United States. Latin American countries owe much to their Western roots, but they differ significantly enough that it is convenient to follow Samuel P. Huntington[1] and classify them as non-Western.

We Westerners have always assumed that there is essentially one way to live: ours. Anyone who lives differently just needs some time, and perhaps some advice from us, to develop properly. This mind-set has shaped not only the West but also, to a great degree, the entire world. Half a millennium ago, European colonial powers began bringing the "three M's" to peoples around the globe: the military to subdue them, markets to realize a profit, and missionaries to tell them how to live and think like we do.

These habits persist. The global economic system, modeled after Western capitalism, propels "developing" countries down a path of rapidly rising resource consumption. The automobile fleet on Delhi streets doubles every few years, even though the air is already thick with pollutants. The World Bank and International Monetary Fund use unpaid debts as leverage to obtain further Westernization of national economies, with mixed results. After the fall of the Soviet Union, Western consultants flocked into Russia to try to install an economic system that runs contrary to almost every aspect of Russian history and culture. Its total failure became a spectacle that humiliated the Russian people before the world. Even the recent Asian financial crisis was arguably less an Asian than a Western failure, because investors tried to impose Western financial practices in a part of the world with a very different tradition.

Why are we Westerners like this? We live in the age of CNN and the Internet. Air travel is cheap, and business is global. Given so much contact with the world, why can we not appreciate that others have their own very different and legitimate ways? Part of the answer is that our encounters with other cultures are often inauthentic. TV, movies, and English-language Web pages provide a highly filtered version of life elsewhere. If they are to hold our interest, they must be intelligible and must therefore reinterpret reality to fit our worldview. Tourism keeps us in a managed world of hotels, restaurants, and tourist attractions. The protective bubble lets in some of the sights, sounds, and flavors of a foreign country but insulates us as much as possible from the culture itself, which travelers tend to find confusing and upsetting. Because so many travelers view culture as consisting of little more than its surface features, they do not sense the loss.

Business, however, brings many Westerners into direct and intimate contact with other peoples, and it has not been without its effect. In the old days Western business made little concession to the host culture, due to its economic hegemony. But Japan changed everything. During the 1980s, Japan built a formidable economic machine that set the standard of quality for the world, and the hegemonic balance began to tip. Northwest Airlines scheduled direct "auto executive" flights between Detroit and Tokyo. Business leaders worldwide began taking Japan seriously, and later the entire Pacific rim as Japanese investment spawned highly competitive industry in that part of the world. Conscious of their economic power and wary of foreigners by nature, Japanese business people expected Western visitors to make cultural adjustments. Those who refused hit a brick wall.

Western business people absorbed some genuine cultural lessons during this period. A stream of books on cross-cultural management appeared, and continues unabated. Corporations and consulting firms organized workshops on the same topic, and MBA programs offered courses in Japanese and Chinese. But even here, the primary reaction was to reduce culture to matters of language, customs, and etiquette. The cross-cultural guides warn that in Latin America one should not be offended if kept waiting for forty-five minutes, or if one's host takes care of other business simultaneously. In Germany one should keep the office door shut. In parts of Africa one should greet associates in the hallway, even if this means saying hello to the same person several times a day. If someone offers a business card in Japan, one should receive it with both hands, study it, and perhaps place it on the table in front of oneself.

Business people are willing to observe rules of etiquette, but too often only because offensive behavior can distract attention from the business at hand. Too many regard the business itself as the same game whether played in Boston or Bangkok. In reality, deeply held cultural assumptions shape both etiquette and business. Latin Americans tend to be late because their underlying conception of time is different. Germans have their own sense of space that requires order and privacy. For many Africans, human existence is irreducibly communal; failing to acknowledge another person is subhuman. Japanese build their society on group harmony; whence the importance of respecting others through business card rituals and a thousand other courtesies.

Business is likewise grounded in culture. It owes its existence to the fact that people have certain attitudes toward commitments, authority, work, and community. Only something as deep and pervasive as culture can inculcate these behaviors, and business simply takes advantage of them. It is a ripple on an ocean of culture.

The question remains: why do Westerners resist the fundamental differences between themselves and others, even others with whom they work closely in the business world? It is because our universalism is an essential component of our culture. It is inextricably related to our sense of time, the way we process information, our faith in reason, our reliance on technology, our belief in progress, our egalitarianism, our secularism, our romanticism, our neglect of courtesy, our missionary impulse, our exploitation of nature, our expansionism and colonialism, our respect for law, our guilt complex, our fascination with natural science, our mechanisms for dealing with stress, and even our peculiar sense of humor. These elements support one another, much as the organisms in an ecosystem do.

All cultures are systems of this sort, and I will undertake to describe some of them. Only this will, I believe, fully reveal how radically cultures differ and prepare us to deal with the differences.

Culture and Language

When I step off the plane in Guangzhou, I cannot understand a word of the Cantonese dialect spoken there. Yet the language is only part of the system of practices and institutions that make up Cantonese culture. Why should I expect everything else to be transparent? The whole culture is likely to be as strange as the language.

Cultures differ as radically as languages because they themselves are, in part, extended languages. The set of behaviors we call "language" is a subset of a larger set of meaningful behaviors that help to define a culture. A culture bestows meaning on all of its practices in the very same way that it gives meaning to words.

This view traces to the philosopher Ludwig Wittgenstein, about whom I will say more in Chapter 4, but a brief explanation is possible now. Suppose I scratch my head. If someone just asked me a difficult question, this may mean I am perplexed. If I am sitting in a Sotheby's auction, I may have just bid £10,000. If I am driving alone, it may be nothing more than relieving an itch. The gesture obtains its meaning from the role it plays in a social practice and the way people respond to it. Its meaning may therefore vary from one situation to another, or it may have no meaning at all.

The meaning of a gesture can vary across cultures as well as within a culture. Pounding one's fist into one's hand emphasizes a point in the United States but is obscene in Singapore. A woman in the United States who wears a scarf may simply be protecting her hair from the wind. A woman in Germany who does the same identifies herself as Muslim.

Wittgenstein emphasized that words receive their meaning contextually, just as gestures do, rather than by dictionary definitions. The same principle applies to more complex behaviors and even institutions. Think about what it means to wear a white dress, say "I do," and receive a ring while standing in a church, versus what it means to do the same while standing on the stage of a playhouse. Marriage means what it does because of the practices and expectations that surround it. Culture gives them meaning in the same way it gives meaning to words, gestures, and attire. Culture is a maker of meaning. The meaning of the whole is likely to be no less obscure to an outsider than the meaning of the part we somewhat arbitrarily call "language."

I may protest that when I step into the culture of Guangzhou, Westerner though I be, I am quite well aware of how different it is. The traffic is chaotic and frightening, the sewers leak (or do not exist), and the high-rise flats are appallingly crowded. But the Westerner in me writes these off to a lack of development. Chinese are still basically like Americans, or least they will be once they learn better. This is why Bill Clinton can travel to Beijing and tell President Jiang how to run his country.

This is not to suggest that only Westerners have a sense of superiority. Most peoples regard others as inferior. The Chinese themselves call their country *Zhōngguó* (central kingdom), because they traditionally consider themselves the center of civilization and see Westerners, for example, as close to barbarism. The very word *barbaric* reflects the ancient Greek taunt that foreigners say nonsense syllables ("ba ba") because they are too ignorant to have a coherent language. The Western sense of superiority differs because of its universalist twist: it regards other cultures as less developed.

It sees the nations of the world as more or less advanced on a single ladder of development (with Western nations obviously on the upper rungs), rather than as advancing in fundamentally different directions. Only Westerners would describe as "developing" a nation that was already ancient and highly developed when European civilization was still in diapers.

This attitude reflects our own cultural needs more than arrogance, but it gets us into trouble. If I am in Guangzhou on business, for example, my failure to acknowledge how different it is can lead to increasing frustration and anxiety. I attend my first meeting, but no one seems to be serious about making a deal. Back home I can negotiate with people I met only yesterday, but here it is best to build a long-term relationship (*guānxi*) with my business partners. At home, agreements are based on a legal framework that presupposes the universality of rules and law. Westerners, bless their hearts, can believe in this, but Chinese ultimately cannot. For them a piece of legal paper is worthless, and deals are grounded in flesh and blood, that is, in personal relationships of trust and mutual obligation. I may eventually convince my partners to sign a Western-style contract, but the next day they want to renegotiate. To them, the idea of slavish adherence to what is written on paper, when the world changes daily, is perverse. As the business gets under way, my associates may want to put their relatives in key positions. To my mind nepotism is bad business and probably unethical, but here contractual obligation to a firm is a concept with little meaning, whereas loyalty to the extended family has powered a great civilization for five thousand years. My associates expect me to keep an eye on lower-level employees constantly, even though I am accustomed to giving instructions at the beginning of the day and checking on things occasionally. It has not occurred to me that internalized rules and guilt play a more important motivational role in my own culture than in China. Here in Guangzhou, employees are equally responsible, but they respond to people rather than guilt. I have concerns about how the business is run, but when the president of the firm is in the room, everyone simply agrees with what he says, and no one wants to bring up problems in the company. Authority is conceived in a very different way here.

In addition to these mounting frustrations, I seem to be unable to predict what my associates will say or do next. Sometimes they seem perfectly reasonable, but moments later they come up with irrational and inexplicable ideas. The irrationality of the system itself, as I see it, almost defies belief. Every company action requires approvals from layers of bureaucrats who seem to know little about the business and who sometimes want something in return. Worse, the process drags on interminably. I cannot understand why the Chinese people would do this to themselves.

Yet the Chinese built a civilization that has flourished for eons. It also occurs to me that my own country might appear equally dysfunctional to a

Chinese visitor. Every news broadcast is saturated with reports of crime and violence; poverty and despair persist amid incredible affluence; and perhaps most shockingly to Chinese sensibilities, elders often languish in institutions without financial or personal support from those who owe them their being. Yet one can see these as flaws in a greater system that has much to recommend it. One can presumably achieve a similar perspective in China, if one understands how the culture works.

Such is the purpose of this book. It attempts to prepare the reader to understand and cope with a strange country by explaining how its system is put together, much as a grammar text prepares one to learn a language.

Cultural grammar can be viewed as the way people solve life's basic problems. One particularly thorny problem is stress, which results from our lack of control over what happens to us. Westerners turn to science and technology for a sense of control. This is why we have so much technology—not because we are smarter or more highly developed. Chinese organize themselves around strong families, respect for age and authority, *guānxì*, superstition, and rituals. Chinese developed such key technologies as the compass and gunpowder, but only the West felt the need to use them to control their environment, for instance by colonizing much of the world. If we view cultures as stress-management mechanisms, incomprehensible behavior begins to make sense. Even better, we can use this understanding to cope with life as the locals do.

How does one learn a culture? Much as one learns its language. It is best done with a combination of intellectual preparation and immersion, as neither method alone seems optimal. One can learn a foreign language in orderly, intellectual fashion on home shores, but only with diligent study and much discipline. Alternatively, one can learn it by absorption, particularly when cast into an alien environment and survival demands it. There are teaching methods that eschew all intellectual treatment and try to duplicate the learning process of a child. But for adult learning, it seems better to use the intellectual resources that adults have and children do not. Systematic study can lay the groundwork for later learning by immersion.

Why Understand Culture?

Our age calls for cultural awareness at both the social and the professional levels. Socially, we sense that culture is somehow at the root of the major issues of the day. The reasons are evident enough. Immigrants of widely different backgrounds pour into Western countries in unprecedented numbers. At the same time, the Western economic system stretches its tentacles into every corner of the earth, restructuring economies and cultures.

The result is cultural change and disruption around the globe. One cannot pick up the daily newspaper without reading of ethnic struggle on several continents. The growing concentration of wealth exacerbates the tension between rich and poor. Resentment of cultural change and Western economic dominance inspires terrorism and the rise of militant fundamentalism. Western nations struggle with the task of holding their diverse populations together. People in the United States, the most multicultural of nations, talk of culture wars, fear resurgent racism, flee crime and violence, and come to blows over such social issues as abortion. Anyone who doubts the power of culture can think about how some ordinary, decent people in the Balkans became monsters overnight when ethnic hatred was unleashed.

Culture is the theme of our age. Our most pressing issues are profoundly cultural in nature. We try to address them, but without an appreciation of how deeply culture determines our worldviews, we can only grope and fumble.

On a professional level, cultural understanding helps us adjust to unfamiliar environments in which we must work. The term *culture shock* is unfortunate, because it suggests that there is an initial shock when one gets off the plane, and it goes away after a few days. The initial shock may or may not happen. One who has always lived in an affluent nation and flies into Conakry, capital of Guinea, is in for a shock. However, one who flies into Beijing is more likely to be delighted and impressed than shocked during an initial period. The problem is adjusting over the longer term. Dealing with the stress of not understanding the language, never really knowing what is going on, and having to deal with behavior that seems strange, annoying, or downright insulting requires an enormous amount of energy. Initially one operates on an adrenaline high and can deal with it. But eventually one's body and psyche want to return to a more normal state. One begins looking for a way out.

If one intends to live or work in a new cultural environment, previous experience can be misleading. Long and extensive travel without adjustment problems is no indication of what it may be like actually to live or work in a strange culture. As already mentioned, the typical traveler is insulated from the indigenous society that supplies the cooks and the maids. Even the international backpacker may have no idea what it means to work in an unfamiliar country. Hitching rides in rural Kazakstan can be physically and emotionally demanding, but it is a different kind of challenge. A backpacker interacts with the locals primarily on the basic level of obtaining food, shelter, and transport. There is little real engagement with a culture. In fact, the backpacking experience is much less an encounter with other cultures than a rite of passage in the backpacker's own culture. It is no accident that almost all international backpackers are from northern

Europe, North America, and Australia. By contrast, a person who lives and works in a culture, negotiates agreements, supervises employees, and develops a market must engage the culture at a sophisticated level.

One strategy for avoiding burnout is to seek out aspects of the culture one can learn to appreciate or enjoy, and then make the most of them. This obviously works best when one knows something about the culture. This is an obvious strategy in such matters as food, for instance in China, internationally known for its advanced cuisine. But it is important to know what one is doing. Not only are bad restaurants legion, but Chinese food can be very different in China than elsewhere. I have eaten soup that is indistinguishable from newsprint and hot water ground to pulp in a blender. (I will forgo a description of the sea beetles and tendon sheath.) But food that is amenable to one's palate is almost certain to be better than the daily fare back home. This is something to which one can look forward every day to help get past the rough spots.

This strategy can be generalized, and one can take it a certain distance even without a deeper knowledge of the culture. In India there is a wide selection of English-language newspapers, written with eloquence and intelligence; one should not miss the letters to the editor, a favorite pastime for would-be writers. In Scandinavia cyclists can pursue their hobby on bicycle-friendly streets. Tokyo is a huge, crowded city, but one can explore without fear of crime. In Mexico a request for assistance in broken Spanish receives a friendly response. If one seeks them out, these small pleasures will accumulate and help convert an overall negative experience to a positive one.

Small pleasures cannot, however, carry the full weight of cultural adjustment. Stress is ultimately generated by a feeling that one has no control over the situation. Knowledge of the culture helps create a sense of mastery that relieves much of the stress. Furthermore, every culture has its own distinctive mechanisms for dealing with stress. This is an aspect of culture so fundamental that it can serve as a principle around which one's understanding of a country is organized. It can be a great relief to plug into a society's stress-management mechanism, particularly if one moves from the relatively weak postindustrial mainstream culture of the United States, which provides little support in this area, to a strong, traditional culture. But doing so requires a rather deep knowledge of how the culture works.

A bonus of cultural knowledge is the favorable impression it makes on one's hosts. Most peoples are quite sensitive about perceived attitudes toward their culture. A lack of knowledge or enthusiasm may be interpreted as an insult, as a signal that their culture is not worth learning about. They are likely to respond warmly, on the other hand, to active interest and involvement. In most of the world, developing personal relationships is absolutely essential to getting anything done. If people sense respect for their culture, this is likely to go a long way toward building indispensable professional relationships.

Is the World Westernizing?

The case for understanding world cultures is multifaceted and over-whelming. Yet many people remain unconvinced, for at least two reasons. One is the belief that world cultures are converging to a Western standard, at least at the upper echelons of society. Knowledge of Western culture is therefore quite enough to succeed personally and to understand world events. Others argue that even if residual differences persist, countries interact primarily on the level of trade and commerce, where the bottom line and the laws of economics govern irrespective of culture. Both arguments are fallacious.

It is understandable why one would gather the impression that world cultures are converging. The spread of capitalism is apparently bringing a single economic way of life to peoples around the world, and everyone knows that culture is profoundly shaped by how people make a living. Global business supplies the entire world with basically the same products and services. High-tech communication systems pipe the same Western-style entertainment into homes everywhere and link the world with the Internet. English is the language of business and air traffic control around the globe.

Not only do global business and communications homogenize the world, but there is another factor at work. Money attracts. The elites in any country instinctively gravitate toward the culture that represents wealth and power, and the lower classes follow to the extent they can. For the last few centuries the center of gravity for many has been the West. Ambitious people learn European languages, cultivate Western connections, send their children to Western universities. They adopt the manners and mores of the West not only to lubricate this process but also to increase their prestige at home.

Because world cultures are converging to a quasi-Western state, so the argument goes, there is little need to learn about other cultures. The convergence of cultures thesis, however, simply does not square with the facts.

Consider, for example, the claim that capitalism is homogenizing the world. Even if we grant that capitalism has the power to homogenize, countries with a stock exchange may be capitalist only in the nominal sense in which some nations with a parliament are democratic. Quasi-socialism in Sweden, fierce competition in the United States, *keiretsu* in Japan, *chaebol* in South Korea, corruption in Venezuela, and cronyism in Indonesia make for very different economic systems that require wholly different skills from its participants. There is a mini-industry of books, workshops, and consultants that help international business people acquire these skills. It is one reason I write this book. It is a testament to the primacy of culture that this diversity remains despite Western efforts to install its economic philosophy worldwide.

As for Western products and media, do they Westernize? At one level arguments of this sort are almost humorous. Many people actually fear that McDonald's restaurants endanger their culture, although this concern rarely extends to the Chinese and Italian restaurants that cover the globe. The source of these attitudes is the common habit of trivializing culture, of reducing it to such surface matters as cuisine. When I tell my students that Chinese culture would be essentially the same if everyone in China ate *sauerbraten* and *spätzle* rather than *miàn* and *shāo mǎi* (noodles and dumplings), they are outraged, particularly those of Chinese descent.

On another level, however, an influx of Western consumer goods can transform lifestyle. If skyscrapers and traffic jams replace villages and rice paddies, something has changed. But they replaced villages and farms right here in the West, many things changed, and yet we are still Westerners. Cultures can change without losing their identity. Jakarta looks like Atlanta from the air, and life there is very different from life in the provinces. But on the ground, it is still very much Indonesian and cultural light years from Atlanta. As for media, consider that Europeans have been exposed to a steady stream of Hollywood movies and TV shows for half a century. They complain bitterly about degradation of their culture, but they remain very much Europeans.

The analogy of an ecosystem is helpful. If someone introduces Mexican plants into Hawaii, they may very well bring change. They may find their own niche in the system, or grow uncontrollably, or just die out. In no case does Hawaii become Mexico. It is still Hawaii, perhaps altered, perhaps damaged, or even enhanced. So it is with cultural influences.

The West may admittedly change cultures beyond recognition if its influence is large enough and lasts long enough. But they will all change in different ways. In fact, this lesson is already before us. Islam exerted a powerful influence on the Middle East, northern Africa, and parts of Asia. Yet these regions remain vastly different culturally. It is true that the European colonial powers achieved greater homogenization in regions of North and South America. But this is only because they systematically suppressed the indigenous cultures and brought smallpox and other European diseases that decimated the native populations.

The attraction of Western prosperity, however, may be viewed as a more insidious influence. Not only do elites worldwide drive Mercedes automobiles and watch the Disney Channel; some deliberately set out to immerse themselves and their children in Western culture. Yet this influence lasts only as long as the West remains economically dominant. The 1980s reminded us that the tables can turn. Asian economies achieved growth rates unprecedented in the West, and Japanese industry had American executives shaking in their boots. Huntington[2] points out that even during this short period, Asians began to reject Western cultural dominance. Their leaders noted that the Philippines, a former U.S. protectorate, remained an economic basket case while the nearby Tigers were flourishing. For them this illustrated the superiority of Asian values. Singapore's Lee Kuan Yew, who built his country partially after the Western example, developed new interest in his Chinese heritage. Even in the West, people began studying Asian languages, took up chi gong (in Chinese *qìgōng,* which roughly means "energy exercise"), experimented with acupuncture, and decorated their apartments according to the ancient guidelines of *fēng shuǐ.*

The Asian financial crisis of the early 1990s seems to have convinced many people that the Asian boom was hollow and that the West will continue to rule economically. Before jumping to this conclusion, it is wise to examine the crisis a little more closely. I suggested earlier that it resulted not so much from Asian failure as from a misguided attempt to impose the Western financial system. Consider Asian manufacturing, which is a spectacular success. Even though manufacturing is a global activity, portions in Asia have been customized to Asian culture, particularly in Japan and South Korea. International finance, however, is more difficult to localize than manufacturing. Traditional Asian finance is based on investment in trusted friends and family members, which is in direct contradiction to Western practices. Too many investors, from both East and West, relied on equity markets and Western-style loans without cultivating the necessary relationships. The problem was not too much cronyism, as the Western press tells us, but too little. (More accurately, the old ways were too much altered by outside influences to work properly.) It is no wonder that disaster ensued. The situation would be roughly analogous to one in which all the major players on Western stock exchanges began using inside information.

Interestingly, China and Taiwan largely retained family-based finance, thanks to investment cash that poured in from relatives in Hong Kong and the Chinese communities of Southeast Asia, Vancouver, Toronto, and San Francisco. I have never seen it mentioned in the Western media that these two countries fared much better than most of their neighbors during the crisis. Perhaps the rest of Asia will in time learn to attract foreign capital on its own cultural terms. If it does, Asian economic recovery will accelerate, and the center of gravity will perhaps again move east.

Few even claim to have predicted the Asian crisis a week before the Thai currency collapsed. How can we predict that Western economic dominance will endure long enough to cement its influence? From a broader historical perspective, we see that cultural fads can come and go in the upper classes without much effect on the society at large. When France was the dominant European power, many elites in Europe and North America learned French and sent their children to Paris to study. Now it is all forgotten.

An even more transient phenomenon is youth culture. Its sameness around the world is admittedly remarkable, alarming to some. Teenagers everywhere wear the same blue jeans and sneakers, admire the same performers, and watch the same movies and TV shows. I have been told that every young person in Beijing and Shanghai saw *Titanic* two or three times. But youth culture is not culture; it is a passing phase in the larger culture, the one that holds society together. Even in northern Europe, the epicenter of post-1960s Western youth culture, young people suddenly grow up at about age twenty-seven, stop sleeping in youth hostels, start using formal second-person pronouns, and join mainstream adult society. Countless establishment Chinese once belonged to the Red Guards, another 1960s phenomenon, and perhaps the largest and most extreme youth movement of the twentieth century. (One businessman told me that the major preoccupation of his youth was finding enough glue to put up Maoist posters.) Cultural identity is primarily forged during early and middle childhood, not during rock concerts or Communist Party meetings.

Global business and media not only fail to homogenize the world, but the net effect of their influence may be precisely the opposite. Benjamin Barber was one of the earliest to recognize the full implications of this in his prophetic book *Jihad vs. McWorld*. Barber marveled at how the supposedly centripetal forces of business and media seem to go hand in hand with the centrifugal forces of religious and ethnic separatism. He asked, how can the world continue to fragment along ethnic lines when the very participants in ethnic struggles are plugged into the same global market, and their thinking is influenced by the same "infotainment telesector"? He grimly remarked that the bodies of young victims on opposite sides of the Balkan struggles were found clad in the same brand of tennis shoes and jeans.

Barber proposed an explanation. Global business and media weaken the nation state and the civic institutions it represents by making them increasingly irrelevant. More ancient forms of social organization fill the void, as nation states fracture along ethnic and religious lines. The growing irrelevance of the nation state is clear in everyday life. Many immigrants have little interest in citizenship as long as they can obtain a work permit. Newcomers to the United States, for instance, can get a green card, a job, and a share of U.S. prosperity without being a citizen. Certain welfare benefits are tied to citizenship, but aside from this, little rides on it except the right to vote. Even this is of minimal concern in the United States, as most eligible voters do not bother to exercise this privilege. They do not bother because, again, the nation state and its political subdivisions are becoming less relevant. Geographical proximity, which once bound people into the community of discourse that is so vital for civic institutions, no longer matters so much. Furthermore, the quality of life is determined primarily by the products, services, and jobs available. These, in turn, are a function of global economic forces that nation states have limited power to influence. In fact, no government can stand between the consumer and the global market for very long. The Soviet Union collapsed ultimately because it did just this. The same forces that destroyed the Soviet Union are eating away at authoritarian and democratic states alike around the world. As ethnic and religious allegiances supplant nation states, it becomes more difficult for people to let go of their cultural identification even when they want to do so. The cohesion of their society now depends on it. Cultural differences are cemented into place.

Interestingly, the media now seem to be increasingly shaped by culture rather than vice versa. News and other broadcasts are often tailored to regional audiences with common interests and viewpoints. CNN, once a window on the world, is now so regionalized that it has lost much of its value as an international news source.

The decline of the nation state is by no means the only mechanism that retards the Westernization of the world. Another is simple distaste for what is perceived as Western decadence or immorality. True, the craving for Western media and consumer goods is nearly universal, and societies undergo massive change as they build the kind of economic system that can satisfy these appetites. At a physical level they look increasingly Western, as skyscrapers go up, streets clog with automobiles, lives are cluttered with consumer goods, and per capita resource consumption rises ominously to Western levels. But change is not the same as convergence, and physical resemblance does not imply cultural homogeneity. In one nation after another we see a struggle to import the baubles and bangles of the West while keeping its questionable culture at arm's length. One thinks immediately of the Islamic world, but parts of the Confucian realm equally fear contamination with Western drugs, crime, and licentiousness.

Business Is Business

Those who acknowledge the reality of cultural difference may nonetheless insist that it does not matter. Business and trade drive the world today. They respond to the laws of economics and the imperative of the bottom line. A stock market is a stock market, whether it be the Copenhagen bourse or the NASDAQ exchange. A deal is a deal, regardless of the accents of the negotiators. Anthropologists tell us about the wide variety of trade rituals among traditional societies, but once a market system evolves, the laws of the marketplace take over. The adjustment of prices to equilibrate supply and demand is a dynamic that follows the internal logic of exchange. It operates as surely as the law of gravity. The internationalist's job is therefore to understand business and economics, not anthropology.

Let us grant for the sake of argument that world affairs reduce to business and trade relations between nations. It still must be shown that business and trade can be explained apart from culture. They cannot.

The desire to find universal laws is a deeply embedded trait of Western culture. Sometimes the search is successful, and in the case of the marketplace there is indeed an internal logic at work. Western economic science has made a major contribution by describing it. Its yearning for universality, however, has prevented it from appreciating the extent to which these economic laws under-determine economic behavior.

Perhaps it is best to begin with parables. Cooking proceeds according to the same laws of chemistry in a Manhattan microwave oven as over a Pakistani dung fire. Yet within the framework of these basic laws, and to our great delight, a stunning variety of cooking styles can evolve. It is quite a stretch to suppose that the laws of chemistry explain the development of *boeuf bourguignonne* regardless of cultural input. One who thinks otherwise should take care not to say so in earshot of a French chef.

Or consider the behavior of drivers on city streets. There is a certain internal logic to vehicular traffic. Two automobiles cannot occupy the same place at the same time, short of mutual destruction. This implies an inherent efficiency in traffic patterns in which vehicles on opposite sides of the street move in opposite directions. (Perhaps a thoroughgoing Westerner will deduce at this point whether drivers will keep to the left or the right!) Due to physical constraints on reaction times and stopping distances, a vehicle or pedestrian cannot arbitrarily cross a stream of vehicles without disastrous results. Some provision must be made for yielding to others. One might therefore expect to see certain regularities in traffic patterns around the world.

Now consider driving behavior in two cities I have visited, Chicago and Chengdu. To cross Chicago's Lake Shore Drive, one must traverse several lanes of fast-moving cars, trucks, and buses. One option is to press a button on a traffic signal. When the signal eventually changes, nearly all of the drivers will stop, perhaps with some annoyance. One must simply watch for any who do not. If there is no signal nearby, it is necessary to wait for a gap in the traffic and dash across. Any oncoming cars will expect pedestrians to stay out of the way. If they do not, the driver will slam on the brakes at the last instant, and a serious or fatal accident is possible.

Now consider the task of crossing Chengdu's Renmin Xi Lu. A very few years ago this major city and capital of Sichuan Province had few traffic signals, and crossing at one was probably not a realistic option. Pedestrians had somehow to make their way through a constant stream of bicycles and rickshaws, then through a stream of motorcycles and three-wheeled vehicles, then through a stream of cars, taxi vans, overloaded buses, and enormous roaring trucks with broken headlights and unsure brakes, and then through the same sequence in reverse order as they approached the opposite side. The vehicles did not organize themselves into lanes, although the great majority of vehicles on a given side of the centerline moved in the same direction; this, at least, was predicted by the universal laws of traffic. If ignorant visitors attempted to wait for a gap and dash through, their lives were in danger, and this remains true today. Rather, pedestrians must negotiate their way across. The cyclists and drivers will see them and make a certain limited allowance for their passage. Motorists must anticipate when and how much to yield, and pedestrians must pace themselves to be at the right place when they do so. Motorists work their way through an intersection much less by observing traffic rules than by one-on-one negotiation.

Superhighways recently replaced the "two-lane" rural highways that once surrounded the city, but no one will soon forget what the old roads were like. Two cars abreast might pass a third car simultaneously. Vehicles approaching from the opposite direction had to veer onto the shoulder, despite the fact that it was lined with pedestrians, farm animals, and agricultural products laid out to dry on the pavement. Somehow it worked, although the same behavior would be unthinkable and deadly in the United States. Part of the difference is in the superior skill of Chinese drivers, a greater fraction of whom are professionals. The rest lies in a different set of cultural conventions.

Go to another country and the conventions are different. Drivers in Indian cities, for example, rely heavily on their car horns. Here the polite driver honks constantly at other drivers who are about to weave in front of him. Some vehicles even display signs in the rear imploring other drivers to sound the horn. The horns are navigational beacons that help drivers find their way through interstices in the traffic. It is remarkable to observe the peaceful and unperturbed expressions of drivers as they pound on their horns. One can imagine the flow of adrenaline and clogging of the arteries that would accompany this behavior in Chicago.

The point, again, is that universal physical laws govern traffic behavior but radically under-determine it. Culture does the rest. So it is with economic behavior. Western economic analysis is based primarily on the assumption that the economy consists of atomistic, utility-maximizing individuals. The assumption is particularly explicit in neoclassical economics, which is the reigning economic orthodoxy of First World nations. (Ironically, it provides the basis on which the World Bank and International Monetary Fund have imposed austerity measures on *non*-Western "developing" nations—such measures as national debt ceilings that the Western world itself would not and could not observe.)

There is a certain internal logic about exchange that neoclassical economics correctly identifies. If there is a shortage of cooking oil, then other things being equal (an infamous phrase in economics), its price will rise. But the very language, "its price will rise," falsifies the situation. Prices do not rise as does the pressure of gas in a heated vessel. As George P. Brockway points out in his book, *The End of Economic Man,*[3] price is the result of conscious decisions on the part of human beings. Neoclassicists will doubtless respond that, yes, human beings may consider many factors when making economic decisions. But in the end and on the average, we act in our individual self-interest. If there is a shortage of cooking oil, some individuals will find it advantageous to bid higher, and oil will sell at a higher price. But here again, even in this simplified scenario, there is a fundamental mistake. Perhaps one individual will break into the store and take all the cooking oil, making the bids of others irrelevant.

The neoclassicists respond that they are describing the behavior of an orderly and honest marketplace, not anarchy. Adam Smith himself emphasized that the invisible hand can operate only in a context of certain moral sentiments.[4] Yet moral sentiments are a cultural phenomenon, and they may not match neoclassical assumptions. The community may organize a boycott to protest what they see as price gouging and set up a picket line to discourage anyone who would pay the inflated price. Boycotts, respond the economists, are "externalities." Naturally the laws of the marketplace will not operate when people interfere with the market. It is not hard to see where this is going. Any behavior that violates the basic assumptions of the field is by definition not the behavior of the marketplace. By making this move, economic theory denies itself the possibility of answering its own fundamental question—does it describe the real world or a fictitious one?

To answer this question, one must observe the culture and try to understand how it supports economic behavior. One can occasionally find behavior in real societies that approximates that of independent, self-interested individuals bidding on goods and services. But economic and business activity involve much more than this. The single most important determinant of economic behavior is what people want, that is, the desires that create the demand side of the supply-demand equation. The economy would be vastly different if people wanted to spend most of their money on lifetime learning rather than consumer goods. The anthropologist Mary Catherine Bateson suggests that the more affluent societies may in fact be moving in this direction.[5] These are matters that classical economics never attempted to explain. In other words, the whole issue of marketing, whose importance few businesspeople doubt, was never under the economics umbrella in the first place. It has always been a matter of culture and psychology.

Beyond marketing is the issue of work. The fact that a specific fraction of people want to work at all, rather than accept support from relatives, the state, or criminal activity, is culturally determined. The same holds for how long they work, how hard they work, what is considered useful work, and what is considered work at all. I once frequented a coffee stand in India that employed three people sitting side by side at a table: one who sold tickets for a fraction of a rupee (about five cents U.S.), one to take tickets from customers, and one to pour delicious, aromatic, fresh coffee, grown just outside of town, into tiny cups. In India this is a natural and unquestioned employment of labor. Ah, but it only reflects a labor surplus and is therefore explicable by economic law, says the neoclassical economist. Historical economic conditions no doubt influence cultural attitudes, but they are cultural nonetheless. If this seems doubtful, let me ask: would a Westerner hire three people to operate one coffee pot at an outdoor stand, even if he or she could employ them for ten cents an hour?

There is more. The types of work people are willing and prepared to do, whether it be cleaning toilets or running a corporation, depends in large part on the roles assigned their social class. Supply-and-demand equilibration does not explain why some people risk their jobs by showing up late repeatedly while others are punctual by nature. It does not explain firm loyalty: whether workers will flit from one employer to another for slightly better salaries or working conditions, or whether they prefer a lifetime commitment to one firm. Nor does it predict whether employers are willing to reciprocate this commitment. A large, hierarchical organization peopled by professional managers with considerable autonomy, so common in Europe and the United States, is hard to find in China's private sector, where most organizations are flat, authoritarian, and family controlled. Economic theory has little to say about this or other organizational matters. It does not predict whether firms prefer written or oral contracts, whether agreements will be kept, whether they are considered final or subject to continuous revision, or least of all what kind of negotiation is necessary to forge them. All of these matters are of central concern to the business person, and all are culturally based.

This could go on for the rest of the book. In fact it does. Ultimately the best way to be convinced that Western-style economic theory radically under-determines economic behavior is to examine specifically the role played by cultural factors.

The Rest of This Book

The ideas surrounding culture cannot be presented sequentially. Like the organs of a body, they must be understood through their relationship to one another. This is why the text constantly makes reference to concepts that have not yet been fully explained. There is no alternative. One must be patient and wait for the picture to emerge gradually.

The arrangement of chapters is based on what seems to work best in classroom and workshop experience. Chapters tend to alternate between descriptions of specific cultures and more general discussions, although every chapter contains concrete examples. The country-specific chapters provide a brief introduction to the language(s) of the country. Much of the material reflects field experience, a characteristic that tends to distinguish anthropological literature. Whereas the West's "low context" culture expects documentation by numerical data and publicly available sources, most countries have "high context" cultures in which one can glean significant information only by living there. I draw from the fieldwork of others, and cite it when I do, but I also rely heavily on my own experience, both to obtain firsthand information and to acquire some judgment about which secondary sources are reliable.

I begin with a cross-cultural discussion of time, space, and information, because these concepts are relatively easy to grasp and nonetheless have a good deal of practical value. I then take on the issue of whether rich countries are rich because of their culture and say a good deal about the Japanese economy. This will help develop the important distinction between rule-based and relationship-based cultures. Next I return to a more general discussion of how cultures are different from races, ethnic groups, and sub-cultures. Following this are in-depth studies of Mexico in one chapter, and Germany and Denmark in the next. Chapter 7 then presents various schemes for classifying cultures, each of which is questionable on some ground but useful in providing conceptual framework within which to think about culture. Chapter 8, the central chapter of this book, develops the idea of culture as a stress-management system and integrates the ideas so far presented into this framework. This lays the foundation for discussing the massive Chinese and Indian civilizations in the next two chapters. Chapter 11 takes up Western culture, which can now be seen in perspective. I believe that the intellectual puzzle pieces of culture will begin to fall into place at this point. The next two chapters analyze Turkey and Zimbabwe, respectively, with the benefit of the full conceptual framework. Chapter 14 takes up the issue of cultural relativism: is it possible to judge other cultures by an absolute standard? When is it ethical to "do as the Romans do"? The last chapter takes up the issue of multiculturalism, with emphasis on the United States. For those who wish to study the culture of a specific destination, the book ends with a reading list organized by 125 countries.

Finally, a caveat. The discussion to follow is somewhat frank about world cultures, as it must be if it is to be true to the subject. I take a clinical approach, much as one would do in medical school. This is not to suggest that one should discuss culture in frank terms, or in any terms at all, with associates, any more than one would ask about a friend's hemorrhoids. Most people around the world have a strong ego involvement with their culture or ethnic group and are extremely sensitive about the subject. My advice is to say absolutely nothing, good or bad, that can be interpreted as reflecting on the local culture. Even a comment that seems flattering is, at best, likely to come across as patronizing.

It is perfectly acceptable to say that one had a productive visit in Taipei or was impressed by the pyramids at Teotihuacan. These describe personal experience. But to be on the safe side, one should not say that Taiwanese are productive, or that Mexico has an impressive cultural background. U.S. nationals must exercise particular caution. Their multiethnic nature leads them to underestimate how intensely people from more homogeneous countries can identify with their national culture.

Although candid, my comments are not intended to reflect positively or negatively on any culture. Cross-cultural judgments may be possible in principle, but my purpose here is simply to understand. I have neither the wisdom nor the desire to pass judgment. For me every culture is a source of fascination, because it must encompass all of life and give it meaning.

Notes for Chapter 1

1. Samuel P. Huntington, *The Clash of Civilizations and the Remaking of World Order,* Simon and Schuster (New York, 1996).

2. Ibid., 93.

3. George P. Brockway, *The End of Economic Man,* 3d ed., W. W. Norton (New York, 1995).

4. Adam Smith, *The Theory of Moral Sentiments,* Library Classics (Indianapolis, 1982).

5. Mary Catherine Bateson, *Peripheral Visions,* HarperCollins (New York, 1994).

2 *Space, Time, and Context*

Space and time are objective properties of the physical world that have nothing much to do with culture. At any rate, this is the Western view. It is mistaken, and its mistake helps to teach a central lesson of this book: assumptions that seem obvious and inevitable, in this case assumptions about the nature of space and time, need not hold across cultures. A study of space and time also provides a good deal of practical guidance for navigating unfamiliar cultures.

The Navajo people, who live in the southwestern United States, illustrate how radically cultural conceptions of space and time can differ. For most of us, the world consists of objects that are arranged in space and endure a certain amount of time. We can scarcely conceive of anything else. For the traditional Navajo, however, the world is made up of processes.[1] If I put a plate on a table, then in my worldview two objects are involved: a plate and a table. The Navajo conception is hard to describe in English, but basically there is a single entity involved, a process of putting. The Athabascan tongue of the Navajo reflects this metaphysics. It is organized almost entirely around verbs, one of which may have more than a hundred inflections. Rather than put a plate on the table, I simply put. The inflection of the verb indicates, along with the context, what is being put and where it is being put. The language is so alien to outsiders that, reportedly, no adult has ever learned it with any degree of fluency. The metaphysics it embodies has some interesting parallels in the speculations of Western philosophers, such as the monadology of Wilhelm Gottfried Freiherr von Leibniz and the process philosophy of Alfred North Whitehead, but it is completely foreign to our normal mode of thought.

The Truk Islanders of the southwest Pacific have an equally remarkable understanding of time.[2] They share our conception that objects endure through time, but they reckon the passage of time in a very different way. Cultural anthropologist Edward T. Hall reports an incident that occurred during the U.S. occupation of the atoll at the end of the Second World War.[3] A man burst excitedly into the military governor's headquarters. Out of breath, he said there had been a murder, and the murderer was running around loose. The officer in charge was about to send out military police to apprehend the culprit when he inquired about exactly when the assault occurred. It gradually surfaced that the crime occurred seventeen years previous, and that the perpetrator had never been caught. The Trukese make no distinction between the recent past and the distant past.

Most cultures do not differ so radically in their spatiotemporal frame-work, but they differ nonetheless. Hall, just mentioned, is one of the best-known students of cultural time and space. His observations are useful to architects and urban planners as well as to people who work across cultures.[4] He also speaks of high-context and low-context cultures, a dis-tinction that rings true and is of particular value to Westerners who may find a high-context society bewildering.

Space

Hall describes the spatial consciousness of Germany, the United Kingdom, the United States, France, Japan, and Arab countries in order to illustrate how it varies across cultures.

Germany is characterized by a strong sense of private space. Office doors are normally kept shut. If an approaching visitor can see the occupant of a room, perhaps by standing near the threshold, that person is considered to have entered already. It is as rude to glance through an open door in Germany as it is to walk in unannounced in the United States. More gener-ally, looking directly at a person in a public place is tantamount to walking up to him. Doors not only are kept shut but also tend to be heavy and soundproof. The same goes for partitions between offices, apartments, or hotel rooms. Scandinavians have a similar preference for soundproofing, although they may be more casual about intrusions at work. The German sense of privacy is uncomfortable with sharing facilities, such as offices or computer work stations. Children prefer a room of their own, and adults prefer a partitioned space to an open room full of desks.

Spatial order is important. Furniture, for example, has an assigned place, and it is not a good idea to move chairs around the room. Hall speaks of a German expatriate in the United States who had the visitor's chair in his office bolted to the floor, so that his American colleagues could not adjust its posi-tion. Restaurant employees may be unwilling to move tables together.

The United Kingdom has a different sense of privacy. Children are obliged to share rooms, and adults on the job commonly have no office of their own. Whereas Germans need some private time to hole up in a room by themselves, the British may simply stop interacting with the people around them (a practice also used in Japan and elsewhere). When they do speak, they tend to do so at low volume, to preserve the privacy of their conversation.

The French, by contrast, are comfortable with much noisier and more crowded environs than the British, as in a popular cafe. The governing principle is one of sensory involvement. Whereas many in the United States prefer a quiet, smooth ride in a large automobile; the French prefer to ride close to the road, hear the engine, and feel the wind. They want to savor the world and have developed legendary discrimination in taste. This is a Mediterranean trait that dates back at least to the ancient Minoans, whose artifacts show a keen aesthetic sensibility. It is reflected not only in art and cuisine but also in the urban environment. Gigantic U.S. skyscrapers and urban freeways assault the senses, while a French city is built on a human scale. I once stayed in a Dallas hotel that was totally encircled by freeways. It was literally impossible to walk away from the place, not only because pedestrians are prohibited on freeways but also because it would have been suicidal to cross them. To reach a newsstand or restaurant, I had to hire a taxi and ride a considerable distance through oppressive traffic. When staying in a Paris hotel, I need only step out the front door to find a patisserie, *tabac,* café, Metro stop, or pleasant park nearby.

Hall notes the popularity of radiating star designs in France. Urban avenues radiate from a plaza, as intercity highways radiate from Paris. Hall sees this as a reflection of the French centralizing tendency (also remarked by Fukuyama; see Chapter 3). Just as all roads lead to Paris, all power radiates therefrom. The sort of decentralization that is periodically fashionable in U.S. business is very unnatural for the French. Decisions of any significance typically must be ratified in Paris.

Radiating stars also occur in Japanese cities. The hubs are used as landmarks for navigation, because the streets themselves rarely have names. Building numbers, when they exist, are more likely to reflect the order in which the buildings were constructed than their location. Even natives can have difficulty finding their way around. On my first visit to Tokyo, I had to direct my cab driver to my hotel, even though I was the one who was semiconscious with jet lag.

Tokyo is the only city in which I have become totally lost, and the story illustrates several aspects of the culture. One morning I was to catch a tour bus in front of a certain hotel at a certain hour. Because this hotel was across town from my own, I left very early in the morning to allow time for unforeseen difficulties. When I emerged from the subway, I found myself completely disoriented. As luck would have it, a thick overcast prevented navigation by the sun. I began by exercising my best map-reading skills, using the low-context Western way of orientation (more on this later). Due to the absence of street names, however, Western-style analysis left me as baffled as ever. So I showed several people on the street the name of the hotel. Eager to help, each person sent me off toward a different point of the compass. In Japan, courtesy demands that when a question is posed, some kind of answer be given, even if it contains a certain amount of fabrication or equivocation. One can lose face by admitting ignorance.

Eventually I came across the grounds of the Emperor's Palace, a piece of land said to be worth more than the state of California during the 1980s real estate boom. This aligned my mental compass and directed me to the hotel. Greatly relieved, I arrived precisely at the minute the bus was scheduled to depart. The driver, however, was furious. Everyone else was there, waiting for me. Bewildered, I mentioned that I thought I was on time (which I was). The driver told me that I should have been early. Why the reaction? This is examined in the next section.

The Japanese sense of privacy is similar to that of the British, only more intense. The Japanese can be alone by erecting an invisible wall around themselves. Everything and everyone outside the wall is ignored. This is why Japanese partitions could traditionally be made of paper, and many today are not much more substantial. Foreign guests may be annoyed by clearly audible conversations in the adjoining hotel room, but Japanese are accustomed to this. The value of these skills in a spatially compressed society is obvious. Even the public bath can be experienced as private, as the bathers do not acknowledge each other's presence. Those who avail themselves of these facilities should keep this in mind.

Public areas are equally crowded in Arab countries, but here the sense of space is quite different. Pushing, shoving, and close contact are normal in public, but Arabs prefer spacious private homes. Whereas Japanese can tolerate cramped quarters, and Germans prefer to be separated by partitions, Arabs prefer togetherness in one, large, high-ceilinged room. Arabs in conversation are comfortable with across-the-room separation or with close contact, but not with the slightly standoffish conversational distance characteristic of the West. When Westerners instinctively back off, Arabs get the sense of an effort to avoid them. I confess that I have been in the comical situation in which an Arab conversant keeps approaching as I retreat, so that together we make a path across the room.

Hall suggests that Westerners take ownership of the space immediately around them while standing still, whereas Arabs assume spatial rights while moving. It is an affront to a stationary Westerner to approach too closely, whereas people in a moving crowd on a sidewalk or in a subway station may pass and maneuver around each other at very close quarters. (Standees on a subway car often have little choice about where to position themselves.) Conversely, an Arab would feel no compunction against standing right up against someone seated in a waiting room; in fact, this may be done to encourage that person to relinquish the seat.

Hall has an explanation for why Arabs tolerate close proximity. He suggests that unlike a Westerner, for whom the self is bounded by skin or clothes, the Arab's self is tucked somewhere inside the body. The extremities of the body are not really part of the self. This permits a certain amount of shoving and pinching in public without violation of selfhood. It may, Hall speculates, have traditionally made the amputation of a thief's hand a more tolerable punishment. In private it encourages close contact. The historical explanation for this behavior is presumably the inhospitable desert environment, which compelled people to cluster in protective towns or tents.

Close contact magnifies the olfactory element. Arabs traditionally converse face-to-face and breathe on each other during the process. The odor can convey information about the other's emotional state, and one person may comment on another's smell. Hall states that matchmakers historically sniffed a prospective bride to check for anger or resentment that could impede the marriage.

The emphasis on body odor is in stark contrast to the United States, where odors are masked by chemical deodorants and toothpaste. A hiker who spent an entire summer walking the Appalachian Trail in the eastern United States confirmed this fact to me in a striking way. Weeks in the wilderness accustomed him to natural odors. When he occasionally left the trail to buy provisions at a grocery, he was nearly asphyxiated by the chemical soap and deodorant residues on the bodies surrounding him in the checkout line. This behavior relates to the Puritan strain in Western culture, which is particularly strong in the United States.

Time

Hall's characterization of "monochronic" and "polychronic" cultures may be his most useful contribution to the cross-cultural professional. This is because our conception of time affects nearly everything we do and determines to a remarkable degree what everyday life is like. It also shapes our organizations in surprising ways.

Australia, Canada, New Zealand, northern Europe, and the United States are monochronic. People do one thing at a time, whence the name. Time is partitioned into intervals, each dedicated to a separate activity. People make appointments, keep them, and are expected to be on time. Time is viewed as a measurable substance. It can be spent, saved, wasted, and made up. In a polychronic culture, people do several things at once. There is less tendency to view time as a measurable quantity of sand in the hourglass. People may make appointments, but they may show up late and may be obliged to share their time slot with others.

One way to identify a monochronic or polychronic culture is to observe how people form queues. Consider, for example, the process of checking into a hotel. In monochronic countries people queue up in orderly fashion at the desk. The clerk takes care of one guest at a time, following a strict first-come, first-served discipline. A polychronic queue is not a queue at all. It is a mob crowding around the counter. As soon as one guest speaks to the clerk, someone edges his or her way up to the desk and addresses the clerk. This can be quite irritating to Westerners. Worse, the clerk responds to the intruder as though the former guest were no longer present. The clerk may deal with three or four guests before finally handing the first a key. This may seem rude, but it is regarded as courtesy, because each guest is as acknowledged as soon as possible. It may actually reduce waiting time, because the clerk can start one person's business while waiting for the computer or bellhop to respond for another. The courteous aspect may evaporate in other situations, however, as when people push and shove to board a bus all at once. Anyone who is timid about joining the fray will be left standing on the curb.

As in all cultural matters, there are exceptions. Check-in queues may be orderly at international airports and hotels even in polychronic countries, because they wish to please Western visitors. I once patronized a British bank in Africa where Western-style queuing was the norm, but because everything else about the bank was polychronic, a queue of five or six people meant a wait of three hours at least. I had to set aside an entire morning to cash a check. The endless queues at bus stops in Havana, Cuba, follow a strict first-come, first-served regimen, even though the country is strongly polychronic. Why? It is an interesting question. Explaining little anomalies like this can help one go a long way toward understanding a culture.

The United States is perhaps the world's most thoroughly monochronic society, at least as gauged by slavery to the clock. A visitor must explain if five minutes late for an appointment; even three minutes may call for a brief or mumbled apology. There must be a really good excuse for being ten to fifteen minutes late, and the host will not adjust his or her schedule to accommodate the tardy visitor, who should also have telephoned ahead if possible about the delay. (Somehow the punctuality rules do not apply to students in my early morning classes.) I was reminded of my subjugation to the American clock when my wristwatch recently stopped running. I found myself constantly glancing at time readouts on VCRs, microwave ovens, computers, and other peoples' watches to relieve my anxiety about the time of day. I recalled with fondness my stay in polychronic Africa, where queues are slow but a wristwatch is primarily a status symbol. Its owner may not even bother to set it to the correct time.

In a polychronic culture, time is elastic. A visitor with an "appointment" should not be surprised if kept waiting forty-five minutes. This should not be considered an insult, although it *may* reflect the fact that the host is of higher rank. When the visitor's turn finally comes, it becomes evident that there is really no concept of "having a turn" at all, because the host will probably have someone else in the office simultaneously. He or she will interrupt business to take telephone calls, confer with the secretary, and so on. The host may not be present at all; the appointment may have been canceled or postponed without notice because of family matters.

On many occasions it is necessary to discuss sensitive matters, but other people are in the room. The question arises as to what is the polite way to ask for privacy. There may be no polite way. Usually the solution is to bide one's time until a tête-à-tête is feasible. If the relationship has been cultivated properly, an opportunity will soon come, perhaps at lunch tomorrow, or on the golf course.

Punctuality alone is not a reliable indicator of monochronicity. People are usually on time in polychronic China and are often late in monochronic Russia. In fact, it is a mark of Hall's insight that he identified the structuring of time, rather than adherence to the clock, as the essence of monochronic time consciousness. It is a good idea for Westerners to be on time in any part of the world, because people may expect it. On a visit to Mexico I was invited to a restaurant dinner party. The other guests were told to arrive *a las siete hora americana* (at seven o'clock American time, meaning promptly at seven), because an American professor was coming and would be punctual. Meanwhile I was enjoying the company of some Mexican friends who were unaware of this arrangement. I recall thinking how nice it was not to have to worry about being on time. We arrived at the restaurant at eight, only to find everyone else waiting. To make matters worse, the kitchen operated on *hora mexicana* and served the meal at ten o'clock.

Hall mentions Latin America, the Middle East, and parts of southern Europe as polychronic cultures. India, China, and Africa are also polychronic. Chinese time is slightly more structured, perhaps due in part to the regimenting activity of the government. Its control of time is symbolized by the fact that the entire country is required to use Beijing time, even though this means that extreme western provinces can see very late sunsets. Japan is historically polychronic but adopted enough monochronicity to deal with technology. Transportation schedules, for example, are strictly observed.

Monochronic culture sees time as an empty vessel to be filled with activity. This is parallel to the idea of empty space, which seems to have originated with the classical Greek philosophers and is a characteristically Western idea. The atomic theory of matter, for example, originated with Leucippus and Democritus, postulates that matter consists of tiny indivisible particles moving through a vacuum. The more ancient view is that vacuum is an absurdity because matter *makes* space; space is the extent of matter. The temporal analogue is that activity makes time. Time is how long the activity lasts, and time does not pass when one is idle. Clock-conscious Westerners might well envy this state of affairs, and polychronic time can in fact help to manage stress if properly understood.

Both kinds of time consciousness have some advantages, even from the point of view of the other. No one in a polychronic culture likes to be kept waiting; the German Swiss point out that even their Italian compatriots appreciate trains that run on time. Conversely, no one in monochronic culture likes to be interrupted just when things get interesting. Indeed, it seems that just when I am beginning to make progress on this book, I am obliged to shift to some other task. Psychologist Mihaly Csikszentmihalyi describes "flow" experiences, during which human beings are happiest and most productive.[5] These are absorbing activities in which one loses track of time. The clock, however, does not lose track, and it soon jerks the hapless Westerner back into the reality of monochronicity.

A polychronic Latin American TV network intersperses commercial breaks throughout the hour, while monochronic European TV used to cluster them to avoid interrupting the programs. U.S. TV mercilessly irritates its monochronic viewers by dispersing commercials in polychronic fashion.

Monochronic travelers make arrangements well in advance. Perhaps Scandinavians are the most extreme. One spring, when my family and I were living in Denmark, I booked a July passage on a ferry to Norway. When my confirmation came in the mail, it showed a booking for July of the *following year*. I telephoned the booking office to report the mistake. I was informed that the idea of obtaining a berth three months in advance was ludicrous. Everyone books ferry space more than a year in advance.

Polychronic travel arrangements tend to fall into place at the last minute. On one of my trips to India, I applied for a business visa, several months in advance, because I was familiar with the glacial pace of Indian bureaucracy. I wanted to take no chances, because any delay would upset complicated travel plans. I had purchased a half-inch stack of airline tickets. I waited and waited, and the visa did not come through, despite repeated inquiries from me and my Indian hosts. They patiently worked through connections (another polychronic habit, discussed later) to expedite the visa. The day before my departure, I received a telephone call from none less than the Indian consul in New York City, whom I convinced to approve the visa. The visa arrived by air courier the next day, approximately one hour before I caught a taxi to the airport.

This kind of brinkmanship can be extremely stressful for someone who lives monochronically, as it was for me. My Indian colleagues did not understand why I had a problem with it. After all, I got the visa. An analogous situation occurs when the deadline approaches for completion of a project.

Westerners become nervous and speed up the pace. In a polychronic culture, it is like any other day. Westerners reason that time is money, and the longer the meter runs on a project, the more it will cost. They set milestones and measure their success in part by whether they are reached in a timely fashion. Monochronic time is in fact money, because one task must be completed before another can be taken up. One's polychronic counterparts are in no particular hurry, because they can fill their time with the many other activities in which they are involved.

Western managers on assignment abroad, particularly those from the United States, are placed in a difficult bind when the home office expects results on a monochronic timetable. They are also handicapped in negotiations. Business people around the world learn at their mother's knee that U.S. nationals are impatient and ruled by deadlines. All one has to do is wait until the deadline approaches, and the Americans will cave in.

Mary Catherine Bateson points out another key difference between monochronic and polychronic experience.[6] The former tends to have a high rate of stimulation, especially when compared to more traditional polychronic societies. Monochronic people are accustomed to a constant stream of sensory input. No one is caught in traffic without reaching for the mobile phone or tape deck. No one jogs without wearing earphones attached to a radio or tape player. No one rides the train without reading a book or newspaper. When the airliner reaches altitude, dozens of laptop computers (including mine) appear. Available technology is obviously a factor here, but equally important is the monochronic tendency to reach for the technology. It is essential that moments do not slip by unfilled. In traditional cultures, waiting is much less a burden. While living in Africa, I noticed that people would wait hours outdoors for a tardy bus with no sign of irritation, an experience that would send many Westerners into an apoplectic fit. For Africans there is no need to make use of this time, because there is no time to use. Time grinds to a halt.

Bateson reports that when she returned to the Philippines to visit friends she had made while doing fieldwork, the slow pace of events was intolerable. During her fieldwork she had occupied herself with observation and learning. This suggests that impatient Westerners can occupy their minds, productively at that, by being as observant as possible. It works for me.

Another technique I have found useful is to practice being patient, as preparation for travel to a polychronic culture. While stuck in traffic or a long checkout line, one can review the day's activities rather than fret about time lost. Better yet, one can live in the present for a few moments, perhaps by observing people, meditating on one's good fortune in life, or if one is religious, praying for others less fortunate. As with any skill, practice is the key.

Polychronicity has implications outside the realm of time. One is broader interests. The monochronic academic, for example, is likely to be highly specialized, publishing perhaps only in the area of real estate inheritance tax, and talking about little else through much of the day. One Latin American academic I met, who is not atypical, is officially an engineer but spends considerable time writing poetry and going to meetings on new age philosophy. I myself am a bit suspect in the eyes of some Western colleagues because I write in both mathematics and culture.

Life in polychronic cultures is also very much wrapped up in relationships with others. People tend to spend the day interacting with a wide circle of friends and acquaintances, whereas in monochronic cultures it is more common to focus on tasks. Hall points out the organizational implications of this tendency. Polychronic organizations are likewise based on relationships rather than tasks. One manages people rather than projects. In Hall's view, this is because polychronic managers are capable of interacting with and therefore managing many people at once. Monochronic managers cannot do this and therefore manage tasks. The tasks themselves are organized in a hierarchical fashion, which gives rise to an organizational chart. The president interacts only with a few vice presidents, each of whom delegates to a few subordinates, and so forth. By contrast, polychronic organizations are flatter, because the boss can keep tabs on many people at once.

Hall goes on to characterize monochronic organizations as governed more by rules than by people. If an employee in Chicago wants time off for a vacation, he or she will probably consult company policy on the matter and perhaps file a written request. An employee in Bogota is more likely to ask the boss about it, or call on a friend who has influence. In general, things get done by working through friends, family members, or other connections. There may be many complex procedures, and it may be necessary to observe them to the letter, but this may be of little avail unless a friendly expediter pulls the right strings. A monochronic organization tends to ensure more or less equal treatment to employees of a given rank. It is no coincidence that fairness tends to be a key organizing principle in monochronic societies. A polychronic organization gives the boss greater flexibility to take into account the individual situations of employees. This is consonant with the greater "power distance" typical of polychronic societies, where the decisions of the boss are less likely to be questioned.

This suggests that there are more factors at work here than time consciousness. Not only is there the fairness issue, but more importantly, a fundamental distinction between rule-governed and relationship-governed cultures comes into play. Hall is probably right to suggest that polychronic organizations tend to be flatter because managers can deal with many matters simultaneously. This is supported by the fact that flat organizations are rare in monochronic societies. Monochronic organizations, however, are rule governed and task oriented because the larger society is rule governed, not because it is monochronic. It is rule governed because of a belief in universalizing rationality that is deeply rooted in its history. Monochronicity and fairness principles derive from the same historical origins but along different routes.

Because there are many boxes on each level of the organization chart, a polychronic bureaucracy tends to be sprawling and unstructured. Westerners complain about sluggish bureaucracy in their own countries, but their burden is light by polychronic standards. Because there is no well-organized hierarchy to set procedures, bureaucrats vie with one another for a piece of the action. Everyone wants to make sure that nothing happens unless he or she signs off. As a result, the procedures may be irrational and involve functionaries who have no logical connection with the project. The sheer volume of procedures multiplies as well. A study of one joint venture in pharmaceuticals revealed that the U.S. government required the filing of 26 documents in the course of 9 administrative procedures.[7] For the same type of venture, Japan required 325 documents in 46 administrative procedures, and South Korea required 312 documents in 62 administrative procedures. The joint venture was undertaken in South Korea, where the paperwork required two years and nine months to complete.

Monochronic bureaucracies, on the other hand, are monolithic and tend to take on a life of their own. They may continue to follow their mandate long after they have outlived their usefulness. One thinks of the massive czarist bureaucracy, which seems to have survived two Russian revolutions more or less intact. My favorite example is the Pennsylvania Turnpike Commission. Its expensive bureaucracy continues to collect tolls and make repairs fifty years after the completion of the turnpike, when maintenance could easily be folded into other highway operations.

What accounts for polychronic and monochronic tendencies in general? Hall is not explicit on this point but makes an interesting suggestion: Western reliance on guilt tends to reinforce punctuality. Westerners internalize what they regard as a universal moral code, and guilt results from violating the code. The Western habit of adhering to internal conscience is naturally extended to a habit of adhering to an internal clock. One finds a different sort of consciousness in polychronic cultures. One of my students related an incident in which a Latin American friend missed his plane. He did not say that he missed the plane, however. He said, "The plane left without me." There was no guilt.

Japan enforces punctuality despite its polychronicity, due to its social decision to adapt to Western-style technology. Because Japanese culture is not based on guilt, it appeals to its efficient social discipline. People, rather than a guilt complex, must urge everyone to be on time. I got a taste of this discipline when the Tokyo bus driver rebuked me for almost being late. In Germany, it is not necessary for the bus driver to say anything. A guilty conscience propels one to catch the bus.

Hall seems right about the connection between guilt and monochronic time consciousness, but there is a more fundamental dynamic at work. Both monochronic and polychronic time have stress-management roles. Monochronic time is not so much a stress-relieving device itself as a part of a larger strategy. A Westerner, particularly one of northern European cultural ancestry, takes control of life by taking control of the environment, largely through technology. Nature is bulldozed and restructured to build power systems, transportation systems, and planned cities. Even the grass and trees are kept under control by mowing and trimming. The society is structured around an economic system, a welfare system, and an educational system. By surrounding oneself with order, the Westerner is reassured that the elements are under control.

Part of this order is the structuring of time: daily schedules, calendars, and deadlines. Meeting the schedule imposed by structured time imposes its own stress that partially offsets the stress relief obtained by an orderly environment. Yet it is apparently worth the cost, even in the frenetic United States. Polychronic cultures find security and control elsewhere and need not be enslaved to the clock. People may or may not be punctual, depending on whether other factors require it. As noted earlier, the structuring influence of the Chinese government calls for a certain regimentation of time as well, and a fair amount of punctuality results. The opposite extreme is illustrated by an experience that Hall relates. He drove a long distance across a rural road to attend a Christmas dance one evening at a Pueblo village near the Rio Grande. He and some other visitors stood shivering outside the church where the dance was to take place. The concept of clock time does not exist in the Pueblo culture, and no particular time had been set for the dance. In past years it had started at various times. Occasionally one or two Pueblo would emerge from the church, a hopeful signal that the festivities were about to begin. But nothing happened, and by two o'clock in the morning the visitors were exhausted and ready to head home. At about this time people suddenly began to converge on the church, the doors opened, and the party commenced. To the Pueblo the matter was simple; they started the celebration when they were ready to start it.

Lax time reckoning not only avoids stress in most polychronic cultures but also can be used to reduce stress. Latin American life was historically fraught with unpredictability. Any sense of control over one's immediate situation, even in small ways, could be therapeutic. A minor functionary could at least govern events in his office by deciding when he would see each visitor. Someone kept waiting was someone over whom he had momentary control.

Tardiness need not indicate an effort to control, however. In Indonesia it is customary for the most highly ranked participants in a meeting to arrive half an hour late (the ritual excuse is "bad traffic"). Tolerating their late arrival does not give them control but is a way of acknowledging their authority, much as one would do with deferential language or lowered eyes.

Context

One who gets off the plane in Stuttgart, Germany, walks into a low-context environment. Signs in multiple languages tell exactly where to pick up luggage. Maps and posters explain various routes to the city. Travelers choosing rail transport, for example (which is mostly above ground in Stuttgart), find a detailed system map, schedule, and instructions for operating the fare machines. Similar information is available at every stop along the way.

The system is even more elaborate in Scandinavia, for example Denmark. Every urban bus stop is provided a posted timetable. For a modest price one can buy a master schedule book that contains detailed maps of every intercity bus and rail route in the country, plus complete schedules for every day of the year. There is even an indication of the walking distance between a town's bus and train stations.

Passengers deplaning in Mumbai (formerly Bombay), India, find themselves in a totally different predicament. There are few signs, and the ones that exist are probably wrong. After a long wait in the customs line (and guessing which one to join), the bewildered visitor tries to follow the other passengers, but they quickly disappear into the crowd. Everyone else seems to know what to do. The visitor's confused look is immediately noticed, and a number of people approach with various kinds of propositions: hotels, taxis, even joint business ventures. There is a bus service of sorts to the domestic terminal some kilometers distant, from which the connecting flight departs, but no indication of it is visible. At the street exit, a number of boys crowd around travelers, some offering taxi service. The airport in Delhi has a counter at which one can pay the taxi fare to avoid unscrupulous drivers, but most travelers are unaware of this unless someone tipped them off in advance. If the hapless visitor manages to find the bus, the driver will be noncommittal about when it will depart. He seems to be waiting for local passengers who have no luggage and are apparently hitching a ride to some point along the route.

India is a high-context culture. A substantial amount of background information is necessary for one to know what is going on and what to do. The lesson is obvious: one should not go until finding out what to do from people who know the system.

In a low-context culture like Germany's, information is given explicitly. Everything is spelled out. The world's only low-context cultures are those with northern European backgrounds, expect perhaps Singapore, which is low-context to the extent it is because it is the creation of former Prime Minister Lee Kuan Yew, who was educated at Cambridge and known in those days as Harry Lee.

Negotiations and contracts tend to be very different in low- and high-context cultures. A Western-style contract is probably the most thoroughly low-context artifact in the world. Lawyers attempt to foresee every possible contingency. I once told an audience in China that, back home, I had to sign a contract containing three pages of fine print to rent a bicycle for a day. They looked at each other in disbelief (or disgust). This kind of detail is necessary, because if there is a dispute, it will be resolved by appealing to the letter of the contract. Even then there are disputes as to how the contract is interpreted, and these are resolved by appeal to thick volumes of case law in which every conceivable distinction is explicitly drawn. Because the letter of the contract governs, a signed contract is engraved in stone. It can be abrogated only by drawing up another contract, equally dense, that supersedes the first agreement by mutual consent.

A high-context contract varies from one culture to another. The written contract has been adopted almost everywhere, but one must be careful about what it means. In parts of Latin America it may not represent the real agreement, which is concluded with a handshake. In Confucian cultures it may be too vague to specify what the deal is. It may be viewed as a preliminary agreement that evolves as the situation changes. The signing of a contract may mark only the beginning of the negotiation process.

In high-context cultures, people are accustomed to having a socially defined understanding. They have developed efficient signals for communicating what people are supposed to do. There is no need to write out the details. Low-context cultures rely more on an internalized disposition to obey the rules. Behavior is more easily regulated or changed by laying down rules. Even in low-context cultures, however, surprisingly much is implicit. It is interesting that as the United States moves from a northern European mainstream culture to greater multiculturalism, reliance on regulation, law, and litigation—that is, on making things explicit—increases as a common cultural support while shared cultural assumptions diminish.

Contextuality can be observed even by going no deeper into a high-context country than the international airport. In a typical situation there is a departure lounge with several doors leading to the aircraft or to buses that take passengers to the planes. However, there is no clear indication of which flights leave from which door. Or if there are signs, they quickly become obsolete as flights are delayed or switch gates. As waves of passengers enter the room and crowd around various doors, confusion seems to reign. An airline employee may occasionally announce something while standing at a door, but only those at the front of the crowd can hear anything above the din. Western travelers become uptight as they try to ascertain what is going on, perhaps by collaring an airline employee and trying to extract information that the employee most likely does not have.

The locals in the room, however, somehow seem to know which door to crowd around and when to do it. They have spent a lifetime picking up on social cues. Perhaps they can tell where people are going by their conversation, accent, mannerisms, or dress. They may have noticed who checked in at the same counter and instinctively stay with this group. In high-context cultures, one is much more alive to the social environment (who am I traveling with?) than the physical environment (which gate?). It is necessary only for a few people to hear the announcements or overhear conversations between employees. This is why airline staff do not bother to announce over a public address system or post signs.

What to do? Cope as the locals do, of course. Foreigners perhaps cannot decipher the language or subtler clues because of unfamiliarity with the country. But they can peek at boarding passes; I do it all the time. They are printed in Roman letters around the world. I also use the trick of remembering who was ahead of me in the check-in line. Languages spoken or printed matter in hand may give a clue (flight attendants are taught to notice these). Sometimes I just ask or show someone my boarding pass.

Fortunately, the most intensely high-context country in the world, Japan, provides a low-context environment in airports and many other public places. Yet everyday life is another matter entirely. The well-known Japanese indirection is a product of their high-context culture. Japanese are loathe to say anything directly, particularly if it is negative. They seem evasive to outsiders, but the aim is to maintain harmony. Highly refined consensus-building skills provide a rich context of background information. Because everyone knows a good deal about what the other is thinking anyway, only subtle verbal cues are necessary. Participants in a meeting can sit in silence a full minute, which makes visitors squirm.

It is much easier to immigrate from a high-context culture to a low-context culture than vice versa. Western countries, which are struggling with massive immigration, unwittingly provide a double inducement. Not only does their material wealth attract, but their low-context culture eases the adjustment. A wealthy high-context culture such as Japan experiences almost zero immigration, partly of course because of legal restrictions but also because the adjustment is hard. A corollary is that Western businesses may have difficulty opening a market in Japan, whether or not the government imposes restrictions. The Japanese themselves would be hard pressed to articulate how to go about it, because it is part of their cultural background knowledge they take for granted.

Ethnic groups in a low-context culture are commonly high context. As I write this I am sitting in a lobby occupied by people of a mainstream Western culture and a high-context subculture. All speak the same language. Posted on the door of the men's room is a small sign stating that the facilities are out of order and another restroom is available on the third floor. Without exception, every man belonging to the mainstream culture has noticed the sign, and every member of the subculture has ignored it and entered the restroom. (Perhaps I was wrong when I said that all cultural patterns have exceptions.) One group lives in a world of instructions and is alert to them. The other lives in a rich context of culturally transmitted information. At this point the question is: do the men who enter find the facilities out of order, or have they been tipped off that everything is fixed and someone forgot to remove the sign?

Hall traces Western low contextualism to the role of logic and reason in the culture. Actually it is usually a product of how behavior is regulated. Relationship-based cultures regulate behavior primarily through personal supervision and influence. One absorbs behavioral norms from parents, older relatives, neighbors, and persons of authority. There must be an efficient means to communicate information directly through these relationships. The culture is therefore rich in context. Because of the efficiency of this mechanism, information of all kinds tends to be transmitted contextually rather than explicitly stated as rules, schedules, or policies.

Rule-based cultures teach children to obey certain rules even when they are unsupervised. The penalty for violation is guilt as well as shame. It is therefore less urgent to transmit information through relationships, and the system can work with less contextualism. When behavioral changes are needed, it may suffice simply to promulgate new rules. Rule-based cultures can therefore be low-context cultures and can tolerate a greater degree of cultural diversity. Yet much information must be stated explicitly, and a certain critical mass of the population must be disposed to pay attention and obey the rules. Obviously both rule-based and relationship-based mechanisms operate to some extent in many cultures, and it is a question of which is dominant.

A final conclusion Hall draws is that low-context cultures tend to minimize the importance of culture. This is largely true and is in fact why I spent so many pages in Chapter 1 trying to convince Western readers of its importance.

Yet this disregard seems to stem from the Western tendency toward universalism rather than from its low-context culture.

Notes for Chapter 2

1. Robert W. Young and William Morgan, *The Navajo Language: A Grammar and Colloquial Dictionary*, University of New Mexico Press (Albuquerque, 1987).

2. I use the present tense, but it is the "ethnographic present." It describes the situation at the time the culture was observed, in this case at the end of the Second World War.

3. Edward T. Hall, *The Silent Language*, Doubleday (New York, 1959).

4. Ibid.; *The Hidden Dimension*, Doubleday (New York, 1966); *The Dance of Life*, Doubleday (New York, 1983).

5. Mihaly Csikszentmihalyi, *Flow: The Psychology of Optimal Experience*, Harper & Row (New York, 1990).

6. Mary Catherine Bateson, *Peripheral Visions*, HarperCollins (New York, 1994).

7. Boye Lafayette De Mente, *Korean Etiquette and Ethics in Business*, NTC Publishing Group (Lincolnwood, Ill., 1994).

3 Culture and Prosperity

In a world preoccupied with economic development, the relationship between wealth and culture quickly becomes an issue. Opinions tend to extremes. Economists tell us that cultural factors are "externalities" that may have marginal effects but do not explain prosperity. At the opposite extreme we hear people say that any Third World economy could be fixed by shipping in 10,000 Swiss.

The truth lies, not in between, but along a different dimension. If economic activity rests on culture, as argued in Chapter 1, then every culture should have its own distinctive way of generating wealth, even its own kind of wealth. Culture is therefore related to prosperity, but not in so simplistic a way that one can send in Calvinists to obtain it. One must design products and modes of production that suit the culture. As a corollary one should expect the West to be better at producing Western products in the Western way than the rest of the world.

There is no romantic suggestion here that wealth can be whatever a culture takes it to be, or that all cultures are wealthy as measured by their own value system. Although cultures value different kinds of wealth, whether it be goats or concubines or stock certificates, it is nonetheless wealth that they value. There is something recognizable about wealth that usually allows us to spot it in a given culture. The same is true of poverty. Some cultures are poor by any reasonable measure, and some endure abject misery. Most familiar is Third World poverty, which generally results when global forces disrupt a traditional economy but supply no viable substitute. In a typical scenario, people leave their traditional farms to work in factories or mines, which are subject to the vicissitudes of market prices. The people become dependent on a cash economy and have little recourse when prices drop and workers are laid off, except perhaps cultivation of illegal coca or poppies. A person in this predicament might be rich in terms of family support or spiritual contentment, but I am talking about material wealth, and in this sense they are poor.

Wealth is therefore recognizable across cultures to some extent, but the age of globalization has universalized the concept in a further sense: there is only one way to be rich. One must own Western consumer goods. Indeed, the lure of Western goods has seeped into almost every culture, and many people who once regarded themselves as relatively well-off feel poor because they lack them. A craving has swept the world for automobiles, microwave ovens, VCRs, pocket phones, computers, and other technology-based goods that the West is good at producing. Traditional people commonly spend their first cash earnings on a TV rather than plumbing or a better roof. This preference for consumer goods gives the West a natural advantage and raises the question as to whether other cultures can be clever enough to generate Western-style wealth in their own way but just as efficiently.

The question is largely unanswered, but a few countries seem to have done so. Japan rose from the ashes of the Second World War to set the world standard in manufacturing. The dictator Park Chung Hee launched South Korea on a path of economic growth that is spectacular by any standards, Western or other. Lee Kuan Yew brought Singapore from a sleepy island to a sleek, shiny, First World economy in three decades. One might argue that Singapore used something resembling a Western approach. But Japan relied on its social discipline, it ability to achieve group harmony, its *keiretsu* and *keidanren,* and its lean manufacturing techniques to create an industrial sector that was unique in the world and matches its cultural talents. South Korea took an approach so different from that of the West that the concept of the "bottom line" plays almost no role in its business. Yet Koreans created the all-important *chaebol,* their modification of Japanese *keiretsu,* and built a highly productive manufacturing sector. Even Lee Kuan Yew relied on his culture's acceptance of authoritarian government.

The connection between culture and prosperity is too complex to analyze in a single chapter, but it is helpful to cover a few basic lessons. One is that we probably know even less about wealth creation than we imagine. Culture influences how we think about wealth, as well as how we create it, in ways of which we are unaware. This is a good point at which to call on the services of cultural anthropology. An examination of cultures based on very different assumptions can convince us to question our own assumptions. The story of the cargo cults in the southwest Pacific is oft repeated, but it serves this purpose well.

A second lesson is that the measure of wealth itself probably depends on culture more than we think. On this point cultural anthropology provides the fascinating examples of the Tlingit, Kwakiutl, and other northwest coastal peoples of North America—the people of the potlatch.

With this preparation, we can turn to Francis Fukuyama's recent book, *Trust: The Social Virtues and the Creation of Prosperity.*[1] He aims to show that prosperity in today's world rests on cultural as well as macroeconomic variables. His analysis of trust requires some revision, but he is right in his basic thesis. Even an exposure of his errors can help elucidate the distinction between rule-based and relationship-based cultures, which I am developing gradually in these pages.

Finally, a brief account of Japanese manufacturing will illustrate how a culture can beat the West at its own game, at least for a while—not by importing Swiss workers, but by exploiting its own cultural traits.

Wealth and Cargo

The cargo cults of New Guinea and Melanesia provide one of the most absorbing stories in the annals of anthropology. The account given here is based on Marvin Harris,[2] who relies largely on the fieldwork of Peter Lawrence[3] and describes the situation after World War II.

During this period some of the mountain villages of Papua New Guinea have their own airports. A typical airport is equipped with hangars and a radio shack with thatched roofs, and a tower made of bamboo. An aircraft, made of sticks and leaves, might be parked on a dirt runway. Villagers man the facility around the clock, maintaining a bonfire at night to serve as a beacon. At the sound of an approaching aircraft, one of the villagers rushes into the radio shack. He gives landing instructions over a tin-can microphone that is attached to an antenna of string and vines. No one is surprised when the aircraft lands at the airport in the valley below. The whites are sending out messages that trick the plane into bringing cargo to them rather than the intended destination.

The villagers believe the airplanes to be occupied by dead ancestors who will come to life when the planes land. They are bringing cargo to their progeny—food, clothing, consumer goods. In the old days they brought it in canoes, later in steamships. Western missionaries explain to the natives that wealth comes, not from cargo planes, but from factories and hard work. The natives, however, note that all evidence is to the contrary. The Europeans and Americans, in fact, receive their provisions in the form of cargo and must therefore know the secret of cargo. They know how to convince the ancestors to come in ships and planes. Their own sacred literature tells of an ancestor, Noah, who came in a ship.

Some years earlier the natives agreed among themselves to cooperate with the missionaries, but only with the ulterior motive of learning the secret of cargo. They renounced their own ancient rituals in favor of prayer and church attendance. They assented to the view that human beings descended from Adam and Eve rather than such animals as cats, dogs, and monkeys, as the natives themselves believed. They worked for colonial employers for a few cents an hour. Unfortunately, the whites not only cling to their secret but continue in their duplicity. One occasion, for example, they took the cargo prophet Yali to Australia. They wanted to convince him that the cargo beliefs were false, so that he could return home and persuade his followers likewise. They showed him the factories, mills and farms where wealth is really created. Yali noted, however, that the wealthy whites seldom set foot in a factory. He visited a museum in which whites reverently view the sacred ritual objects of his own culture, carefully mounted behind glass—objects that the missionaries had described as works of Satan. He observed that the Australians treat dogs and cats as though they were human relatives. He was shown a textbook that depicted the descent of human beings from monkeys.

The cargo cults are revitalization movements, which are efforts of a dying culture to reclaim its former vigor in the last moments before extinction. The cults come in several forms. One of the best known is the John Frum cult in the New Hebrides, apparently named for a medic in the U.S. military during the Second World War. The name may be a contraction of "John from America." John Frum is said to have promised to return with cargo but so far has not arrived. His followers set up shrines containing red crosses and related items, some of which they reportedly still maintain. They point out that Christians have waited more than two thousand years for their Savior's return.

Westerners find these stories amusing and somewhat pathetic. We marvel at how the cultural presuppositions of cargo cult adherents prevent them from understanding the true origin of wealth. Yet there is no simple explanation for why one nation is wealthy and another poor. It may seem obvious to us, but it was equally obvious to people living in New Guinea. Perhaps what is obvious is our own set of cultural presuppositions. Before we smile at the cargo cults, we might consider whether our own understanding is equally myopic.

Wealth and Prestige

The Tlingit, Kwakiutl, Chinook, and some twenty-five other groups who once occupied the northwest coast of North America provide what may be the world's most remarkable object lesson in the meaning of wealth. Before European settlers came, the natural riches of this region handed its inhabitants a generous living, asking little labor in return. Every year salmon choked the rivers as they struggled upstream to freshwater spawning areas. At other times the rivers teemed with halibut, herring, cod, and trout. The Pacific Ocean offered such bounty as whales, seals, and porpoises, and at low tide one could walk the beach and help oneself to shellfish. This environment supported affluent and complex societies that may have spent more time redistributing their wealth than earning it.

The pivotal institution of these cultures is the potlatch, made famous by Ruth Benedict's landmark book *Patterns of Culture*.[4] The potlatch is an elaborate banquet that is months in preparation. Guests travel long distances to attend the celebration, which might last a week. On approach they see the host's enormous "totem" poles decorated with carved emblems of his clan and other creatures. The host entertains them in a lavishly furnished hall, adorned with intricate artwork and attended by persons in luxurious dress. In addition to sumptuous feasts day after day, the host presents his guests with hundreds of blankets and other gifts neatly lined up in stacks. The most valuable and prestigious gifts are copper plates with designs beaten into them. The host might also give away slaves, or have them ceremonially killed by throwing them into a pit. He may build a bonfire inside the hall, fueled with the abundant oil of the candlefish. The fire sometimes ignites the building and reduces it to rubble.

Meanwhile the beneficiaries belittle the host's extravagance. They dismiss the piles of gifts and talk about how much more they have at home. They try not to be impressed by the feast or the sacrifice of slaves. If the building burns to the ground, they resolve to stage an even more elaborate potlatch themselves.

The purpose of the potlatch is to enhance the host's prestige by impressing his guests. His leadership position is at stake. People support leaders who can demonstrate their status in the form of exorbitant wealth. The most convincing demonstration is the ability to give away or destroy possessions with abandon.

This is an extreme case of an institution whose most famous example is the "big man" system of Melanesia but that occurs in various guises worldwide. It was the dominant form of political organization before governments developed. A big man retains power by giving things away. In modern Western nations the practice survives in the form of patronage or state benefits given in exchange for support. Marvin Harris suggests that the big-man system endured because it had the effect of redistributing resources from those temporarily more fortunate to those less fortunate, thereby insuring families against the ups and downs of weather, disease, and other contingencies.[5] Early civilizations copied the idea by taxing the population for a fraction of their production and redistributing the goods from royal warehouses. They may have developed the first written languages in order to inventory government stores.

More relevant here is what the potlatch says about the intimate connection between wealth and status. Totem poles and copper plates have little utilitarian value except to enhance status, much as expensive art on the walls of an upscale San Francisco apartment. Wealth therefore need not be practically useful in the normal sense. One might maintain that copper plates and Utrillos are simply status enhancers rather than real wealth, but this is unconvincing, since they are exchanged for such clear examples of wealth as blankets and yachts. Even materially useful items need not derive their value from their utility, as demonstrated by the Tlingit and comrades, who gave away or destroyed their material goods for the sake of status.

Status value helps to explain the global spread of Western consumer goods. These gadgets seem to have almost universal appeal—one point on which the universalizing West got it right. In many ways they offer practical value, but status is an important element. I recall that when pocket phones were new in Asian cities, people could be seen on street corners proudly talking into their phones, making sure that everyone noticed. I suspected that they arranged for their secretaries to call them. Some time later, a cellular transmission antenna was erected near my residence in Zimbabwe, where I again noticed important people using their phones in public. I later learned that the signal had not yet been turned on, and they were talking into dead phones. Status was obviously more important than utility.

The upshot is that since wealth is in part status value, a culture can to a great extent determine what counts as wealth. In a sense, Western cultures have done just this by giving social value to consumer goods, a fact that helped to create a middle class. Technology allows modern factories to produce consumer goods with remarkable efficiency, while services remain expensive. One reason for this is that manufactured goods are gifts that keep on giving. A recorded song entertains many times for about the same cost as a single live concert. Thus, if people value manufactured goods, wealth can be spread to a large segment of the population. Henry Ford's assembly line, for example, multiplied the labor productivity of automobile manufacture by a factor of eleven. But productivity increased only because people wanted the new cars. There was prestige in owning an automobile, even though it was sometimes more trouble than a horse and got mired in the mud. Things are not altogether different today. Recently a Hong Kong friend showed me the luxury cars parked in the basement garage of his apartment building, each sitting in a parking spot that cost the owner more than the vehicle. Without prompting from me, he remarked that many of these cars seldom leave the garage, because of the congestion and lack of parking in the city. The vehicles, he told me, are coveted status symbols. Again, cultural values and efficient production combine to help enrich the middle class.

Even though consumer goods can confer status, one might imagine that their practical utility is still enough to ensure their popularity. Yet even their practical value falls as they increasingly clutter one's life. As a wry commentary on this trend, someone gave my father-in-law an electric fork for his birthday. It was an ordinary serving fork with a functionless electric cord attached to the wooden handle. The joke, of course, is that nobody cares whether the fork has any use, because it goes into a kitchen stocked with more gadgets than one would ever use. Yet consumers continue to value their easily produced gadgets and therefore continue to grow rich. The much-remarked efforts of the advertising industry to create demand for frivolous consumer goods may represent a certain sort of wisdom. They make people richer by convincing them to want easily produced manufactured items rather than expensive services.

By learning to crave the consumer goods advertised on TV, populations worldwide have changed their definition of wealth. This gives them a shot at creating or maintaining a large middle class, but if they wish to achieve prosperity comparable to that of the West, they must do one of two things. They must either compete with the West on its own turf in the production of Western consumer goods, or they must buy Western goods with goods and services they produce more efficiently (i.e., they must exploit their comparative advantage). Non-Western nations have tried both strategies. As mentioned, Japan and South Korea have done rather well beating the West at its own game. One might also mention India's foray into software development. Others have tried the latter strategy by offering beautiful tourist beaches, fashionable craft items, and so forth. But this strategy relies on strong demand in the West. Some Westerners are willing to pay premium prices for Italian vacations or African sculpture, but Western demand for consumer goods dwarfs these specialty markets. If everyone wants only what the West produces efficiently, the old strategy of comparative advantage does not go far.

Prosperity and Trust

At the age of twenty-five, An Wang emigrated from Shanghai to the United States. He founded Wang Laboratories of Lowell, Massachusetts, in 1951. His genius for entrepreneurship gradually became evident. By 1972 his firm had 2,000 employees. By 1984 it was one of the largest employers in the Boston area, with 24,800 people on the payroll and annual revenues amounting to $2.28 billion. At this point he retired from his leadership position. The following year the firm showed its first loss. Within four years 90 percent of its market was gone, and within eight, by 1992, the firm had filed for bankruptcy.

Francis Fukuyama uses this story to illustrate a difference between Chinese and U.S. organizational styles. A non-state Chinese firm is typically run by the family that owns it. It is likely to have a hub-and-spoke organizational structure in which a central figure personally oversees as much of the day-to-day operation as possible. Wang himself followed this pattern.

In 1972, when Wang Laboratories had 2,000 employees, 136 reported directly to him. When Wang retired, he gave the mantle of leadership to his American-born son Fred, passing over several more senior managers, including John Cunningham, whom most insiders believed to be the logical successor. This display of nepotism induced several experienced managers to leave the company. The elder Wang eventually fired his son, but the damage had been done.

Large corporations tend to have a multilayered hierarchy of professional managers. A single family may own a sizable share of the company, but its management is generally left to others. Fukuyama points out that, allowing for a few exceptions, such corporations are based in Europe (particularly Germany), North America, South Korea, or Japan. In particular, it is difficult or impossible to think of a large, private Chinese corporation or a well-known Chinese product brand. Taiwan, Hong Kong, and Singapore likewise specialize in small- and medium-sized firms. This is not to be explained by the level of development. South Korea is roughly on a par economically with Taiwan, for example, but such Korean firms as Hyundai and Samsung are on the order of five times larger than the biggest private firms in Taiwan.

Fukumaya's primary explanation for this phenomenon is the level of trust in the respective societies. China is a low-trust society, whereas Germany, the United States, and Japan are high-trust societies. A high level of trust leads to "spontaneous sociability," which in turn facilitates the formation of voluntary, nongovernmental associations. These include civic clubs, churches and other religious organizations, and most significantly for economics, large business corporations. These, operating in a high-trust environment, generate the kind of prosperity to which the First World is accustomed. But it is best to consider this argument one step at a time.

A high level of trust has obvious efficiencies. In the United States one commonly finds a row of newspaper vending boxes on downtown streets. By dropping in a coin, one can open the door and take a newspaper from the top of the stack inside. Seeing such a row of boxes, an Italian friend once remarked to me that, in Italy, the first buyer would take the entire stack. Newspapers there are sold only at newsstands, which incurs higher labor costs and is less convenient. It is a small inefficiency, but multiply it by millions of transactions that must be monitored more carefully.

Monitoring is expensive. Bureaucracies impose procedures to accomplish it, procedures that must themselves be audited. Guards must be hired, inspections conducted. Safeguards must be built into contracts to ensure compliance, and interminable legal actions undertaken to enforce it. These burdens are recognized even in the traditional economic literature, where they are known as "transaction costs."

Distrust also hampers negotiation. The purpose of negotiation is to identify an exchange in which everyone receives goods that are more valuable to oneself than to the other parties. This obviously works better when both parties are forthcoming about what they really have to offer. Some degree of good faith is necessary.

In a high-trust society one is inclined to take any reasonably well-groomed person wearing a business suit at face value, unless there is a particular reason to be suspicious. In a low-trust society one must establish a long-term personal relationship, in order to build trust, before business can be discussed. This not only consumes time and energy but also imposes a severe constraint on with whom one can do business at any given time.

Ironically, business people in high-trust societies are sometimes less likely to acknowledge the role of trust in their dealings than those in low-trust societies. They are likely to point to an incentive system that keeps people in line. For example, there are reputation effects, to use the neoclassical economist's term. Business people are trustworthy because they want business in the future. Or they are agents for a firm that wants future business. For transitory relationships there are third-party enforcers for whom reputation is important, whether it be bonding agencies, insurers, or the legal system. This view does not explain, however, why these incentives fail to operate in low-trust societies until one establishes a personal relationship. It seems more likely that the incentives reinforce a mode of behavior that would not exist were it not already culturally predetermined.

A similar principle applies in law enforcement. For the most part, people in high-trust countries obey the law because they are predisposed to do so, not because the existence of police and legal courts gives them an incentive. Except in an authoritarian police state, the criminal justice system can only take care of a few people at the fringes who do not absorb the cultural norms. If people were generally inclined to break the law, police and judges would likely behave no differently than anyone else. A colleague told me a story of a vacationer in Rio de Janeiro who was robbed of his beach bag while sunbathing. As he chased the thief, he spotted a police cruiser on Avenida Atlântica and asked the officers inside for help. One of the officers inquired whether the sunbather's money was in the stolen bag. "No, thank goodness; it's hidden in my shoe." At this point the officer drew his revolver and said, "Hand it over."

Fukuyama points out that the much-vaunted business possibilities of the Internet likewise presuppose trust. The Internet can link sellers and buyers with unprecedented efficiency. Customers need only run a search engine to find a vendor, anywhere in the world, who offers precisely the desired product. The Internet allows small, widely dispersed firms to organize themselves into supply and distribution chains when travel and coordination costs would otherwise be prohibitive. But the essence of Internet business, as we now know it, is doing business with strangers. The whole affair presupposes an extraordinary reservoir of good faith. The Internet is touted as community-building technology. In truth, its effectiveness presupposes community.

This lesson was actually available rather early in the game. Academics were among the first to use the Internet, years before it was called the Internet, to send E-mail messages. Their correspondence showed a level of courtesy and respect that had always characterized scientific correspondence. But when the use of E-mail broadened to groups of people without preestablished community, the practice of "flaming" quickly developed. It was characterized by rude and insulting language, often in the form of trenchant criticism. Tellingly, flaming was often used to browbeat the recipient into conforming to some behavioral norm the Internet "community" viewed itself as having established. As Internet users discovered the impossibility of building community in this fashion, the invective became steadily more intense. In one well-publicized incident, a U.S. law firm violated the etiquette of the time by broadcasting advertisements over the Net.[6] When it ignored entreaties to cease and desist, Web vigilantes overwhelmed its electronic mailbox with thousands of flames. Unsurprisingly, their censure was to no avail, and the firm continued a practice that was acceptable by preexisting legal and social norms. Not only has the Internet proved itself incapable of spawning community, but in more recent years its antisocial possibilities have become increasingly evident.

It is normally assumed that the Internet will overcome cultural barriers and establish electronic commerce worldwide. Yet consider that relatively few countries have major mail-order businesses, primarily those Fukuyama classifies as "high trust". The same factors that discourage ordering from strangers by mail may discourage E-commerce even more strongly, due to the relative ease of putting up Web sites that one can take down quickly when caught in fraud. Naturally, international E-commerce can proceed in and between Western multinational corporations, or between firms with a preestablished relationship. Third-party seals of approval may also help, and there may be ways to design E-commerce to facilitate the relationship-based practices of most of the world. But E-commerce will not proceed internationally in the same fashion it has in the West.

At the center of Fukuyama's analysis of trust is its role in the kind of spontaneous sociability that is necessary for the formation of large, professionally managed private corporations. Germany, the United States, and Japan were able to invent this type of corporation because they are high-trust societies. They are well endowed with "social capital," which he understands to be habits of trust that are no less foundational to economic performance than material capital.

Fukuyama attacks the received view that the United States is individual-istic in contrast to more communitarian traditional societies. He echoes Alexis de Tocqueville's famous assessment of the United States as a land of joiners, of people who are always willing to form voluntary associations. Similar collectivist behavior is evident in Japan and Germany. On the other hand, traditional societies that are often described as communitarian are in fact atomistic. Except when mandated by the government, communal ac-tion seldom extends beyond the family. Fukuyama's assertions notwith-standing, the United States is individualistic in a way that China is not, but this is consistent with a tendency to form voluntary associations. Voluntary associations require trust. A church or civic organization has a treasury to which members are willing to entrust their resources. A Boy or Girl Scout troop has leaders to which families entrust their children. A business cor-poration has managers to which the owners are willing to entrust their investment and ultimately their livelihood. (Contrary to Fukuyama's char-acterization, book discussion clubs and whatnot are not uncommon in China, but he would be right in pointing out that not much is at stake in these associations.)

Private business firms obviously exist in low-trust nations, but the key management positions are almost always held by family proprietors. The firm can grow to a respectable size if family members have the talent and energy to supervise a large number of employees personally. But this kind of talent is rare, and a firm is subject to the law of regression to the mean: the sons who inherit the business are not likely to be as talented as the fathers who started it, as the story of An Wang painfully illustrates. Large firms, even when they occur, are not long-lived. In a high-trust soci-ety, the family can turn management over to a hierarchy of professionals, and the firm can continue to grow.

The government can of course step in to create large enterprises, as it does in nearly all Pacific Rim nations. This results in a U-shaped distribu-tion of firm sizes: some state operations at the high end of the scale, many family firms at the low end, and practically nothing in the middle. This same pattern is found in France, where the government has been held in sufficiently high regard to attract talented people and organize some rather successful industrial enterprises. In other low-trust areas the government is less active and the high side of the U is missing. Central Italy, for example, is similar to Hong Kong in its large number of successful small firms, ini-tially in machine tool manufacture but more recently in other areas as well. But Italians distrust government, and large government-run corporations have not played the major role they have in France.

South Korea is a special case to which Fukuyama directs considerable attention, because even though it has a strongly Confucian culture, it nonetheless has an impressive collection of large private corporations, namely, Samsung, Hyundai, Lucky-Goldstar (now LG), Daewoo, and Ssangyong. Fukuyama argues that the South Korean government has in fact played a key role in the growth of these corporations. President Park Chung Hee, a major figure in South Korea's economic ascent, took Japanese industry as his model. He was impressed not only with its activist government but also with the central role of Japanese *keiretsu,* or "networked organizations" that unite firms. (Fukuyama points out that Korean *chaebol,* its counterpart of the *keiretsu,* is represented by the same two Chinese characters that represent *zaibatsu* in Japanese, an older name for *keiretsu.* Taiwan also has network organizations, but they play a much smaller role.) The South Korean state not only owns a sizable fraction of the country's industry but also tightly regulates the remaining firms by controlling access to credit, granting of subsidies, and protection from foreign competition. Inside the large Korean firm (*chaebol*), says Fukumaya, lurks a Confucian family business that would quickly revert to Chinese ways without government leadership.

A nation such as Taiwan, Thailand, Indonesia, or China can go a long way with small- and medium-sized firms, particularly in software and some other high-technology industries. But the absence of large private firms may impose a glass ceiling on economic development. Such key industries as computer hardware and aerospace require the organizational size and complexity of a giant corporation. First World prosperity ultimately rests on such organizations. Large corporations developed historically in the United States, for example, because only they could supply the wide-scale coordination necessary to operate railroads, which are essential to modern industry.

Trade could conceivably obviate the need for large private corporations within the boundaries of China or another low-trust society. The government could provide the necessary coordination, as in South Korea or Singapore. Yet the economic efficiency of the Chinese government has not inspired a great deal of admiration to date. As for trade, a small state can certainly rely on it to supply the products of large corporations. But a major power, on which the economy of an entire region primarily rests, cannot supply First World prosperity as we know it, in Fukuyama's view, without supplying the corporate structure on which it depends. If he is right, China may face fundamental obstacles, cultural obstacles, in its path toward becoming an economic superpower.

Fukuyama is right to focus on trust as a key ingredient in economic activity. His distinction of high-trust and low-trust cultures is somewhat misleading, however, because trust is as much a part of one as the other. The difference lies in how trust is built. In fact, it should now be evident that Fukuyama has discovered the distinction between rule-based and relationship-based cultures. Rule-based cultures facilitate trust by inculcating respect for standard operating rules. One can make deals with near-strangers because the chances are high that they subscribe to the same rules. One can obtain honesty from most staff by laying down the rules and making the penalty for violation clear. Guilt will normally carry the burden of enforcement while the boss is not looking. Relationship-based cultures, on the other hand, build trust through personal relationships. More direct supervision of employees is necessary, because people are motivated more by other people than by internalized rules.

Fukuyama incorrectly analyzes Japan, which is a strongly relationship-based culture and should therefore be classified with low-trust nations. Trust is built by cultivating relationships in elaborate old-boy networks. While classmates at the University of Tokyo or elsewhere, young men form bonds. They maintain contact over the years in karaoke bars and on golf courses, which are regular features of professional life. A member of the network can bring in a friend who is not a member by vouching for his honor. The networks therefore tend to grow and large organizations can result. In addition, there are the highly developed Japanese skills for fostering loyalty to the group and maintaining harmony therein. In short, trust must be built through relationships, just as in other low-trust countries. There is no justification for calling Japan "high trust" except that it produces large private organizations, which begs the question at issue.

Finally, Fukuyama's analysis is predicated on the assumption that prosperity is measured by the ability to produce Western-style goods that require large-scale enterprises. It is conceivable that low-trust nations could learn to operate small enterprises more efficiently than the West, using their networking skills and family connections. Then they could profitably trade their goods for the output of large corporations. (They have a cost advantage even today, but it is normally due to historically low wages rather than inherent efficiency.) The non-Western world could also take major steps to mold demand to match its strengths, as Western corporations have done for decades, rather than simply accept the dictates of tastemakers in the West.

Prosperity in Japan

The Western world likes to talk about the long-term recession underway in Japan. Perhaps it helps us to forget about how Japan was in the economic driver's seat in the 1980s. Even when our memory serves us, we convince ourselves that Japan succeeded by adopting Western ideas. Did not W. E. Deming take quality control concepts to that war-torn country in the 1950s? Were not the Japanese so grateful that they named a prestigious national award in his honor?

Japan in fact borrowed much from the West, just as the United States was to borrow much from Japan three decades later. Yet that country would not have overtaken and, for a time, outperformed its American rival in manufacturing without homegrown methods. It would take us too far afield to give a complete account of this, but four items can be mentioned: continuous improvement, suggestion boxes, just-in-time inventory management, and fuzzy control.

Continuous improvement is a simple idea. If workers use moments of spare time to find and implement small ways to improve things, the results may be negligible in the short run, but over a decade or so they can spell the difference between failure and success. The approach has other advantages. It makes the job more interesting and gives workers "ownership," to use a popular term in U.S. business, in what they do. The cost is zero, or even negative, because workers conceive and implement their ideas at times they would otherwise be idle, and their output may even rise because they are more engaged. Japanese sometimes use the analogy of wading across a swimming pool (or, in their case, a public bath). One can rush across in a crash program to reach the other side, but it requires much effort, since the friction of the water increases rapidly with speed. Or one can ease across very slowly, which is effortless due to very slight friction, and yet reach the same goal.

Continuous improvement is a natural idea in Japanese culture, which takes the long view and ascribes responsibility to the group rather than the individual. It is less attractive to Western industry, which relies on individual incentives for managers and workers. The contribution of an individual worker in a continuous improvement effort is probably too small to show up in production statistics or catch the attention of a floor manager looking for a promotion or bonus. The measurable gains come only in the combined efforts of many workers. The manager therefore does not know whom to reward. More fundamentally, Westerners control their work environment, and their environment generally, through cause and effect. Science reveals the connection between cause and effect, and technology manipulates the effect by manipulating the cause. Causes are the handles by which one can get a grip on things. Continuous improvement does not provide visible handles, because the factors that actually caused improvement cannot be isolated. The manager knows only that the little changes somehow added up. Another barrier is impatience, particularly in the United States. The U.S. manager wants to see results in the next quarterly report, whereas the real benefits of continuous improvement may require years to materialize.

Suggestion boxes symbolize group harmony, which is the social mechanism that makes continuous improvement possible. If a Japanese worker proposes a change in the workplace, via a suggestion box or otherwise, that proposal is taken seriously and implemented if possible. But it is not done to improve efficiency so much as to maintain the health of the group.

It is essential in any workplace to get everyone to work together toward a common goal. The authority of the boss is of course one way of doing it, and deference to one's superior is an important principle in all Confucian societies. Yet Japan has not relied on this alone.

Another approach is to talk through disagreements in order to arrive at some kind of compromise. This usually involves appeal to principles of what is fair or efficient, an approach that can work in rule-based Western cultures but is alien to Japan. In fact, the single greatest barrier to a Western professional's adjustment to Japan (or Korea) is the relatively minor role played by rationality, conceived as fairness or efficiency, in everyday decision making. T. R. Reid relates an incident in which his American daughter entered a Japanese elementary school and was assigned to a small group for classwork.[7] On the first day, while Reid and his wife watched from the sidelines, the group was asked to determine the capital of the United States. Most of the children thought it was Hollywood, and the young American pointed out the error. Although she was obviously the authority on the matter, the group agreed upon Hollywood as the answer. Maintaining group harmony was more important than making the rational choice.

In Japan, courtesy replaces appeals to rationality as a principle of social cohesion. If there is an emotional clash, there is no recourse to fairness or efficiency arguments to iron out the problem. The best policy is not to provoke anger, embarrassment, or hurt feelings in the first place. This is called "saving face."

One way to save face is to take everyone's ideas seriously. I was once on a multicultural committee whose task was to produce a planning document. The Japanese colleague who headed the committee wrote a first draft and asked for committee input. He carefully incorporated every suggested change into the document, along with annotations as to who suggested the change and what the original text was. As the memo went through several rounds, the annotations became longer than the document, but everyone's contribution was respected. The process reflected the old Japanese practice of *nemawashi* (roughly, "turning the roots"), which involves everyone in decision making. Everyone edits circulating drafts (*ringi sho*) of a memo and stamps them with his monogram (*hanko*) to indicate that his view has been incorporated.

Toyota and other firms adapted the same principle to the factory by considering and respecting ideas from the floor. As it happens, workers often make useful suggestions, because they are close to the job and understand its subtleties. Improvements, large or small, are therefore put into practice day after day, even if it would be impractical to install a direct economic incentive.

Just-in-time inventory management, perhaps the most famous Japanese innovation, is a direct outgrowth of Japanese social organization. Japanese business is typically done by working through an old-boy network, and the identification of suppliers is no exception. Executives that supply auto parts to Toyota, for example, may be golf buddies of the executives who purchase the parts. They trust each other enough to let engineers from the two firms work together and make sure that the parts have the right specifications. Because the commitment is long term, Toyota can count on the availability of a part as long as it is needed. Production scheduling can also be closely coordinated, so that the parts are manufactured when they are needed in the assembly plant, that is, "just in time." This prevents the buildup of parts inventories, which is expensive because it occupies space and, more importantly, ties up capital. Small inventories also allow faster response to market changes and easier correction of defects in the supplied parts.

The whole affair rests on personal commitments that executives will not breach because it would mean loss of honor and ostracism from their peer group. It is true that Japan's compact geography also contributes, because it makes delivery times more predictable. The fact that so many businessmen live in Tokyo makes it easier for them to gather in groups for business and pleasure, an essential part of trust maintenance. But the system could not exist without Japan's unique culture.

Western businessmen also form old-boy networks, and there is talk of interlocking boards of directors. But these connections do not dominate business decisions and are regarded with suspicion if they become too extensive. The result is that Western supply chains (aside from those influenced by Japanese practices) are very different from Japanese. American firms, for example, historically take bids from several suppliers. The contacts contain detailed engineering specifications that must be drawn up in advance of production, because engineers are normally denied sufficient access to the other firm to permit close cooperation. If the contract runs out or is disputed, a new round of bidding may be necessary, making the price and availability of parts unpredictable. Just-in-time delivery is hard to achieve, since supplier and customer relate to each other essentially through legal documents. The long transport distances on the North American continent compound the difficulty, as do recent upgrades in antiterrorism safeguards, which threaten some of the lean manufacturing practices that have developed since the 1980s.

Japanese networking also facilitated the growth of *keiretsu* (known in prewar days as *zaibatsu*), or vertically integrated corporate networks. Personal connections also link the *keiretsu* to each other and to the government. A related phenomenon is the emergence of industrywide trade associations, which exist partly to agree on industry policies and ward off government regulation. There are even businesswide organizations known as *keidanren.*

Fuzzy control presents a particularly interesting case in which Japan not only adopted Western technology but also, for cultural reasons, used it more successfully than the West for a decade. Fuzzy control began with Lotfi Zadeh's paper on fuzzy logic, in which propositions are not definitely true or false, as in classical logic, but have degrees of truth.[8] It is inspired by the perception that most statements in everyday life are vague and tend to be more or less true.

The idea of fuzzy logic attracted limited attention until the 1980s, when expert systems became popular in the United States. They were originally conceived as a way of capturing an expert's knowledge in a set of rules, for example, "If the patient has a sore throat and a throat culture reveals streptococcus, then prescribe penicillin." The dream was to automate expertise and thereby make it much cheaper. It was quickly realized that expert systems cannot replace experts but are well suited to automatic control. A steam engine, for example, may be regulated by turning up the heat when the pressure falls, and vice versa. The rules might say, "If the pressure is slightly low and rising slowly, then do not adjust the heat," or, "If the pressure is very low and steady, then increase the heat substantially," and so on, with rules for every situation. Naturally a "slightly low" pressure is not well defined, and this is where fuzzy logic comes in. The condition "slightly low pressure" is associated with a "membership function," which indicates to what degree the pressure is slightly low. If it is 10 psi too low, the condition "slightly low" may be 90 percent true, but if the pressure is 30 psi too low, the condition may be only 20 percent true. A rule is applied with a level of confidence equal to that of the least-confident premise. So if it is 20 percent true that the pressure is slightly low, and it is 50 percent true that the pressure is steady, then it is 20 percent true that one should not adjust the heat. When all the rules have been applied ("fired"), one has a set of different instructions, all of which apply to a certain extent. Perhaps it is 20 percent true that the heat should remain steady, 60 percent true that the heat should increase substantially, and so forth. These instructions have their own membership functions and are combined ("defuzzified") in a fairly straightforward way to obtain a specific number for how much the heat should be changed (e.g., increase by 1,000 Btu per hour).

Fuzzy control encountered a storm of criticism from the Western scientific establishment, which preferred classical control based on scientific laws. In classical control, one writes down the equations that describe heat transfer, the production of steam, and so forth. One then applies sophisticated mathematics (optimal control theory) to calculate how the heat should be adjusted to achieve the desired pressure. Fuzzy control, however, is ad hoc. The rules represent not physical law but common sense. The membership functions are chosen simply because they seem reasonable and have no grounding in theory. Western engineers largely rejected fuzzy control during the 1980s.

Japan, meanwhile, had a love affair with fuzzy control. Perhaps the approach had no theoretical basis, but it worked remarkably well if one sufficiently tweaked the rules. This was enough for the Japanese. They used fuzzy control (implemented by computer chips) to provide a smooth ride on trains, automatic focus in cameras ("fuzzy focus," an interesting oxymoron), and climate control in buildings. They put fuzzy controllers in clothes dryers, rice cookers, and many other products. Rice cooking is no easy task, incidentally, because Japanese have a discriminating taste that can be satisfied only by monitoring the cooking process carefully through several stages. By the 1990s the Japanese success had convinced Western engineers that they were missing a good thing, and Western industry quietly began installing fuzzy (and "neuro-fuzzy") control in a host of products.

There were various theories for why Westerners rejected fuzzy control and Japanese accepted it so readily. Many fuzzy control proponents saw selfish motives in Western science. Engineers who had struggled with the rigors of classical control felt threatened by novices who could easily pick up fuzzy control, which is mathematically trivial. Zadeh's rivals believed that he did not deserve to be famous for inventing so simple an idea, and so forth. These may have been factors, but one must explain why Japanese engineers were not governed by the same motives. It is also interesting that the first commercial application of fuzzy control was developed, not in Japan, but at the University of Odense, Denmark, where it was applied to cement manufacture. This is a process for which it is essentially impossible to construct a mathematical model based on physical law. One must simply stand over the vat, adjust the heat, and stir as indicated by the consistency of the slurry. In this case, at least, Western science had no objection to fuzzy control, and it was a case in which scientific principle was unavailable.

As for Japanese enthusiasm, it was said that the fuzziness represented a "feminine" logic due to the lack of sharp distinctions and was therefore more suited to Asian culture than the male-dominated West. This was a curious explanation in view of the fact that Japan, by any criterion, has the most masculine culture on earth (see Chapter 7). A slightly more sophisticated view was that fuzziness harmonized with the concept of yin and yang in Asian Buddhism, which implies, among other things, that nothing is wholly A or wholly not A; it is always a mixture. Perhaps, but fuzzy logic had a remarkable cult following in the West, too, even while it was scorned by scientists and engineers. One might just as well argue that fuzzy logic satisfied the Western desire for order by bringing the vagueness of everyday life into a formal system.

I suggest that the Japanese used fuzzy control because it was easy to implement, it worked, and most importantly, its unprincipled nature was simply not a concern to them. The Western scientific and engineering communities, on the other hand, were bound by a tradition of rigorous discipline in the study of nature. As much as anything, their investigations provide the foundation of Western culture today, because they are the basis on which Westerners control their environment. By refusing to cave in to the ad hoc approach of fuzzy control, Western scientists and engineers were carrying out their almost priestly duties as custodians of the scientific tradition. The Japanese, however, have no need of such a tradition. They are free of the Western burden of making nature intelligible, because their culture does not rest on science-based technology. For them, technology is a choice, not a necessity. Ironically, this allowed them to choose a successful technology that the West felt duty bound to reject.

I have tried to illustrate how a non-Western nation can take advantage of its cultural characteristics to create Western-style products with efficiency and quality. It is not a question of whether "Asian values" or "Western values" are better; it is a question of whether those values are properly matched to production and finance.

An irony of the Japanese story is that Japanese innovations found their way to the United States, partly through the agency of W. E. Deming himself, where they helped Americans to restore their dominant position. The U.S. manufacturing scene of the 1980s was dominated by Japanese ideas and buzzwords, many of which were fads, but others of which were successfully adapted to U.S. culture. They brought the U.S. manufacturing sector through a revolution that is obvious to anyone who walks into the factory of today. Just-in-time inventory management, for example, became part of the "lean manufacturing" approach, which uses Toyota's *kanban* system as well as some non-Japanese ideas, such as a "theory of constraints" that focuses attention on production bottlenecks. It has also become common to build close relationships with two or three suppliers rather than regularly take bids from many. Due largely to Japanese ideas, all-important setup times in factories have been reduced by orders of magnitude. The Japanese group-oriented approach is alien to the United States, but it was transformed into "worker empowerment," as popularized by

NOTES FOR CHAPTER 3   57

Tom Peters and others.[9] Worker empowerment gives workers some authority to make improvements at their own work station, thus implementing a
form of continuous improvement by appealing to the sense of equality and
individualism in the United States. This creates a sense of enfranchisement,
which encourages further innovation. Managers encourage teamwork in an
individualistic society by giving team bonuses for good work, which build
up peer pressure within the team that discourages free riders. Given that the
manufacturing sector is by far the most productive segment of a First World
economy, it is hard to overestimate the importance of the Japanese contribution to the U.S. economy.

Japan itself has fallen behind, largely due to overinvestment and other
financial problems. As I remarked earlier, it is more difficult to adapt a non-
Western culture to the global financial system than to global manufacturing. But it is far too soon to conclude that it cannot be done.

Notes for Chapter 3

1. Free Press (New York, 1992).
2. *Cannibals and Kings: The Origins of Culture,* Random House (New York,
1977).
3. *Road Belong Cargo,* Manchester University Press (Manchester, U.K., 1964).
4. Houghton Mifflin (Boston, 1961, orig. published 1934).
5. Marvin Harris, *Our Kind,* Harper & Row (New York, 1989).
6. Jared Sandberg, "Phoenix Lawyers Irk Internet Users Again By Broadcasting
Ad," *Wall Street Journal* (June 22, 1994), sec. B, p. 5, col. 1.
7. *Confucius Lives Next Door: What Living in the East Teaches Us about
Living in the West,* Random House (New York, 1999).
8. Fuzzy Sets, *Information and Control* 8 (1965): 338–53.
9. Tom Peters, *In Search of Excellence: Lessons from America's Best-Run Companies,* Warner Books (New York, 1988).

4 *What Is Culture?*

While teaching a class in cross-cultural management, I asked the international students in the room to contrast their country with the United States. One French student immediately spoke up. The main difference, she explained, is that her home country "has more culture" than the United States.

Leaving aside the truth or falsehood of her remark, it speaks of culture in a different sense than I use in this book. The French student's idea of culture as refinement or high civilization can be traced at least as far back as the Victorian poet and social critic Matthew Arnold. A related sense identifies culture with art, music, and literature, as when we refer to a concert as a "cultural event."

For our purposes, however, culture has a much broader scope. It is the way that human beings learn to live with one another and their environment. There are many different cultures, because culture is learned and human beings are flexible enough to learn vastly different ways of living. The most fascinating aspect of culture is that it gives *meaning* to practices and institutions. A study of culture must always involve interpretation, or a determination of what things mean.

This definition of culture was popularized in the early twentieth century by anthropologist Franz Boas and reflects the mainstream view of cultural anthropology over the last several decades. Boas emphasized that all cultures are equally worthy of study and respect, an idea that traces to the eighteenth-century German philosopher Johann Gottfried Herder. Herder criticized European colonialism for its failure to grant the legitimacy of non-European cultures. Ironically, the same thinking planted the idea that European cultures, too, not only are legitimate but also deserve to exist in a purified state. This helped fuel romantic European nationalism and justify such practices as "ethnic cleansing."

What Culture Is Not

Culture, as already noted, is not identified here with the arts or refinement. Another popular sense of culture is reflected in talk of "corporate culture," and by extension the culture of other kinds of organizations. It might refer to the pinstripe formality of IBM, the business-casual atmosphere of Silicon Valley, or almost anything related to behavioral norms in an organization. This again is not the sense of culture I employ here, because a corporation does not have a culture of its own in the anthropological sense. The fact that an organization has distinctive practices does not show that it has a culture. The people of Muncie, Indiana, behave very differently in church than at the bowling lanes, but this is not because the churches and bowling teams have their own cultures. On the contrary, they work together with other institutions to constitute a single U.S. Midwestern culture. Culture addresses the fundamental issues of family, sex, power, and death. A workplace is only one strand of this fabric.

Still another interpretation of culture appears in the cultural studies movement on campuses in Britain and the United States. It got started in the early 1960s at the University of Birmingham, where it was strongly influenced by the work of Raymond Williams and Richard Hoggart. One of its agenda was to provide a neo-Marxian political analysis of Western culture, for which it draws inspiration from the late-nineteenth-century Italian Marxist Antonio Gramsci, and more recently the French philosopher Louis Althusser. It is not difficult to tell when one is reading the literature of the field, because it achieves a level of obscurity that puts Kant and Hegel to shame.

Cultural studies soundly rejects the idea of high culture, or culture as refinement, which it views as a political tool of the ruling class. It prefers to analyze popular culture promulgated by mass media. In the United States it is part of a larger movement that took university humanities departments by storm, one that involves semiotics, poststructuralism, feminist theory, and radical views of interpretation. It views culture as "text" to be interpreted as literary text, and interpretation often takes the form of deconstruction. The process of deconstruction, or hermeneutics, is credited to Jacques Derrida, but it was anticipated by methods for interpreting holy scripture. It looks beneath the surface meaning (if any) to ulterior political motives that produced the text. It gave us the popular journalistic term *subtext* and banished the study of "dead white males" from some college curricula in favor of feminism and multiculturalism.

Cultural studies has a skeptical attitude toward cultural anthropology and its concept of culture. It deconstructs anthropology as a tool of colonialism or neocolonialism, and it suspects talk of cultural otherness to be a smokescreen for political oppression or racism. Anthropologists might describe a woman's role in Saudi culture in neutral terms and hesitate to apply such Western ideas as gender equality. Cultural studies, by contrast, calls it an "unjust society marked by exploitation of women." If the anthropologist protests that Saudi culture is too different from ours to apply Western concepts, cultural studies reads this as code language for the belief that Saudis are racially inferior. At root, it denies the radical otherness of other cultures because it wants to apply Western political and ethical categories to them—a clear demonstration of Western universalizing tendencies. Adherents of cultural studies differ from most Western academics, however, in that they make no pretense at detached objectivity. They view all discourse, including their own, as being at the bottom political and therefore feel justified in giving their scholarship over to a political cause.

Enthusiasm for cultural studies peaked years ago, but many anthropologists remain sympathetic with the movement and have drifted away from the traditional Boasian paradigm. This book, however, continues to speak of culture (and cultures) in the classical sense developed by anthropologists. It takes the view that making a good faith attempt to understand culture, or anything else, in an objective and apolitical way is part of what is meant by *understanding*.

Culture, Nature, Personality, and Ethnic Groups

Culture is normally distinguished from human nature on the one hand and personality on the other. Human nature is the common genetic heritage of humankind. We all share a need for food, shelter, and nurturing. We all cling to our parents, love our children, and grieve over the loss of loved ones. We all smile when we are happy and weep when we are sad (although Indonesians may laugh when angry). We all enter the world in the same way and find our visit cut short. The fact that we are self-conscious beings presents us with an additional set of fundamental problems: coping with our inability to realize or even justify our aims, and coming to terms with our mortality. Although this book says much about differences, it builds its analysis on this fundamental commonality.

Culture, by contrast, is cultivated. It is based on a set of behaviors, attitudes, and ideas that human beings *learn* while living together. The analogy with cultivation is a good one because it reminds us that human culture can be deliberately cultivated as can a garden; we can teach ourselves to think and behave in certain ways rather than others. This can be an important element in the survival of human societies, and it is becoming more important.

Personality consists of the traits that are unique to an individual human being. It is partly genetic and partly learned. Because much of personality is acquired, it is strongly influenced by culture. Yet a very wide range of personalities can develop within a given culture, whence the danger of placing too much emphasis on "national character." There is some truth to the notion that Japanese are polite and Israelis are not, or that British are reserved and Brazilians are fun loving. But one must always be prepared to meet a rude Japanese or a boisterous Englishman. A little story may clarify the relationship between personality and culture. When I took an apartment in Zimbabwe, the neighbors made it clear that I should hire a maid, because people need work. It is against my egalitarian nature to hire a maid, but I acquiesced. I paid her ten Zim dollars a week (at the time, about seventy cents U.S.) to come in once a week, which was somewhat excessive. When I left for work on her first day, the apartment was strewn with books and papers that I had been using to prepare the courses I was teaching. When I returned from work, the maid had already left, and the apartment was completely bare. My paraphernalia had vanished. One might think that thieves had cleaned out the place, but I had an inkling. I began to look into cabinets and closets. There I found neat little stacks of books and papers. What is more, they were accurately sorted by subject. One stack was statistics, one was operations management, and so forth. The next week I remarked to the maid that she did a really fine job. Her response: "So you were impressed, were you?"

My maid might well have been a corporate executive if she had grown up in Switzerland, where order and system are foundations of the culture. Organization is less important in Zimbabwe, and she is a part-time maid. It is therefore misleading to say that the Swiss are organized and Africans are not. There are disorganized people in Switzerland and, as my maid demonstrates, compulsive organizers in Zimbabwe. It is just that either culture rewards and encourages the type of personality needed to make its system work.

Culture is not the same as personality, then, although certain personalities may thrive better than others in a given culture. In Japan, courtesy and deference are an essential part of the mechanism that enables people to live and work in harmony. In Israel, where interpersonal relations are ideally regulated by internalized universal moral law, few courtesies are necessary. In Brazil, raucous parties and festivals play a central role in stress management. This sort of behavior is not likely to evolve in a cold northern European climate that keeps people in their homes. Of culture, human nature, and personality, culture is the only one that has no genetic input.

A culture can also be distinguished from an ethnic group. The latter term generally refers to a subpopulation of a state that has a common cultural background historically. Examples are people of Chinese background in Indonesia, or people of Turkish background in Switzerland. The boundaries of ethnic groups may be blurred, as for example in the United States, where peoples as diverse as Puerto Ricans, Chileans, and even Portuguese-speaking Brazilians may all be regarded as "Hispanics." Ethnic groups usually form when large numbers of people immigrate, or when a state expands its control to lands occupied by exotic cultures.

A subculture is a group that differs in some cultural respects from the larger society. I use the term *society* to refer to people who live in the same geographical area and interact with one another much more than with people outside the area. A society normally has a dominant culture, and I will argue in Chapter 15 that it must for long-term survival. Yet a society can tolerate and even benefit from minority groups that differ culturally in some respects.

Unlike an ethnic group, a subculture may be identified with no particular national heritage. A religious commune, for example, may over generations develop a subculture without ethnicity. An ethnic group, on the other hand, may be scarcely distinguishable culturally from the mainstream population. In the United States, for example, people of Irish background may cultivate a certain amount of ethnic consciousness, wear green on Saint Patrick's Day, and so forth, but their culture is essentially mainstream. Because ethnic groups often find themselves assimilating to the mainstream culture, they may try to emphasize their difference and even fabricate ethnic traditions to foster a sense of solidarity. This is a form of revitalization, although when it occurs, cultural identity tends to be beyond recovery. I live in Pittsburgh, which is historically a stronghold of such Scots as Andrew Carnegie and so-called Scotch-Irish. The university at which I teach likes to make much of its Scottish heritage, for instance with its tartan colors and its team of kilted pipers. It is one of the world's few universities that offer a major in bagpiping. As it happens, the kilt was apparently introduced by English businessman Thomas Rawlinson in the nineteenth century, on the grounds that it was more suitable garb for his employees than the traditional robes (many Scots, unsurprisingly, dispute this claim). The conventional identification of certain plaids with clans is pure fiction. Even the bagpipe is hardly unique to Scotland but is found in many areas once dominated by Celts. The Highland drone can be heard even today as far away as Hungary or northern Spain.

Race

Race, as understood in the West, consists of biological traits that correlate with geographic region, such as skin color. Although cultures tend to be racially homogeneous—and even here one can point to many exceptions, such as Latin America—there is no necessary connection between a culture and the race of people that practice it. A person of any race has the capability to become a fully functioning participant in any of the world's cultures. A racially different person may of course be ostracized because of appearance, but the same can happen just as easily to people of unusual appearance belonging to the same race. The lack of a necessary connection between race and culture should be no surprise, because any culture already accommodates a wide variety of individual traits, much wider than any variation attributable to racial background.

I emphasize the weak coupling between race and culture because the West has so long assumed the opposite. In the current era it is politically incorrect to view race as a determinant of intelligence, creativity, personality, moral character, or industriousness. Yet this is precisely the historical Western view. These traits in turn explained cultural differences in wealth, literacy, social organization, and level of "development," resulting in a thoroughgoing racial determinism. Its origin is no mystery, as it flows directly out of the West's universalizing rationality. The dynamics of this inference provide an instructive, if ultimately tragic, lesson in how culture shapes our thinking.

The Western concept of race began to develop when colonialism exposed Europe to world cultures. One can trace the mental steps that a universalizing European of, say, the Victorian era might take to try to understand the vast differences among these cultures. First, since there is but one rational way to live, there is but one developmental path. European culture is clearly superior and dominates the world, and it must therefore have advanced further along this path than the others. (Most people regard their culture as superior to others, and Europeans are no exception.) Now a troubling question comes to mind: why are cultures older than the West less advanced? Furthermore, why do ethnic groups living in the West lag behind, when they have been exposed to a more advanced way of life? The Victorian may consider various explanations. The inferior climate and natural resources of some regions may account for their backwardness, yet this does not explain every case, nor does it explain retarded ethnic groups. Racial discrimination unfairly holds back minorities living in the West, but this is not an explanation that naturally comes to mind, as the West sees itself as upholding justice. In any event, racism in the West does not explain the historically slow development of non-Western countries. The European, and later the European American, are therefore drawn to what seems the inevitable conclusion: nonwhite races must be biologically inferior. This seems to explain everything.

Another attraction of the racial point of view is the Western preference for explanations that reduce matters to natural science. They are easier to universalize and can be expressed in terms of cause and effect, which supports the West's reliance on technology. Biological determinism fits this bill much better than cultural interpretation. Stephen Jay Gould tells us in his immensely popular book, *The Mismeasure of Man*,[1] how Victorian science supported racism. The field of craniometry claimed to predict

human intelligence on the basis of skull capacity. Conveniently, members
of nonwhite races (and women) were measured as having smaller skulls.
Anthropometry asserted that people with "apelike" features tend to have
low intelligence. These features include a thick skull, fewer cranial sutures,
large jaws, a large face, long arms, precocious wrinkles, a narrow forehead,
large ears, the absence of baldness, darker skin, greater visual acuity, di-
minished sensitivity to pain, and absence of blushing. It was widely assumed that nonwhite races possessed these traits to a greater degree than
the white race. The early twentieth century saw the rise of eugenics in a
United States that had recently been swamped by immigrants from southern and eastern Europe. Eugenics emphasized selective breeding and even
sterilization to favor Nordic stock and thereby improve the national gene
pool. The idea was endorsed by some of the leading intellectuals of the day,
such as Theodore Roosevelt, Alexander Graham Bell, Margaret Sanger,
Oliver Wendell Holmes, and the founding editors of *The Nation* and *The
New Republic*. The movement fizzled in the United States in the 1930s,
after some of the finest examples of the Nordic race were seen jumping
from windows during the Wall Street financial crash. Unfortunately, it
found new devotees in Nazi Germany.

We can and should ridicule nonsense parading as science, but the basic
premise of Western racism—the inferiority of nonwhite races—is more
deeply rooted than this. It need be viewed, not as the result of pseudoscience, evil intent, or even arrogance, but as the natural outcome of a universalizing rationality that has no other ready explanation for persistent
cultural differences. Despite our political correctness and other efforts
to expunge it, it persists. As Jeremy Rifken points out in *The Biotech
Century,*[2] biological determinism and eugenics have resurfaced in the ex-
citement surrounding the new biology. There is no denying the importance
of genes, but again we overlook the profound effect of culture on individuals of any genotype.

Ethnic Conflict

People in the United States tend to think of ethic conflict in terms of
race, no doubt due to its violent history of race relations. More often than
not, however, race plays little or no role. One thinks of Muslims and Serbs
in Bosnia, Catholics and Protestants in Ulster, Ukrainians and Russians in
Ukraine, Hutus and Tutsis in Rwanda, or Hindus and Muslims in India.
The differences are purely cultural. There are Russians versus Chechnyans,
Sinhalese versus Tamils, Chinese versus Tibetans, Spanish versus the Basque
minority, Indians versus Pakistanis, Temne versus Mende (Sierra Leone),

Davaks versus Mudarese (Borneo), Indonesians versus East Timorese, Shiite Iranians versus Sunni Iraqis, the various factions of Afghanistan, and even Francophones versus Anglophones in Quebec, and in each case, racial differences are minimal. In fact, it is hard to think of long-standing ethnic conflicts, other than those involving Westerners, in which there is significant racial difference, although the violence against ethnic Chinese in Indonesia comes quickly to mind.

Ethnic hatred often seems most intense when even the cultural difference is minimal. While working in India, I visited the home of friends who, like many middle-class Indians, employ guards. They remarked that the night guard would not come that evening, because he had been beaten up on the street the previous day. Sectarian riots had recently broken out all over India, sparked by the destruction of a mosque located in the town of Ayodhya. The Hindu perpetrators justified their action on the grounds that the building stood on the holy birthplace of Lord Rama, a Hindu deity. The newspapers reported several hundred deaths from disturbances in the city where I resided, many spurred by police action. (Interestingly, the state compensated the families of rioters killed by riot police, paying them a sum that was fairly substantial by Indian standards.) Hindus had attacked the night guard as part of the general mayhem. Yet even my hosts, who were native Indians, expressed bewilderment that the assailants could tell that he was Muslim. There was nothing about him in either appearance or mannerism that should provide a clue.

Perhaps similar peoples tend to end up in conflict because neighbors tend to be similar, and conflicts typically involve neighbors. Yet why should conflict between neighbors be accompanied by the intense hatred and unthinkable atrocities that so often characterize ethnic strife? One possible explanation is an ecological theory of warfare, to be discussed shortly.

How to Understand Culture

Before continuing with the main business of this book, I would like to take a moment to examine an issue that constantly lurks in the background: what it means to understand culture. It is an issue that is deeply contested among anthropologists, and much of the field's history can be seen as a series of attempts to resolve it. I would like to explain my position on this issue, to avoid misunderstanding of what I am trying to do in this book.

Because culture gives meaning to its practices, they must somehow be interpreted. This seems to call for a method of study that is very unlike chemistry or mathematics, perhaps something akin to literary criticism.

The study of culture becomes particularistic, since it considers each culture on its own terms. It appears that one must either ignore meaning, the heart of culture, or sacrifice generality.

To make this more specific, suppose that we would like to understand why the Cherokee and the Choctaw peoples of North America were at one time constantly involved in skirmishes. One approach is find out how they explained it, or what the whole affair meant to them. Perhaps it was something to do with redressing certain grievances. The Cherokee attacked the Choctaw because the Choctaw ambushed a Cherokee warrior. The Choctaw ambushed a Cherokee warrior because the Cherokee hunted on Choctaw land, and so forth, through an endless regress, much as we see today in the Middle East. But this explanation seems incomplete. Even once we know the meaning of it all, we still wish to know why this cycle of violence had to occur. Here is one explanation: tribal warfare creates a no-man's land between belligerent groups and therefore prevents overexploitation of natural resources. It ensures that a certain amount of land is allowed to lie fallow and regenerate itself. Tribes fight because the peaceful ones depleted their resources and no longer exist. This is an explanation based on a general principle of cultural evolution and might therefore qualify as science.

Views on how culture should be understood cover the full gamut, from interpretation to science. At one pole is the "symbolic anthropology" school, often associated with Talcott Parsons and particularly Clifford Geertz, for whom the aim of cultural anthropology is to uncover the meaning of practices and institutions.[3] At the other might be Marvin Harris, who proposes "cultural materialism" as the only foundation on which a science of culture can rest. He is sympathetic, for example, with the ecological theory of warfare just presented, on which he considerably elaborates.[4] The position taken here is that interpretation must have a place, in fact a central place, in one's understanding of culture. At the same time, however, some form of generalization is possible as well, based on the fact that all cultures address certain fundamental problems: how to wrest an existence from the earth, how to get along with one's fellows, and how to cope with the stress and frustration of self-conscious experience. It is difficult, if not impossible, to state in general terms how cultures solve these problems. Cultures are complex systems, much like ecosystems, that are organized in very different ways. Their solutions cannot be grasped without analyzing each on its own terms. Yet one can at least say that these systems will be organized around the basic tasks that any culture must accomplish. This is not a law of nature in the sense of the second law of thermodynamics, but it at least provides some structure to one's thinking.

The obvious question at this point is, why must I make general statements about culture? Why not settle for case-by-case interpretation? Perhaps I am succumbing to the Western trait I criticize so much, namely, insisting on universality where there is none. I concede that my approach is unabashedly Western inasmuch as I look for patterns that hold across all (human) cultures. I do this partly for its own sake, and partly because I am speaking primarily to Western readers, who rely so thoroughly on universalizing rationality. I therefore seek universality of a sort, but it is another thing to insist on universality where there is none. My criticism of the Western understanding of culture is, not that it generalizes, but that in its pressing need to find universality, it generalizes too quickly. Arguably the West's greatest achievement is its ability to universalize, while its greatest tragedy is its tendency to universalize its own peculiarities. Hasty generalizations can at times carry out their cultural task even when they are false, but in a shrinking world they have become maladaptive. I therefore propose an account of culture that I think not only is more sensitive to the complexity of the world but also shows Westerners how their very universalism meets a cultural need.

Culture and Meaning

How does one find out what things mean in a culture? If understanding culture is like interpreting literature, what is to prevent people from having a wide range of interpretations?

One of the strongest proponents of the literary approach is Clifford Geertz, who argues that a layered and nuanced interpretation of social practices is the stuff of cultural understanding. He calls it "thick description," borrowing a term from philosopher Gilbert Ryle. Geertz's views foreshadow the more radical interpretive approach of cultural studies, already discussed. It is not necessary to go as far as cultural studies, however, to recognize the basic truth that culture must be interpreted. In fact, one can perhaps obtain more insight from one of Geertz's own intellectual mentors, Ludwig Wittgenstein. I briefly alluded to Wittgenstein's views in Chapter 1 as a key to understanding how culture can bestow meaning. Now is a good point to examine them more carefully.

Suppose I arrive at the office for my first day of work. When I meet another employee who is already at work, that person pulls his or her left ear. I respond in kind, also saying "mmm" if the she is female and "ooo" if he is male. I soon observe that if a superior initiates the greeting, I should also wink while responding. After a few days, just as I begin to master this peculiar practice, the employees begin tugging at their right ears. Eventually I realize that this is done when the weather outside is cloudy or rainy.

In Wittgenstein's view, when I learn how to participate in this practice, I understand what it means. An ear tug has meaning in the very same sense, and receives its meaning in the very same way, as the word *bachelor*. It receives its meaning from its role in the larger context of social behavior, that is, from the set of occasions on which people tend to use it. This runs counter to the traditional view that words have meaning because they are defined to mean something, and similarly for gestures. In the traditional view, the word *bachelor* is meaningful because it is defined to mean an "unmarried man." Some words, such as *red,* cannot be defined in this way. But they are defined "ostensively," for example by pointing to a red object.

It is tempting to imagine definitions for the words and gestures of the office ritual. Pulling the ear seems to say something about the weather. The "mmm" and "ooo" might be rendered, "Good morning, sir," or, "Good morning, madam." Perhaps a wink is a sign of deference. But in Wittgenstein's view, no such interpretation is uniquely determined by the meaning. A similar "postmodern" view was expressed by the philosopher and logician Willard Quine, who carefully analyzed what it means to translate a language. He regarded such interpretations as "analytical hypotheses" that may help an outsider grasp the language but that are under-determined by the meaning of the words or gestures. Analytical hypotheses can be concocted for one's own language. Dictionarians do it for a living. However, the meaning of the words they define consists in their role in the overall "language game," to use Wittgenstein's phrase, not in their "definition." This can even account for the meaning of such technical language as, "the spectral line has a wavelength of 4,000 Ångstroms." Roughly speaking, the meaning of this statement resides in the fact that scientists assent to the statement when certain experiments with spectrometers have certain results and reject it otherwise. This theory also accounts for the meaning of what are traditionally regarded as ostensively defined words, and does so more satisfactorily. When one points to a red thing, the pointing finger does not distinguish whether the color, texture, or weight of the object is meant. The notion of color is captured in the fact that an orange object of the same texture and weight is not called "red."

The postmodern view that reality under-determines its description, that different theories can be equally legitimate, may provide a way for universalizing Westerners to deal with cultural difference. For the moment, however, it suffices to examine some immediately practical implications. One is that the way to learn what practices mean is to learn when it is appropriate to engage in them. There is no harm in imposing an interpretation of one's own, expressed in one's own concepts and language, as long as one recognizes that another's interpretation may be equally valid. Some south Indians, for example, use a certain twisting motion of the head during conversation. It clearly does not mean "yes" or "no." It may mean something similar to "uh-huh" in U.S. English, but this does not seem quite right either. Anglophone Indians are no doubt prepared to give their own account of what it means. Yet to understand what it means, it is enough to learn when to do it.

If this view is correct, then there is a certain latitude in how one may interpret meanings, in the sense that different analytical hypotheses can be equally appropriate. The meaning of a practice is far from arbitrary, however, because one does not know it until one has learned when and how to engage in the practice.

Not all behavior is meaningful. Sometimes I scratch my head to indicate puzzlement, and on other occasions I scratch it to relieve an itch. Only the first type of scratch is meaningful, but what makes it so? In Wittgenstein's view, it is not meaningful because I am thinking, "I am puzzled." It is meaningful because people commonly scratch when they hesitate, screw up their faces, ask for advice, and so forth, and because people *learn* to indicate puzzlement in this way. Some people scratch their heads in the morning, but this behavior is not meaningful because others do not learn to express the time of day by scratching.

This view leads to two further practical implications. One is that to understand another culture fully, it is not necessary to get inside the heads of the people. It is not necessary to think as they think or feel what they feel. This is fortunate, because it is probably impossible to do so. (Nor is it clear that it is always possible, even in principle, to *know* whether one is doing so. How can one tell, for example, whether the next person experiences "red" the same way? Such considerations, known as the "private language argument," helped drive Wittgenstein to his account of meaning.) The second implication is that to discover what things mean, one must become sufficiently immersed in the culture to learn the practices and interpret them in whatever way helps one know what one is supposed to do. Does this mean that to understand the Chinese practice of *fǎlún gōng,* I must engage in it? At a minimum I must know how to use the phrase correctly in everyday discourse: how to explain it, how to recognize when people are doing it, and so forth. One way to learn all this is to engage in the practice.

Culture is a collection of habits and practices that fit into the grooves of the human learning mechanism. The practices must hang together or relate to each other in a way that makes them assimilable, as a group, by ordinary human beings. Perhaps this is why Latin Americans are fond of saying that one cannot understand their culture until one speaks the language, savors the food, hears the music, and enjoys the parties. Latin Americans have worked out a way of wresting an existence from their environment and a coexistence with one another. The behavior patterns that help them adapt must be learned and retained by a single human being. They must cohere in a single lifestyle. I have emphasized that there is much more to culture than language and lifestyle, because we Westerners so often reduce it to these. Yet they are not irrelevant, because they form part of the coherent, learnable system that constitutes a culture.

Language, in particular, is conditioned by learnability. We tend to think of language as a kind of literary Morse code in which any speech pattern can in principle be associated with any meaning. This is wrong not only in its supposition that words get meaning in the way that code does, for example by defining *dit-dah* to mean "the letter A." It is doubly wrong by supposing that linguistic patterns are arbitrary, when in fact only certain ones are likely to be learned. Noam Chomsky's famous views on universal grammar are in this vein.

More generally, the way we talk about the world, whether it be in everyday language or in specialized scientific discourse, is subject to learnability. As Immanuel Kant emphasized, the world becomes intelligible only when patterns are recognized. A computerized algorithm might analyze the data and pick out any number of patterns that could serve as the basis for scientific theories. But only certain ways of organizing the data seem assimilable by the human mind. When a theory resonates with our faculties, we say it is elegant and enlightening. It seems to make sense, to hang together. This is not unlike the experience of learning a culture.

A final implication of the Wittgensteinian view of language, mentioned in Chapter 1, is that because cultural practices in general receive their meaning is the same way language does, we should be prepared for the possibility that a strange culture is as unintelligible as its language. We must learn the culture just as we must learn its language, and we must learn it in the same way: by learning how to participate in meaningful practices.

Notes for Chapter 4

1. Stephen Jay Gould, *The Mismeasure of Man,* W. W. Norton (New York, 1981).

2. Jeremy Rifken, *The Biotech Century: Harnessing the Gene and Remaking the World,* J. P. Tarcher (New York, 1998).

3. Clifford Geertz, *The Interpretation of Cultures: Selected Essays,* Basic Books (New York, 1973).

4. Marvin Harris, *Cultural Materialism: The Struggle for a Science of Culture,* Vintage Books (New York, 1980).

5 Mexico

Mexican culture is one of the most colorful, complex, and conflicted in the world. Its uniqueness stems partly from its origins in an extraordinary and tragic encounter between Americans and Europeans. More important, however, is the fact that Mexico, perhaps of all Latin American countries, has most nearly achieved a cultural union of European and indigenous peoples. This tenuous unity contributes to political stability but creates a society beset with stresses and fault lines, much like the landscape it inhabits.

Mexico in its complexities may therefore seem an unlikely place to begin a tour of world cultures, and yet it illustrates some key concepts, particularly the distinction of rule-based and relationship-based cultures, the idea of a high-context culture, and the role of culture in managing stress. It raises again the issue of how prosperity relates to culture.

Mexico tends to be characterized in economic terms; it is the "economic problem" of North America. Undeniably, there are few places where the economic gradient is steeper than along the U.S.-Mexican border. By one estimate the average worker in Mexican *maquiladora* plants on the Mexican side of the border earns about one-eleventh as much as the average U.S. worker a few miles away. The cultural difference is equally sharp. U.S. nationals look, sometimes longingly, toward the warm, sensual, family-oriented culture to the south but are hesitant about the crime, harsh class divisions, and massive economic problems. Mexicans look, sometimes longingly, toward the affluent, happy, and youth-oriented colossus to the north but are repulsed by what they experience as selfish individualism and the flat coldness of the people. In the end the economic difference provides stronger motivation, as throngs of Mexicans emigrate north, legally and illegally, although many of them resolve to return to the culture they vastly prefer as soon as possible.

Mexico has taken giant economic strides since the 1960s and continues to develop a Western-style economy at a rapid pace. Not only has it become a major trading partner of the United States; it has become a favored plant site for U.S., Japanese, German, and Taiwanese firms in search of low-cost but industrious labor. As Mexican wages have begun to rise in the last few years, some of these firms have turned their attention to Southeast Asia and elsewhere. Yet Mexico's economic momentum continues, despite the precipitous fall of the peso in the mid-1990s.

Several factors make this economic growth possible. Aside from unrest in the southernmost state of Chiapas, the country has been more or less politically stable since the late 1960s. The 1965 *maquiladora* agreement provided another boost. It permits the United States to ship parts to Mexico for assembly and import the finished products to the United States, while paying export duty only on value added. The more recent North American Free Trade Agreement, a pact between Canada, the United States, and Mexico, has somewhat augmented the effects of the *maquiladora* treaty. Mexico is also a popular vacation and retirement destination for *gringos* (a Mexican word for "foreigners," particularly Yankees, that derives from the Spanish for "Greeks").

Mexicans are acutely aware that the rising macroeconomic statistics touted by the government mask major social problems. The lion's share of economic growth devolves to the upper class. The 1994–95 economic crisis increased unemployment, and everyone talked about rising crime. Newspapers ran cartoons suggesting that troops went to Chiapas to quell the unrest because they were afraid of the criminals in Mexico City. This city, the world's largest, continues to absorb migrants from the hinterland in search of a livelihood. It struggles to provide basic services and to alleviate some the world's worst air pollution.

Nonetheless, one senses a resilience and determination among Mexicans. Despite much-bemoaned government and police corruption, people care about public institutions, from city parks to universities to archaeological sites, and heavily endow them with public funds. The government employs dedicated civil servants who have upgraded the infrastructure immensely, including a reliable and well-managed power grid and a system of super-highways along which "green angels" rescue motorists with engine trouble. People joke that the rail system still uses original nineteenth-century equipment installed by Porfirio Díaz, but the intercity bus system is far better than that of the United States. Travelers can choose from several competing lines that dispatch clean, spacious Mercedes vehicles to points all over the country.

There is every reason to be optimistic about Mexico. One worries, however, that the intense colors of its cultural fabric will fade under the increasing glare from the north. Some Mexicans already grumble that inhabitants of the northern city of Monterrey, a symbol of the new Mexico, are not true Mexicans. Yet for the time being, Mexican culture remains radically different from that of many of the internationals who do business there.

The heart of Mexico is its unique mestizo culture. Fused in a historical cauldron of violence and instability, it is neither European nor indigenous. Western culture never prevailed, because the conquering Europeans created conditions too oppressive for their own culture to survive. To understand

Mexico properly, we must appreciate how the country still labors under the burden of its history. We therefore probe history more deeply in Mexico than in other countries we examine.

Los Conquistadores

Our first encounter with travelers from another planet may be less dramatic than the European discovery of Mesoamerica. At least we can hope so. When Hernán Cortés arrived in Central America in 1519, the native population was some 25 million, including 17 million Aztecs. By the end of the first century of Spanish occupation, it had been reduced to 1 million. To understand how this was possible, a little background is necessary.

This morning I watched a contingent of soldiers raise the gigantic Mexican flag that dominates La Plaza de la Constitución, known locally in Mexico City as the Zócalo. Between green and red fields, the flag depicts an eagle with a serpent in its beak. Seven centuries ago, the Aztec deity Huitzilopochtli instructed his people to settle on the spot where they saw such a creature. The Aztecs, migrating south from their mythical homeland of Aztlán, spotted the symbolic eagle on an island in Lake Texcoco, which lies some 2,500 meters above sea level in a great basin ringed by mountains. They built the imperial city of Tenochtitlán on the site of today's Mexico City, with its great temple-pyramid located almost precisely where the Zócalo is today. Their dominant tribe, the Mexica, gave Mexico its name. Tenochtitlán's wealth was based partly on an ingenious system of floating gardens in Lake Texcoco and partly on plunder from people subjugated by the Triple Alliance, consisting of the cities Texcoco, Tlacopan, and Tenochtitlán. In subsequent years emperors Moctezuma I and Moctezuma II extended Mexican domination and further enriched the capital. It was during the reign of Moctezuma II that Cortés entered the scene.

The question returns: How could 508 Spanish conquistadores subjugate a powerful civilization of 17 million Aztecs, twice the population of Spain? A key factor is the Aztecs' own subjugation of their neighbors, who were forced to hand over slaves and sacrificial victims as well as tribute. Conquered and yet-to-be conquered peoples were more than willing to form alliances against the Aztec overlords. In addition, the extravagant Aztec civilization placed an environmental strain on the Valley of Mexico. Dwindling resources pressured them to squeeze more out of their weakened subjects in order to maintain their lifestyle, intensifying resentment.

There are of course other factors: the superiority of European weapons, the effectiveness of cavalry against foot soldiers, and Moctezuma's much-quoted belief that the arrival of the Spanish fulfilled a prophecy, thus allowing Cortés to gain Moctezuma's initial confidence. The Europeans' motivation likewise had a mythical component. They were after gold, of course, but at a deeper level they were driven by their romantic conception of travel, which enriches the tourism industry to this day. Christopher Columbus, for example, recorded in his ship's log several sightings of mermaids and other fantastic creatures. Gonzalo Pizarro, brother of the famous conquistador, trekked through Amazonian rainforests to find El Dorado and his city of gold, whose existence in this hostile environment a sober head could only doubt. The very name *Amazon* apparently refers to a tribe of female warriors reported by Pizarro's comrade Francisco de Orellana, but its reality has never been confirmed. This magical sense of adventure, combined with an unshakable religious faith, inspired the conquistadores to extraordinary feats of bravery and determination.

The Spanish may have been advantaged in other ways. One is that Mesoamerican culture was in its twilight years. The great civilizations of the region—Olmec, Mixtec, Zapotec, Toltec, and especially the Maya—had come and gone. It was what Mexicans call the "postclassical period." The Aztecs themselves, by their own account, borrowed much of their culture from the Toltecs, who had occupied the Valley of Mexico before falling to outside invaders some two centuries earlier.

Still another factor is that Mesoamericans were familiar with violent conquest, and domination by the Spanish was not altogether a new experience. In fact, the Spanish and the Aztecs were remarkably similar in some respects. Both were very much male dominated, intensely religious, and violent. The Aztecs and other Mesoamerican peoples drew desperately on their religion for salvation from the stress of dwindling resources and the terror of earthquakes and volcanoes. The steps of pyramids were thickly encrusted with the bloody residue of human sacrifice. Cortés was repulsed by the practice, but it served a ritual function similar to that of the European practice of burning thousands of witches at the stake (a parallel that the Spanish doubtless did not see). It granted some sense of control over uncontrollable fate. If witches could be identified as a source of evil or misfortune for Europeans, their sacrifice could perhaps improve the situation. Mesoamericans hoped that human sacrifice would appease the gods and convince them to call off natural calamity. No smaller gesture sufficed, as the Aztecs imagined their deities to be cruel and taunting. A codex from the period, written in the Náhuatl language still spoken in parts of central Mexico, describes them as follows. A Romanized spelling of the Náhuatl appears first, followed by an English translation.[1]

Teca papaqui; teca huehuetzcatica tetennecuilhuitica in tlalticpac, amo tle nelli; auh amo nelli in quitoa, in quitenehua: zan tetennecuilhuitica.

They mock the people on earth. They are happy at the mishaps of men; they make fun of the people on earth. Nothing is true. Nothing they express, nothing they say, nothing they reveal to the people is true: they are only deceiving the people.

After the conquest, New Spain (as the Spanish called it) settled into a brutal system based on *encomiendas* (large land grants made to influential Spanish families). Indigenous people living on the encomiendas, or working in gold and silver mines, succumbed to deprivation and disease visited upon them by Europeans.

Meanwhile the Roman Catholic Church worked diligently to convert the natives to what they considered the one correct understanding of God. This can be regarded as arrogant, but it can also be regarded as the inevitable behavior of a universalizing culture and religion. Although the church became a major power broker and landlord in Central America, it must be said that power was not the only motivation. Many priests and friars were sensitive to the local culture, learned the languages, tried to benefit the people as best they could, and passed down to us much of what we know about them.

This encounter of two strongly religious peoples launched a period of creativity that incubated nothing less than a new religion. Its birth can perhaps be identified with the appearance of the Virgin of Guadalupe (Nuestra Señora de Guadalupe) in 1531, an event with much symbolic power in Mexican consciousness.[2] A poor indigenous farmer traditionally named Juan Diego was approached by a beautiful dark-skinned Lady who spoke to him in the Náhuatl language. She told him to go to the priest in a nearby city and relay her instructions to build a shrine in her honor. When the priest declined to see him, he returned home only to be admonished during a second apparition to try again. This time the priest talked with Juan Diego and was sympathetic. He patiently explained, however, that the parish was very poor and could not afford to divert resources from the needs of the people. Note that the priest is not a villain in the story; the note of reconciliation is key to its meaning. When the Lady appeared a third time she directed Juan to a rosebush that was blooming impossibly out of season. The rose is a European import, but flowers play a central role in Aztec myth. Juan took some roses to the priest in the frocklike garment his people wear. When he released the frock and let the roses fall at the feet of the astonished priest, an image of the Virgin was visible on the frock where the roses had been.

To this day the same image of this Mexican version of the Virgin Mary can be found in practically every Mexican church. She is sometimes depicted standing on the moon against a field of stars, with the sun behind her; all three are references to Aztec religion. Similar blends of native and

Catholic imagery can be found in the painting and sculpture that decorate churches, as well as in rituals and religious celebrations. This has been described as syncretism, or a mixture of religions, but it can also be viewed as an indigenous faith enriched by a fresh infusion of imagery. In any case, their religion has been an essential part of the support system that has brought Mexicans through five centuries of turmoil.

Anyone who doubts the power of the cult of Nuestra Señora de Guadalupe today can watch mothers wait in line for hours in Mexico City to have their babies blessed on the Virgin's day, December 12. A rock concert may command similar devotion, but then rock concerts are essentially religious events. They provide the kind of ecstasy that ancient Greeks obtained from Dionysian rites and evangelical Christians still obtain at revival meetings.

The encomienda system lasted about three hundred years, during which several racial subpopulations developed:

peninsulares – persons born in Spain

criollos – persons of Spanish descent born in Mexico

mestizos – persons of mixed Spanish and indigenous parentage

indígenas – indigenous persons

mulattos – persons of mixed Spanish and African descent

zambos – persons of mixed indigenous and African descent

Africans

A class hierarchy persists today, but it is only loosely related to race except at the extremes. Persons with a strong European appearance are likely to occupy upper classes, and the many native subpopulations that survive, particularly those who speak their ancient languages, are on the bottom rung of the social ladder. The social standing of people in the large mestizo population is determined as much by family history as by race.

Independence

The old order began to break up about 1810 with the appearance of Miguel Hidalgo y Costilla, a priest who rallied *indígenas* and mestizos under the banner of the Virgin of Guadalupe and fomented revolt. A bloody and confusing series of events followed, too complicated to recount here but marked by independence from Spain in 1821. In its first twenty-eight years of existence, the new state had twenty-five presidents who seized power in every conceivable fashion. The famous General Santa Anna himself became president of Mexico eleven times.

Having rid itself of Spanish rule, Mexico had now to deal with a newly imperialist United States of America. Until recently, Anglos in the United States used the term *wetbacks* to refer to illegal Mexican immigrants who swim across the Río Bravo into the United States, where the river is known as the Rio Grande. Ironically, the term originally referred to immigrants *from* the United States who illegally crossed the Sabine River into Texas, then part of Mexico, overwhelming the Mexican population. Disputes over this issue led to the secession of Texas from Mexico in 1832 and its annexation to the United States in 1845 to avoid recapture by Mexico. As retaliation for the latter, in 1846 Mexican troops fired on U.S. cavalry camped on the Río Bravo, which at the time was well inside Mexico. The U.S. border was along the Nueces River to the north. Nonetheless, U.S. President James Polk viewed this as a provocation and sent General Zachary Taylor to seize Mexican territory in retaliation, resulting in foreign occupation as far south as Puebla. The end result was the U.S. annexation of what are now California, Nevada, Utah, most of Arizona, and parts of Wyoming, Colorado, and New Mexico, for which the United States later paid Mexico a trifling sum of $15 million. It is curious that the writer Henry David Thoreau is well known in the United States for having gone to jail for civil disobedience, but not for the subject of his protest, which was U.S. aggression toward Mexico. In any case, it is a sensitive matter for Mexicans, and U.S. visitors to Mexico would do well to avoid any discussion of history or relations between the two nations.

The next epoch in Mexican history was marked by the installation in 1864 of Ferdinand Maximilien von Habsburg as the emperor of Mexico by Napoleon III. It is from this era that we obtain the *Cinco de Mayo* celebration, which receives so much attention among Hispanics in the United States and helps to illustrate how subcultures define themselves. The celebration recalls the French attempt in 1862 to send an army from coastal Veracruz inland to take Mexico City. On the fifth of May (*cinco de mayo*) it was stopped short and soundly defeated by Mexican troops in Puebla. It is an event of only moderate importance for Mexicans, no doubt because it was a momentary victory. A year later the French dispatched a larger force that successfully laid siege to Puebla and marched on to take the capital. A junta installed by the French, following Napoleon's dictates, chose the Austrian archduke Maximilien as monarch. In Mexico today, the *Cinco de Mayo* is an observance of secondary importance except in the State of Puebla. Some Mexicans complain that Hispanics in the United States have forgotten their history and confuse May 5 with the date of Mexican independence, September 15. In any event, it is common for subculture revitalization movements to sacrifice historical accuracy for cultural ends. The *Cinco de Mayo* is to Mexican Americans what kilts are to Scots.

In one sense, however, the fifth of May fed into the mainstream of
Mexican history. One of the victorious commanders was a young brigadier
general named Porfirio Díaz Mory, who ushered in a new era when he
became Mexico's president fourteen years later. Díaz restored stability and
introduced some degree of industrial development, but at the cost of an oppressive right-wing dictatorship. This was the age of robber barons in the
United States, and Díaz encouraged the Guggenheims, Rockefellers, and
Hearsts to invest in Mexico by granting enormous concessions and privileges to foreigners, even the right to commit serious crimes against
Mexicans without consequences. Foreigners praised Díaz for his progressive leadership, but the maldistribution of wealth worsened. By 1910,
90 percent of arable land was tied up in 834 haciendas controlled by
wealthy families, while the 10 million peasants (*peones*) owned no land.[3] A
mounted force of thugs known as *Rurales* maintained order in the hinter-
lands but brutalized the people.

A New Mestizo Culture

The Universidad Nacional Autónoma de México, or UNAM for
short, enrolls a quarter of a million students at any one time. Its impressive
and sprawling campus, Ciudad Universitaria, was built in Mexico City's
southern suburbs in the 1960s, although the institution itself dates back
450 years. The university is known for a leftist bent that is out of step with
the Mexican mainstream, but its curious motto expresses an idea of central
importance to the country: *Por mi raza hablará el espíritu.* The literal
English translation, "The spirit will speak through my race," is scarcely
intelligible, partly because the Spanish *raza* has a meaning closer to the
English *people* than to *race*. Here it refers to the concept of *raza cósmica*
developed by the motto's author, José Vasconcelos, who was Minister of
Education in the 1920s. Vasconcelos first clearly articulated the concept
that Mexicans are in fact a single people, a single mestizo culture, despite
their disparate backgrounds. This ideology seems in fact to have fostered a
sense of Mexican nationalism that survives to this day. It is partly responsible for melding Europeans and natives to a degree that distinguishes
Mexico from the rest of Latin America. It also inspired a remarkable tradition of ideological mural painting, examples of which can still be seen on
the exterior of UNAM buildings, particularly the library.

Vasconcelos rose to power in the wake of the Mexican Revolution,
which erupted in 1910 and spawned a bloody and complex sequence
of events, as well as a pantheon of revolutionary heroes. By far the most
romantic was Emiliano Zapata, a man of humble origin who could speak

Náhuatl with his supporters. His name was revived in the 1990s by the self-described *Zapatista* rebels in Chiapas, an impoverished region of Mexico with a largely indigenous population. In typical Mexican fashion, the rebels cultivated an air of mystery by their allegiance to a masked leader known as "Subcommandante Marcos" but otherwise unnamed. Some doubted that he was a real person, but I have seen him (masked) on European TV. It is reported[4] that he is actually Sebastián Guillén Vicente from Mexico City, but in Mexico there is not always a clear distinction between the real and the imagined.

The revolutionary period ended in 1929 with the installation of the so-called Institutional Revolutionary Party (PRI), which remained in power until Vicente Fox assumed the presidential office in 2000. Although the PRI brought political stability, its rule has not always been benign. Even as late as the 1960s, political murders and harsh police actions were a fact of life, including a massacre of several hundred protesting students just before the 1968 Olympic Games in Mexico City. This legacy of violence continues to haunt many Mexican families. This was impressed upon me when, on one occasion, I was invited to a private home. As we talked in the living room, my hosts, who like most Mexicans are sensitive to body language, noticed my longing glances at the grand piano in one corner of the room. For me, one of the more serious deprivations of international travel is separation from Western music. Someone invited me to play, and I chose a volume of Beethoven from the well-stocked musical library. As I began to play, I was shocked to find the piano grossly out of tune. I said nothing, of course, but later asked a friend in the family why the instrument had been neglected. She explained that a young man who grew up in the house had studied to be a concert pianist but was assassinated by Communists during a political struggle more than twenty years ago. His parents could never bring themselves to sell the instrument, and it has sat unmaintained and seldom used ever since.

Avoiding Stress in Mexico

Mexicans have evolved several mechanisms for dealing with the historical uncertainty of their environment (see Table 5.1). Religion, already discussed, commands remarkable devotion among the lower classes who need it most. Among its assurances are the regularity and predictability of the church calendar, the social solidarity built by elaborate preparations for festivals (such as the annual village festival day), and of course the benefits of liturgy and prayer. Religious experience can become quite intense. There are celebrations of Holy Week in which a man has literally been nailed to a cross, in a re-enactment of the Passion of Jesus Christ.

TABLE 5.1
Stress-Management Mechanisms in Mexico

Mechanism	Contribution to Stress Management
Religion	Assurance from above; regularity and predictability of ritual and holidays
Dionysian lifestyle: intense experience, raucous festivals, blurring of reality and imagination	Escape from harshness of everyday existence
Strong extended family, friendship	Support in time of trouble
Machismo	For men, sense of control over their lives; for women and families, some degree of security, since men are obliged to protect them
Courtesy and indirection; wearing of "masks"; role of symbols	Less exposure to danger

Religious intensity is part of a larger pattern. It illustrates the distinction of Apollonian and Dionysian cultures. Mexican life tends toward the Dionysian, meaning that people often escape from the pressures of life through intense experience, whereas an Apollonian culture would take a more practical approach of keeping life routine and under control. Mexicans seek intensity of experience not only in religion but also in festivals, noisy parties, and singing, all of which provide temporary escape. On the *Día de los Muertos* (Day of the Dead), Mexicans even confront death in a festive mode. Personal and family relationships are intense and emotional, and displays of emotion are accepted for men and women alike. In years past, political differences could quickly escalate to anger or violence. The Spanish language itself is pushed to the extremes of expressiveness. One should not be alarmed when Mexicans speak in a way that seems overwrought. They prefer high levels of stimulation; the radio or TV on the bus is usually loud. Even the food is intense, as Mexicans are connoisseurs of countless varieties of peppers having every degree of piquancy. The Dionysian element also surfaces in a certain dreaminess and confusion of imagination and reality, as witnessed by the phenomenon of Subcommandante Marcos.

Mexican imagination can be frustrating to Western visitors, particularly when combined with a strong sense of fatalism inherited from indigenous peoples. Mexicans can think big about the future, but when it comes to implementation, very often there is pessimism about what can actually be achieved. The Western concept of history sees it as subject to human control, and to a great extent Westerners cope with life by going out to change the world. The United States in particular emphasizes personal responsibility and convinces itself that one can take control of one's fate by taking responsibility for one's life. The traditional Mesoamerican sense of history sees it as cyclic and predetermined, giving rise to a fatalism that persists in Mexico.

The role of polychronicity in relieving stress has already been discussed. Mexicans also deal with the exigencies of life by relying on relationships of mutual dependency, between friends as well as family members and between men as well as women. Contrary to some popular misconceptions, Latin machismo does not imply rugged independence. It is perfectly acceptable for a man to ask his amigos for help, and they will go to any length to oblige. Dependency relationships are taken for granted between family members, but they must be cultivated between friends. In particular, persons who do business must develop a relationship of mutual trust.

Still another cluster of stress-avoidance techniques stem from a historical fear of speaking openly. Mexicans have an uncanny ability to read body language, for example. They will remark that I seem tired or upset when I am unaware of it myself. Courtesy and affability avoid sending unintended signals of hostility. It is impossible to say, *"por favor," "para servirle," "muchas gracias,"* and *"muy amable"* too often. When leaving the room or walking in front of someone, it is polite to say, *"con permiso"* (with permission), and before asking a question, one says, *"Una pregunta por favor"* (May I please ask a question?). Residents of Mexico City (to which Mexicans often refer simply as México, or México D.F.) put the lie to the excuse often heard that it is the size of a city, not the character of the people, that explains the rude behavior one finds there. Denizens of the world's largest city are happy to take time to listen to halting Spanish and give directions or advice. There is at least one exception to this all-around courtesy, however: some shopkeepers are very stingy with small change, since there seems to be a perpetual shortage (a common problem around the world).

Mexico's polite manner of speech also has a dark underside: a rich vernacular of obscene and insulting language. While so much of the world is content to parrot the Anglo-Saxon obscenities that saturate Hollywood movies, Mexicans reach into the shadows of their historical psyche to build their own vernacular. Rape is a common theme, as reflected in a whole lexicon of unofficial meanings for the verbs *chingar* (to hate, hurt, destroy, rape, etc.) and *coger* (to grab, sexually assault, etc.), which reflect the Mexicans' view of themselves as the product of rape.[5] Shortly after Hernán Cortés arrived in Mesoamerica, a Tabasco chief presented him with a mistress/slave, the Aztec princess La Malinche. At some level, Mexicans view their mestizo culture symbolically as the bastard child of Cortés and La Malinche. Christened "Marina" by the Spanish, La Malinche contributed much to Cortés' success, due to her brilliance and multilingual abilities, and today *malinchista* is an epithet applied to a traitor or lover of foreigners.

Mexican writers have long emphasized that Mexican courtesy and indirection are actually mechanisms for masking the harsh realities of Mexican life. Even Subcommandante Marcos is quoted as saying that he would remove his famous mask when Mexico stopped masking the reality of oppression. A similar theme courses through *El Laberinto de la Soledad* (*The Labyrinth of Solitude*), the celebrated reflection on Mexican culture written by Nobelist Octavio Paz.[6] There is much insight in Paz's work, and I quote him on the frontispiece of this book. Yet courtesy and indirect speech characterize many relationship-based cultures around the world. They also tend to surface as regulative principles in Western cultures where justice and rule-based mechanisms have broken down, as in the slavery-ridden antebellum South of the United States. I prefer to interpret Mexican courtesy along these lines. I always warn my students that sources may give misleading information about their culture, because culture shapes how we think about culture. Mexican intellectuals are not immune to this phenomenon.

Another important mechanism is the use of symbol, whose meaning and power in the Mexican psyche is difficult for many outsiders to grasp. Camera-toting Westerners and Japanese emphasize image rather than symbol. For them, the look of a thing can be more important than the thing itself. An image might be defined as an abstraction of a concrete object, whereas a symbol makes an abstract concept more concrete. An image reduces a movie star or politician to a stylized collection of traits, while a symbol brings religious ideas down to a human level. Visitors to the media-saturated United States complain that when they try to get to know someone, it is often impossible to get past the image he or she wishes to project. In Japan, the appearance of a meal is more important than its taste (which may explain why so many Japanese prefer Chinese food to their own). A nation with Mexico's heavy reliance on religion and political ideology, on the other hand, can be expected to invest in symbols. More pertinent here is the fact that symbols provide an indirect means of expression that can reduce exposure to danger.

One might convey the power of symbol to people in the United States by using the example of a symbolic issue. The abortion issue, for instance, excites remarkably intense feelings and dominates many political campaigns. Pro-life advocates harass clients at abortion clinics, and pro-choice advocates take to the streets in protest. Physicians who perform abortions have been attacked and even murdered. Without minimizing the moral importance of the abortion issue per se, one can nonetheless acknowledge that it symbolizes a cluster of issues that are of crucial importance in the United States. It stands for the opposition between a conservative, family-oriented culture and an affluent, professional lifestyle. It therefore represents the major schisms in U.S society except race: traditionalism versus feminism, religious faith versus secularism, family versus individualism, working class versus professional class, making ends meet versus affluence. These issues are large, abstract, and difficult to think about, but the abortion of a pregnancy is as close to flesh and blood as one can get.

The story of Fidel Castro's ascent to power in Cuba may help illustrate the role of symbol in Latin culture. In the weeks before his victory, Castro was encamped in the mountains above Santiago de Cuba with twelve disciples. Cubans did not overlook the parallel with the twelve disciples of Jesus Christ. When his revolutionary party prevailed, Castro traveled to Havana by highway and made a triumphal entry into the city, riding not in a bulletproof limousine but in an ordinary jeep. The analogy with Jesus' triumphal entry into Jerusalem upon a mere donkey was obvious enough. While Castro gave his victory speech with Che Guevara at his side, one of the doves that had been released as part of the celebration perched on his shoulder and remained there for the duration of his speech. (This event is not apocryphal, as I have seen it on film.) As the new nation and its new ruler were thus christened, the religious mind could scarcely avoid seeing a parallel with the baptism of Jesus, during which, according to the New Testament, a dove descended from heaven. None of this means that Cubans think Castro is Jesus Christ. Yet the symbolic aspect of Castro was in a sense more real to Cubans than the man himself, just as the image of a presidential candidate is more real to U.S. voters, or least more important in influencing their vote, than the man himself.

Finally, the topic of machismo deserves special attention. It has been traced to eighth-century Moorish Spain but took a particularly violent form in the New World. *Machismo* can be defined as "manly virtue" (*virtue*, incidentally, has the Latin root *vir*, or "man," and in Roman times referred to "manly strength" or "courage"). It is historically associated with honor, bravery, violence, a hunger for power, and a double standard for women that idolizes them even while abusing them. Men actually have had little choice in the matter; historically, those who were not machos were ostracized.

The inescapability of machismo suggests that it has an essential function in the culture. The violence and oppression it has created seem dysfunctional enough, but it has a constructive side that helps men and women alike deal with the stress of adversity. The essence of machismo is the willingness to endure any hardship, any deprivation, any degree of suffering in defense of oneself and, particularly, one's family. Life can be harsh and painful, and training in the virtues of manliness can help prepare a boy for what is coming. Machismo, like many effective cultural defense mechanisms, makes a virtue of necessity: what would otherwise be only the inevitable misery of hardship is elevated to the manly honor of enduring hardship without flinching. Women are subjugated to men, but in exchange they can rely on

men to shield them while they carry out their nurturing role. Machismo
deals with stress, and in particular with the lack of control over adversity,
by *taking* control—of others and oneself. This leads to lust for power over
one's peers and over women, which may be sought by violent means, but
ultimately it is a struggle for power over one's own fear, the kind of fear that
can render one helpless when adversity threatens.

Today the character of machismo varies across the social classes. In the
lower classes it is still associated with violence and abuse of women, particularly in combination with drinking, as it is to a surprising extent in
some other cultures. In the upper classes, however, it represents honor,
courage, and devotion to one's family.

The Mexican sense of honor is too often underestimated by outsiders.
Respecting a man's honor is not unlike saving face in Asia. One must take
care not to criticize or embarrass a colleague in front of his peers, or even
in private. I am aware of one instance in which a Mexican employee of a
U.S. firm was summoned by his superiors to discuss his candidacy for a
promotion. However, the employee not only failed to appear but missed
work due to "illness." For two or three weeks he responded to neither telephone calls nor a registered letter sent to his home. His disappearance
baffled his superiors, but it is easily explained to someone familiar with
Mexican honor. He had heard office scuttlebutt that his promotion would
probably be turned down. He did not want to suffer such humiliation in
front of his colleagues. This Mexican sensitivity to criticism raises obvious
management issues that I will take up shortly.

First Meeting

Mexican culture is polychronic. One should not take offense if kept
waiting for an appointment, even forty-five minutes, or if the host takes
care of other matters in one's presence. Family matters may take precedence
over a business appointment, and the host may have been called away to
pick up a child at school or attend a funeral. It is important to arrive on
time for an office appointment, however, particularly if a person of higher
rank is expected. One can be more lax after learning the habits of one's
associates. Some Mexicans, particularly in the north or in Mexico City, are
beginning to use *hora americana* (American time) rather than *hora mexicana* when dealing with foreigners. They may expect punctuality. For an
affair at a private home, however, on-time arrival could be embarrassing, as
one may catch the hosts in curlers or in the shower.

Mexico is the most formal of Latin American countries. It is best to wear
a dark, conservative, expensive-looking suit. Three-piece suits are not uncommon for men. Visitors should sport a fashionable watch, shine their

shoes, and make a habit of patronizing the most expensive restaurants and hotels they can afford. Visible wealth is interpreted as a sign of success. The formality of dress decreases with altitude, however, and simply a pressed shirt and slacks are appropriate in warm, humid climates. Also, too much ostentation could be poorly received in smaller cities. In a business meeting, the business card should be offered with the right hand immediately after introductions. Business cards should be kept pristine in a case. Mexicans do not follow the Asian custom of receiving a business card with both hands, but one should nonetheless read the card before putting it away.

Titles are expected both orally and in correspondence, such as *Doctor, Profesor,* or *Señor* (*Doctora, Profesora,* or *Señora* for women). When in doubt about which title applies, it is better to err on the higher side, whereas in Germany, for instance, an error in either direction is unacceptable. *Licenciado* (abbreviated *Lic.*) can be used to address any college graduate, although the term is more commonly applied to lawyers and government employees. The title *Ingeniero* (engineer) is appropriate for professionals in technical fields. Hispanic surnames should be treated with care: Carlos Rodríguez Vargas should be addressed as Señor Rodríguez, *not* Señor Vargas. Rodríguez is his father's family name, and Vargas his mother's family name. Occasionally he might write his name Carlos Rodríguez V. If Ana María González Barros marries Señor Rodríguez, she traditionally becomes Ana María González de Rodríguez (or Ana María de Rodríguez), while her professional name may simply be Ana María González. Their offspring might be Jesús Rodríguez González and Consuela Rodríguez González. A young woman whose marital status is not known may be addressed *Señorita* (abbreviated *Srta.*), whereas an older woman or woman in a position of responsibility may be addressed *Señora* (*Sra.*) regardless of marital status.

Mexicans commonly embrace and/or kiss when they meet (*abrazar*), but this behavior is normally reserved for good friends or family. If unsure about what to do, it is best to let them initiate. If they do initiate, one can take satisfaction in having been accepted into their circle of affection.

One or more of the Mexicans present will be prepared to converse in English if the visitors speak little or no Spanish, in which case the latter should apologize for their ignorance of the language. Those who speak some Spanish, however, should not hesitate to use it, as the Mexican hosts will be pleased by this interest in their culture. Mexicans are patient with visitors who struggle with their language and will tolerate any number of mistakes. Their sense of honor, however, may prevent them from speaking English if it is flawed. On one occasion I was asked to give a series of technical lectures at a Mexican conference. As I often do when speaking abroad, I spoke in English but used transparencies in the local language. At meals between sessions, however, I found myself conversing with only one or two colleagues who happened to be fluent in English. So I began to inflict my mediocre Spanish upon some of the other people around the table. After hearing me stumble a few times, they loosened up and began to respond in equally compromised English. If I, the "big shot" professor, were willing to make a fool of myself, they would do likewise. From then on we enjoyed a lively albeit awkward bilingual conversation.

When conversing in English, it is best to speak slowly and avoid colloquial expressions. I use hand gestures and make important points two or three ways. I always try to use as many words with Latin roots as possible. Mexican hosts will probably say nothing if they fail to understand, again due to their sense of honor. One can discretely test for comprehension by asking a related question. It is useful to provide Spanish versions of written materials and have a Mexican national on the team, although this person should not serve as an interpreter, which is a position of lower rank. Some say that visitors from the United States should avoid bringing a Mexican American, who could also be regarded as belonging to a lower social class, although I cannot confirm this personally.

As in all high-context countries, speech in Mexico is often indirect. People rarely say no directly but are more likely to respond by saying "maybe" (quizás), by saying they will "think about it," or by changing the subject. Yes (sí) is more likely to mean "I understand you" than "yes."

Cultivating Relationships

Despite its Western roots, Mexico is a relationship-based culture, and professionals must develop bonds of trust and friendship with other individuals. This kind of professional/personal relationship has a somewhat different character in every culture that relies on it; the Mexican version, at its best, tends to be based on genuine friendship and affection. Interaction will begin with social chitchat, perhaps over a long lunch. There is no problem finding a topic of conversation, because the perfect topic is always available: one's family. Visitors may talk about their children, parents, siblings, and aunts and uncles and nieces and nephews. The Mexicans will love it. Those who like to show photos of grandchildren can take this chance to indulge themselves with an appreciative audience. The Mexicans will of course do the same, and one can respond with equal interest. This talk of family not only plants seeds of friendship but also provides assurances that the visitor is a responsible person. A family man can be trusted to take obligations seriously. He is a man of honor. (I use the masculine gender because this concept of honor is part of machismo and traditionally applies to men.)

The key to building relationships is *simpático* (showing genuine concern for the welfare and feelings of one's companions). While Western professionals tend to get wrapped up in abstractions and forget about the concrete human situation, in Mexico it is essential to keep the emotional radar in operation at all times, even in the middle of a business negotiation. This means reading body language and constantly looking at things from another's emotional perspective. Mexicans know instinctively that we are human beings first and professionals second. Western visitors can acquire this perspective with practice, which incidentally can be a very useful way to operate, not to mention a humane one, upon returning home.

The classical mistake of Western visitors to Mexico is trying to short-circuit the process of relationship building. It is true that business is often discussed at breakfast (*el desayuno*) or lunch (*el almuerzo* or *la comida*). Dinner (*la cena*) can be either a light affair at home or a heavy meal later in the evening, and the latter may involve some serious talk. Business may also come up at an evening party in a private home. But whatever the occasion, one should be content with small talk until the host brings up more-serious topics. This could take two or three days. Even when the time comes, it is wise not to get too wrapped up in shoptalk, particularly at a party.

These social interchanges are by no means a waste of time. Building trust and friendship is at least as important to a Mexican as factual documents and accounting statements are to a Westerner. One should by all means enjoy the food, the atmosphere, and the mariachi musicians if they come round to the table. (They normally charge by the song.) When someone finally brings up more serious matters, it may seem unnatural to do business while relaxing. Yet with some practice it is quite possible to use good professional judgment while enjoying oneself. Greek businessmen provide a good example, as they are probably the world masters of this skill.

In some cultures, dinners and parties and other sorts of hospitality are intended to loosen people up or induce them to feel obligated to make business concessions. Koreans and Russians are notorious for this tactic. In Mexico, however, this is normally not the intent. Hospitality is part of the culture and builds a relationship.

Westerners often sense a conflict of interest when doing business with close friends, because friends may expect special favors. In Mexico one *must* do business with friends in order to build trust. The relationship is genuinely personal as well as professional. Mexican professionals do not expect associates to compromise their business judgment for the sake of the friendship and will not do so themselves. There is, however, a mutual expectation that both parties will honor their friendship by negotiating in good faith and following through on commitments. It is the only alternative in a country where legal enforcement is unreliable. It is also acceptable to ask for help if one is in a bind. Perhaps one needs an extension on a delivery deadline, or a quick decision from the owners on whether the deal will go through. In such cases it is appropriate for a friend to ask for assistance, provided one is prepared to reciprocate if called upon. One must go to great lengths to oblige a friend's request, even if it involves personal hardship. A refusal to do so can be deeply insulting. If the request is unethical or impossible to fulfill, one can explain the situation and possibly offer an alternative. Because the relationship is based on trust, the Mexican counterpart will probably accept the explanation. Obviously, one who breaches this trust may as well pack up and go home.

Decision making is slow in Mexico. Rather than try to push for an answer, it is better to keep the contact alive, perhaps by making additional trips. The decision will eventually come through. Mexicans may be dilatory about transferring payments or delivering services, perhaps for reasons beyond their control. It is perfectly acceptable to remind people about payments due. However, the best approach is to build reciprocity into the agreement. The visitors deliver A, then the Mexicans deliver B, then the visitors deliver C, and so forth. After all, the reason most people pay their electricity bill is that the power would be cut off otherwise. When the Mexicans do not deliver B, the visitors would do well to contact the people in the Mexican firm who are expecting C. This gives them an incentive to lean on those responsible for the delay.

In general, the hard-driving U.S. or northern European professional must become accustomed to the fact that business is not the top priority in Mexicans' lives, and they will not pretend otherwise. This is a perspective, after all, that has much to recommend it.

Law, Corruption, and Crime

Laws and regulations serve a ritual function in Mexico. Although the legal system is largely dysfunctional, legal procedures must be followed in precise detail. Mexican culture is what Geert Hofstede calls "uncertainty avoiding."[7] Uncertainty-avoiding cultures are risk averse and often prefer to be reassured by predictable rituals and procedures. The elaborate rituals of the Aztecs have evolved into the bureaucratic tangles of today's Mexico, which serve basically the same purpose: providing a sense of predictability and order. Chapter 8 will show how precise execution is often essential to rituals, and the Mexican bureaucracy is no exception.

It is important that foreign visitors ratify agreements in a written contract, in case there are legal problems. This is not to deny that countless business deals among Mexicans are made orally (perhaps to avoid taxes). In fact, even where foreigners are concerned, the real contract is ultimately a mutual understanding reinforced by personal relationships. Legal enforcement is difficult and should not be considered in advance as a realistic option.

Mexican law is based on the Napoleonic code, introduced by Maximilian. It relies on statutes and judicial discretion rather than juries and precedent. Unlike Anglo-Saxon law, in which any business activity is legal unless it violates a law, in Mexico no business activity is legal unless it is explicitly recognized by statute. Formalities and document filings must be observed to the letter (often with originals, not copies). This is obviously a specialized skill and requires the services of a Mexican lawyer.

Bribery (*la mordida,* or the "bite") is widely practiced in Mexico, but it is not ubiquitous. As in much of the world, police officers commonly request payment on the spot to settle a traffic ticket. In certain industries, bribes are necessary to obtain permits and the like. Mexicans despise bribery and consider it immoral, even many who practice it. They tend to blame it, along with many social ills, on their political leaders. Yet bribery is a grassroots activity that goes back centuries. Any fair observer would have to give former President Ernesto Zedillo credit for making a good faith effort to clean up corruption in government, with a modicum of success.

Whereas bribery serves a structural function in some cultures, nothing about Mexican culture seems to require it. The system should be able to operate primarily on the basis of personal relationships, particularly through family and friends. Bribery seems to be the product of dysfunctional political arrangements inherited from the old days, and there is no obvious reason why reform efforts coupled with economic growth cannot bring substantial success, much as did reform efforts in the United States during the era of Theodore Roosevelt. One might predict a declining role for bribery in coming years. In any event, foreign visitors should avoid it whenever possible, if only because it is risky and possibly illegal. One approach is for the foreign firm to postpone its choice of Mexican contractors until it has spread the word that it is looking for those that can get things done without side payments.

Crimes against persons remain a serious problem in Mexico City and Ciudad Juárez, and to a lesser extent in some other cities. Part of respecting a culture is respecting its dangers, and it is foolish to be cavalier about crime. The first rule is to try not to look like a tourist. Mexicans can spot gringos a mile away, but the locals may assume that people in business attire (and without cameras) are residents or frequent visitors and know what they are doing. It is always safer to be accompanied by a Mexican associate. This is especially important in areas frequented by tourists, such as streets around the extraordinary Museo de Antropología in Mexico City. Fortunately, Mexican hosts always take their guests on tours of some of the best attractions.

When moving about the city, I avoid crowded buses. I have used the Mexico City subway several times, but I never carry cash, credit cards, or documents unless I absolutely need them, in which case I use a hidden money belt. It is not unusual to see riders carrying bags and purses bearing stitches where they were slit open by thieves, probably gangs of young *panchitos*. The safest bet is to take a registered taxi. When walking, I stick to streets with heavy pedestrian traffic, particularly at night. I ask my Mexican friends about which areas to avoid. "Help!" translates as *¡Socorro!*

Health

This is as good a point as any to take up the subject of health. By far the most frequent health hazards for travelers are contaminated food and water. In Mexico, and many other countries, it is an ever present risk, for natives and visitors alike. Health is a cultural as well as a medical issue, because American, European, and Japanese travelers so often insult their hosts with comments and questions about the safety of food and water. It is a good exercise to imagine being a guest in someone's home and asking whether the food on the table is safe. This is scarcely worse than asking similar questions in a restaurant, because the locals read it as an insult to their country and therefore to themselves.

Nonetheless, the health hazard is real and must be addressed. Affluent Mexicans themselves are careful about what they eat. They patronize hotels and restaurants with private water supplies and good reputations. They may take offense when you decline certain items, but they will take still greater offense if you fall ill and are unable to eat anything the next day. (Being Mexicans, they will also sympathize with you and find the whole situation embarrassing.) I therefore offer the following advice, which applies in most countries around the world as well as Mexico. I am no physician, but having hosted a large fraction of the world's malevolent gastrointestinal organisms, I can speak with some authority.

First, I do as affluent Mexicans do by eating in upscale establishments when possible. I avoid street vendors entirely, no matter how tantalizing the food. I favor busy restaurants, because there is less chance that the food sat around or was reheated. I ask friends about good places to eat. I drink only bottled water, coffee, hot tea, canned soft drinks, or alcohol; the bottled water should be a reputable brand. (One reason for the global popularity of Coca-Cola is that locals everywhere know it is safe.) I religiously avoid salads, raw fish, and other foods that have not been exposed to high temperature. I think about how the food might have been prepared, taking particular notice of whether impure water might have been used after the last cooking stage. I avoid ice like the plague, even if someone tells me it was made with purified water. If I have cooking facilities, I use them to prepare my own food.

That said, I do try to be as discreet as possible when passing over risky foods. If the restaurant is serving drinks with ice, for example, I quietly tell the waiter, *"Sin hielo, por favor"* (no ice, please). If my hosts want to make an issue of this, it is their choice to do so.

Some people seem to be blessed with immunity to food poisoning. If I break any of my rules, however, I am likely to get sick, which brings me to how one should deal with illness. I stop eating the moment I feel something coming on. This may be culturally difficult to do, but if I have an imminent dinner engagement, perhaps I can bow out on grounds of illness. If I continued to eat, recuperation would only be longer and more unpleasant. I also take note of my incubation period, which can help to identify dangerous foods by counting the hours back from the first symptoms. The period is longer than one might think, usually about thirty-six hours. I carry a "survival kit" with remedies that I have found to work. I use the pink bismuth-based preparations, which help me feel nearly human enough to keep my wits about me. It also helps protect me from food I must eat to avoid giving grave offense. I also carry gut-paralyzing pills (e.g., Imodium) to relieve diarrhea symptoms, but I use them only when on the move, on which occasions they can be a gift from the gods. (I have heard physicians scoff at such remedies because they only treat symptoms. Yes, exactly.) If the illness induces a fever, I sleep as much as possible. If I absolutely must be up and about, I take aspirin to reduce the fatigue, disorientation, and queasiness that come with fever. I continue to drink bottled water or clear juices to avoid dehydration. After the initial attack, I must begin to eat a little, or the debilitation due to lack of nourishment will become as serious as the illness. I always carry some bland snacks in my survival kit to get me through this period, and I return to a normal diet little by little. I search around the neighborhood for innocuous foodstuffs, or inquire about what locals eat in case of illness. In India, for example, widely available coconut milk is excellent for this purpose (I drink it straight from the coconut), as is yogurt, which is said to help restore intestinal microorganisms. I have found, oddly enough, that scrambled eggs are tolerated by almost any diseased stomach. If I return to normal eating too soon, the relapse will be nearly as serious as the initial attack and will postpone recovery.

Even when I take all the precautions, however, I get sick occasionally. This seems to be unavoidable, short of fanatical antisocial behavior. I have also learned that gastrointestinal distress is not limited to "developing" countries. I endured one of my worst episodes in Denmark, where I was bedridden for a week and could not return to a normal diet for six weeks. My worst bout ever, however, was in India.

Some Western travelers carry elaborate medical kits containing needles, syringes, bandages, and various drugs. Although this technological approach is only natural for Westerners, I have never been so prudent. However, I get the recommended vaccinations and take a malaria prophylactic when traveling in infested areas; the latter can induce some pretty interesting dreams. Beyond this, I avoid taking unnecessary chances that could land me in a hospital with unsanitary needles and no reliable blood supply. Hospitalized patients in many countries rely on relatives to bring in food or provide blood transfusions. When in trouble, it obviously pays to get a message to local friends as quickly as possible. They will take care of the situation.

Employees and Organizations

Some years ago a U.S. manufacturing firm installed a material requirements planning (MRP) system in one of its Mexican *maquiladora* plants. On the face of it, this appears to be a serious mistake. An MRP system is a computer program designed to order hundreds or thousands of parts in such a way that they are in the right place at the right time for assembly. These systems tend to be difficult to maintain even in U.S. plants that are accustomed to computerization. The workforce may not be disciplined enough to keep the computer's data base current, and expediters end up placing key orders by hand. The expedited orders make the updating task even harder, the data base gets even further behind, still more orders must be expedited, and the MRP system may eventually become little more than window dressing.

As it turned out, however, the MRP system was the best thing that ever happened to this particular *maquiladora* plant. The system itself was of course a miserable failure, since Mexican workers have no stomach for the kind of regimentation required to keep it going. It served, however, as a convenient scapegoat. Due to the Mexican sense of honor, it simply was not practical for either U.S. or Mexican managers to point out problems in the plant, because any such criticism would reflect on the supervisor in charge. However, the MRP system was fair game. Everyone could point to problems in the factory by blaming them on the computer, and once the problems were identified and discussed, they could be addressed.

Mexican sensitivity to criticism may explain the tendency to blame all problems on the president of the country. Talk of local police corruption might offend a friend's uncle, who happens to be the police chief, but it is all right to refer to it obliquely by talking of corruption in Mexico City.

I was treated to an amusing instance of this while visiting the ruins of Teotihuacán. I paused to listen to a teacher who was lecturing his junior high school class, seated near the steps of one of the pyramids. Mexican teachers tend to be quite good, and this one told his class the fascinating story of how the ancient priests ripped the beating hearts out of their sacrificial victims on these very steps. Although talking out of turn is less acceptable in Mexico than in the United States, the kids immediately shouted, "Maestro, this should happen to [former] President Salinas," a proposition with which *El Maestro* readily agreed. At that time Carlos Salinas de Gortari, accused of corruption and gross mismanagement, was the MRP system of Mexico.

Reluctance to accept criticism is a perennial problem for Mexican organizations, since improvement is less likely without it. Westerners tolerate criticism because they separate professional and personal life. Rationality rules on the job and asks one to subjugate personal feelings to legal and financial imperatives. For Mexicans, however, life is life and cannot be compartmentalized into the professional and the private. Professional liaisons, at their best, are fully human relationships based on friendship and mutual concern, rather than Western-style technical relationships that serve mutual convenience. Business negotiation is inseparable from the richness of human conversation in general. Decisions are based on the heart as well as the head. Since Mexicans believe in this holistic approach, they make no attempt to exclude their emotional reactions from professional or work life. The feelings of managers and factory workers alike must therefore be respected. There is no really satisfactory way to criticize in Mexico, but the most common approach, other than identifying a scapegoat, is to speak with the person privately or to work through a trusted third party.

The need to respect feelings reflects a broader need to acknowledge the dignity of individuals of all stations. Despite the overwhelming importance of the family, there is a surprisingly strong individualistic strain in Mexican culture, and people want their individual worth to be recognized. Professionals from the United States are sometimes seen as disrespectful due to their casual dress, informal manner, and failure to use titles. This behavior may send a positive message of unpretentiousness to their U.S. associates, but it makes Mexicans feel unimportant. On the other hand, the egalitarianism of U.S. nationals gives them a distinct advantage in their relations with common people, who crave respect as much as anyone. Whereas the Mexican upper class can be dismissive with waiters, secretaries, and the like, U.S. nationals instinctively make friends by treating them with respect. This can be particularly valuable when secretaries control their bosses' appointment books.

Mexican individualism also surfaces in a strong sense of craftsmanship and an aversion to regimented quality-control procedures. They want their work to be meaningful on a personal level, and they are less likely than northern Europeans to accept the Marxian alienation of labor that so marked industrialization in the West. Theirs is not a rule-based culture, and they are less susceptible to the Western imperative to conform to a system, whether it be an MRP system or a quality-control system.

Several factors have contributed to the erroneous perception that Mexicans lack a work ethic. Polychronicity always creates this impression with time-conscious Westerners, who may fail to understand that hard work need not be done on a particular schedule. Mexicans may seem lazy because many are idle, due to unemployment or connections with a well-heeled family. The overwhelming importance of personal connections in many organizations, as opposed to achievement, may make hard work an irrational activity. Given a minimal incentive, however, Mexicans are both industrious and ambitious. The universities are packed with students who study hard, respect their teachers, and diligently attend class (perhaps the reader can sense my envy as a professor in the United States), even though only a small fraction will obtain jobs worthy of their education. Mexican workers accept on-the-job training with enthusiasm, not only for self-advancement but also out of their culture's historical respect for learning.

Professional Women

A professional role is entirely possible for international women in Mexico, even if it often remains difficult for Mexican women. Visiting women will generally be treated with courtesy and respect, as required by upper-class machismo, a fact that can sometimes give them an advantage over visiting men. Women are also said to be more adept at Mexican skills of reading moods and body language. This, too, can be an advantage. Attempts to break out of the role of honored guest, however, for example by trying to be "one of the boys" or trying to take an aggressive stance, are likely to fail. The bond between men that means so much in Latin countries is inaccessible to women, but it can be roughly approximated by professional and trustworthy conduct over a period of time. Married women with families can strengthen ties by talking about this aspect of their lives.

The role of women in the larger society is difficult to describe because it is rapidly changing, particularly in the universities and among college-educated people. Until recently, young women seldom traveled alone unless accompanied by their children, but this is changing at least in the more cosmopolitan cities. In any case, women should dress and conduct themselves conservatively and expect behavior that in the United States or northern Europe would be considered patronizing or demeaning.

It is common for Westerners to visit other countries with a mission, perhaps to fight just this sort of patronizing behavior. My advice to those who feel they must do so is to avoid Mexico. Their campaigns will fail, and their careers will suffer. A case study well known in business schools tells the following story.[8] A female bank employee in the United States asked to be transferred to a branch in Mexico City. Her Mexican associates were polite and accommodating enough, but she encountered patronizing attitudes from male coworkers. Her clients were none too subtle about their lack of respect for her professional competence. Her dilemma was whether to acquiesce in this aspect of Hispanic culture or fight it. She chose the latter. As a result, superiors gave her lukewarm evaluations and her career began to bog down. Women sometimes report greater success than this, but it would be wise not to count on it.

The patronizing attitude toward women does not imply that women are inferior, only that they have a different role. They nurture the family while men shield it from danger. In fact, the flip side of machismo is *Marianisma* (after Mary, mother of Jesus), which views women as morally superior to men. What Western women experience as demeaning, traditional Latina women accept as a sign of respect. *Marianisma* and the cultural system it supports may allow one to develop a side of oneself that would be problematic in the cold, competitive, politically correct world back home: a different kind of relationship with the opposite sex, affection and friendship for associates, and greater devotion to family at the expense of job duties. Men, of course, can reap similar benefits.

The Western habit of viewing other cultures as less advanced, as in need of missionary zeal, is inadequate and stifling. Different peoples have made different trade-offs and arrived at different solutions to life. Every solution favors certain human virtues and develops some aspects of human potential while suppressing others. A Westerner who simply resists a culture that seems retrograde misses an opportunity to develop a part of his or her humanity that is neglected at home.

Languages . . . and Mathematics

Spanish is the only official language of Mexico and, fortunately, a relatively easy language to learn for much of the world. Much of its vocabulary is already familiar to the millions who speak romance languages or English. Spelling and syntax are entirely straightforward. The only real complication is the unwieldy verb conjugation scheme that burdens all Latin-based languages, but Mexicans tolerate almost any sort of usage they can understand. Mexicans normally do not speak more slowly for foreigners, but it is rarely necessary to understand every word. After all, one commonly hears no more than a word or two of what is said when conversing in one's own language, and context says the rest. One can rely on this same interpretive skill when learning a new language. Mexicans, always ready to assist, can help gringos with their language studies. School children in Mexico often approach foreign visitors and ask if they may practice their English by posing such questions as, "What is your name?" "Where are you from?" and so forth. Mexicans are similarly tolerant of visitors who want to practice their Spanish.

The Spanish language comes in various flavors across Latin America, and Mexican Spanish is distinctive. It borrows some words from the indigenous language Náhuatl, such as *aguacate* (avocado), *chocolate* (*choco* is the bean, *atl* is "water"), *coyote, guacamole, ocelote, tamale,* and *tomate,* all of which have been absorbed into American English as well. Mexicans are said to weaken their vowels, unlike Venezuelans or Caribbeans, who weaken final consonants, or Colombians who supposedly speak the clearest Spanish, at least to foreign ears. Whatever the case, Mexican Spanish differs no more from Castillian Spanish than American English from British English, and mutual intelligibility is rarely a problem.

Náhuatl is most often associated with indigenous Mexicans, but the country is actually a treasure trove of native American languages. Some 8 percent of the population collectively speak 56 native languages in 286 dialects (according to the 1990 census), and slightly more than 2 percent do not even speak Spanish. Table 5.2 lists the more important native languages, most of which are spoken in several dialects.

Some 1.5 million Mexicans speak 26 dialects of Náhuatl. The chief dialects are East and West Huasteca Náhuatl, spoken by some 800,000 people. The correct name for the language is actually *Nāhuatlahtōlli.* The stem *nāhua* refers to "clear or intelligible speech," and the suffix *tl* creates a noun, so that *nāhuatl* refers to "a person who speaks well." The *h* is not pronounced but indicates a glottal stop, much like the glottal stop that replaces the *t* when some British say, "Bri'ish." Otherwise one can pronounce Náhuatl words by reading them as though they were Spanish words, with a few exceptions: *x* is pronounced *sh,* and *ll* is pronounced as in English rather than with a *y* sound as in Spanish. Note, however, that the ancient Mixtec (*meesh-tek*) city of Oaxaca is pronounced *wa-ha-ka.* Also the Spanish sounds *hu* (English *w*) and *cu* (*kw*) are spelled *uh* and *uc,* respectively, when they occur as final consonants of Náhuatl words. The macron over the first *a* in *nāhuatl* (written as an accent in Spanish) indicates a long vowel. Náhuatl speakers often sprinkle their conversation with Spanish, resulting in a mixed language sometimes called "Mexicano" (the early Spanish word for the Náhuatl language).

TABLE 5.2
Native Language Groups of Mexico

Language Group	Primarily Spoken In
Ch'ol	Chiapas
Huasteco	San Luis Potosí, Veracruz
Maya	Campeche, Quitana Roo, Yucatán
Mixteco	Guerrero, Oaxaca
Náhuatl	Guerrero, Hidalgo, Puebla, San Luis Potosí, Veracruz
Otomí	Hidalgo
Purepecha	Michoacán
Totonaca	Puebla, Veracruz, Zacatlán
Tzeltal	Chiapas
Tzotzíl	Chiapas
Zapoteco	Oaxaca

This table lists the languages spoken by more than 100,000 people (according to the 1990 census), and the states in which they are primarily spoken.

The Mayan language has attracted much interest because its ancient hieroglyphics were only recently deciphered. This breakthrough provides a window on a great civilization whose descendants continue to speak their ancestral language in Mexico and Belize. The primary modern dialect is Yucatán Maya, which is spoken by some 700,000 people throughout the Yucatán peninsula. Tourists who visit the fascinating Mayan ruins of the area will encounter a number of people who speak only Maya, for instance in Mérida and Chetumal. About 40,000 people in the State of Quintana Roo speak two Maya dialects (Yucatán and Chan Santa Cruz) but no Spanish.

Mayan codices reveal not only a complex civilization but also a level of mathematics that achieved precision and sophistication far beyond any practical need. Today's astronomers can verify that their Mayan counterparts predicted celestial events thousands of years into the future, within a fraction of a second. This may be compared with the West's Julian calendar, which Pope Gregory had to correct only fifteen centuries later by removing ten days. The lives of the Maya were governed by a 260-day sacred calendar (*tzolkin*), a 365-day seasonal calendar (*haab*), and a 360-day long count calendar (*tun*), the first two of which coincided every fifty-two years. They kept track of many other cycles, all of which consisted of 13 Mayan time units times a power of 20, since they used a base-20 number system (except that one *tun* is 18 rather than 20 *uinals*). The longest calendar cycle measured the 26,000-year orbit of the solar system around Pleiades.

Like all Mesoamerican peoples, the Maya felt a deep need for predictability in an uncertain environment. Self-consciousness induces anxiety about what will happen next, and the advanced level of self-consciousness produced by the complexity of Mayan civilization led, at least among the intellectual elite, to an equally advanced reckoning of what the future may bring. It is ironic that the early inhabitants of what is now a strongly polychronic country shared the modern Western need to structure their lives by structuring time. We cannot know for sure, but it is very likely that they arrived at rituals and festivals on time. The Maya differed from Westerners in that they viewed time as cyclic and predestined, and simply wanted to be aware of what was coming.

Mexico's indigenous languages symbolize the enduring influence of ancient civilizations on Mexican culture today. If Mexicans lack the Mayan preoccupation with time, they nonetheless continue the traditional reliance on ritual and religious devotion as antidotes to an uncertain environment. The Western components of the culture may strengthen as political stability becomes more reliable, but it is likely that this unique fusion of European and American elements will continue to characterize Mexico.

Notes for Chapter 5

1. Alfredo López Austin, *The Human Body and Ideology: Concepts of the Ancient Nahuas, I,* University of Utah Press (Salt Lake City, 1988), 52–68.

2. Louise M. Burkhart, "The Cult of the Virgin of Guadalupe in Mexico," in Gary H. Gossen and Miguel Léon-Portilla, eds., *South and Meso-American Native Spirituality: From the Cult of the Feathered Serpent to the Theology of Liberation,* Crossroad (New York, 1993).

3. Robert Ryal Miller, *Mexico: A History,* University of Oklahoma Press (Norman, Okla., 1985).

4. Gary H. Gossens, "Maya Zapatistas Move to the Ancient Future," *American Anthropologist* 98 (1996), 528–38.

5. Boye Lafayette De Mente, *Mexican Etiquette and Ethics,* Phoenix Books (Paradise Valley, Ariz., 1997). See also Boye Lafayette De Mente, *NTC's Dictionary of Mexican Cultural Code Words: The Complete Guide to Key Words That Express How the Mexicans Think, Communicate, and Behave,* NTC Publishing Group (Chicago, 1996).

6. Octavio Paz, *El Laberinto de la Soledad,* Ediciones Catedra (Madrid, 2000).

7. Geert, Hofstede, *Cultures and Organizations: Software of the Mind,* McGraw-Hill (New York, 1991).

8. Thomas Dunfee and Diana Robertson, "Foreign Assignment," in Thomas Donaldson and Patricia H. Werhane, *Ethical Issues in Business: A Philosophical Approach,* 5th ed., Prentice-Hall (New York, 1996), 377–78.

6 *Germany and Denmark*

While waiting in the Hamburg Altona station to board a German train to Denmark, I studied the other passengers on the platform who were waiting for the same train. About half were Danish and half German, and it was clear who was who. Aside from the fact that they were speaking the soft tones of Danish rather than the crisp rhythm of German, the Danes nearly to a person wore the same multicolored *fritidstøj* (leisure outfit), carried the same Räven backpack, munched on the same high-calorie snacks, and were all fashionably thin. The train soon arrived in Altona, precisely on time, of course, and sometime after our departure it reached the Danish border. At this point, passengers were obliged to walk through immigration control and board a Danish train on the other side. The seat numbering was supposed to be the same on the second train as on the first, but for some reason the Danish railroad had provided cars with a different layout. Quite a few tickets, including my own, bore seat numbers that did not exist. Almost without exception, the Germans scurried from one car to another in search of a matching seat, upset about the lack of *Ordnung* (order). The Danes, meanwhile, were totally unperturbed. They simply plopped down in a convenient seat and continued to *slappe af og spise* (relax and eat).

Everyday events of this kind can speak volumes about a culture. This one highlights the homogeneity of Denmark and the role of order and system in Germany, both of which are fundamental stress-management mechanisms in the respective countries. Both peoples offer textbook cases of Western culture. Both rely, in their own ways, on an environment that is highly structured and rationalized through technology to obtain a sense of security—the essence of the Western approach to life. Danish behavior may be casual, but their workplaces are as neat as a pin, designed for maximum efficiency, with a place for everything and everything in its place. This is why they can take so much time to relax, eat, and participate in sports that keep them thin and fit. The Germans may express their individuality in dress and personal manner, but they conform religiously to a complex system of rules that regulate a highly efficient state.

This chapter attempts to introduce the reader to Western culture by briefly touring two contrasting instances of it. Along the way it provides practical advice for professionals who find themselves in Germany or

Denmark. Much of what I say about German culture applies as well to Austria and the German-speaking portion of Switzerland. My remarks on Denmark require some modification for other Scandinavian countries, which I will briefly indicate. With these and subsequent concrete examples as background, Chapter 11 provides a deeper analysis of the West and its cultural origins.

A Culture of Engineering

Engineering lies at the root of German society as well as its industry. *Engineering* might be defined as the "application of science and technology to bringing nature under control." It not only builds engines that harness natural forces but also surrounds us with order and system: heated dwellings, irrigated agriculture, power and transport grids, and medical technology. It transforms an unpredictable natural environment into systems that respond to human wishes. In this way it addresses a fundamental cause of stress: the inability to predict and control one's situation. It is little wonder that engineering projects can be found in almost every civilization, and civilization arguably arose in order to build them. Yet it is the West that relies most thoroughly on engineering, that invests most heavily in the scientific research that underlies it, and that conforms its lifestyle most completely to its demands. Of Western nations, Germany most clearly exhibits this tendency.

German engineering goes far beyond precision-built Mercedes automobiles and indestructible *Autobahnen* (highways). Living in a German-speaking country is like living in a gigantic social machine. Trolleys and trains tick along with the precision of a Swiss watch. One day while waiting on a platform in Basel, Switzerland, I watched train after train close its doors at the scheduled minute of departure, on each occasion just as the second hand crossed the 12 on the station clock. Intricate laws regulate every part of German economic machinery, down to the size of screws with which one mounts a storefront sign.[1] The universally admired German apprenticeship system trains young workers for maximum efficiency. Vacation periods are staggered so that not everyone rushes to the beach at the same time. Detailed zoning laws make sure that Alpine villages have that picture-postcard look. Little is left to chance, as in one hotel I frequented in Ulm, where an exhaust system removed odor from the toilet bowls.

Germans are said to thrive on hard work. One hears the aphorism: *In Frankreich arbeitet man um zu leben, aber in Deutschland lebt man um zu arbeiten* (In France one works to live, but in Germany one lives to work).

Germans take their work seriously, but their reputation as workaholics is far from accurate. While U.S. or Japanese prosperity may rest on long hours and stress, Germans produce by planning ahead and working smart. Labor unions won a 35-hour work week in 1984, and the government mandates a 30-day paid vacation for many workers. Volkswagen adopted a 28.8-hour week in 1994. Germans excel by making the most of their brief hours on the job.

A key component of German productivity is the apprenticeship system. About two-thirds of students graduating from secondary school enter the "dual system" (*duales System*), in which they spend about two days a week at vocational school and three days working as company-sponsored apprentices. (Many among the remaining third enter the world-class German university system.) Apprentices spend three or more years training for any of some 325 job categories, ranging from geriatric nurse to sales clerk. A company's investment is considerable, particularly since trainees make no commitment to continue working for the company that trains them. It has been argued that a company's net cost of training an apprentice was essentially a wash until 1991, due in part to tax breaks, but labor costs have risen and the advantages of hiring apprentices are less compelling today.[2] Nonetheless, the system remains in place as a kind of social contract. If companies cannot hire their own apprentices, they may be able to hire someone else's. Since nearly everyone's full potential is realized, German workers can collect high salaries while putting in a short week.

Aside from replacing the natural environment with a controllable artificial one, the engineering approach has three additional characteristics that shape German culture: safety, structure, and science. The hankering for safety is evident in German risk aversion. The proverbial rule of thumb for building a bridge is to calculate the amount of steel required—and double it. Germans extend this principle to life in general. The German business person does not propose a new product with a sales pitch. He or she lays out a detailed production and marketing strategy, with contingency plans for everything that might go wrong. The German consumer pays a premium for quality, because well-built products provide greater protection against the unplanned. German decision making is slow, not in order to preserve group harmony or avoid loss of face as in Asia, but to make sure every possible outcome is considered, just as an engineer would factor in any possible traffic load or wind stress on a bridge. Germans are reluctant to enter new markets but specialize in established industries in which they define the standard of quality. One thinks of BMW automobiles, Siemens electrical equipment, Braun appliances, and Merck pharmaceuticals. Perhaps this explains why computerization was remarkably slow to develop in this land of technology.

A Structured Society

Structure is another key component of engineering, and Germans impose structure on their time and society as well as their physical environment. This is the source of their monochronic time consciousness, discussed in Chapter 2. The day is under control when neatly partitioned into periods, with one task assigned to each period. In particular it is bifurcated into work time and personal time. One thinks of Wemmick in Dickens' *Great Expectations*, who crossed a drawbridge to enter his home every evening, leaving the world of work behind. It is not much different in Germany or in northern Europe generally, where one rarely brings work home. While living in Denmark, I learned that it was impossible even to dial up the campus computer from my apartment and check my E-mail, because nobody does such things at night.

Much of the separation between work and personal life is mandated by law. Factories must get special permission to run their machinery on weekends, because labor law ordinarily prohibits it. Closing laws can be a major nuisance for shoppers, although Germans are accustomed to planning ahead and manage their shopping with similar foresight. The original 1956 closing law required shops to close by 6:30 p.m. during the week and by 2 p.m. on most Saturdays. I remember a late afternoon shopping trip in Munich on the last business day before Christmas. I half-assumed the closing law would surely make some exception for the holidays and did not watch the time carefully. Yet upon the chiming of the legal closing hour, the bustling city almost instantly became a ghost town. I was stranded with no possibility of finding a gift by Christmas, even though it was two days hence. The closing laws have been relaxed somewhat in recent years, allowing shops to remain open until 8 p.m. on weekdays and 4 p.m. on Saturdays (6 p.m. on the four Saturdays before Christmas), but many if not most shops retain the old hours. When in a pinch, one may be able to find something open in the train station.

Structure is equally visible in German social organization. *Ordnung* receives top priority. There is even a government bureau called the *Ordnungsamt* (Office of Order). Equally important is the northern European penchant for compartmentalization. It is clearest in the Netherlands, which copes with differing viewpoints in a densely populated country through a system of "pillarization," a kind of segregation. The original pillars were Catholics, Protestants, liberals, and socialists, each of which ran its own political parties, labor unions, and newspapers. The most famous instance of pillarization is the former system of apartheid in South Africa, where the Dutch colonists dealt with native Africans in the same way they dealt with divergent groups back home: by compartmentalizing them. The pillars, however, are historically supposed to have equal status, which of course was not the case with blacks and "coloreds" in South Africa. Another well-known example of compartmentalization is the Christiana neighborhood of Copenhagen, where drug use, graffiti, and other disorderly elements are allowed to thrive amid the neat and clean surroundings of mainstream Danish life.

Germans similarly compartmentalize their lives, not only in the separation of work and personal time already mentioned but also in the distinction between professional and personal acquaintances. While Mexicans prefer to do business with personal friends, Germans make a sharp distinction between a personal friend and a business associate. On one occasion I remarked to a German colleague that a certain person with whom I had worked was *ein Freund von mir* (a friend of mine). When I saw the surprised look, I realized my mistake. I should have said something like *guter Bekannte* (close acquaintance) rather than *Freund*.[3]

As in many languages, the divide between formal and familiar is marked by pronouns. *Sie* is the formal "you" and *du* the familiar "you," which at one time corresponded respectively to *you* and *thou* in English. Germans use *du* only to refer to family members (whence the term *familiar*), children, and intimate friends. It is customary to use *Sie* even with professional associates one has known for decades, although *du* is beginning to gain currency among young adults at the office. The *Sie/du* marker is a helpful guide, because one should not ask those addressed as *Sie* about their personal or family life, nor in most cases refer to them by their first name. Some Germans, particularly when visiting the United States, are self-conscious about their reputation for formality and affect a casual manner, in which case one can respond in kind.

Compartmentalization also affects the social status of immigrants, without doubt a topic of worried dinner-table conversation in western Europe. Germany began admitting large numbers of *Gastarbeiter* (guest workers) in the 1960s to alleviate its labor shortage at that time, and many additional immigrants, perhaps too many, took advantage of Germany's once liberal provisions for political asylum. Beyond this, those who can prove German descent (*Aussiedler*) may become citizens on that basis alone. To my knowledge, Germany and Israel are the only countries in the world with such a policy. The net effect is that Germany has accumulated a significant subpopulation of *Ausländer* (foreigners). Germans do their best to maintain a liberal attitude toward ethnic minorities, despite their historical discomfort with them. Painfully aware of their country's anti-Semitic past, they try to compensate with demonstrations against skinheads and neo-Nazis. Always admiring of good work, they acknowledge the contribution that Turks and others have made to German prosperity. Yet compartmentalization ensures that these immigrants, other than those of German ancestry, will never be regarded as Germans. The original *Gastarbeiter* were assumed temporary residents, and Germans were caught unprepared when many settled down and started families. The tight job market remains particularly difficult for applicants with dark skin or an accent. Apartment ads are often marked *keine Ausländer* (no foreigners), which really means no foreigners with Mediterranean or Middle Eastern roots. Around the dinner table one may hear talk about how immigrants misunderstand the nature of wealth. Too many, it is said, believe that the German *Wirtschaftswunder* (economic miracle) was somehow a gift from heaven rather than the result of effort and organization.

Life of the Mind

The third component of Germany's engineering approach is science and mathematics, the foundation of technology. German science goes far beyond its long list of such luminaries as Leibniz, Euler, Gauss, Cantor, Hilbert, Helmholtz, Hertz, Gauss, Mach, Heisenberg, Planck, Schrödinger, and Einstein. It extends to a rigorously intellectual approach to life in general. One need only visit Deutsches Museum in Munich to sense the height of the German intellectual plane. Most science museums simplify the material for the general visitor, but this museum seems to find little condescension necessary. I recall one exhibit that allows the visitor to reproduce the Millikan oil drop experiment of quantum physics in its full authenticity and presents without apology the mathematical analysis that Millikan himself performed.

The same principle applies to professional life. I once attended a talk by a chemical engineering professor on the occasion of his promotion to an academic chair sponsored by Bayer AG. Although several top Bayer executives were in attendance, the professor gave a technical talk intended for an audience of faculty and Ph.D. students, and the transparencies were packed with mathematical notation. While business executives in much of the world are expected to be generalists, the Bayer executives asked astute questions that not only demonstrated their understanding of the material but also proved challenging for the professor. The lesson here is that anyone who makes a presentation to a German professional audience should feel free to demonstrate his or her command of the field in its full sophistication, to the point of displaying mathematical models or technical details. A second lesson is that Germans value intelligent questions and the ability to answer them. One who makes a presentation without thorough advance preparation is taking an unacceptable risk.

Germans support intellectual inquiry both because it is useful and for its own sake. The German respect for the utility of science has led to the world's most efficient system of technology transfer. While U.S. executives tend to dismiss many academics as useless eggheads, German industry-sponsored institutes fly the same academics across the Atlantic and pick their brains for anything that might pay off. This emphasis on the practical coexists with an equally strong emphasis on the intrinsic value of knowledge. The German mind, for example, has developed a formidable intellectual tradition in philosophy and theology, which one may assume contributes little to industrial output. As a close student of this literature myself, I can attest to its remarkable originality and depth. If the German corpus consisted solely of Immanuel Kant's writings, the nation could take pride in its achievement.

Getting Along with Germans

Several German traits conspire to create for some visitors the impression of a cold, unwelcoming people. One is the sense of privacy. So much as looking at another person can be an invasion of personal space. Pedestrians tend to stare straight ahead, like New York City subway passengers, and office workers keep their doors shut, suggesting aloofness. Due to the sharp separation of private and public life, people open up only to their families and best friends. The intellectual bent can lead to an arrogance that does not suffer fools gladly. The rule-based society leads people to chide others about lapses in compliance with written and unwritten rules. A favorite pastime, for example, is to criticize neighbors for not keeping their front steps clean.

Germans are better described as shy than aloof, however. Some observers have tried to capture this by contrasting German "coconuts" with American "peaches." Germans are hard on the outside but agreeable on the inside, whereas Americans are soft on the outside but cold and hard inside. In a similar vein it is said that Americans are all smiles but do not mean it, whereas European friendship, once it develops, is real. The European bias in both observations is obvious enough, but both are right in the sense that most Germans are not the cold fish they may seem and warm up to acquaintances over time.

Germans are also inhibited by insecurity which traces partly to their sense of historical guilt. Western cultures can be regarded as guilt based, as opposed to shame based, and the power of guilt is nowhere stronger than in Germany. Although most Germans alive today were born after the Nazi era, they feel a collective responsibility for its horrors. Many suppress all displays of patriotism, as they believe that their nation is not worthy of flaunting itself. Shortly before the reunification of East and West Germany, I asked someone whether the official name of the unified country would be "Bundesrepublic Deutschland," the name of the old West Germany, or simply "Deutschland." The response, given in utter seriousness, was this: "My country does not deserve a name."

Intellectual arrogance certainly thrives in Europe, but in my experience it is less pronounced in Germany, due perhaps to the sense of guilt just mentioned. It is most noticeable in the desire for getting things right. Germans do not like to make mistakes and are prone to correct others' lapses. Germans who speak English, for example, aspire to speak it perfectly, and many come close to the mark, aside from the accent. On one occasion I had the amusing experience of having my English "corrected" by a German (I am a native speaker of the language). He was unaware that the English taught in Continental classrooms is not always up to par, for example in the usage of perfected and continuing tenses. Nonetheless, it is important for Germans to believe they have it right, since getting things exactly right is one way of getting things under control.

European hauteur is also selective in its target, as U.S. nationals will experience more of it than Asians, for example. Part of the explanation is that it is fashionable among educated classes to voice disdain for those provincial and Puritanical Americans, much as it is fashionable in American universities to look down on conservative Christians. A deeper reason has to do with the role of aristocracy in Western culture. Societies that emphasize individual rights or equality require their own unique rationale for why some people should have authority over others. Historically the European solution has been aristocracy, literally the rule of the excellent. Power is legitimated by superior ability or moral character. Those who exercise power must remind others of their superiority, whence the haughtiness often associated with aristocracy. In the judgment of many Europeans, however, the United States displays neither the sophistication nor the superior character that would justify its superpower status, and there is a tendency to remind American visitors of this fact. There is also the matter of wounded pride, as most European states once ran empires or colonies of their own. The fact that today's superpower was once a collection of European colonies only rubs salt into the wound.

Americans do not understand the European objection to their superpower role, because their view of power is quite different. Although a leader should be competent, leadership in America is passed around. Leaders have power because it is their turn to take charge, not because they are inherently superior to everyone else. Americans might argue that they simply took over from the British when the world situation required their services. Probably the only way for Americans to get respect in Europe, however, is to qualify for their hegemony by aristocratic standards. A good start would be to acquire a deeper knowledge of world affairs, and world cultures.

Professional Etiquette

German professional life is all about being professional, which means being serious and competent. Bankers in much of the world wear conservative business suits to reassure customers of their probity and stability. German professionals wear many "business suits" to provide similar reassurance in a risk-averse culture: punctuality, total preparedness, thoroughness, conservatism, and yes, a generally dour and humorless disposition. Germans object strenuously to the last characterization, but it does not deny a German sense of humor—it denies only that humor should be displayed in the workplace.

My students sometimes perform skits to illustrate how not to behave in a given cultural context, and a recent one on a German business meeting makes the point well (with some modifications by the instructor). An American business woman rushes into a German office suite for her appointment with Günter Schmidt and colleagues. Spotting Herr Schmidt through a slightly open door bearing his name, she calls out, "Hi, Günter, I'm Linda. Sorry I'm late. My kid has the flu and I had to get him to a doctor." The subject of the meeting is an American proposal to market the Dodge Caravan in Germany. Endeavoring to fit into the local culture, Linda begins her presentation with a joke about neo-Nazis. She then moves to her first Powerpoint slide, which bears the inscription "A Fantastic Opportunity" in large red print, followed by three or four exclamation points. The presentation continues with various photos of Caravans flanked by attractive women in scenic surroundings. When the audience asks about marketing research, Linda apologizes for not having the data at her fingertips but promises to fax it over that afternoon. At the conclusion of her talk, the members of the all-male audience rap their knuckles on the table, rather than offer applause, and Linda suspects this to be some kind of sexist gesture.

The proposal to sell Dodge Caravans is probably dead on arrival, since American minivans are too large, too fuel inefficient, and too American to appeal to the German market. The main point here, however, is that Linda manages to be unprofessional in almost every possible way. Tardiness is a sign of carelessness, which does not reassure risk-averse Germans. Looking through an open door is tantamount to bursting into the office unannounced. Colleagues are addressed by surnames and titles, and introductions are brief but formal. In this case Herr Schmidt, once notified by the receptionist, might emerge from his office with the greeting, "Good morning. Günter Schmidt," to which the response might be, "Pleased to meet you, Herr Schmidt. Linda Gonzalez." One does not discuss personal or family affairs in a business setting. Although meetings in the United States commonly begin with a joke to break the ice, such attempts fall flat in Germany. The Nazi era is a hypersensitive topic that should never be broached. American-style pizzazz and such superlatives as *fantastic opportunity* or *terrific deal* come across as juvenile and irrelevant. It is good that the presentation is slick and colorful, but it should replace the fluff with engineering specifications and marketing data, generously illustrated with plots and graphs. Obviously Ms. Gonzalez should be prepared to answer marketing questions in detail. The fact that she is female imposes on her an added burden of convincing male colleagues of her competence. The rapping of knuckles on the table, however, is standard practice in meetings and has nothing to do with the gender of the speaker.

No decision is likely to be made during a meeting. The Germans will want to research the issue further and examine every angle before making a commitment. Once made, however, the commitment is ironclad, and the Germans will expect similar reliability from their foreign partners.

Visitors may be invited to dinner, most likely in a restaurant rather than a private home, due to the strong German sense of privacy. The meal may run long, perhaps even to midnight, as the diners amuse themselves with wide-ranging conversation, smoking, and drinking. Nonsmokers may be expected to tolerate the fumes in silence, although smokers are beginning to ask permission to light up. Teetotalers can fit in by drinking *alkoholfreies Bier* or *Mineralwasser*. Business is not discussed in any important way. I have known restaurants to carry monochronicity to its logical extreme by serving the guests one at a time. In such cases it is perfectly acceptable to eat one's dinner while it is hot. If the affair does run late, one should not presume that it is all right to stagger in late for work the next morning, despite the rather early business hours that are customary in Germany.

German cuisine is heavy on red meat and calories but by no means limited to wurst and sauerkraut. Cooking is highly regional, ranging from *Eisbein* in Berlin (literally, "ice leg," or pickled pork) to *Spätzle* (literally, "baby sparrows") in Stuttgart. *Spätzle,* one of my favorites, are chewy noodles that can be regarded as the potatoes of Swabia, but with melted cheese make a respectable meal in themselves. Visitors with religious objections to pork should note that the famous *Wienerschnitzel* (Vienna cutlet), which visitors generally identify with veal, is more likely to be pork.

Making Connections

Germany is the precise opposite of a relationship-based culture. I enjoy telling my Asian students that German Chancellor Gerhard Schröder's half-brother was unemployed in 2001—and watching their jaws drop. Cronyism is practically unknown, and attempts to cultivate personal relationships with professional associates may be viewed with suspicion. Except at the highest levels, one interacts with an organization, not the people in it, and one may in fact negotiate with different people on each visit. In a bureaucracy, it is the position that matters, not its occupant. This is not to deny that one should go out for beers with the boys, since male camaraderie is expected and business entertaining is standard practice. But such rituals are primarily for recreation, or for the satisfaction of some primal urge for male bonding, rather than for the development of long-term business relationships. Although one should certainly make acquaintances on such occasions, they are not for the purpose of building trust as in Asia or Latin America. It is just that someone who becomes acquainted with a person may also become acquainted with his or her product. Relationships are practically never cemented by bribes, which are *streng verboten* (strictly forbidden) for government officials and highly unsavory for anyone. Gifts should be kept small and presented only at Christmas or other special occasions. Appropriate gifts are a bottle of *Sekt* (champagne) or other liquor, a small item bearing the company logo, or an inexpensive product of the company.

Given that Germans are so averse to the personal approach, the question arises as to what is the German equivalent of making connections. Chapter 3 discussed the German tendency toward spontaneous sociability and the creation of private organizations. It should be no surprise that the key to entry in German professional life is forming an organization, and establishing relationships with other organizations. In business, one forms a German corporation, which can come in either of two varieties. A newcomer generally forms a GmbH, or *Gesellschaft mit beschränkter Haftung* (limited liability corporation), which is roughly parallel to a privately held corporation in the United States. This is normally arranged through one of the German banks, which are the lords and masters of the business scene. Although private corporations in the United States are often equity financed, a GmbH is normally underwritten with bank loans. The average debt-to-equity ratio for German corporations has traditionally been about twice as high as in the United States.[4]

The other type of corporate entity is an AG or *Aktiengesellschaft* (business corporation), whose shares can be traded on the open market. The AG structure is strictly regulated and is appropriate only for such large, established corporations as Bosch or Siemens. Aside from corporations, one can form an OHG or *Offene Handelsgesellschaft* (general partnership), a KG or *Kommanditgesellschaft* (limited partnership), or the popular GmbH & Co KG (limited partnership with a GmbH as one of the partners). However business is organized, its traditional purpose in risk-averse Germany is much less about making profit than accumulating enough surplus to continue. Entrepreneurship exists but is a much more limited activity than in North America.[5] Entrepreneurs tell me that the pool of venture capital is relatively small and even smaller in Scandinavia.

The second step, after incorporation, is to exhibit one's products at some of the innumerable trade fairs (*Messen*), which are constantly underway in Hannover, Frankfurt, and other cities. One can wander the aisles, hand out business cards, and pitch one's wares to potential customers. The fairs are run by trade associations, which proliferate like mushrooms in Germany. The bank can put one in touch with the relevant associations and make other useful contacts. The associations themselves associate to form such "peak organizations" (*Spitzverbände*) as the BDI or Bundesverband der Deutschen Industrie (Federation of German Industry) and the BDA or Bundesvereinigung der Arbeitgeberverbände (Federated Union of Employer Organizations). As in Japan, one purpose of peak organizations is to organize voluntary self-regulation as a way of warding off governmental regulation.

Romanticism

Romanticism is one of the defining traits of Western culture and reaches its zenith in Germany. It can be summed up as a reaction to secularism. The West regards nature as a secular realm to be manipulated by technology, rather than a divine realm that one tries to control by appealing to the spirits that dwell in it. Secularism implies a disenchantment of nature, which leaves Westerners lonely in a dead world of molecules and physical forces, rather than the world of life and spirit familiar to most traditional cultures. Re-enchantment is attempted through any number of means. One is to view nature as a sublime realm whose grandeur bespeaks a divine architect, even if it is not itself inhabited by that architect. This kind of romanticism inspires, for example, the wilderness values of the Sierra Club and public parks that attempt to preserve nature in its pristine state.

One mark of romantic cultures is a tendency to exploit and despoil nature on the one hand and a contradictory tendency to revere an unsullied environment on the other. The former reflects the need to manipulate a secular world, and the latter is the romantic reaction to secularity. Not far from my house in Pittsburgh is the preserved nineteenth-century mansion of Henry Clay Frick, a business associate of steel magnate Andrew Carnegie. Frick, son of a German immigrant to the United States, operated hundreds of coke ovens in the western Pennsylvania countryside in order to fuel the furnaces of Carnegie's steel mills. He was part of an industrial machine that assaulted the natural environment to an almost unimaginable degree. Coal-mining operations and slag heaps not only defaced the land-scape but also leached poisonous chemicals that stain streambeds to this day. Coke ovens, blast furnaces, and railroad locomotives belched noxious fumes and black smoke, so polluting the air that Pittsburgh was at times obliged to burn its street lamps at noon. Social Darwinist Herbert Spencer, whom Carnegie invited to Pittsburgh to admire his industrial empire, hur-ried home as quickly as possible, lest the hellish surroundings drive him into depression and suicide. Visitors to Frick's mansion, however, see a very different vision of nature. The misty waterfalls and glorious sunsets of ro-mantic landscape paintings adorn the walls throughout. A nearby gallery houses additional nature paintings from Frick's collection. The stark con-trast with Frick's industrial activities is no accident. As nineteenth-century industry intensified its brutal exploitation of nature, nineteenth-century art became all the more romantic.

The romantic reaction is obvious enough in Germany. Until recently the Rhine was an industrial and agricultural sewer, at one point losing almost all ability to support aquatic life. Acid rain severely damaged the famed Schwarzwald (Black Forest). The reaction has taken several forms, such as the rise of die Grünen (the Greens). First organized as a radical environ-mentalist movement in the late 1970s, die Grünen has become the third-largest political party in Germany and entered the national ruling coalition in 1998. In 1991 they and other groups pushed through the most visible manifestation of German environmentalism: its recycling program.

Recycling has attracted remarkable grassroots support in much of Europe and North America, but Germans do it with a vengeance. The 1991 law, extended in 1996, requires German companies to recycle packaging and worn-out products. They can do it themselves, but the business com-munity soon developed a second option, the nonprofit corporation Duales System Deutschland (DSD). Companies pay DSD to let them put the fa-mous green dot (grüner Punkt) on packaging that DSD will recycle. DSD supplies color-coded recycling bins to companies and private homes across the land, including yellow ones for plastic and metal, brown ones for food waste, plastic sacks for old clothes, supermarket bins for beer and milk bot-tles, boxes for spent batteries, and black bins for miscellaneous trash. There is also a paper bank for discarded paper and a bottle bank for empty wine bottles. The German system has been faulted even by some environmental-ists for going overboard, on the ground that so extensive a collection effort costs more than it is worth. Others say it is based more on ideology than useful environmentalism, since in many cases there is no satisfactory way to recycle the stuff that is collected. The recycling laws are one reason that business people mutter about the impractical romanticism of die Grünen and similar groups. Yet the technologists of the right and the romantic tree huggers of the left are two sides of the same secular coin.

Another sign of re-enchantment in Germany is its enthusiasm for pets, which is shared by much of Europe and particularly North America. Pets are anthropomorphized and treated almost as members of the family, since animals are much-needed companions in a lonely, secular world. Germans take their pets very seriously in a very German way, inasmuch as pet laws reportedly fill a volume several inches thick.[6] The well-known writer Thomas Mann provided in his novella *Tobias Mindernickel* a somewhat pathological explanation of the relationship between Germans and their pets.

A third manifestation of German romanticism can be found in one of its most remarkable achievements: music. German-speaking countries produced an outpouring of musical superstars that arguably has no parallel in any age or culture: Bach, Händel (employed in England but raised in Germany), Haydn, Mozart, Beethoven, Schubert, Mendelssohn, J. Strauss, Schumann, Brahms, Wagner, Bruckner, Mahler, R. Strauss, and Schönberg. It is amusing to speculate on why this run of musical genius occurred when and where it did. Certainly the development of a fertile musical idiom was a factor, as suggested by the fact that great music began to peter out when, by Schönberg's day, the possibilities of the idiom had been mostly exhausted. Yet the same musical system was known to all of Europe. Germany's musical tradition seems to rise from its peculiar blend of passionate romanticism with a rigorous intellectual bent. It is true that composers prior to Beethoven are said to be preromantic, a concept which I always found confusing when performing their music, until I realized that it is nonsense. Styles change, but all great Western music is romantic. The very concept of musical genius is a romantic notion. If one examines Bach's *Mass in B Minor,* Mozart's *Jupiter Symphony,* or the Brahms *Requiem,* one finds passion inseparably combined with a rigorously designed musical structure. Their irresistible appeal is based on their successful integration of those two fundamental Western traits that are normally so at odds: the calculating rationality that controls a secular world through technology and the passionate individualism of the romantic response to secularity. For a few musical moments, the schizophrenic Western psyche enjoys wholeness.

Managing Stress in Germany

Germany's engineering approach is a stress-management mechanism. It gives one a certain sense of control to adopt an analytical, problem-solving approach to life. One might recall from childhood how absorbing and satisfying it was to build a house of blocks or draw one with crayons. This is perhaps because the house is first designed in one's imagination, where one has considerable control over matters. If the mental plan is conceived carefully and thoughtfully, it is more likely to work in practice, thus enhancing one's success in the real world as well. The general idea is to make plans, get organized, and take control.

In 1889 a massive flood nearly destroyed Johnstown, Pennsylvania.[7] A dam upstream from Johnstown on the Little Conemaugh River broke during torrential rains, releasing a 40-foot-high wall of water that thundered down the narrow ravine toward the unsuspecting city below. The relentless wave hit with the force of a locomotive and scattered buildings like toys. Terrified residents clung to the roofs of floating houses or searched in vain for children who had been swept away into the night. Finally a mountain of mud, debris, and countless bodies piled up against a stone railroad bridge that withstood the onslaught. The death and horror were beyond comprehension. When morning revealed the hellish scene, survivors were faced with the question of how they would deal with the unthinkable. Almost all of northern European stock, they took the cue from their culture. Day had scarcely broken and they were already getting organized. One group was assigned to set up a morgue, one to distribute food and water, and one to oversee treatment of the wounded. In reality there was not much the survivors could accomplish until help arrived, but the organization efforts must have given them some sense of control in the midst of chaos.

Getting organized and taking control is a coping mechanism that people use worldwide. In the West it is a dominant behavior pattern, and Westerners go a step further by restructuring the environment to ensure control: rivers are dammed, pests are exterminated, streets are laid out in a grid, lawns are trimmed, and time is compartmentalized. Germany's engineering approach is a particularly elaborate implementation. Here, as much as in any Western culture, organization and system stand between human beings and the abyss. Table 6.1 summarizes Germany's stress-management tools.

Newcomers can have difficulty adjusting to the German approach, not only because it may require a change in personal behavior but also because Germans engineer their society as well as their individual lives. The rules and regimentation can seem oppressive. One way to deal with this is to understand the purpose behind the rules, as a construction worker might consider the larger scheme behind the complicated pipes and wiring that must be installed. Another approach is to take advantage of the benefits of a regulated society. One must invest energy in the learning and observance of rules, but in return one lives in a stable and well-organized environment, not to mention an affluent one. Freed from concerns about whether one's job will be there tomorrow, or whether one can get to work safety, or whether one can afford to educate the children, one can move up the Maslovian scale and focus one's attention on more enjoyable pursuits.

TABLE 6.1
Stress-Management Mechanisms in Germany

Mechanism	Contribution to Stress Management
Engineering approach to nature and society	Predictable and controllable environment
Order and system	Sense that life is under control
Monochronic time consciousness	Part of orderly environment
Work-oriented approach	Allows one to take charge and have the sense that one is master of one's fate
Separation of personal and professional life	Regular escape from work stress
Highly regulated state	Security; help in time of need
Emphasis on correctness	A form of stoicism; control of one's own behavior even when events are out of control

This raises the general question as to whether making adjustments to a strange place will dilute one's cultural identity. I believe it actually strengthens an awareness of who one is. Some Israeli students, for example, recently told me that while living at home they scarcely regarded themselves as Jewish, but a year spent in the United States broadened their perspective on their own heritage and induced them to start attending temple services. Adjustment to a strange culture requires adoption of some new habits, but the same is true of any new life experience, whether it be college, marriage, employment, children, or retirement. Far from weakening one's identity, these changes define and enrich one's character when dealt with properly. The same holds for an encounter with another culture, which has the added benefit that stress-management skills essential for success abroad may be useful at home.

The German Language

The German language reflects the culture's fondness for precision and complexity. Precision derives from a large vocabulary replete with technical terms. Good diction is important, particularly in contracts, technical specifications, and regulations.

The complexity appears in the grammar and syntax, which impose a rather high start-up cost for students of the language, even those who speak another Germanic language. One must struggle with three genders, four cases, and a goodly number of irregular verbs. The genders are only sometimes predictable, plurals are irregular, and one must memorize which prepositions take which case. (I still remember reciting to myself as a beginner that *aus, ausser, bei, mit, nach, seit, von,* and *zu* take the dative.) Adjectives must be inflected to reflect the case, gender, and number of the noun or pronoun they modify, and the inflection depends on whether the adjective is preceded by a definite article, indefinite article, or no article.

Syntax can be even worse. Verbs in a dependent clause tend to pile up at the end. A particularly devilish device is the separable verb prefix, which is sometimes detached from the verb stem and placed at the end of the clause. I have seen instances in which the separable prefix literally appears halfway down the page from the verb. One reason for such long sentences is that a descriptive clause can function syntactically as an adjective that precedes the noun it modifies, leading to a nesting of clauses. Some say that the syntactic complexity encourages the woolly philosophizing for which Germans are known.

Pronunciation is fairly straightforward, since the letters represent more or less the same sounds as in English. There are exceptions: *Stuttgart* is *shtootgart* because the *s* precedes a consonant, but *sauerkraut* is *zourkraut* because it does not. *Bach* (literally, "brook") rhymes with the Scottish *loch*. A voiced consonant (*b, d, g*) is usually unvoiced when it appears as the final sound of a word (*p, t, ch*), so that Sigmund Freud is *zigmoont froit*. The psychologist Jung is *yoong,* the theologian Barth is *bart,* the composer Mozart is *moat's art,* and the automobile Volkswagen is *folk's voggen* (VW is *fow vay*). Vowels are pure: *a, e, i, o, u* are *ah, eh, ee, oh, oo*. An umlaut (*ä, ö, ü*) indicates a rounding of the lips when pronouncing the vowel. A final *e* is neutral; the philosopher Nietzsche is *neat-shuh,* not *neat-shee*. One often sees a letter that looks something like a beta (ß). It is short for *sz* (pronounced *ess-tset*) but is now commonly written *ss,* a spelling recently made official. Small words can run together to make big ones, as in *Arbeitgeberverbände* (*Arbeit-geber-verbände,* "work-giver associations"). The stress on syllables can depend on grammatical function; *gestern* (yesterday) is *GUESS-tern,* but *gesterben* (dead) is *ge-SHTEHR-ben* because *ge* is a participial prefix. Old books are printed in an ornate font called *Fraktur*. Good luck reading it.

Regional variations are surprisingly severe. I have serious problems with the Bavarian dialect, and Swiss or Austrian speech is even further from *Hochdeutsch* (high German). Professional people in any region, however, can speak standard German.

German formality is reflected in constant please's and thank you's (*bitte* and *danke,* or more elaborately *bitte schön* and *danke schön*). Greetings include *Guten Morgen* (good morning), *Guten Tag* (good day), and *Guten Abend* (good evening). Remember, *Tag* is *tock,* and *Abend* is *ah-bent*. If one walks into a Bavarian shop and hears *Grüss Gott!* (Greet God!) from the sales clerk, this is no attempt to evangelize; it is simply a hello. "Excuse me" is *Entschuldigen Sie mir,* or *Entschuldigen* for short. When taking leave, one might say, *"Auf Wiedersehen"* (till next time), or *"Gute Nacht"* (goodnight), or more informally, *"Tschüss"* (bye). "I don't speak German" is easy: *Ich spreche kein Deutsch.* Perhaps the most welcome phrase is *Alles ist in Ordnung* (all is in order). After *Ordnung,* the most important word in the language is *Pflicht,* whose sound suggests its meaning: duty. Interestingly, the traditional word for "sex" in this guilt-based culture is *Geschlecht* (*schlecht* means "evil"), but Germans now use the English *sex.* Let no one say there is no word for "fun"; it is *Spass,* formerly *Spaß.*

Practicing one's German can be a problem, since German-speaking associates will switch to English as soon as they detect lack of fluency. They do so to be accommodating, practice their English, or show off. The only reliable way to get experience is to take intensive courses or converse with people who speak no English. In fact, it is probably best not to speak German with colleagues until one is fairly proficient. Germans try to be patient with foreign speakers but honestly have difficulty dealing with imperfection. Fortunately, everyday conversational German is not particularly difficult to master once one gets past the initial grammatical barrier. As with any language, true fluency requires years of immersion.

The Danish Language

Language provides a useful pivot on which to turn to a discussion of Denmark. The complexity and formality of German contrast with the simplicity and casualness of Danish, much as the cultures contrast. The egalitarian Vikings handed down an earthbound language with little tolerance for circumlocution, or fancy talk, as one hears little of it even today. A particularly earthy characteristic is that Danish does not distinguish "dirty words" from more polite expressions for frustration or bodily functions. Some Danes are unaware of this Puritanical strain in English, and it is amusing to hear them sprinkle their English with Anglo-Saxon epithets they pick up from Hollywood movies, even in polite company.

Danish is something like an average of German and English in respect of vocabulary, but it is closer to English in two ways: simple syntax and totally unpredictable spelling. Students of English complain that the old Gaelic *ough* can sound like *oo, oh, ah, off,* or *uff,* but Danish presents similar conundrums. The syllable *af* is pronounced *ay* in *slappe af* (relax), *au* in *afdeling* (department), and *off* in *aften* (evening). Danish is also every bit as illogical as English, as a little story illustrates. One weekend I took my son to a destination in the countryside by public transport, which is possible because bus and train routes cover the land like a fishnet. I had no worries about catching a bus back home, because the printed schedule indicated that the bus ran *hverdag* (literally, "everyday"). I had forgotten, however, that *hverdag* means "weekday," while *hver dag* (two words) means "every day." We were stuck with a long nocturnal hike to the nearest train station—one of the few occasions on which public transport let me down.

Danes are shy and uncomfortable about speaking to strangers. Before learning this lesson, I made the mistake of saying, *"God morgen"* (Good morning) to my next-door neighbor. From his startled look one would think I had pulled a gun on him. One exception to this tendency is that people ask for practical information, such as directions or the time of day. The latter question is *Hvad er klokken* (pronounced something like *vah ehr kloggen*), to which one can respond by showing a wristwatch. Thanks (*tak*) are commonly expressed, but courtesy is not very important in Denmark. People rarely say "please" (*værsåvenlig;* literally, "be so kind"). There are certain phrases, however, that Danes love to say all the time. *Godt nok* (good enough) is roughly equivalent to the American *OK*, although people say OK as well. Everything is either *deilig* (*die-lee*) or *dårlig* (*doi-lee*), that is, "nice" or "nasty." Sometimes every sentence seems to end with *ikke osse?* (*ig-oss*), meaning "right?" A curious Danish habit is to utter the word for "yes," *ja*, while inhaling. "Cheers" for drinking is *Skål* (pronounced *skole*). "See you later" is *på gensyn* (pronounced *poe gen-soon* with a hard g).

Scandinavian languages affix definite articles to the end of nouns. An example of this that survives in English is *helmet*. The Danish word *hjelmet* is literally "the helmet," since *hjelm* means "helmet" and the suffix *et* means "the." Confusingly, *et hjelm* is "a helmet." The definite article changes when preceding an adjective, so that "the old helmet" becomes *det gamle hjelm*. Similarly, "the mermaid" is *havfruen,* but "The Little Mermaid" is *Den Lille Havfrue.* This, incidentally, is the famous fairy story penned by Hans Christian Andersen, native of Odense (pronounced *ohn-suh*) and probably Denmark's best-known writer. The sculpture of The Little Mermaid in Copenhagen is a nice illustration of tourism as pilgrimage. It is an unimposing piece in an unattractive industrial section of the harbor, but it is a must-see for every vacationer in the country.

All Danes study English from an early age, and quite a few speak it well, so there is no great motivation for foreigners to learn the language. It is essentially unspoken outside tiny Denmark, whose entire population (four million plus) would scarcely fill up a quarter of Mexico City. Yet Danes are flattered when visitors learn even a few words or pronounce names correctly. Linguistic competence can be useful, as I found that most shopkeepers, waiters, hairdressers, and bank tellers in my suburban community had forgotten any English they may once have learned.

The greatest barrier to learning Danish is the sound of the language. Germans say Danes speak as though they have a hot potato in their mouth, an apt description. Proper pronunciation is nonetheless important, as Danes have difficulty with foreign accents. Particularly challenging for foreigners are the soft consonants: *d* as in *mad* (food), *g* as in the name Jørgen, and *t* in the suffix *et*. Outsiders can scarcely hear the last two, much less pronounce them correctly. The phrase *rødgrød med fløde* (a delicious dessert of berries and cream) was reportedly used as a password during the war because German spies could never say it correctly. This hypersensitivity to accents only reinforces the aversion to immigrants, who rarely master Danish pronunciation. While I was taking out the garbage one day, a woman asked me for directions. When she heard my foreign accent, I thought the poor lady would faint from shock. Foreign tourists downtown are nonthreatening because they will soon leave, but foreign residents in a suburb are troubling.

The Welfare State

When people talk about Scandinavian cradle-to-grave security, they are not joking. The Danish government not only pays for hospital maternity care and both paternity and maternity benefits at home, but it also sends a nurse to the home afterward to check on the infant's health—and to make sure the parents know what they are doing. The state provides free education at all levels, right up to the Ph.D. It even pays doctoral students a stipend to keep them alive while they study, whether it be in Denmark or elsewhere. It is a great way to experience another country at public expense. Inability to find a job after graduation has only a marginal effect on one's living standard, due to the generous unemployment benefits. In fact, there is a certain advantage in being unemployed, since one can move to Copenhagen rather than reside in a less interesting city where jobs are available. When the young person marries and starts a family, free day care is available. If illness or disability strikes, the government provides health care and living expenses as needed. Retirement benefits are paid out, and yes, burial expenses are borne by the state. Granted, the system is not perfect: dental care is only partially subsidized.

The welfare state creates what in some senses can only be regarded as utopia. Poverty literally does not exist. When Jesus Christ said that the poor will always be with us, he was not talking about Denmark. There is very little crime, due in part to universal affluence and in part to Denmark's nonaggressive "feminine" culture. One can walk through the loneliest park late at night without fear. Youngsters think nothing of riding the city bus alone to school or to any destination in town. Aside from some domestic altercations resulting from alcoholism, violence is rare. The most violent act I have ever seen on a Danish-produced TV show occurred when one person pushed another onto a sofa.

The welfare state, of course, has a catch. The income tax rate (some 60 percent) would incite armed revolution in the United States, and there is value-added tax as well. Danes impose upon themselves an automobile tax that more than triples the price of a car. Yet there is remarkably little grumbling about the tax burden. Why should people complain, when the nation's standard of living is among the highest in the world and everyone has a fair share? Besides, the taxes do not just disappear into a black hole as in many countries; they buy something. Aside from lifetime security, one can enjoy one of the world's finest infrastructures. There is a magnificent system of bike lanes, so that one does not have to sacrifice safety to take advantage of a healthy mode of transport. Public transit is a marvel to behold. Trains and ferries run frequently and on time, and one can usually take along a bicycle for use at the other end. Buses are immaculate, well designed, and densely routed. Ground transport at the airport is scheduled to coordinate with aircraft departures and arrivals. An inexpensive 1,000-page schedule book shows timetables for every intercity bus stop and train station in the land and even indicates how many meters one must carry one's suitcase between the bus station and the train station.

Danes enjoy leisure as well as affluence. They knock it off early, play a vigorous game of soccer at the community recreation center, and come home to eat and watch TV. This is possible because intelligent design, rather than hard work, powers the economy. The world is familiar with well-designed Scandinavian furniture, but this is only the tip of the iceberg. The whole environment, like a Toyota automobile, is saturated with design forethought. There is a fractal structure: good design remains visible as one zooms in, from large-scale land-use patterns, to public utility systems, to building layouts, to furniture and tools, to the tiniest features on the most insignificant pieces of hardware. While riding the bus, I played a little game of focusing on some artifact in the vehicle, a bracket, a window, or whatever. If I contemplated it long enough, I would discover the clever idea in its design. While bicycling to work, I asked myself why the traffic signal for the bike lane turns green a second or two ahead of the traffic signal for automobiles. (Yes, some bike lanes have their own traffic signals.) Eventually the answer occurred to me. Since the bike lane is to the right of the roadway, cars making a right turn must cross the bike path. They are required by law, however, to yield right-of-way to cyclists. If the cyclists begin to move a bit early when the light changes, motorists are reminded to wait for them to pass. Thousands of little ideas like this one add up to a lifestyle of prosperity and leisure.

Public and private systems are highly rationalized. A computer in Århus maintains a dossier for every pig in Denmark (and there are more pigs than people). Each morning farmers can log in and find the optimal diet for each pig on that day. In many areas homes are heated by waste heat from power plants, delivered through insulated water pipes installed at public expense. Rather than purchase and maintain an expensive furnace, homeowners need only install a valve and water meter. Fuel cost, of course, is zero. This kind of efficiency is possible in Denmark because people are willing to invest through taxes rather than privately.

Design expertise even appears in food. I have never heard international gourmands sing the praises of Danish cuisine, but it has its virtues. The staple is hearty *frikadeller,* sometimes referred to as "Swedish meatballs." There is much pork and smoked fish. The *Danbo* cheese everyone eats has a mild but rich flavor that perfectly complements the hard, dark brown *rugbrød* (rye bread), leavened with beer. (I joked with friends that *rugbrød* has the advantage that it tastes the same whether fresh or stale.) The sweet pastry known in the United States as a Danish is an omnipresent temptation. The most Danish of dishes, however, is *smørrebrød,* because it evinces the Danish talent for design. Although the word literally means "butter bread," it actually refers to a small piece of *rugbrød* or other bread with two or three items on top—perhaps slices of smoked fish, egg, ham, cucumber, or any of a dozen other delicacies, tastefully arranged. In the cafeteria where I often took lunch, the kitchen staff must have enjoyed welcome relief from the monotony of dishwashing and floor mopping when they assembled trays of *smørrebrød,* each piece artfully designed and slightly different from any of the others.

Homogeneity

It would be easy for Danes to abuse the welfare state. Rather than work, they could plead lack of jobs or disability and collect generous benefits. Rather than pay exorbitant taxes, they could do business under the table. Danes believe their system works because they have a common value system. They are all brought up to respect the free rider principle: if I ride the bus, I should pay my fair share to keep it going. If I benefit from a system that works because others voluntarily obey the rules, I should do likewise, even if no one is looking.

The task presented to Danish culture is to convince an egalitarian, individualist population to buy into this collectivist argument. This is accomplished partly through a sense of *folkelighed,* which might be inadequately translated as "patriotism" or "national solidarity." Danes claim to be the first to have adopted a national flag, the *Dannebrog* (Dane's cloth). Every *sommerhus* (summer house) is expected to have a flagpole, and thousands of Danes raise the cloth every morning when in residence. The monarchy is retained, much as in the United Kingdom, to foster a sense of patriotism. Presumably patriotic citizens are more inclined to work toward the common good.

A second mechanism is a guilt-based culture that takes rules seriously, particularly rules that emphasize a collective point of view. Danes lose all shyness around strangers when they see an infraction. One who would like to experience this aspect of Danish society need only walk for a moment on a bike path; the passing cyclists will immediately apprise one of the necessity of moving aside. People are normally scrupulous about the rules, however, without being told. My wife brought a heavy envelope to the post office for weighing. The clerk remarked that if it were one gram lighter, the rate would be much less. Rather than cheat the government a gram, the clerk asked for permission to clip off a corner of the envelope and tape over the hole so as to reduce the weight. There is also a strong sense of political correctness, which seems related to patriotism as well as to rule enforcement, for instance in the area of environmentalism. It is admirable and patriotic to take an *aktiv ferie* (active holiday), meaning one that focuses on such healthy and nonpolluting activities as hikes and bike rides. Visitors can be advised to acknowledge Danish values by getting around on bicycle and bus, as I did, rather than by automobile. The health benefits are undeniable; after a few weeks I had built up enough stamina to keep up with Danish seventy-year-olds on the bicycle path.

A third mechanism is a feminine culture that favors cooperation over competition. The Swedish automaker Volvo pioneered cooperative work teams, which since have become common in industry. The hard sell is unknown. A U.S. automobile dealership may give its sales force a pep talk every morning to fire them up, but this is inconceivable in Scandinavia. Not even MBA students are competitive. There are no power lunches or power ties, nor for that matter many neckties at all. There are no buzz words and no rush to get ahead.

If any of these mechanisms were missing, the Danish welfare state could break down. Danes must therefore have a good deal of social conditioning in common, which in the Danish mind calls for homogeneity. Their thinking is that people will tolerate generous transfer payments if they believe the recipients have the same work ethic they do. People are less likely to cheat the government if they believe others are honest. We therefore see a fourth mechanism: conformity, at least in some areas of life. Children are expected to participate in sport teams, scout troops, and clubs, which help to homogenize values in a climate of individualism. Conformity is visible even on the surface, as people dress alike, towns look alike, and everyone eats the same narrow range of foods—as illustrated in the prize-winning Danish film, *Babettes Gæstebud* (*Babette's Feast*). The general attitude is that if one wants something different, the border is not far away. There is said to be a colony of 10,000 nonconformist Danes in England.

A corollary of this thinking is that there is no for place for multiculturalism or immigrants. Nonetheless, a small community of Muslims and other minorities has gathered in Denmark for much the same reason as in Germany. Danes agonize over the "immigrant problem" in public forums and private conversation alike. There is a clash of values, as Danes see immigrants as habitually on the dole, prone to have irresponsibly large families, and reluctant to adapt to Danish culture, while immigrants see Danes as selfish individualists who put their jobs ahead of their kids, salt away their parents in public institutions, and indulge themselves in pornography. There are no mosques in Denmark (specifically built as such); city officials oppose them on the ground that they would broadcast prayer calls and wake everyone up at daybreak. A right-wing organization, Den Danske Forening, is said to harass immigrants. The underlying problem is that Danes fear that immigrants are genuinely threatening to their homogeneous culture. I recall a raucous celebration that occurred a few years ago in Copenhagen after a Danish victory in World Cup soccer. Throngs of drunken young people choked the streets, leaving behind piles of beer bottles and other refuse in a very un-Danish mess. There were few police on the scene, and yet no violence occurred. Several of my colleagues remarked to me that this incident teaches a lesson. If Denmark were open to immigrants, a celebration of this sort would get out of control due to their presence in the mob.

If Danish society is so feminine and peaceful, one might wonder what happened to the swashbuckling Vikings. Actually they survive in the form of bikers, or young men who emulate the Hell's Angels motorcycle-based lifestyle they see in Hollywood movies. Every morning I cycled past a biker compound located incongruously in a neat, middle-class suburban neighborhood. I could not see inside, as it was surrounded by a high wooden fence topped with barbed wire and floodlights. A surveillance camera guarded the entrance. Like other residents, I pretended to ignore it. I never saw any action around this particular compound, but the news media regularly report wars between Scandinavian biker gangs. Aside from bikers, there are skinheads and neo-fascists, doubtless encouraged by high unemployment among young men. Tucked away in picturesque Ålborg, a small city in northern Jutland, is said to be one of Europe's major neo-Nazi cells, with its own radio station. Scandinavian culture seems to be dealing with its masculine and violent elements by isolating them in a fashion that resembles Dutch pillarization.

The drunken celebration in Copenhagen is another relic of the old masculine culture, although people today seem to drink more out of boredom than bravado. The safety, security, and sameness of Denmark are reassuring but unexciting. Picture postcards labeled "Denmark at night" show nothing but pitch black, and they are not far from accurate. The long Nordic winters compound the problem. The clean lines and primary colors of Danish modern architecture ultimately cannot dispel the gloom. I can remember when thick fog saturated the city for days on end, with the light level alternating between darkness and a murky twilight. It is the kind of environment that can drive one to depression and drink. At the university where I taught, some classes reserved Fridays for beer, including a class that met across the hall at nine in the morning. Someone would haul in several cases of warm Tuborg beer, and the students would sit and nurse their bottles for an hour in virtual silence. I made it a point to visit the men's room on Friday morning before the line started to form.

Equality

In Scandinavia, equality is real. The secretary may have an office just as large, with just as many windows, as the boss. I recall visiting a famous professor whose office was so small that it would hold only his books. He worked at a small desk in the hall, while his secretary luxuriated in a spacious windowed office. This contrasts with an incident I heard about in the United States. A government employee was assigned to an office that had too many windows for his pay grade, because no other office was available at the time. The agency boarded over the extra window.

One of my son's school friends in Denmark dreamed of becoming a garbage man, not because he liked the smell of garbage, but because he liked the smell of money. Sanitation workers earn one of the higher salaries in the land, in compensation for the nature of the work. It is expensive to eat out, even at fast-food restaurants, because the minimum-wage law ensures that cooks, waiters, and busboys earn a decent living. The lack of authoritarianism is reflected in a strong labor movement. The union trains employee representatives in nonconfrontational negotiation techniques, and they are likely to have their fingers in many management decisions. The pro-labor orientation is reflected in the nation's political rhetoric. When I attended a political rally on one occasion, it was like passing through a time warp to hear the New Deal Democrats that governed the United States in the 1930s. Equality seems to reign even in consumption of news. By far the most popular newspaper in the country is the sensational tabloid *Extrabladet*. Everyone from construction workers to college professors reads it unashamedly. No one feels obliged to be seen with something sophisticated like *Die Zeit* (German), *Information* (Danish), or *The Wall Street Journal* (U.S.). It is amusing to see little old ladies reading *Extrabladet* on the bus, with a full-page nude splashed across the backside of the newspaper.

It is important to observe Danish equality in professional situations. Salaries for different ranks may be surprisingly similar. People expect to receive the same respect, whether they happen to be janitor, secretary, or CEO. Titles are rarely used. There may be equivalents for *Mr.* or *Mrs.*, but I have never heard them spoken. It is very common to refer to a person simply by their first and last name, such as Lars Sørensen or Gudrun Jensen. In some contexts people are called by their full name, as in Lars Åge Sørensen, but this is because there are so few distinct Danish names (there may be two or three people in the building named Lars Sørensen), and not due to any love of formality.

Equality plays a key role in Denmark's welfare society because it fosters a sense of enfranchisement. People who feel they are an integral part of a cooperative effort are inclined to pitch in and make it work. People who feel they are serving someone else's system are more likely to milk it for what they can get. Denmark takes the first approach.

Privacy

Denmark illustrates the strong sense of privacy that sometimes develops in cold climates. One normally avoids discussing personal or family issues except with intimate friends. If a business associate's husband has been ill, it may prudent not to inquire about the situation, unless she broaches the issue. Better to risk showing unconcern than risk invading one's privacy. Walls between hotel rooms or apartments are soundproof, and I could play my piano without fear of disturbing the neighbors. Unlike the situation in Germany, however, office doors are generally left open. Alternative lifestyles, such as living with a gay or lesbian partner, are accepted, but this does not mean that it is all right to talk about it. One's private life is precisely that—private.

An emphasis on privacy does not dampen natural human curiosity, and Danes have some interesting ways of satisfying theirs. Dinner guests are often given a tour of the entire home, including closets, bathroom, and attic, a ritual that presumably satisfies curiosity. (There is more entertaining in the home than in restaurants, presumably because of the high cost of dining out.) Danes are habitually nosy, and it is best not to leave personal correspondence lying around. When I sent my own correspondence to the printer in the hall, I always found someone reading it when I arrived to pick it up, no matter how fast I scurried over from my office.

Managing Stress in Denmark

An orderly, safe, and secure environment, along with the comfort of living in a homogeneous population, are the more obvious stress-management tools in Denmark (see table 6.2). Visitors can obviously take advantage of the former. The latter can be more difficult, but Danes can eventually accept, as one of their own, outsiders who speak their language fluently and share their basic values.

There is also a sense of fun, even of magic. Several cities have a *tivoli* (amusement park), the largest and most famous being in Copenhagen. Children worldwide have played with Lego blocks, invented by a Danish carpenter in 1932. The word comes from the Danish *leg godt,* or "play well." Tourists flock to Legoland in Billund, where one can view miniature cities constructed entirely from Lego blocks. There is also an appreciation of fantasy that may be inherited from ancient Vikings and Celts, who lived in a magical world. Some Danes say half seriously that they believe in elves (*nisser*). The *Nissemand* (a kind of Santa Clause) comes at Christmas, a holiday Danes observe with gusto. My family and I joined a gathering to sing carols around a Christmas tree and were impressed to find that the others knew dozens of verses by heart. I suspect it is no accident that the most renowned Danish author, Hans Christian Andersen, wrote fairy stories. Travel, a favorite activity since the age of Vikings, has a magical element. The word for "fairy story," *eventur,* is the same as the word for "adventure." In fairness I should also mention that Danes have a dour and serious side, reflected in a high incidence of depression and suicide. Their second most famous author, the theologian Søren Kirkegaard, helped to found the gloomy existentialist school of philosophy.

By and large, however, Danes are relaxed and even tempered. As already mentioned, work hours are short, and amateur sports relieve any tension

TABLE 6.2
Stress-Management Mechanisms in Denmark

Mechanism	Contribution to Stress Management
Well-designed infrastructure	Predictable and controllable environment
Neatness and efficiency	More time to relax; less stress
Welfare state	Security; help in time of need
Homogeneous population	Assurance of shared values; possibility of welfare state
Separation of work time and personal time	Regular escape from work stress
Sense of fun and make-believe	Diversion from orderly life

that might exist. Danes are strongly monochronic but will not tolerate time pressure. One should never contact a colleague after hours on a business matter, no matter how urgent. In general, Danes do not take themselves or life too seriously, a refreshing contrast with Swedes and Norwegians. Visitors would do well to lighten up and relax with the locals.

Religion plays a very minor role in Denmark, despite the interest in Christmas. A surprisingly large number of students get theology degrees, but this is due to cushy job opportunities in state-supported Reformed Lutheran churches. Most Danes choose to pay church taxes, but only to preserve the right to have a church wedding and to record their children in the *Kirkebog* (registry of Christian names). The vast majority sleep through Sunday morning church bells.

Scandinavia

Denmark, Iceland, Norway, and Sweden form the core of Scandinavia. Finland is admitted to the club by courtesy, despite its very different ethnic background. There are also Denmark's Faeroe Islands and Greenland, although the latter is very nearly autonomous and its people are primarily Inuit.

Scandinavian countries in general share most of Denmark's characteristics: a welfare state that works, homogeneity, an emphasis on neatness, feminine culture, and egalitarianism. The universalizing side of Western culture is very much in evidence. Norwegians and Swedes regard themselves as internationalists and brokers for peace, and for the Swedes it seems quite natural that they should judge world science with Nobel prizes. Scandinavians are heavily involved in aid organizations that work internationally. Danes might be distinguished in the group by their easygoing nature and somewhat lighter touch when it comes to state regulation.

When people from different Scandinavian countries gather, they tend to speak their own languages, which the other Scandinavians can generally understand (although many have problems with Danish and its hot-potato pronunciation). Exceptions include Icelanders and Finns, who speak Swedish or Norwegian on such occasions. Many Scandinavians speak English and are quite proud of it.

The dominant Norwegian language is essentially Danish spoken more clearly, although one should never point this out in the presence of Norwegians. It is a sensitive point, as Danes imposed their language on Norway during the Middle Ages. Norway recognizes two official written languages: Bokmål (book speech) represents the Danish-like dialects spoken in urban areas, while Nynorsk (new Nordic) is closer to Swedish and represents dialects spoken in towns and rural areas. Norwegian culture is similar to that of other Scandinavian countries, but beyond this the cultural picture seems as complex as the linguistic one. Norwegians differ from Danes by placing less emphasis on informality and fun and more on privacy. It is not unusual for a Norwegian to spend the summer alone in an isolated mountain summer house. There is a strong aversion to time pressure, and working hours are short. I have seen shops that are open four or five hours a day. The cost of living is very high, but I suspect this is due less to high taxes than people say. A cold climate and egalitarian wages elevate prices as well.

In Sweden, Western rationality works itself out as a highly regulated social welfare system. There seems to be a government regulation to fix every problem in life except death and alcoholism, and the state is working valiantly against these as well. The health system is highly developed, and Swedes are known for keeping the world's best data base of medical records. Some public officials in other countries look admiringly at Sweden's optimized lifestyle, but it is not easily exported. Ubiquitous regulation imposes a high social cost that may not sit well with another population. Swedes are willing to invest in a highly organized social environment because it is their primary source of security, whereas most countries have already invested in other mechanisms.

The Swedish commitment to equality is very strong, as even the royal family and the prime minister behave much like ordinary citizens. A possibly legendary but plausible story has it that when Swedish King Carl Gustaf went Christmas shopping and tried to pay by credit card, he was asked for identification. The monarch was unable to convince the cashier that he carried no identification card because he was the king. He finally won the day by pointing out his likeness on a one-krona coin in the cash drawer. The tendency to total equality bore tragic fruit one evening in 1986, when the much-admired Prime Minister Olof Palme walked to the cinema with his wife. On the way home he was shot dead by an assailant that has yet to be identified. It was a profound shock to his country and the entire world, as it seemed to demonstrate that peace and security are not even possible in Sweden.

If Sweden emphasizes a rational social system a bit more than other Scandinavian countries, Iceland emphasizes homogeneity. It is said, not entirely in jest, that all Icelanders can recognize each other on the street, so that an outsider is instantly spotted. The Icelandic language is guarded from foreign influence even more fiercely than French, as linguists search ancient Viking texts for words and phrases they can apply to computer technology. Icelanders are as proud of their culture as any Scandinavian. They are known to remark that the harsh climate of their island weeded out all but the hardiest specimens of humanity.

Finns are linguistically related to Saami (Lapps), Estonians, and Magyars (Hungarians). The language is non-Indo-European and a mystery to other Scandinavians. Finns are known for a strong sense of personal autonomy and respect for the autonomy of others. The Saami live in the northern reaches of Norway, Sweden, and Finland, although many have migrated to the larger cities of these countries. Estonia could with justice be regarded as part of Scandinavia, since Estonians are ethnically related to Finns and speak a mutually intelligible language.

The salient common theme of Scandinavian cultures is the search for security in a rationalized social welfare apparatus. The same tendency characterizes Germany and much of Europe, but it is strongest in the northern countries. The Swedish automobile Volvo, built like a tank, serves as a metaphor. An automotive engineer once told me that the Volvo relies on passive safety, while a car like the Italian Ferrari favors active safety. Volvo passengers are surrounded by a protective system that absorbs shocks from the outside. The driver of a Ferrari relies on the car's maneuverability to get out of the way of danger. Scandinavians, in general, prefer the protection of a well-built social system, while Italians distrust the government and call on their own wits for survival.

Notes for Chapter 6

1. Richard Lord, *Succeed in Business: Germany,* Graphic Arts Center Publishing Company (Portland, Oreg., 1998), 20.

2. Karin Wagner, "The German Apprenticeship System After Unification," report no. 1011-9523, Wissenschaftszentrum Berlin für Sozialforschung (January 1998).

3. The common closing in letters and E-mail, *Mit freundlichen Grüssen* (with friendly greetings), does not necessarily imply an intimate relationship and can be used in any informal communication between acquaintants.

4. Colin Randlesome, "The Business Culture in Germany," in Collin Randlesome, William Brierly, Kevin Bruton, Colin Gordon, and Peter King, eds., *Business Cultures in Europe,* 2d ed., Butterworth-Heinemann (Oxford, 1990), 28.

5. Ibid., 1.

6. Richard Lord, *Culture Shock: Germany,* Graphic Arts Center Publishing Company (Portland, Oreg., 2000).

7. The Johnstown Flood National Memorial in South Fork, Pennsylvania, brings the disaster to life in exhibit and film.

7 Classification of Cultures

Brazilians are fun loving, Israelis are brusque, and British are reserved—we have been cautioned against this sort of cultural stereotyping often enough. There is even talk of national diseases that reflect the culture: British constipation, French liver disease, and flu in the United States, the last perhaps due to stressful overwork that lowers resistance to infection.

Granted, any culture contains a wide range of personality types, or diseases for that matter, and it should not be identified with any particular one. Yet if we are to understand and talk about cultures, we must characterize and classify them somehow. Fortunately, this can be done without stereotyping. The key is to classify cultures by their structural properties rather than the personality traits of their peoples. Certain personalities may be more evident because they tend to thrive in a given culture, as explained in Chapter 4. But culture is primary, and personalities secondary.

Cultural classification has several benefits. It can bring to consciousness differences that might otherwise be overlooked. It can caution a visitor not to take umbrage if an Israeli seems rude, a Brazilian distracted, a Japanese evasive, or a European arrogant, because these are manifestations of a culture at work rather than responses to a particular foreigner. Brazilian culture is Dionysian (a concept to be discussed shortly), an important subculture of Israel is strongly rule based, and Europe relies on aristocracy in the classical Greek sense. Fun-loving personalities therefore fit well into Brazilian life, and rudeness is common in Israel, as witnessed by a typical session of the *Knesset*. A certain aloofness helps to distinguish aristocrats. But the underlying mechanisms, not the personalities they favor, should provide the basis for characterizing cultures.

Classification schemes provide a useful cultural vocabulary, even if they do not classify very well. Most are based on cultural mechanisms that one can arrange in pairs of opposites, such as masculine versus feminine, rule based versus relationship based, Dionysian versus Apollonian, and so forth (see table 7.1). If a given mechanism, such as rule-based behavior, assumes a key role in a given cultural system, one can refer to that culture as "rule based" as opposed to "relationship based." But a characteristic can also coexist with its opposite, in which case the classification scheme may become muddled, even if the cultural mechanisms on which they are based remain useful to explain how the cultures work.

TABLE 7.1
Classification of Cultures

Relationship based—individual behavior governed by relationships	*Rule based*—individual behavior governed by rules
High power distance—subordinates accept their position	*Low power distance*—preference for egalitarianism
Collectivist—primary loyalty is to the family or other group	*Individualist*—primarily loyalty is to oneself
Polychronic—comfortable with multi-tasking, involvement with several tasks at once	*Monochronic*—preference for structured time, one task at a time
High context—information transmitted implicitly through cultural norms	*Low context*—information transmitted explicitly
Polite—primarily concerned with feelings of others	*Rude*—justice takes precedence over courtesy
Shame based—motivated primarily by approval or disapproval of others	*Guilt based*—motivated to a large extent by internalized conscience
Humor as amusement—finds humor in twists and turns of everyday life	*Humor as jokes*—finds humor in irony and violation of rules and rationality
Masculine—emphasis on aggressiveness, competition	*Feminine*—emphasis on nurturing, cooperation
Uncertainty avoiding—preference for stable environment, reluctance to take risks	*Uncertainty tolerant*—ability to deal with unpredictable environment, willingness to take risks
Apollonian—finds security in equanimity and well-ordered lifestyle	*Dionysian*—finds escape in intense experience

The classifications above the horizontal line tend to correlate with those in the same column.

Perhaps the best-known scheme surveyed here is Geert Hofstede's classification of cultures along four axes: power distance, individualism/collectivism, masculine/feminine, and uncertainty avoidance. An even more fundamental distinction is that between rule-based and relationship-based cultures, which is related to Hall's distinction of low and high context (as discussed in chapter 2). It also gives rise to a distinction of guilt-based and shame-based cultures, rude and polite cultures, and even has implications for a culture's sense of humor. Finally, Ruth Benedict's characterization of Apollonian and Dionysian cultures has an important kernel of truth.

Power Distance

Geert Hofstede's original classification of cultures is based on a 1970s survey of employees in IBM subsidiaries located in fifty countries.

He analyzes the results in his book *Cultures and Organizations: Software of the Mind*.[1] He defends his IBM sample on the ground that the respondents are similar in respects other than cultural background, in the sense that they are white-collar employees of a conservative U.S.-based corporation. This presumably helps to isolate culturally specific traits from other traits. Each employee surveyed completed the same questionnaire. The responses were coded on a scale of numbers, usually 1 to 5. After the results were in, Hofstede used them to rate each country on the four dimensions mentioned. The choice of dimensions was based partly on previous work in the literature and partly on Hofstede's own interpretation of the results. It is important to understand that Hofstede did not stipulate a priori how the responses would determine a country's placement on each of the four scales. Rather, he associated questions with national traits after the results were in, and did so in such a way that an intuitively appealing classification of cultures would result. Hofstede is completely straightforward about this, and perhaps it is for the better. Surveys alone cannot explain a culture; interpretation is always necessary.

Power distance helps to explain how societies regulate the behavior of their members. One way for a society to govern itself is for a few members to exert power over everyone else. How individuals acquire power is a fascinating question, indeed the fundamental question of politics. One way it can occur is for subordinates to *accept* the dominance of superiors. This is what occurs in a society with large power distance, as defined by Hofstede. A society in which people involuntarily chafe under the power of a few does not satisfy this definition, as when Denmark was ruled by Germans or Hungary was a police state. If people are willing to grant power to a village elder, a boss at work, or a government potentate, however, it is probably because this is a mechanism their culture has evolved to maintain social order. In Hofstede's words,

Power distance can . . . be defined as the extent to which the less powerful members of institutions and organizations within a country expect and accept that power is distributed unequally. "Institutions" are the basic elements of a society like the family, school, and the community; "organizations" are the places where people work. Power distance is thus explained from the value systems of the less powerful members.[2]

In large power distance countries, children are typically required to be obedient and respectful to parents. As they grow older they are expected to be deferential to teachers and to their elders in general. Employees rarely challenge their superiors directly and may be reluctant even to discuss problems or concerns. An ideal boss is a benevolent or fatherly autocrat (the boss is rarely female). There are large differences in salary and skills between superiors and subordinates. There may be a rigid class structure with limited upward mobility.

In countries with low power distance, children are allowed to contradict their parents. There is more two-way discussion in classrooms, as students ask questions and even challenge the teacher. Discipline may be a problem, and when it is, parents are more likely to side with the child than with the teacher. Corporal punishment is not likely to be used. In the workplace, superiors may consult with subordinates before making a decision. Employees can bring concerns and grievances to the attention of management. The ideal boss inspires the workers to strive voluntarily toward a common goal. The workers may be organized in labor unions. Salary differences are smaller, and workers may resent excessive perks on the part of executives.

Hofstede measured power distance by responses to three survey questions:

• Answers by nonmanagerial employees on the question: "How frequently, in your experience, does the following problem occur: employees being [sic] afraid to express disagreement with their managers?" (mean score on a 1–5 scale from "very frequently" to "very seldom").
• Subordinates' perception of their boss's *actual* decision-making style (percentage choosing either the description of an autocratic or of a paternalistic style, out of four possible styles plus a "none of these" alternative).
• Subordinates' *preference* for their boss's decision-making style (percentage preferring an autocratic or paternalistic style or, on the contrary, a style based on majority vote, but *not* a consultative style).[3]

This leads to the ranking of countries by power distance displayed in table 7.2. Although a list of this sort masks major differences in the role of power across countries, it seems remarkably accurate as a ranking. Confucian and other East Asian cultures are in fact authoritarian; younger people defer to their elders, women to men, and employees to bosses that are almost always older and male. Japan is the least authoritarian in this group, as middle management for example tends to take initiatives that are ratified by senior management. Power distance in Latin American countries (and the Philippines) is accompanied by strong class differences that date back to colonial days. Costa Rica is well known to be a partial exception, as the table indicates. Southern European countries, aside from what is now northern Italy, are historically characterized by strong central governments. The lowest power distance is found in northern Europe and its cultural offspring. Here internalized rules carry more of the burden of social regulation, and there is less reliance on the exercise of personal power. Israel is presumably classified with northern European countries because the IBM survey was completed by *Ashkenazim* (European Jews).

TABLE 7.2
Ranking of Countries on Power Distance Scale, Highest to Lowest

East Asia	Latin America	Other	Southern Europe	Other Western*
Malaysia				
	Guatemala			
	Panama			
Philippines				
	Mexico			
	Venezuela			
		Arab countries		
	Ecuador			
Indonesia				
	India			
		W. Africa		
			Yugoslavia	
Singapore				
	Brazil			
			France	
Hong Kong				
	Colombia			
	El Salvador			
		Turkey		
			Belgium	
		E. Africa		
	Peru			
Thailand				
	Chile			
			Portugal	
	Uruguay			
			Greece	
S. Korea				
		Iran		
Taiwan				
			Spain	
		Pakistan		
Japan				
			Italy	
	Argentina			
		S. Africa		
		Jamaica		
				U.S.A.
				Canada
				Netherlands
				Australia
	Costa Rica			
				W. Germany
				U.K.
				Switzerland
				Finland
				Norway
				Sweden
				Ireland
				New Zealand
				Denmark
		Israel		
				Austria

*N. Europe, Canada, U.S.A., Australia, New Zealand
Data Source: Hofstcde, page 26, which provides numerical scores as well.

Western nations tend to become less authoritarian over time; the 1960s marked a particularly sharp change. This biases the survey's ranking of the United States and perhaps other countries. Corporate America, where the survey data were gathered, tends to be more conservative and therefore to reflect more of the authoritarianism of the past than most institutions. The United States as a whole is therefore less authoritarian than the survey indicates.

Power distance is clearly about social structure rather than personalities. As Hofstede's soundest and most reliable classification scheme, it describes a very real cultural phenomenon that professionals must confront every day. When northern Europeans, Americans, or Australians, for example, work in high–power distance countries, they may have difficulty believing that most people on the bottom genuinely accept their position. In their own countries some people lord it over others, but only provisionally. Bosses must earn their position and hold it for a limited time, while subordinates may resent their lowly status. In much of the world, however, it is generally accepted that a few are destined to rule and many are destined to follow. Bosses may be expected to show some degree of competence or wisdom or willingness to consult, but within reasonable bounds failure to meet expectations does not destroy their authority. It is not difficult for Westerners to get used to this when they are in charge, but it is a different matter altogether when they are on the receiving end. One scenario is for a Westerner to be accused of some offense. The first instinct is to prove oneself innocent and demand one's rights, but the only recourse may be to grovel before some official, apologize for what seems a perfectly legal act, or pay a bribe.

The adjustment is equally awkward in the reverse direction. Professionals who emigrate to the West must become accustomed to justifying their authority anew each day, both at work and at home. Their employees may expect to be consulted about decisions and perhaps won over to the boss's point of view. The greatest conflict, however, is likely to appear in the family. The children mingle with peers who talk back to their parents and expect a great deal of freedom in their choice of career and spouse. Yet they must come home to a family that expects the same respect and obedience as in the old country. This family drama is a constant refrain among Muslim immigrants to Europe and Asian immigrants to the United States.

The basic dynamic of a high–power distance society is that people respect authority because there is no viable alternative. The boss is a fallible human being like the rest of us. But if a boss loses authority whenever this fallibility shows, no mortal can command allegiance, and everything will fall apart. We therefore see a number of mechanisms that conceal or varnish over the boss's human frailties. In much of Asia and elsewhere, people take care that the boss does not lose face. They do not mention the boss's errors, or even problems in the company, because their existence is an embarrassment to the boss. Bad news filters upward sooner or later through trusted third parties. This can cause problems when time is short, of course, such as in the construction of the new Chep Lap Kok airport in Hong Kong. According to some press reports, those in charge were unaware that air freight operations would not be ready by the mid-1997 opening date. Since the date had been moved up to coincide roughly with the handover of Hong Kong to China, there was apparently no time for the information to percolate upward through back channels. The opening was a disaster for air freight operations and companies who use them, as tons of produce and other merchandise sat rotting on the tarmac.

In Japan the boss has an ambiguous role in decision making, which helps protect him from the dishonor of making bad decisions. The role of Emperor Hirohito in formulating Japan's wartime policies, for example, is murky to this day. In some parts of the world, such as the Middle East, leaders sometimes take on legendary status and are credited with extraordinary abilities. I was told that the founder of a university at which I taught could speak twenty or thirty languages, including obscure African dialects. People still say that Mustafa Kemal Atatürk, founder of modern Turkey, could miraculously foretell the future. And of course there was Mathusaleh of Jewish Scripture, who we are told lived 980 years.

A key question remains unanswered: if high–power distance societies govern themselves by deferring to superiors, how do low–power distance societies do it? In most cases, they rule with rules. As we will see shortly, these societies try to inculcate in young people a respect for basic rules of justice and rationality. They also formulate additional rules as needed, which people tend to obey when the rules can be seen as consistent with the basic rules and as emanating from a legitimate source, such as a parliament. Yet power-preserving mechanisms appear even in low–power distance Western countries, since even there, someone must take charge at times. An old conundrum of Western culture is how an egalitarian society can endow certain people with power. Even the ancient Greeks were acutely aware of the problem, and they addressed it with the concept of aristocracy, or rule of the excellent. The ruling class distinguishes itself through greater abilities or higher character.

Ironically, aristocracy can alienate the ruling class from subordinated people in a fashion that may not occur even in high–power distance societies. Westerners have at times regarded their slaves as subhuman, for example, in order to reconcile slavery with egalitarian principles, which presumably apply only to human beings. Thus people who grew up in a low–power distance society may hesitate to relate to maids or laborers on quite the same level as peers, because they are uneasy about their ability to justify their superior position and lifestyle. In a high–power distance society, on the other hand, it may be entirely possible for one to relate to subordinates as fellow humans, without posturing or pretense, because no one questions who is in charge. This principle should not be pushed too far, but one can observe that in China, for example, it is common for bosses to invite their drivers to join them around a restaurant table, or for the maid who prepares dinner at home to eat with the family. Such behavior is less likely in Europe or Latin America, due to their aristocratic heritage. This is not to deny, of course, that high–power distance societies may have rigid class structures that tend to separate people, India being a salient example.

When relating to subordinates in a high–power distance society, it is important not to confuse common humanity with common station. I am reminded of the advertisements in which Dave Thomas, founder of Wendy's fast-food restaurants, is pictured with rolled-up sleeves and apron, as though he is in the kitchen frying hamburgers. Americans and Australians admire a boss who will pitch in and work alongside everyone else. High-power distance societies do not admire this pretense of equality, since they view status as reflecting the order of nature rather than personal merit. Superiors must observe this order no less than subordinates, or else lose respect. In some countries, for example, I must be careful not even to be seen making photocopies, as this is secretary's work. Occasionally I sneak into the office when no one is looking and make the copies. I am told that some Latin Americans do the same. There may be such prohibitions in low–power distance countries with a strong labor movement, but the cause is of course totally different.

Individualism and Collectivism

Hofstede distinguishes individualist and collectivist societies as follows.

Individualism pertains to societies in which the ties between individuals are loose: everyone is expected to look after himself or herself and his or her immediate family. Collectivism as its opposite pertains to societies in which people from birth onwards are integrated into strong, cohesive ingroups, which throughout people's lifetime continue to protect them in exchange for unquestioning loyalty.[4]

The distinction is problematic, because a society that is individualist on one level may be collectivist on another. A collectivist society is presumably one in which people are loyal to some group beyond themselves, usually the family. Yet as discussed in Chapter 3, people in an individualist country may exhibit spontaneous sociability by forming voluntary organizations or displaying a sense of civic responsibility. Suburban dwellers in the United States, for example, feel guilty when they do not know their neighbors by name, whereas family-oriented Asians see no problem in this lack of connection to the community. Perhaps a collectivist society is distinguished by a strong and unquestioning group loyalty that goes beyond community-mindedness. Yet citizens of individualistic cultures have on many occasions sacrificed their lives in voluntary military service, which would seem to demonstrate maximum loyalty. It may well be that the sense of civic responsibility is declining in the United States, and its population is becoming more atomistic, but this is not the issue. The issue is whether a country that is civic minded can also be classified as individualistic. Since the answer is apparently yes, it is unclear what is meant by *individualism* and *collectivism*.

Another angle is to interpret individualism as self-reliance. I should know something about this, since I came from one of the most fiercely self-reliant subcultures in the world, the people of the southern mountains in the United States. My ancestors chose to isolate themselves by migrating to wilderness areas in which nearly total self-sufficiency was the only option. As folk tradition puts it, if they were in earshot of their neighbor's rifle, it was time to move on to some place even more remote. They spun their own cloth, churned their own butter, and wrested from the earth all of life's necessities and creature comforts except iron, guns, and coffee. Even then, they smithed their own tools and often used chickory as a coffee substitute. Exceptions to self-reliance, such as barn raising and common self-defense, were forced by pure necessity. This tradition still resonates with many people in the United States, but I am unsure how much explanatory value it has for cultures in general. It seems related to U.S. interest in self-help books, propensity to do-it-yourself jobs, sometimes radical distrust of government, and the "lone ranger" characters of popular literature. But even in the United States, individualism seems as much a historical result of personality selection—the tendency of nonconformists to migrate to a strange land—as a structural property of the culture. One might say that Western cultures are individualistic because they produce such nonconformist minorities. Yet one of the classic expressions of Western nonconformism is to build such radically communal societies as the Shakers, Mormons, Moravians, and Mennonites. Such communities seem to be an outgrowth of the West's strong rule-based orientation (to be discussed shortly), rather than individualism, because they are normally based on a set of principles that are at odds with mainstream behavior.

The difficulty of the individualist/collectivist polarity is reflected in Hofstede's inability to identify survey items that measure it.

The survey questions on which the individualism index is based belong to a set of fourteen "work goals." People were asked: "Try to think of those factors which would be important to you in an ideal job"; . . . When the answer patterns for the respondents from 40 countries on the 14 items were analyzed, they reflected *two* underlying dimensions. One was individualism versus collectivism. The other came to be labeled masculinity versus femininity. . . .[5]

The preferences that were taken to indicate individualism are appropriate enough:

1. *Personal time.* Have a job which leaves you sufficient time for your personal or family life.
2. *Freedom.* Have considerable freedom to adopt your own approach to the job.
3. *Challenge.* Have challenging work to do—work from which you can achieve a personal sense of accomplishment.[6]

But the preferences indicating collectivism have little to do with collectivism:

1. *Training.* Have training opportunities (to improve your skills or learn new skills).
2. *Physical conditions.* Have good physical working conditions (good ventilation and lighting, adequate work space, etc.).
3. *Use of skills.* Fully use your skills and abilities on the job.[7]

The ranking that results appears in table 7.3. The individualistic United States appears on top, and countries with strong family ties tend to appear near the bottom. The particulars of the ranking are puzzling enough. Japan, for example, appears near the individualist pole despite its strong group orientation. India is similarly ranked, even though extended family ties are the glue that hold the country together. The individualist ranking for Italy, where family is sacred, may reflect the northern part of the country.

The overall ranking might be interpreted as revealing a polarity in which Maslovian self-actualization, a characteristic of affluent societies, lies at one extreme and family loyalty at the other. Yet this does not explain why affluent Singapore and South Korea should lie near the collectivist pole, or indeed why rich Indians are as loyal to family as anyone.

The only clear characterization of the results seems to be that countries in the bottom two-thirds of the chart exhibit strong extended family ties, and the others do not. Yet from a broader point of view, the individualist/collectivist polarity is not the central issue. What is important is the mechanism by which a society hangs together. The extended family, for example, is paramount in Latin America, the Middle East, India, and China, among other places. Latin America and the Middle East also rely on various types of friendship, as China does on relationships of mutual obligation (*guānxì*). Japanese and Koreans are loyal to employer and the state as well as the

TABLE 7.3

*Ranking of Countries on Individualism/Collectivism Scale,
Individualist Countries First*

Other Western*	Southern Europe	Other	East Asia	Latin America
U.S.A.				
Australia				
U.K.				
Canada				
Netherlands				
New Zealand				
	Italy			
	Belgium			
Denmark				
Sweden				
	France			
Ireland				
Norway				
Switzerland				
W. Germany				
		S. Africa		
Finland				
Austria				
		Israel		
	Spain			
		India		
			Japan	
				Argentina
		Iran		
		Jamaica		
				Brazil
		Arab countries		
		Turkey		
				Uruguay
		Greece		
			Philippines	
				Mexico
		E. Africa		
	Yugoslavia			
	Portugal			
			Malaysia	
			Hong Kong	
				Chile
		W. Africa		
			Singapore	
			Thailand	
				El Salvador
			S. Korea	
			Taiwan	
				Peru
			Costa Rica	
		Pakistan		
			Indonesia	
				Colombia
				Venezuela
				Panama
				Ecuador
				Guatemala

*N. Europe, Canada, U.S.A., Australia, New Zealand
Data Source: Hofstede, page 53.

family, whereas many Westerners respect rules of fairness even while neglecting their families. I have oversimplified these loyalties here but will return to them when discussing individual countries. It is important to understand them, because without them societies would disintegrate.

Masculine and Feminine

Masculinity and femininity are slippery concepts in the West. They are entangled in an ideological movement toward feminism among elite groups and reactions to it among other more traditional groups. Hofstede himself admits that he favors feminine cultures and is pleased that his native Netherlands is so classified. The cultural distinction of masculine and feminine is real enough, and anthropologists have studied it around the world. Their findings are complex, however, and they seldom support the simplistic generalizations that Western popular culture would like to make.

Hofstede portrays the masculine/feminine polarity as a tough/tender polarity.

Men . . . are supposed to be assertive, competitive and tough. Women are supposed to be more concerned with taking care of the home, of the children, and of people in general; to take the tender roles . . .

Male achievement reinforces masculine assertiveness and competition; female care reinforces feminine nurturance, a concern for relationships and for the living environment.[8]

Masculine/feminine is not the same as male/female; a person of either sex can exhibit both masculine and feminine traits. Hofstede identified four job preferences as indicating masculinity.

1. *Earnings*. Have an opportunity for high earnings.
2. *Recognition*. Get the recognition you deserve when you do a good job.
3. *Advancement*. Have an opportunity for advancement to higher level jobs.
4. *Challenge*. Have challenging work to do—work from which you can get a personal sense of accomplishment.[9]

The preferences that indicate femininity are

1. *Manager*. Have a good working relationship with your direct superior.
2. *Cooperation*. Work with people who cooperate well with one another.
3. *Living area*. Live in an area desirable to you and your family.
4. *Employment security*. Have the security that you will be able to work for your company as long as you want to.[10]

Hofstede reports that the masculinity scores of men and women correlate; when men are more masculine, so are women. He therefore ranks a culture by combining the scores for both sexes. He also finds that the gap between men and women on the masculinity/femininity scale is less in more-feminine countries, finally approaching zero in the highly feminine cultures of Scandinavia and the Netherlands. The ranking appears in table 7.4.

One might glean two basic facts from these results. One is that masculine cultures tend to be militaristic. They attack their neighbors (or once did), extol military virtues, enjoy violent sports, and have jingoistic mythologies or national literatures. One naturally thinks of Japanese, Korean, Chinese, Mongolian, Hindu, Arab, Israeli, Turkish, and Germanic peoples in this vein, as well as the northern European subpopulation of the United States. It is a matter for explanation why militaristic Vikings left us the world's most feminine cultures in Scandinavia. Curiously, video games illustrate the distinction rather well. I often propose to my students the hypothesis that, by and large, only boys from cultures with militaristic mythologies are enthusiasts of violent video games (including Scandinavians, interestingly), and the games themselves often reflect those mythologies or fanciful variations on them. Those who are skeptical can reflect on whether any of their friends of southern European, Slavic, African, or Latin American background are hooked on these games in the same way (intellectual games such as Tetris, which originated in Russia, do not count). I am not talking about ancestral lineage, but the culture or subculture in which they were raised. The same hypothesis predicts that few girls from any culture are addicted to these games.

Another fact that emerges from Hofstede's data is that masculine cultures tend to be competitive, while feminine cultures encourage cooperation. Despite their emphasis on group solidarity, for example, Japanese are highly competitive, whether it be in college entrance exams, sports, or rivalries between business executives. On the other hand, there is a marked aversion to competition in Scandinavia, Netherlands, Slavic countries, and many sub-Saharan African countries. In these places it is normally bad form to try to outdo one's fellows or to live an ostentatious lifestyle, although cultural disruption can attenuate these characteristics. The femininity of Mother Russia helps explain why market-style capitalism did not work there. Even now, while the country passes through a chaotic transition in which many cultural traits are in eclipse, braggadocio is resented.

The more closely I look at Hofstede's results, however, the more confused I get. Machismo presents a special problem, because it emphasizes mutual support alongside violence and domination of women. Latin America, although famous for machismo, is markedly less competitive than the countries to the north. Perhaps this ambiguity explains why Latin American

TABLE 7.4
Ranking of Countries on a Masculine/Feminine Scale, Masculine Countries First

Other Western*	Other	East Asia	Latin America	Southern Europe
		Japan		
Austria				
			Venezuela	Italy
Switzerland				
			Mexico	
Ireland				
	Jamaica			
U.K.				
W. Germany				
		Philippines		
			Colombia	
	S. Africa			
		Ecuador		
U.S.A.				
Australia				
New Zealand				
				Greece
		Hong Kong		
			Argentina	
	India			
				Belgium
	Arab countries			
Canada				
		Malaysia		
	Pakistan			
			Brazil	
		Singapore		
	Israel			
		Indonesia		
	W. Africa			
	Turkey			
		Taiwan		
			Panama	
	Iran			
				France
				Spain
			Peru	
	E. Africa			
			El Salvador	
		S. Korea		
			Uruguay	
			Guatemala	
		Thailand		
				Portugal
			Chile	
Finland				
				Yugoslavia
			Costa Rica	
Denmark				
Netherlands				
Norway				
Sweden				

*N. Europe, Canada, U.S.A., Australia, New Zealand

Data Source: Hofstede, page 84.

countries appear all over Hofstede's chart. Equally anomalous is Korea's appearance near the feminine pole, even though martial arts are valued, the military is one of the world's most rigorous, urban women were traditionally forbidden to leave the home during daylight hours, and women continue to play a limited role in business and public affairs.

The distinction of masculine and feminine, although a very real phenomenon, is problematic as a structural characteristic because it seems to be both shallow and deep. It is shallow because gender role differences often serve economic purposes and can turn on a dime when the economic situation changes. Women were rapidly "liberated" from their traditional roles in the United States, for example, when the postwar economy began to take advantage of inexpensive and docile female labor. The role of women in India has changed little because it continues to support an economic system in which marriage profoundly affects family relations, which are in turn the basis for economic relations. Yet there is relatively little aversion to women in the workplace, and their role could change quickly if family and economic relations were decoupled.

However transitory specific gender roles may be, the fundamental dialectic of male and female seems to flow from the deepest levels of human nature. The primal acts of giving birth to and nursing an infant lie at the core of our existence, and women alone can take part in them. One of a child's first distinctions is mama from papa. Ancient mythologies around the world dwell on the male and the female principles, yin and yang, the father sky whose rain impregnates mother earth, and so on in a thousand variations. The idea of male versus female saturates our conscious and subconscious lives. It is difficult to imagine how it could be uprooted without disrupting our humanity beyond recognition.

When explaining a culture, I find it useful to talk about the role of specific gender differences, as well as the balance between competition and cooperation. Yet I prefer to treat general masculine and feminine principles very carefully as the potent and complex ideas they are.

Uncertainty Avoidance

Uncertainty avoidance is the subtlest of Hofstede's categories but the most closely related to the theme of this book. An uncertainty-avoiding culture is one that experiences the stress of uncertainty as a nervousness about life. This nervousness tends to be relieved by adherence to rules and procedures, which are helpful because they serve essentially a ritual function. Ritual is an ancient device for managing stress.

Hofstede discovered the idea of uncertainty avoidance while examining responses to a survey question about job stress.

The question runs: "How often do you feel nervous or tense at work?" with answers ranging from (1) "I always feel this way" to (5) "I never feel this way."[11]

Because the responses did not correlate with power distance, Hofstede concluded that they indicated the level of anxiety or uncertainty about the future. He eventually identified two other questions that he took to measure a similar condition.

... the country mean scores on three questions were strongly correlated:

1. Job stress, as described ... (mean score on the 1–5 scale).
2. Agreement with the statement: "Company rules should not be broken—even when the employee thinks it is in the company's best interest" (mean score on a 1–5 scale). This question was labeled "rule orientation."
3. The percentage of employees expressing their intent to stay with the company for a long-term career. The question was: "How long do you think you will continue working for IBM?" and the answers ran: (1) "Two years at the most"; (2) "From two to five years"; (3) "More than five years (but probably will leave before I retire)"; and (4) "Until I retire."[12]

Hofstede notes that individual responses to the three questions showed no correlation; the country means, however, correlate highly.

Uncertainty avoidance can therefore be defined as *the extent to which the members of a culture feel threatened by uncertain or unknown situations*. This feeling is, among other things, expressed through nervous stress and in a need for predictability: a need for written and unwritten rules.[13]

The rankings appear in table 7.5.

Hofstede clearly seems to be on to something fundamental about culture, particularly in the way he relates stress with uncertainty. His analysis suggests, however, that only *some* cultures need mechanisms for dealing with uncertainty, such as rules and ritual. If the thesis of this book is correct, however, all cultures need such mechanisms and are in large part defined by them. I prefer to view Hofstede as having identified one particular mechanism.

An alternative interpretation of table 7.5 is that uncertainty-avoiding cultures are the risk-averse cultures, that is, they deal with uncertainty by taking few risks. But note that Hong Kong and Sweden are adjacent at the risk-prone end of the spectrum. Hong Kong can reasonably be regarded as risk prone, at least if its lust for gambling on the horses is any indication. But Sweden is risk averse, as noted in Chapter 6. Not only is the society as a whole highly regulated, but safety rules are so strict that, to take one example, the only permissible blood alcohol level for drivers is zero. It is advisable not to drive home after a meal that included bread made with yeast, because this leaves a trace of alcohol in the body. Furthermore, it seems curious to place Japan at the risk-averse end of the spectrum.

TABLE 7.5
Ranking of Countries by Degree of Uncertainty Avoidance, Most to Least

Southern Europe	Latin America	Other	Other Western*	East Asia
Greece				
Portugal				
	Guatemala			
	Uruguay			
Belgium	El Salvador			Japan
Yugoslavia	Peru			
France	Chile			
Spain	Costa Rica			
	Panama			
	Argentina	Turkey		S. Korea
	Mexico	Israel		
	Colombia			
	Venezuela			
	Brazil			
Italy		Pakistan	Austria	Taiwan
		Arab countries		
	Ecuador		W. Germany	Thailand
		Iran	Finland	
			Switzerland	
		W. Africa	Netherlands	
		E. Africa	Australia	
			Norway	
		S. Africa	New Zealand	
				Indonesia
			Canada	
			U.S.A.	Philippines
		India		Malaysia
			U.K.	
			Ireland	Hong Kong
			Sweden	
			Denmark	
		Jamaica		Singapore

*N. Europe, Canada, U.S.A., Australia, New Zealand
Data Source: Hofstede, page 113.

Nor does the table simply indicate the degree to which countries need rules. Sweden is highly regulated, for example, even though it appears at the bottom of the table. But this is as it should be. Such rule-based cultures as Sweden actually want the rules to run things. Uncertainty-avoiding cultures use rules in a ritualized manner to relieve a feeling of anxiety. They tend to be characterized by burdensome and dysfunctional bureaucracy.

So interpreted, the ranking has some degree of validity. Latin American cultures, listed as uncertainty avoiding, are well known to surround themselves with a protective layer of rules and procedures. Yet things actually get done through personal connections, not by appeal to written regulations. A similar statement could be made about some eastern and southern European countries, especially Greece, some African countries (which I believe should be higher on the list), and Russia (which was not surveyed).

One of my former Turkish students told a supposedly true story that illustrates dysfunctional bureaucracy with a bit of humor. It is about a "naïve American" (a common stereotype in the Mediterranean countries) who tried to obtain a driver's license in Greece. The American, Dorian Kokas, possessed a U.S. license that was about to expire and wished to renew it as an EU license. This required eight steps:

1. Get an official translation of the American license at the foreign ministry.
2. Get a chest X-ray.
3. Get an eye test.
4. Obtain a Greek ID or residence permit.
5. Have four photographs taken.
5. Fill out the license application form.
7. Obtain a bill of health from a physician.
8. Ask E.L.P.A. (a motorists' association) to validate the application.
9. Submit the validated application to the Ministry of Transportation.

After completing the first eight steps in a series of misadventures stretching over a period of three years, the naïve American discovered that E.L.P.A. had validated his application (step 8) under the incorrect name Miss Dorina Kokas. He eventually circumvented the problem by donning a wig and bribing witnesses to testify in court that Miss Dorina Kokas and Dorian Kokas are the same person. This enabled him to acquire the coveted license under the name Mrs. Dorian Kokas. The story should not be taken too literally, as Turks are not known for providing a charitable view of Greek culture. Yet it conveys the flavor of dysfunctional bureaucracies that provide a sense of security in much of the world.

Robert Kaplan provides a much grimmer example in his excellent book *The Ends of the Earth,* which describes with stark realism what happens when cultures break down. He had arrived at the Rwandan border with plans to report on the civil war there, and he presented his passport. The passport control station was a small shack that sat in the middle of a scene from hell. Outside the shack, people were stacking human body parts in large piles for incineration. Inside the shack, functionaries examined every jot and tittle of Kaplan's visa to make sure he could enter. Kaplan marveled that Rwandans would care about such trivia when their world was falling apart. But it was precisely because their world was falling apart that they cared. Bureaucratic procedure was the only vestige of predictability in a life reduced to horror and chaos.

Rules and Relationships

The distinction between rule-based and relationship-based cultures has emerged several times. This is to be expected, since it is a fundamental concept that relates closely to several others discussed here: power distance, high and low context, guilt and shame, and polychronic or monochronic time consciousness.

A relationship-based culture is the oldest and most prevalent sort. Individual behavior is regulated by other individuals, sometimes peers but usually superiors, such as parents, older siblings, bosses, or government officials. Children are watched by the entire community. This was dramatically illustrated by an incident related to me by a colleague in Zimbabwe. The colleague noticed a young man stealing something in a grocery. The manager spotted this act (managers in relationship-based countries keep an eagle eye on their customers) and dragged the young man into a back room. Peering through a doorway, my colleague got a glimpse of the manager slamming the shoplifter against the wall and slapping him across the face, with the admonition, "Don't let me ever catch you doing that again." It occurred to me that in my country the manager would land in greater trouble than the thief. Rather than use personal enforcement, he would be expected to call the police and let the system of rules take its course, however ineptly.

In many relationship-based countries it is common to see security guards in front of practically every business establishment as well as many middle-class homes. Guard duty provides a valuable source of employment to young men in these parts of the world, because it requires little training and jobs are plentiful. It must not be assumed, however, that the guards are hired to defend the property. Upon any threat from thieves, they would turn tail and run, since their salary is far too small to compensate risking life and limb. Their function is to do what conscience is supposed to do in the West: to serve as a constant reminder not to steal. Commonly the business or residence is surrounded by a high wall with sharp fragments of glass cemented to the top. The wall is a physical deterrent, no doubt, but psychological as well.

A similar mechanism explains the runaway popularity of mobile phones in much of the world, particularly in Asia. Aside from their general role in reinforcing the personal ties that hold these cultures together, the phones make it much easier for supervisors to supervise. The boss can call from a leisurely breakfast to make sure the employees showed up for work, or check on the shop while traveling or attending a business meeting. Parents can telephone their children from any location to keep them out of trouble. Since relationship-based cultures are almost always polychronic, the constant interruptions from pocket phones are not resented and in fact are usually welcomed. Mobile phones provide an example of technology that reinforces the local culture rather than import Western culture. It is amusing that Westerners, who also like their communication toys, seem sometimes not to know what to do with them. Passengers boarding an aircraft are prone to talk importantly into their phones but, if one actually listens to what they say, babble something like, "I am now boarding the plane. I found my seat. The plane is crowded," and so on with banalities.

Rule-based societies do things by the book. One cannot walk into a park or onto a public beach without seeing a posted list of rules. One cannot get treated in an emergency room without signing a legal release. A church or temple may provide a doorway to heaven, but its earthly existence is defined by the rules contained in its corporate charter. Morality itself is likely to be determined by precepts in a holy book. Commercial agreements are ratified by densely written contracts, and disputes are settled by appeal to volumes of regulations, case law, and statutory law. Lawyers advise those who wish to have an affair with a coworker in the litigious United States to draw up contracts with their lovers, to avoid possible sexual harassment charges.

Although rule-based societies have rules, societies with rules are not necessarily rule based. Rulers often make rules, even in relationship-based societies. The key is how people are induced to follow those rules. In rule-based societies people tend to internalize rules and follow them without close supervision. Germany and Scandinavia provide strong examples. Queuing theorist Richard Larson reported that on one occasion while visiting Denmark, he was stuck in a taxi waiting in a long queue to board a ferry.[14] There was a serious danger of missing his flight. On learning of the urgency, the driver swerved into a lane reserved for emergency vehicles and bypassed everyone else. Larson remarked that this must infuriate the other motorists. "No," replied the driver. "They know I wouldn't do it unless it were really necessary."

China, on the other hand, has a tradition of rules or law (*fǎlǜ*) that stretches back at least 2,200 years to Shang Yang and the Legalist school. Yet the culture is not rule based. Older family members, teachers, bosses, and local officials carry the primary burden of enforcing behavioral norms. When the state wants to enforce its edicts, it must enlist the support of these mechanisms. As in many relationship-based countries, when additional supervision is needed it may create an overbearing police force or intrusive bureaucracy. (Rule-based societies have used a similar apparatus, of course, often to impose norms that run counter to internalized rules.) China also differs in that its concept of law is by no means law in the Western sense, but this is not what makes the society relationship based. Traditionally, "law" was simply the current emperor's will written down; even today, legal argumentation is much less important than in the West. Case law and reasoning from precedent are alien ideas. Yet even if Chinese law followed an Anglo-Saxon or Napoleonic standard, this alone would not create a rule-based society.

Context and Learning

It should now be clear why relationship-based societies are high-context societies (introduced in Chapter 2). If signals from the surrounding culture are to regulate behavior in real time, these signals must be ubiquitous and efficiently delivered. High-context societies are organized to provide the necessary social monitoring. Rule-based societies, on the other hand, can be low-context societies, since they can transmit information about behavioral norms as explicit rules, and people take the rules seriously.

Low-context societies may appear to be better suited for today's complex societies, because their populations are capable of absorbing and acting on written information instantly promulgated to large numbers of people. A corporation that competes in a fast-moving market can change the behavior of its employees overnight by broadcasting an E-mail. Governments can fine-tune an economy by modifying complex regulations. Posted instructions can efficiently direct masses of people through airports or Web sites. Consumer goods can be shipped in fragments with instructions for assembly. Moreover, as suggested in Chapter 2, there is less social overhead than in low-trust societies, where monitoring is expensive and the necessity of building personal trust relationships slows the pace of negotiation.

Low-context mechanisms have disadvantages of their own, however. There are severe limits, for example, on what sort of behavior one can induce by issuing rules. They are a bit like instructions to a hypnotized patient, who will not obey them if they conflict with his or her basic values.

Social rules must generally conform to norms that the population has already internalized, unless one plans to enforce them with an oppressive state apparatus. This is one reason that low-context societies tend to be low–power distance societies.

Rule-based systems also incur their own kind of overhead. As any lawyer or legislator can attest, it is not a simple matter to write rules. They must spell out exactly what sort of behavior conforms with the law. They must allow for innumerable special cases in which the required behavior would be unreasonable or impractical. These complexities often do not come to light until the rules go into effect and have to be rewritten and rein-terpreted. In a relationship-based society, a parent, teacher, or government official simply decides who is wrong. Parties to a disputed contract (if there is a contract at all) renegotiate rather than go to court. Rule-based societies, however, give much more importance to the letter of the law. Laws and contracts become as complex as a Hopi healing ritual; enormous sums are invested in legal specialists and the system they manage.

Rule-based systems also tend to be brittle, because they may rely on a complex delivery mechanism. If the computers that operate flight display screens go down in Chicago's O'Hare Airport, the result is chaos. If they go down in Mumbai's Chhatrapati Shivaji Airport, people will continue to find the right gate through the same contextual cues they were already using.

High-context mechanisms can often be more efficient at transmitting complex and technical information. The young college students who main-tain the computer and local area network may never have laid eyes on a computer manual. Their technical know-how is folk knowledge, passed from one youngster to another as they watch each other work and discuss their projects. Many in fact grew up in high-context societies such as India or Taiwan. Much of the essential knowledge on which high-tech society is based appears nowhere in a technical manual; it is informal oral tradition in technical subcultures. One can go so far as to say that expertise in gen-eral is rarely learned from books and manuals. It is learned from appren-ticeship, by absorbing the art while working around experts over a period of years. It is no different with computer programming than with violin making.

Edward T. Hall makes (still) another useful distinction that helps clarify this point. He identifies three types of learning: informal, formal, and tech-nical. Informal learning is achieved by imitation, as when children learn their native language. Little explicit instruction is given, but the learner eventually "gets the hang of it." It is the kind of learning that relies most heavily on high-context mechanisms. Formal and technical learning involve explicit lessons in which the learner is told to do this or that, much as when a child is told not to say "ain't" or not to use vulgar language. The difference between formal and technical learning, as I read Hall, is that formal learning is normative. It transmits cultural values, whereas technical learning is value neutral. When the language teacher distinguishes a gerund from a participle, either of which may be used, the instruction is technical. But the admonition not to say "ain't" is normative. As Hall puts it, the admonition is given with a different tone of voice to emphasize that there is no choice in the matter.

Most societies take advantage of all three types of learning. However, low-context societies tend to emphasize formal and technical learning, because most people are adept at internalizing explicit formulations. When leaders want to change behavior, they often turn to formal and technical instruction. A curious example is the adoption of "sex education" in many Western schools. Traditionally young people heard about sex almost exclusively from their peers. Partly in order to reduce teenage pregnancy, educators attempted to replace this informal learning with technical learning about condoms, the anatomy of sex organs, and so forth. The example is curious because educators chose value-neutral technical instruction to change behavior, rather than formal instruction, which is designed precisely for this purpose. Interestingly, some conservative groups have in recent years replaced the technical material with formal instruction that emphasizes chastity.

It may again seem that the formal and technical modes of low-context societies have an advantage in today's complex and fast-moving world. Formal instruction can change behavior overnight, because people heed new rules (within limits). Technical instruction can disseminate facts and know-how to a large audience quickly, without distortion along the way. Yet informal instruction has a much greater "bandwidth." It can convey a large volume of subtle information, even information that no one knows how to codify formally. This is perhaps why expertise must often be learned by apprenticeship. The principle is nicely illustrated by Indians, who are well known for their proficiency in computer programming and related activities. Bangalore is one of the world capitals of software development, and a large fraction of the expertise in Silicon Valley and other technical centers is Indian. It should be no surprise that Indians acquire much of their technical knowledge from one another rather than manuals and textbooks. India is a high-context culture in which social networking is an indispensable survival skill. These networking skills enable Indian computer scientists to pick up the tricks of the trade from a large circle of colleagues. Perhaps only this kind of contextual learning can bear the information load of the information age. It appears, then, that both high-context and low-context cultures have advantages in our era.

The Polite and the Rude

Relationship-based and rule-based mechanisms underlie still another distinction of cultures: the polite and the rude.[15] To put it rudely: relationship-based cultures are polite, while the largely Western rule-based cultures are rude.

This may seem wrong on its face. People in Denmark seem very polite, while aggressive shopkeepers and street people harass visitors in India. Australians wait their turn, while Chinese push their way ahead. Canadian drivers courteously yield to pedestrians, while many African motorists ignore them. Tel Aviv is a non-Western city and yet not particularly known for courtly behavior.

Even when the generalization seems to hold, there are inconsistencies. Parisians are rude, and yet France is known for etiquette (the very word is French). Chinese are concerned with saving face and respect for feelings, but they are prone to loud arguments and even fisticuffs in public places. Mexicans are famous for solicitude and displays of affection but tolerate inequality and violence. The Shona people of East Africa charm everyone with their friendly nature and gentle good humor, but superiors bark orders at subordinates.

Nonetheless, there is a pattern here. Because rule-governed cultures can appeal to the rules to settle disputes, it is possible to be open and direct in ways that may offend. Conflicts are resolved by applying mutually agreed-upon principles of justice or efficiency. Other cultures find other ways. Because it is difficult to resolve disagreements and hurt feelings by appealing to rules, people try to avoid giving offense in the first place. They develop a tradition of courtesy, empathy, and deference to superiors.

This is not to say that Westerners are inconsiderate. They are bound by rules that protect the rights of others. This should not be misinterpreted as courtesy, however. Rule-governed behavior respects the rights of any person, or at least any citizen, including those one has never met. It is based on abstract principles of justice. Courtesy respects the feelings of the people at hand and is based on concrete empathy and concern. A rule-governed Westerner might work on behalf of strangers in a distant land while ignoring the feelings of people in the same room.

In the West, it is all right to level criticism at another if it is accompanied with facts or numbers that back it up. The other party is expected to swallow his or her pride. Disputes are adjudged by appeal to fairness or the bottom line. Obviously if Westerners are to subjugate their feelings to abstract principles in this way, they must believe in the legitimacy of the principles. This is the essence of a rule-based culture. In the rest of the world, people put more stock in concrete relationships than intangible rules. To get along with one another, they must maintain harmony by respecting the feelings and pride of their associates, and honoring their superiors.

As always, I am talking about cultural mechanisms, not the psychology of individuals. When I say that Western cultures are rude and others are polite, I do not mean to say that everyone in a given Western culture has a rude disposition. There may be some Western countries in which most people are polite (as well as obedient to rules), due to their particular history and circumstances. My point is that courtesy does not play the necessary integrative role in the West that it does in much of the world. Because the West relies instead on rules of fairness, it can tolerate rudeness.

In some areas the concept of courtesy seems not only superfluous but unknown. Denmark, far from being a land of courtesy, knows it not. When my family and I were living there, my son (who speaks Danish) asked an elderly lady, who was hobbling down the aisle of a city bus, if she would like his seat. The woman refused the offer, responding sharply, "Why? Is something wrong with the seat?" There is no rule that asks one to relinquish a seat. My son's offer was simply an act of courtesy, but since courtesy is an unfamiliar concept, the recipient was unable to recognize it. When Danes seem polite, as when drivers permitted the taxi to enter the emergency lane without protest, their behavior is grounded in rules.

Rules can even require the suspension of courtesy. An acquaintance of mine from the United Kingdom took a job in New Jersey. One day, while driving into the parking lot of his apartment building, he allowed another driver to park close to the door and put his own car in a more distant available space. The other driver met him at the building's entrance. Surmising that he was a newcomer, she harshly criticized his act of courtesy. She pointed out that if he kept up that sort of behavior he could never survive in New Jersey.

What happens when one follows rules of etiquette? Is this not rule-based behavior? Properly speaking, a rule of etiquette is a psychological rule of thumb, a guideline for what sort of behavior respects the feelings of others. It is not a normative rule in the sense used here. It helps one to do what one already knows to be the right thing, while a normative rule defines what is the right thing. (One may of course have other motives for observing etiquette, such as winning influential friends or gaining acceptance to high society.)

We can now deal with some of the apparent exceptions to the aforementioned characterization of rude and polite cultures. We observed, for example, that what appears to be Danish courtesy is rule-based behavior. Yet what about aggressive behavior on Indian streets or in shops? What about the Chinese, who can be abrupt and argumentative in public, despite their concern for saving face? Where is the courtesy? To understand what is happening here, we must recall that the main function of courtesy is to allow people to get along with one another when there is no effective appeal to shared principles. It is clearly more important to get along with one's family or associates than with strangers on the street. One is likely never to see a stranger again but must face family members and coworkers each day. Most relationship-based cultures therefore emphasize courtesy toward associates much more than toward strangers. (There is less emphasis on courtesy toward family members, perhaps because sibling rivalry makes it an impossible goal; the emphasis is rather on deference to older members of the family.)

Thus in many relationship-based countries, such as China and India, strangers on the street more or less coexist without showing much courtesy to one another. (Japanese provide an interesting contrast, as they expect polite behavior toward all fellow Japanese.) Sharp language, honking of horns, and street brawls seem in fact to release tension in China and may help explain the low crime rate. Indians sometimes aggressively pursue customers, although they tend to be rather polite once contact is established, presumably to pave the way for doing business. On MG Boulevard in Bangalore, a total stranger proposed to me a joint business venture but gracefully withdrew when I showed no interest. The Chinese can be equally aggressive in pursuit. On one occasion while I walked through a town in Shandong Province, three or four merchants formed a phalanx in front of me to block my path (others simply shouted, "Hullo, hullo," as Chinese love to do around Westerners). But it was in good fun; part of the motivation was just to get a closer look at the curious foreigner. Once they had a good look and failed to interest me in their wares, they let me pass.

The lack of street courtesy, plus the tendency of polychronic cultures not to form queues, explain the pushing and shoving when one boards a Chinese bus. If Australians queue up nicely, this again is rule-governed behavior. No one ever accused Australians of excessive courtesy, least of all the polite Malaysians and Indonesians who try to do business with their blunt and argumentative neighbors.

Just as a relationship-based culture may not rely on strangers showing courtesy to one another, it may not rely on bosses showing courtesy to subordinates. Courtesy and authority often work in tandem to hold society together. Courtesy helps to smooth over disagreements, but at some point they must be resolved. Since there is no appeal to shared principle, there is normally appeal to a shared authority figure. Thus, when a parent deals with children or a boss with employees, authority plays the integrative role that courtesy would otherwise play. There is no need for courtesy, and the parent or boss may be brusque and even resort to corporal punishment. This explains why the Shona people, with their normally pleasant and gentle disposition, can abruptly turn around and bark orders at subordinates. It also explains the habit of many motorists in Africa of giving pedestrians no quarter. Only the wealthy can afford cars, and those who can afford a car rarely walk. A driver is almost invariably of higher rank than pedestrians and feels no need to extend them courtesy. The pedestrians, for their part, get out of the way. If Canadians behave otherwise, it is because traffic laws require motorists to yield.

Why are the French famous for etiquette and yet so rude? Actually the French are equally famous for rudeness. If the word *etiquette* is French, so is *brusque*. An old name for the French people, the "*Franks,*" gave us our word *frank*. As for why France has a reputation for etiquette despite its frankness, one reason is that etiquette can serve functions other than those related directly to courtesy. For centuries etiquette has been a gatekeeper to the aristocracy, much as knowledge of the arts, fashionable dress, and a proper accent. In the king's court, it pays to be courtly (i.e., courteous). A more specific explanation for etiquette in France, however, may be the tendency for elites in Western cultures to fall back on courtesy for social regulation when justice fails. This occurred in the antebellum United States, where some of the elite discarded justice by enslaving Africans and apparently replaced it with genteel courtesy. It may have occurred in France when the monarchy outlived its time and imposed its arbitrary power on a rule-based society. It occurred on a massive scale in parts of Latin America, where European conquistadores installed an oppressive system that violated many of their own norms. In the absence of justice, many Latin Americans evolved an acute sense of courtesy and friendship, which continue to exist alongside remnants of the violence and inequality that gave rise to them. Finally, if courtesy is unimportant in Israel, admittedly not a Western country, perhaps it is because its Jewish culture is the very source of the West's preoccupation with justice and rules.

Guilt and Shame

A relationship-based culture primarily regulates interactions with people with whom one already has a relationship, particularly peers and superiors—that is, precisely the people who are in the best position to influence one's behavior. The control mechanism therefore naturally tends to be external, a complex of sanctions that can be gathered under the label "shame." A rule-based culture, however, takes more seriously the regulation of interaction between strangers, who may have little influence over one another's conduct. The government or police may of course manage this kind of interaction to a certain extent, but not nearly to the extent necessary, except perhaps in the most totalitarian state. The regulation therefore becomes internal as well as external. Shame plays a role, but children also learn to feel guilty when they break the rules.

I have no desire to advance any particular theory of the psychological mechanisms behind shame and guilt. They may even derive from the same mechanism, conditioned in different ways. Shame, whatever it is, comes into play when children are admonished or punished by their elders, as well as when people lose face or suffer humiliation. The fact that people can experience shame in so many ways, instinctively or after minimal conditioning, makes it a natural tool for regulating conduct. Guilt is a more complicated phenomenon. It obviates the necessity of constant supervision, but it exacts psychological costs, as it tends to torment as much as to motivate. A German American proverb states, *Ein gutes Gewissen ist ein sanftes Ruhekissen* (A good conscience is a soft pillow). What exactly is guilt? I faced this question while I was giving a workshop on cultural differences. A Japanese man approached me during a break and told me that his American wife kept saying that she "felt guilty" about things. He was puzzled by this and asked what she meant. I was hard put to explain guilt to someone who had not experienced it. I finally said that a soldier could feel guilt about killing someone in battle even if everyone praised him for the act. But he could not feel shame unless someone disapproved.

Whatever guilt and shame may be, they have important cross-cultural implications. Japan, a strongly shame-based culture, provides a good example. In November of 1997, Shohei Nozawa, president of Yamaichi Securities, stood before world TV cameras, apologized abjectly, and wept profusely. He had just announced the failure of his firm, one of the most prestigious companies in Japan. It was the largest bankruptcy in postwar Japanese history. Many non-Japanese viewers were shocked or disgusted by the display of tears. It was a time of financial crisis in Japan, and some inferred from Nozawa's behavior that the Japanese had become crybabies and were throwing in the towel. Foreign observers familiar with Nozawa's situation were even more perplexed. He had only recently taken over as president of the firm and had inherited a legacy of corruption and mismanagement from previous executives, some of whom were criminally prosecuted. He was actually beginning to set the firm on the right path. Why should he take responsibility for bankruptcy when his predecessors should bear the guilt?

Actually the incident had nothing to do with guilt. Apology in Japan is a means of restoring harmony, of making amends. Naturally, everyone tries to maintain harmony in the first place by saving face and respecting feelings. But sometimes things go wrong. A jet plane may crash through no fault of the airline, whereupon the CEO personally apologizes to families of the victims. In similar fashion Nozawa apologized to employees and stockholders, even though he personally bore no responsibility. It was not an expression of guilt, as there is essentially no concept of guilt in Japan, but a gesture of reconciliation. The tears reflected the enormity of the disaster, and Nozawa followed up by working hard to find new jobs for Yamaichi employees. Far from being a weak crybaby, Nozawa displayed the traits of a responsible leader.

Westerners are often unaware of the importance of supervision in a shame-based culture. It may be necessary to monitor an employee's work continuously in a situation where a Western manager might simply give instructions at the start of the day. This is not because employees are less responsible. It is just that they respond to *other people* rather than to a guilt mechanism. In a department store, for example, salespeople may give the customer a sales slip indicating the amount of the purchase, which the customer takes to a central cashier. After paying the cashier, the customer returns to the salesperson to exchange the receipt for the item purchased. The aim is to minimize the number of employees who must be closely supervised because they handle money. Supervision is accomplished through paperwork as well as personally. When government employees in Mexico (including teachers) submit an expense voucher to their local employer for the cost of a meal, the restaurant must submit a similar voucher directly to the government. The employer also forwards a copy to Mexico City, where a bureaucrat compares the two copies for consistency and (eventually) authorizes reimbursement.

Supervision can reinforce even rule-based behavior, as though people need to be reminded of the rules from time to time. Unlike supervision in relationship-based cultures, it tends to be given to strangers as much as to acquaintances. The habit seems to be strongest in Calvinist or other historically Protestant cultures. Swiss, for example, are fond of chiding local residents about not keeping their property neat or the grass cut short. Someone related to me his experience in Sweden, where letting an automobile idle is illegal (along with nearly everything else). He was obliged to wait in the car for a few minutes and allowed the engine to run to protect his family from the bitter cold. A nearby motorist promptly walked over and knocked on the window to express righteous indignation at such self-indulgence. My own city of Pittsburgh, historically a stronghold of Calvinist Scotch-Irish, shows the same tendency. A Pittsburgher knows no more satisfying pastime than to deliver little lectures to strangers on the street about what they should do. If a motorist hesitates at the wrong time or makes some minor error, this is good; it provides an opportunity to honk the horn in disapproval and display the appropriate hand gesture. The aim is to occupy the moral high ground. If for most Westerners a clean conscience is necessary for self-esteem, Pittsburghers require a cleaner one than the next guy.

I should say a bit more about this notion of conscience. Actually the idea was articulated (and the word coined) only three centuries ago by an Anglican bishop, Joseph Butler.[16] He meant by *conscience* "a mental faculty that allows one to distinguish right from wrong." It represented part of the Enlightenment intelligentsia's attempt to find a source for moral principle somewhere other than in divine revelation. In popular usage the word has come to denote a tendency to feel guilty about doing wrong, or simply a tendency to do the right thing. Like many psychological traits, it can occur in societies where it plays little structural role in the culture. A dramatic example appears in Jung Chang's historical biography, *Wild Swans: Three Daughters of China*.[17] Her father, Wang Yu, steadfastly adhered to his classical Communist principles despite harassment by Red Guards during the cultural revolution. Not a single individual provided him support or approval, not even his daughter, who joined the Red Guards. He was an example of remarkable courage and conscience, for which he suffered repeated indignities and eventual destruction. It is in fact not hard for conscience to develop in China, due to its sophisticated ideologies and ethical teachings. Yet shame dominates as a means of social control. Indeed, the Red Guards used shame with great effect against Wang Yu.

Cultures cannot be cleanly separated into the guilt based and the shame based. If guilt is a major force, along with shame, in parts of Europe and North America, and if many Asian counties rely primarily on shame alone, it is not clear what to say about Arab countries, for example. The simplistic distinction of guilt and shame does not begin to do justice to the complex practices by which cultures regulate themselves. Nonetheless, they are real phenomena that provide a starting point for a more nuanced understanding.

Humor

Humor is a complex topic, and it is difficult to make generalizations about it. Yet the distinction of guilt-based and shamed-based cultures has implications that extend even into this subtle realm. In guilt-based cultures humor often takes the form of jokes, whereas in shame-based cultures people more often find amusement in everyday life.

Let me explain what I mean by a joke. It is not just a funny remark. A joke derives its punch by providing a bit of relief from the rules. Although the guilt-based West is often identified with freedom, the weight of rationality and obligation constantly burden the Western mind. The freedom sensed by immigrants to the West is illusory, because the control is internal and therefore felt only by natives. A joke provides momentary escape from these constraints. Many jokes are based on twisted or absurd reasoning, logical tricks, or irony; puns are the simplest example. They grant a brief respite from rationality. Other jokes get their punch from a violation of moral standards, as do ubiquitous "dirty" and ethnic jokes. In this view, off-color jokes are, not a distortion of humor, but part of what Western humor is all about. They help to loosen the straight jacket of guilt and conscience.

Western cultures are by no means the only ones in which laughter releases tension. In Indonesia, for example, people may laugh when offended or upset. Jokes, however, are a characteristically Western form of relief. Although humor around the world differs along many dimensions, perhaps the clearest difference is that between cultures that make many jokes and those that make few jokes.

Perhaps some examples will help. The following is one of my favorite jokes, which I learned while growing up in the Southern Appalachian subculture of the United States. A farmer who lives in a mountain hollow above Newport, Tennessee, got word that his rich uncle had died and left him a large sum of money. He didn't trust banks, so he resolved to withdraw the inheritance from the bank and store it where money should be stored: in his mattress at home. He got into his rusty old black Ford pickup truck and drove down to the bank in Newport. After reading the appropriate papers, the bank teller counted out the inheritance in cash while the farmer watched. Upon receiving the stack of money, the farmer counted it again. Unsatisfied, he counted the bills once more, taking care that none stuck together. Finally the bank employee asked, "What's wrong, feller, did I cheat ye?" The old farmer replied, "Nope," and after a pause continued, "But you came damn close to it."

The joke is a joke because of the twist of logic, a characteristic of southern (U.S.) mountain humor. The bit of profanity at the end adds an extra punch. I have found this joke, told with proper timing, to be as reliable a cultural litmus test as any. I first told the joke in the Midwest before a gathering of United Parcel Service managers, nearly all of whom were of northern European extraction. Immediately after the punchline, the audience erupted with side-splitting laughter. Several came up after my talk to tell me they liked the joke. Another spotted me in the airport and bought me a drink in appreciation of the humor. The conference chair wrote my boss to say that he enjoyed my talk and especially the joke at the beginning. I have told the identical joke to several of my classes in cross-cultural management, which tend to be almost entirely non-Western in background. They respond with the silence of the grave. When I tell them that people have actually laughed at that joke, they shake their heads in disbelief.

On another occasion I was enduring one of those interminable flights between Asia and North America, wedged into a seat that seems designed for midgets or amputees. To my delight, the flight attendants began to show several episodes starring the British comedic genius Mr. Bean, who rarely utters a word in his skits. The flight attendants perhaps reasoned that if humor is lost in translation, Mr. Bean's pantomime would transcend the language barrier and appeal to all. An audience consisting almost entirely of Asian passengers stared at the screen in stony silence, while I stifled giggles and laughter. Was it because slapstick has no appeal to Asians? I think not. In fact, on one occasion when I was telling the farmer joke to a class predominantly of Asian students, my desk spontaneously collapsed with a crash and the class roared. At least I got a laugh. Actually Mr. Bean's comedy is not so much slapstick as irony portrayed by actions, which I believe explains the lack of response. In one scene, for example, he is waiting for a stoplight in his tiny automobile. He notices cyclists dismounting and walking their bicycles across when the pedestrian signal changes, which is presumably legal because they are now pedestrians. At this point he steps out of his car and pushes it across the intersection.

In cultures that are not rule based, humor tends to take the form of amusement with everyday situations. The Shona culture of Zimbabwe provides an excellent example. Here mirth is a key coping mechanism that gets one through the day. People develop a talent for enjoying the twists and turns of everyday life. I used to ride a bus to and from work, and the Shona passengers would laugh with abandon the whole way. The few Westerners in the bus may have wished they could speak the language in order to appreciate the jokes. But no one was telling jokes. They found amusement in who boarded the bus, what they did during the day, and almost anything else.

Chinese have a similar taste for amusement, particularly in the form of diversions. They may laugh at a Western joke, but they probably laugh more at the situation than the joke. The spectacle of a foreigner saying silly things could be quite amusing. The very presence of a visitor may strike them as funny, because a visitor is a diversion, something out of the ordinary. I have walked into shops in small towns where the shopkeepers could scarcely count money for giggling at the alien creature who just walked in. On one occasion I arrived at a hotel in Sichuan Province when the elevator was not working. I was obliged to carry my bags up several flights. On the way I passed several people who laughed loudly at my predicament. This was not ridicule in the Western sense, however. The appearance of a Westerner at this hotel was already an exceptional event, but to see a Westerner carrying his own bags up steps was rare enough to merit a good laugh. On still another occasion I was discussing cultural differences before an audience of international students who had just arrived in the United States. At one point I mentioned Confucius, and several Chinese students giggled. I did not intend to crack a joke, and I never found Sage of Shandong Province to be particularly humorous. In this case, however, it was not me or Confucius the Chinese students found amusing. Struggling with the shock of arriving in a strange culture, they were delighted to hear something familiar and comforting. They expressed their delight with laughter. In all of these cases it is important not to interpret the laughter as derision and take offense. The Chinese are enjoying life, and the best response is to do likewise.

Apollonian and Dionysian

Everyone is acquainted with people who live a well-ordered life. Their days consist of routine, predictability, and above all equanimity. The home is orderly, grass and shrubbery neatly trimmed. The property is adequately insured and the automobile is regularly serviced. One may find small figurines on the lawn or white bands painted around tree trunks to protect them from insects. People of this sort rarely raise their voices or show strong emotion. Their children perhaps married high school sweethearts in proper weddings that resulted in several photo albums. Nothing much out of the ordinary seems to happen around the house. Even a death in the family is absorbed into the routine. The burial plot has been purchased in advance, and the business of funeral arrangements and probating the estate diverts attention from the reality of the situation.

Other people seem attracted by emotion and intense experience. They have exciting jobs and such hobbies as sky diving. They linger at noisy parties to the wee hours of the morning. The kids wear tattoos and jewelry on various parts of their bodies and attend raves (dances) with ear-splitting music. Perhaps the younger ones are using the latest drugs, and the older one is shacking up with his or her second or third partner. They all live with gusto and experience life's ups and downs with full intensity.

The first lifestyle is Apollonian, the second Dionysian. The German philosopher Friedrich Nietzsche first drew the distinction in his highly original book *The Birth of Tragedy,* in which he undertakes to explain the uniqueness of this ancient Greek art form. For Nietzsche, the god Apollo represents the penchant for reason and proportion that history attributes to ancient Greece, and its exquisite sense of balance evident in architecture and sculpture. Dionysus, the Greek fertility god, represents a life of excess and intense experience, inasmuch as his followers were famous for their drunken, orgiastic rites. The genius of Greek drama, according to Nietzsche, is the way it fuses the Apollonian and the Dionysian. The principal characters descend to the depths of debauchery, even to patricide, torture, and incest, and yet their story is told within a formal aesthetic framework that represents Apollonian balance and order.

Nietzsche put his finger on a fundamental characteristic of Western art and culture, one that is particularly evident in his own northern Europe. Western-style rules and system maintain Apollonian order on the surface, but Celtic and Teutonic passions seethe underneath. The calm and rational German engineer becomes a warrior from Valhalla after work, as his Mercedes hurls down the autobahn at 160 kilometers per hour. Lest one think this is a trifling matter for Germans, note that former Chancellor Helmut Kohl achieved his last electoral victory on the strength of the slogan *Freie Fahrt für freie Bürger* (free driving for a free people), which expressed his party's opposition to speed limits. In everyday life the Dionysian occurs only after hours and in prescribed places, but the genius of Western art is to find a way to unify it with the Apollonian, to reconcile intense feeling with logic. As Chapter 6 points out, Brahms, Chopin, and Mozart are at once passionate and supremely rational. It all started, says Nietzsche, with ancient Greek drama.

The Nietzschean concepts of Apollonian and Dionysian can apply to cultures as well as to individuals. At least that is the view Ruth Benedict expresses in her famous 1934 book, *Patterns of Culture,* which has been credited with attracting more people to the field of cultural anthropology than any other stimulus. One chapter of the book contrasts what she sees as the Apollonian character of the Southwestern Pueblo people of North America with the Dionysian character of many other North American peoples, particularly those living on the plains. In Benedict's portrait, the Pueblo are a sober and mild-mannered people who spend their days in carefully prescribed ritual and rarely show strong emotion. Benedict demonstrates this in many ways, but we can look at just two examples. Typical courtship behavior is for a young man to approach a girl as she carries water from the well, typically in the early evening. He asks for a drink, and if she likes him, she will give him a sip. It often gets no more passionate than this. Before long the young man visits her father's house to ask permission to marry. After a meal, the father defers to the daughter's will, and if she says yes, the couple retire together that night. Funeral rites, to offer a second example, try to get past the bitterness of death with as little upset as possible. There is no wailing or self-mortification. The priest conducts a poignant but simple ceremony (simple by Pueblo standards). At the end of the ceremony the priest carries prayer sticks, a bowl of food, and the deceased's hairbrush outside the village, symbolically removing memories of the departed from view. He breaks the bowl and hairbrush, and buries them. The breakage is the most demonstrative act in the whole process.

Experts on Pueblo culture have since found some faults with Benedict's portrait, but there is no denying the contrast between the Pueblo's village lifestyle and the plains dweller's taste for intense experience. Many people of the plains sought ecstasy by dancing until they collapsed in a state of seizure or exhaustion, as in the famous Ghost Dance cult. Others subjected themselves to torture or deprivation to reach a higher plane of existence or obtain revelation through visions and dreams. Peyote and other psychoactive drugs might achieve the same goal. One practice that occurred in several tribes was for a man to cut slits in his chest muscles and insert through them strips of wood with ropes attached. He would then swing himself around a tall pole to which the other ends of the ropes were tied, so that the inserts would pull against his flesh. Again the object was to escape the everyday and enter a different mode of experience. Rites of passage were experienced with similar intensity. George Catlin, one of the finest contemporary observers of indigenous Americans, described the funeral rites of the Mandan people.[18] Survivors of the deceased placed the body on a raised platform or scaffold high enough to be slightly out of reach.

Fathers, mothers, wives and children, may be seen lying under these scaffolds, prostrated upon the ground, with their faces in the dirt, howling forth incessantly the most piteous and heart-broken cries and lamentations for the misfortunes of their kindred; tearing their hair—cutting their flesh with their knives, and doing other penance to appease the spirits of the dead. . . .[19]

When the bodies decayed and the platforms collapsed, villagers arranged the skulls in neat rows nearby. Wives and mothers visited the skulls for years, often spending hours a day in conversation with the departed.

The Apollonian/Dionysian distinction provides a rough classification of other cultures as well. As already mentioned, Brazil and Mexico are unmistakably Dionysian. One might contrast Apollonian China with Dionysian Korea. Both are strongly Confucian, but Chinese prefer keeping an even disposition among colleagues, while Koreans are famous for their mercurial temperament. Orderly and sedate Scandinavia provides an Apollonian foil to the Dionysian upheaval and sensuousness of Russia, even though the former once ruled the latter. As Benedict herself admits, however, the distinction may not be helpful in other cases.

Benedict says little to explain why an Apollonian or Dionysian pattern might develop in a culture. Explanation, as opposed to enlightened description, is not what she is about and perhaps, in her view, not what anthropology should be about. Nevertheless, the desire for an orderly and predictable existence on the one hand, and the desire for self-oblivion on the other, can be recognized as coping mechanisms in much of the world. This seems in fact the most natural explanation of their cultural function. They help us to deal with the vicissitudes of life by trying to control them on the one hand, or by somehow escaping them on the other.

It is almost as though human beings are "retrofitted" with self-conscious experience, because it is a poor fit. We are given awareness of the future, and yet we are not given the content of that future. We have the ability to reflect upon our fate, but we lack the tools to control it. We seem to have evolved two fundamental methods for dealing with this predicament: an outer approach and an inner approach. An outer approach might call upon gods or other powers to influence events. Or it might take action to bend the secular world to one's own purposes, a strategy that first took root in the Middle East. The West goes further by using technology to transform the environment into something more orderly. An inner approach tries to remove the uncertainty by changing how one thinks about the external world. One might convince oneself that there is a predictable and coherent reality that lies beneath what appear to be random and meaningless events. In essence, this is mysticism. Or one might detach oneself from the external world and value only what is in one's mind, because one can with proper discipline control the contents of the mind. This is stoicism, which often combines with mysticism. Finally, one might simply find escape from every-day reality by living in a fictitious world that is more to one's liking, or by abnegating one's sense of self altogether.

The Apollonian and Dionysian lifestyles are outer and inner strategies, respectively, but both have an element of denial. The Apollonian approach denies the inherent unpredictability of the world by trying to construct an artificial life of order and routine, or when this fails by substituting pre-dictable ritual for untamed reality, for instance by focusing on funeral arrangements rather than on the finality of death. The Dionysian approach seeks external stimuli to induce a different state of awareness, such as psy-choactive drugs or sky diving, rather than deal with things as they are through self-discipline and meditation. At worst it simply escapes into in-toxication or an ear-pounding rock concert. Yet despite the inauthenticity of these two strategies, we need them. No human can deal with the environment in its full harshness; we must always withdraw somewhat and deal with a simplified piece of it. Our minds are incapable of absorbing all that surrounds us, and we construct a more comfortable version of reality.

The Apollonian/Dionysian classification is different from the other schemes discussed in this chapter, which are based on mechanisms that help people live with one another. Friedrich Nietzsche and Ruth Benedict have identified two mechanisms for dealing with the unpredictability and precari-ousness of life, or in a word, with stress. Cultures are as vitally concerned with stress as with coexistence. The next chapter takes up the theme of stress management as a general principle for understanding culture.

Notes for Chapter 7

1. McGraw-Hill (New York, 1991). The results were originally published in Geert Hofstede, *Culture's Consequences: International Differences in Work-Related Values*, Sage (Newbury Park, Calif., 1980). In 2001 Sage published a second and enlarged edition as *Culture's Consequences: Comparing Values, Behaviors, Institutions, and Organizations across Nations*. A fifth classification related to Confucian ethics was developed by Hofstede and M. H. Bond; "Confucius and Economic Growth: New Trends in Culture's Consequences," *Organizational Dynamics* 16:4 (1988): 4–21.

2. Hofstede, *Culture's Consequences,* 28.

3. Ibid., 25.

4. Ibid., 51.

5. Ibid.

6. Ibid., 51–52.

7. Ibid., 52.

8. Ibid., 81.

9. Ibid., 81–82.

10. Ibid., 82.

11. Ibid., 111.

12. Ibid., 111–112.

13. Ibid., 113.

14. Richard C. Larson, "Beyond the Physics of Queuing," Plenary address, Institute for Operations Research and the Management Sciences (Montreal, Quebec, Canada, 1998).

15. John Hooker, "The Polite and the Rude," *Monash Mt. Eliza Business Review* 3 (1998): 40–49.

16. Joseph Butler, *Fifteen Sermons* (London, 1926).

17. Jung Chang, *Wild Swans: Three Daughters of China*, Anchor Books (New York, 1992).

18. George Catlin, *The Manners, Customs and Condition of the North American Indian*, originally published 1841, republished as Peter Matthiessen, ed., *The North American Indian*, Penguin Books (New York, 1989).

19. Ibid., 84.

8 *Culture and Stress*

We associate stress with the frantic, rushed lifestyle of postindustrial societies, particularly the United States. There is no denying that the United States has a genius for generating its own kind of stress. But stress is a fundamental and universal element of the human condition, no less in traditional, agrarian societies than in complex information societies that are ruled by the clock. To a great degree culture and religion are what they are in order to deal with stress. Far from having a monopoly on stress, the United States arguably has enjoyed one of the less stressful environments of the world. This may explain how it could survive with a relatively weak culture and can afford to generate stress gratuitously.

When living and working in a strange culture, it is doubly important to understand how that culture manages stress, because the ever present stress of existence is only compounded with that of adjustment. This is one of the strongest arguments for understanding the host culture as deeply as possible.

The Biology of Stress

Because the postindustrial world has become so stress conscious, there is a proliferation of literature on the biological effects of stress. It can cause ulcers, hypertension, heart disease, and lowered resistance to infection. All this has been something of a revelation to Western society, which had for so long been under the sway of a Cartesian dualism that is uncomfortable with mingling the mental and the physical.

A dualistic metaphysics holds that mind is a wholly different kind of substance than body, and if the twain shall meet, it is only in a limited and problematic way. Descartes himself suggested that the pineal gland, located at the base of the brain, is the cosmic wormhole through which the two realms interact. Most ordinary people are not metaphysicians, but the dualistic point of view is nonetheless evident in the culture, particularly in medicine. Prior to the recent interest in alternative (i.e., non-Western) medicine, psychosomatic disease, literally mind-body disease, was regarded as less than real. Pain therapy was withheld on the ground that pain is "in the mind" and not truly a state of the body.

Western understanding of stress has broadened along with its metaphysics, although medical textbooks continue to pay homage to Descartes by identifying a metaphysical link between mind and body. The pineal gland is no longer thought responsible, but the nearby pituitary gland is said to generate adrenocorticotropic hormone in the presence of stress. This in turn stimulates the adrenal glands to produce epinephrine. In the short term this hormone heightens the body's defenses. But its long-term presence can lead to many of the physical symptoms associated with stress. One indicator of prolonged stress is enlargement of the adrenals.[1] The bodily reality of stress is reflected in the fact that it operates in animals other than human beings. It is widely recognized to be a cause of disease in farm animals, for example.

Of primary interest here is the role of stress biology in society. Here again its effects surface among animals as well as humans. This was observed in scientific studies as early as the 1950s. Edward T. Hall, whose work is discussed extensively in Chapter 2, calls our attention to a particularly striking study.[2] In 1950 biologist John Christian proposed the idea that animal populations can respond to population density alone, even while food and other necessities are adequate. He tested this idea by observing a herd of sika deer on James Island in Chesapeake Bay, Maryland, which was uninhabited by humans and only about half a square mile in area. A few deer were released there in 1916, and the herd had grown to about three hundred by 1955, which was near the carrying capacity of the island. In fact, there was a substantial drop in population in 1958, at a point when food supply was still adequate. Christian examined deer carcasses throughout the period 1955–60. He found that during the period of overpopulation and 1958 die-off, the animals appeared to be normal with one exception: the adrenal glands were substantially enlarged. Moreover the cell structure of the adrenals showed evidence of severe stress. After the population fell, no such abnormalities were observed.

It is not difficult to see a population-control mechanism at work. If the deer had continued to multiply without check, they would have overgrazed and destroyed the island environment. The likely result would have been extinction of the herd. There is an obvious selective advantage in a control mechanism that kicks in before this occurs. The immediate cause of mortality for the James Island deer is unknown, although two carcasses did show evidence of hepatitis. In any case, the effect of stress on resistance to disease is well documented. Subsequent animal studies have revealed various kinds of dysfunctional behavior that results from the stress of overcrowding, including greater aggression toward neighbors, inadequate care for young, and decreased propensity to mate.

Stress, then, was not invented along with the clock. It is part of our biology and has probably helped us to survive as a species. So if one comes down with a respiratory virus, Epstein-Barr virus, sinus infection, or gingivitis (gum disease)—conditions associated with reduced resistance and overstressed living in affluent societies—one can imagine vultures circling overhead, waiting for nature's population-control mechanism to do its job.

Stress and Lack of Control

As its physiological basis suggests, the essence of stress is being in a heightened state. The body pumps adrenaline to prepare itself to deal with a threat. It takes action, if possible, and the stress is over. In fact, we do not normally refer to this kind of short-term stress as "stress." If no action is available, however, stress in the popular sense sets in. The body continues to stew in its juices and suffers the health consequences.

Stress is bad enough for animals in general, but our human self-consciousness magnifies stress, in two unpleasant ways. First, as conscious beings, we can savor it. We normally experience it as lack of control, continued frustration, or anxiety. It is like driving on ice. None of the control levers work. Something must be done, but nothing can be done. Time pressure is a good example. I must catch a plane in half an hour, but because my schedule is tight, any number of events over which I have no control can make me late: a traffic jam, a parking problem, a shortage of taxis. Note the element of control. Time pressure causes stress because I must be on time, but I have limited control over whether I will succeed.

Second, self-consciousness makes us endure stress longer and more often. A herd of deer becomes stressed when overpopulation actually occurs. A conscious being can reflect on the situation and anticipate a threat before it is realized. It knows that a wild animal may attack in the middle of the night, long before anything happens. It knows that the parched earth can mean crop failure, long before hunger sets in. Because there is no sure way to protect oneself from wild animals, and because rain cannot be summoned, stress becomes a frequent companion. As the threats generalize, stress becomes constant. If one can anticipate wild animal attacks, crop failure, disease, accidents, cold winters, the loss of loved ones, and one's own certain demise, then one has an ever present dread that something bad will happen but nothing in particular. This is anxiety. It is worse than fear, which has an object. If one fears an animal seen in the bush, one can at least run or throw a spear. Anxiety, by definition, cannot be relieved by addressing the threat, because there is no particular threat. It is stress in its uniquely human and most exquisite form.

Perhaps it is now becoming clear why a First World country like the United States presents an inherently low-stress environment for most of its inhabitants, although by no means all. Few need worry about basic food or shelter. The environment is basically stable and predictable. When I rise in the morning and switch on the light, the power grid will oblige. I anticipate no serious problems getting to work. If by some chance I get into an accident, I can count on prompt ambulance service and an efficient hospital to take care of me. When I arrive, there is a high probability my job will still be there. I can eat lunch at almost any restaurant without fear of contaminated food or water. Until recently, one did not have to worry about terrorist attacks on the way home. There are, of course, legitimate fears. People in the United States worry about "random violence," which is stressful precisely because it is random and therefore hard to control. But even here most people can take effective action by avoiding high-crime areas. There is a good deal of anxiety, but perhaps this is because the culture is not providing the support it should.

Compare this to areas of the world where the power grid goes down regularly, the buses may not come in the morning, the blood supply at hospitals (if it exists) may contain hepatitis B or HIV, the food and water are often contaminated, the economy is plagued by hyperinflation and massive unemployment, the government is in a perpetual state of crisis, and terrorists are known to attack at random. This is stress. In an environment such as this, people do not have the luxury of manufacturing stress with tight timetables and high-power jobs. They rely on their culture and their religion to get them through the day. The devastating terrorist attacks of September 11, 2001, gave even the United States reason to draw more fully upon its cultural resources, and several observers have remarked a kind of cultural renewal in the country. The first 2002 issue of the magazine *U.S. News and World Report,* for example, proclaimed "A Nation Reborn" on its cover.

The task before us is to understand how culture enables us to cope. A good place to begin is with the role of ritual and myth in managing stress.

Ritual and Myth

In Western culture, ritual and myth carry the connotation of the irrational and the useless. At the very least they ought to have nothing to do with professional life. Traditional societies, however, are saturated with these practices. People invest a major portion of their time and energy into the maintenance of ritual and myth. How is one to explain such a stark contrast? Is it really plausible to suppose that the entire human race was abysmally ignorant and misguided for a half-million years until a certain few societies finally debunked all such nonsense? Or is it more likely that the equivalents of ritual and myth play indispensable roles in all human cultures, however cleverly they may sometimes be concealed in modern garb? A reasoned response to these questions requires some appreciation of what ritual and myth meant to traditional peoples.

Consider first the Navajo people, already discussed in Chapter 2. The Navajo migrated to the magnificent desert lands of what is now the southwestern United States at least six hundred years ago. Although their language and culture differ radically from those of the fast-paced society surrounding the Navajo reservation, their ritual life contains important lessons for all of us. Fortunately some of their rituals are practiced to this day, including the *kinaalda* (female puberty rite), the three-day *nidaa* (squaw dance, a summer courtship ceremony), and the *yei-be-chei* (a nine-day, winter healing ceremony).

Cultural anthropologists Clyde Kluckhohn and Dorothea Leighton did fieldwork with the Navajo in the 1940s, issuing in an insightful book, *The Navaho,* that has become a classic in the field.[3] They described the central role of ritual in Navajo life, reporting that men devoted one-fourth to one-third of their productive time to ritual activity, and women one-sixth to one-fifth. Shamans or "singers" (*hatahli*) were paid sizable sums for their services. Today a Navajo family, which is not likely to be well-off, may pay $5,000 for the singer and other expenses of a *yei-be-chei*. The fee is well earned.

Prodigious memory is demanded of the ceremonialist. The Singer who knows one nine-night chant must learn at least as much as a man who sets out to memorize the whole of a Wagnerian opera: orchestral score, every vocal part, all the details of the settings, stage business, and each requirement of costume. Some Singers know three or more long chants, as well as various minor rites.[4]

A healing ceremony may involve massage, heat treatments, and a yucca root bath. But most important are the chant and the authority of the singer. The accuracy of delivery is crucial. By saying the right words in the right order, the singer exerts some degree of control over the elements. Note, again, the necessity of control. The ritual gives the feeling of having a modicum of influence over one's fate. It reduces stress.

If the ritual is ineffective, an explanation must be found; otherwise faith in the ritual will weaken. Perhaps there was some minor error in the execution. Or perhaps additional material should have been added. It is not difficult to understand how the ceremonies could become long and exacting.

If the failure of a ceremony cannot be traced to its execution, it may be due to the influence of witches. The Navajo believed strongly in witches (as did Westerners not so long ago) and talked about them constantly. They not only accounted for ineffective ritual but had another function as well. Kluckhohn and Leighton remark that Navajo society experienced at that time a "high anxiety level," due to the problems of adjusting to reservation life. Witches helped to convert anxiety to fear by giving it an object.

Witchcraft lore provides a means of defining and personalizing [the Navajo's] anxiety which will be accepted by others. Beliefs and practices related to witchcraft are thus refuges for those persons who are more under the stress of misfortune than others . . . . [5]

Note the use of the word *stress* in a text written long before current preoccupation with the topic.

Where does myth fit into this picture? One function of myth is to support stress-relieving ritual by putting it into a meaningful context. Every Navajo ritual, for example, has a corresponding story that explains its origin. These stories fit into a vast mythic literature that culminates in a creation myth, according to which the Holy People, a powerful and mysterious race that originally lived underground, created Earth People (the Navajo) and taught them how to survive. The myths may also explain how rituals work. During a healing ritual, for example, the patient temporarily becomes a Holy Person and is cured by virtue of the superior power that Holy People possess.

A second, related function of myth is to help people make sense of life. It is difficult to control events in an inexplicable world in which things seem to happen randomly and for no apparent reason. Perplexity becomes associated with stress, which a coherent mythology helps to relieve. Kluckhohn and Leighton eloquently explain this principle.

The basic function of religion everywhere is to give a sense of security in a world which, seen in naturalistic terms, appears to be full of the unpredictable, the capricious, the accidentally tragic. Someone has said, "Human beings build their cultures, nervously loquacious, upon the edge of an abyss." In the face of chance and the unexpected, of want, death and destruction, all human beings have a fundamental sense of uneasiness. And so they talk and, by making their talk consistent, they assure themselves that "reality" too is consistent. They mask the vast role of "luck" in human life by telling each other that such and such a thing happened because of something a supernatural being did or said long ago. In a world full of hazards, myths affirm that there is rhyme and reason after all. [6]

Another North American people, the Cherokee, provide an equally convincing example of the centrality of ritual and myth in human affairs. When Europeans arrived in North America, the Cherokee maintained a complex and affluent society in the southeastern portion of what is now the United States. Largely due to their early exposure to Europeans, the

Cherokee have forgotten much of their mythology; more is known about their elaborate rituals. To take just one slice of life, consider preparations for battle, as described by Thomas E. Mails in his book *The Cherokee People*.[7] When an enemy threatened a Cherokee village, the village chief sent a messenger to the nation's high priest (*Uku*) bearing a twist of sacred tobacco. If the threat warranted a response, the high priest met with the war chief and his officers to smoke the tobacco and give the order to mobilize. National leaders met with the war chief in the heptagon (council house) to plan hostilities. They painted themselves red, hoisted the red war flag, and appointed healers for each of the four (or seven) companies that would fight the battle.

Back in the villages, the warriors of each company began to prepare themselves. They went down to streams, where priests recited designated prayers to them on four consecutive nights. On the fourth night, the priests gave each warrior a root that they had blessed in a previous ritual. Later, on the eve of battle, the warriors would immerse themselves in a running stream, chew the root, and spit the juice on their bodies to protect themselves from arrows. In the meantime they consulted medicine men who owned divining crystals, always carried in a weasel skin, in order to ascertain their fate in battle.

If the enemy had already attacked by the time word reached the war chief, he could call for a retaliatory strike. If so, he shook his gourd rattle while pacing about the capital city, and sang the chant *U gi wa ne e* four times. His assistant then repeated the performance. Those within earshot relayed the message to towns throughout the nation, where the same performance was executed by local war chiefs. Once mustered, troops from various towns journeyed to the national capital to receive orders and engage in further preparatory rites. Official messengers fetched seven ritual deerskins from the heptagon and brought them to the war priest, who wrapped his divining crystal in them. The war priest then marched through the capital city carrying the sacred ark, a clay pot of hot coals taken from the heptagon fire, in order to bestow blessings on the campaign. When all the warriors had assembled, a day and night of fasting and prayer were declared, during which a number of taboos were enforced. For instance, no warrior or priest was allowed to sleep. No object was allowed to be taken directly from another person's hand; instead, one person must drop the article on the ground for the other to pick up.

On the second night, the warriors did a dance (*A te yo hi*) counter-clockwise around the war flag. The dance continued until shortly before daylight, whereupon the warriors went down to a stream and immersed themselves seven times. At daybreak the war chief kindled a fire from the coals of the ark using seven designated kinds of wood. He first sacrificed rats and worms in the fire. Standing on the west side of the fire with his seven counselors behind him, he threw a deer tongue into the flames, hoping it would burn brightly and be consumed, a propitious omen. If not, additional rituals were performed in the hope of reversing the prediction.

After sunrise, the war priest placed seven folded deerskins on a small table and put his divining crystal on top of them. He placed his hands on the ground and raised them little by little, stopping seven times to pray to the seven heavens. Between each thumb and forefinger he held a bead. If the bead in his right hand seemed to move, victory would be theirs; movement in the left hand signaled defeat. Having come this far, however, the army would proceed even under a gloomy prognosis. The war priest then wrapped his crystal in the seven deerskins and gave them to his assistant, for he would be struck dead if he carried them himself. He washed his hands, because having touched the crystal, he would otherwise break out in sores wherever he touched himself. He then put the hot ashes of the fire into the ark, which prompted the war chief to give the men an inspirational speech. Afterward the war priest prayed to the Three Beings, and the war chief gave the command to march.

The carrier of the ark led the march. Following him were the war chief wearing a raven skin around his neck, the carrier of the war chief's flag, and the chief speaker. After them came seven tribal counselors, followed by the individual companies, one by one, each led by its own war chief, along with the assistant war chief, the speaker, seven counselors, and a number of priests, doctors, musicians, cooks, and of course the warriors. During the march, no one was allowed to speak about trivial matters or women. While the war party was crossing a creek, no one was permitted to stop until everyone had crossed. If a warrior broke a stick or twig, he was obliged to hold it in his hand until reaching camp that night. If the camp was near a creek, warriors bathed before retiring and immersed themselves seven times in the morning. On at least one night during the march, the war chief sent his crystal to the enemy by supernatural transport, and if it returned covered with blood, that was a good sign.

Elaborate rituals such as these may strike us as foolish superstition, but they gave Cherokee warriors the fortitude to get through the day, even to deal with the dread of battle. To the extent that we approach our fate with courage, we rely on ritual and myths that are equally elaborate.

Ritual and Myth Today

Ritual, myth, and superstition help to relieve stress in advanced civilizations no less than in traditional cultures. Take superstition first. This is the pejorative word used in the West for surviving fragments of prescientific myth and ritual. It is bad luck to walk under a ladder, or one knocks on wood to avoid tempting fate. When I was a boy, children would say, "Step on a crack, break your mother's back," as they walked down a paved sidewalk. Even in these fragments, separated as they are from a system that once gave life meaning, one can see stress management at work. Luck and fate represent elements beyond our control. By avoiding ladders and by knocking on wood, control is at least symbolically restored. Children know that bad things can happen to their parents. Walking carefully on the sidewalk might give them a sense of control over the uncontrollable.

Superstition today can be both overt and covert. Overt superstition is alive and well. It is not unusual for sophisticated Indians with Ph.D.'s to avoid travel on inauspicious days. In China gift giving is important, but one should never give a clock. It is an omen of death. Overt superstition persists in the Western hemisphere as well. Seers and fortune tellers do a brisk business in Latin America as consultants to corporate executives.[8] In the United States there have been several reports of the increasing popularity of astrologers among business professionals,[9] not to mention former President Reagan and his wife.

Superstition in Western culture is generally covert, however, because of its questionable status. The parallel between overt and covert superstition is illustrated by the protective role of the Buddha. Across the river from the Chinese resort city of Leshan, in Sichuan Province, sits an enormous Buddha, the world's largest, carved into the rocky bluff overlooking the river. The 71-meter sculpture and the surrounding park attract hoards of Chinese tourists and a few Western visitors. The Buddha was installed twelve centuries ago in order to protect sailors from the dangerous rapids at its feet. The protective role of the Enlightened One is acknowledged to this day, as millions of Chinese keep a small likeness of him in the home.

Westerners might regard all of this as (overt) superstition, but we have our own covert variety. A Chinese expatriate, whom I will call "Haitong," settled a few years ago into an affluent suburban neighborhood in the United States. Soon after moving in, the next-door neighbor remarked to Haitong that he should own a gun. Haitong asked why this was necessary. "Because everyone in the neighborhood has a gun." Haitong dutifully purchased a handgun and brought it home, whereupon his wife asked what they were supposed to do with it. As Haitong did not know, he inquired with his neighbor. "You should keep it in your nightstand drawer, next to your bed." Haitong returned home and told his wife what they were to do with it. They obediently kept the gun in the prescribed place. A mutual friend, who is Chinese, asked me to explain this custom. I think the explanation is clear. Firearm manufacturers do not sell only guns; they sell Buddhas.

Superstition in the form of witchcraft is likewise practiced in the West, in both overt and covert forms. There is a substantial overt interest in the black arts in both the United States and Europe. Any doubt I may have had about this dissipated while I was living in Denmark. I sublet a suburban apartment, which I found to be well stocked with witchcraft manuals and protected by magic crystals that would have impressed the Cherokee medicine men. The phenomenon was not isolated, as the well-educated and middle-class tenants belonged to a witchcraft club.

As for covert witchcraft, instances of it could be observed in the United States in the 1980s when child-care centers were becoming increasingly popular. A rash of shocking and uncorroborated accusations of child molestation were made against child-care workers. The charges ranged from sexual abuse to abduction in flying saucers. In at least one case the accused were imprisoned for several years on the basis of fabricated testimony from children, who were coached by psychologists and nervous parents. This strange phenomenon makes sense when placed in the context of the stress that U.S. families were undergoing at the time. Single-parent families were becoming more prevalent. The U.S. standard of living had recently peaked, and it became more common for both parents in a two-parent family to work outside the home in order to maintain their standard of living. These phenomena triggered a massive shift to day care, which caused anxiety and guilt for parents. Given a breath of accusation, day-care workers could become witches, that is, foci for anxiety. The connection with witches is not drawn capriciously. When the first movie version of Arthur Miller's *The Crucible* was released in 1996, critics immediately remarked parallels with the child abuse panic just described.[10] Miller's play deals with the eighteenth-century witchcraft trials of Salem, Massachusetts. The inspiration for the play was itself an earlier instance of covert witchcraft: the McCarthy hearings of the 1950s, which took place in the United States during a time of anti-Communist hysteria and persecuted a number of innocent individuals for supposed Communist connections.

Religion and Stress

Religion has been at the core of stress management for eons. Although many First World nations have evolved a secular lifestyle, this is a recent development. In much of the world there is still no real distinction between religion and nonreligion. Rather than being relegated to a corner of life, religion permeates all of life.

The First World tends to view religion as a fringe element, as slightly irrational or prone to fanaticism. When one is working in other parts of the world, it is essential to suppress this mind-set. Far from being on the fringe, religion is at the center, holding life together. It supplies reason and coherence to an irrational world. It allows one to see how things are connected, how they are part of a grand plan. The very word means "reconnection" in its Latin origins. Every religion has fanatics, but responsible and well-adjusted people draw sustenance from their faith. The clearest examples are provided by Islamic societies, in which overt religion coexists with work. The trendiest Muslims working with the latest technology might as easily greet coworkers with "God is great!" as with "good morning." The Westernized elite in some countries may appear somewhat secularized, but their understanding of the world is probably conditioned by the religion of their grandparents, in ways of which they are unaware.

The importance of conventional religion may decline as a society becomes more affluent, as Europe and Japan suggest. Yet something must pick up the functions that religion abandons as people lose their ability to take it seriously. It is interesting (and essential) to observe how this works itself out in societies that are growing in affluence. Ethnic solidarity is an important part of the Japanese picture, for example. These issues will be addressed in detail as individual cultures are discussed.

Science as Stress Management

Science has assumed much of the stress-management load in the First World and among the Westernized elite elsewhere. I will not insist that science is literally myth, but it serves many of the same functions. It tries to make the universe intelligible and suggests what actions we might take to control our fate. These actions often have the characteristics of ritual.

Take the matter of healing. Our physicians do not sing to us as in Navajo culture, but they take us through a long and grueling ritual of examinations, tests, and treatments. Precise execution is essential. If the X-ray is slightly off-center, it must be redone. The treatments are important, but the physician and staff are also careful to display their knowledge and authority. The physician uses impressive Latin names for commonplace objects and conditions. Even the nursing staff develop a mysterious jargon that reassures the patient of their expertise: NPO, IV, IM, D&C, PCTA, EEG, EKG, CAT-scan, PET-scan, MRI, EMG, DVT, SPECT. (Occasionally this goes awry. One nurse told an expectant mother that the doctor was going to "section the baby," using nurses' jargon for cesarean section. The mother feared that the fetus would be cut into slices.) The antiseptic rooms, complex electronic equipment, and formalized procedures are often said to be disconcerting, but they are ultimately comforting. They are evidence of the elaborate scientific worldview that underlies the rituals, a worldview that culminates in a general theory of matter, energy, and the origin of the universe. The parallel with Navajo mythology is obvious enough.

When the procedures fail, the physician's work is carefully examined for flaws, because it is important to believe that medicine is usually effective when properly administered. Most societies have cultural and religious supports for people under the stress of disease, in addition to healing rituals. But as these weaken in a secular, multicultural society, reliance on the effectiveness of medical technology deepens. We have seen malpractice suits against physicians rise dramatically, as the need for assurance puts ever greater demands on them, and it becomes ever more important to explain failure.

Some diseases tend to be incurable despite the best efforts of the best physicians. In these cases attention shifts to rituals of diet and lifestyle. The news media proffer daily advice on which foods to shun and which to favor in order to avoid cancer or heart disease. Low-cholesterol foods, antioxidants, fiber, phenols, sterols, terpenes, soy proteins, and vegan diets are currently in favor. People carry bottles of healthy mineral water with them all day, much as ancient warriors carried their protective roots to battle. Practitioners of Western-style yoga are advised to take a cold shower in the morning, recalling the Cherokee's seven morning dips in an icy stream. Perhaps these practices really are beneficial in a medical sense. In any event, they unquestionably benefit their adherents in an existential sense.

Determined efforts to eat the right foods in the right way are reminiscent of the strict diet and dinner-table rituals of Hasidic Judaism. Unlike Judaic law, however, scientific advice is often inconsistent over time, as foods go in and out of favor. The scientific establishment might explain this by pointing out how the news media seize upon their findings and take them out of context. But this only reflects the vigor of public demand for something they can do to control their fate. It is interesting that members of the working class, who tend to be more overtly religious and may receive more support from cultural or ethnic tradition, seem less nervous about low-cholesterol diets and aerobic exercise than professional and technical people. A bumper sticker on a construction vehicle parked on the campus where I work summed it up with the aphorism, "Keep fit, eat right, die anyway."

In addition to diet and lifestyle advice, we are constantly cautioned to avoid circumstances that allegedly cause disease. Very low frequency waves under power lines are said to cause cancer. Small amounts of mercury in silver tooth fillings allegedly lead to any number of ailments, ranging from depression to atrial fibrillation. At this writing these claims are unresolved, but in the meantime they provide alternatives and some small sense of control. Rather than simply worry about the incidence of cancer in the

neighborhood, some people have changed their residence. Rather than simply endure suffering that mainstream medicine cannot relieve, some have
replaced all of their fillings with composites or ceramics. The last procedure
may seem a bit drastic, but no more so than traditional purification rituals.
Cherokee hunters, for example, spent hours of misery sitting on furry
rugs in a crowded sweat lodge; drank a tea of horsemint, cane, and old
tobacco to induce vomiting; fasted the rest of the day; and repeated this
procedure every day for seven days; all in order to purify themselves for a
hunting trip.

Existential Stress

Any successful stress-management tool must address the fundamental anxieties that are inherent in self-conscious experience. The most basic
of these is the sense of mortality. At some point in the distant past, human
beings became aware of their own existence, perhaps dimly and intermit-
tently at first. In particular they began to reflect on their past and plan for
their future. Immanuel Kant taught in his *Critique of Pure Reason* that time
consciousness is an integral part of self-consciousness. People began to
paint animals and hunters on cave walls, such as the famous depictions at
Lascaux, France, perhaps to instruct youngsters in the techniques of the
hunt. The problem with looking to the future, however, is that one sees
the dark at the end of the tunnel. In fact, among the earliest indications of
time consciousness are decorated graves that contain provisions for the
afterlife, for example near Shanidar, Iraq. These are perhaps the earliest
indications of religious activity. As soon as self-consciousness presented its
first insoluble problem, mortality, religion provided a solution, an afterlife.
What has this to do with stress? Dread of death is the ultimate anxiety and
therefore the ultimate stress. In a sense, it lies at the root of all anxiety and
colors all human experience. To use Martin Heidegger's gloomy phrase,
human life is essentially "being-toward-death."

The Christian theologian Paul Tillich, who was strongly influenced by
Heidegger, developed this view in his *Systematic Theology*. In Tillich's
view, religion specializes in the insoluble problems that arise from self-
consciousness. Our awareness of our mortality is one such problem. A second problem is our awareness of our freedom. We cannot escape the necessity of conscious choice, and yet we so often are denied what we choose.
We are given freedom but lack control, and the result is stress. Religions
take various approaches to this problem, such as the use of ritual and
myth, as already discussed. Some religions develop a stoic philosophy. The
word comes from the Greek expression for covered walkways typical of a

marketplace, where "stoics" were often found discussing their views. Stoic religions teach that one should train oneself to desire only what is within one's power to possess. In particular one should outgrow appetites for comfort, sex, wealth, and fame. This is an important part of the monastic life, which is practiced in several faiths. It is also an important element of Buddhist discipline, in which one ideally overcomes one's desire for life itself, conceived as the separate existence of an individual being.

The problem of freedom actually goes deeper than frustration and lack of control. We evolved the ability to choose without evolving a faculty that tells us ultimately what to choose. Our appetites may urge us toward gluttony or sex, but we can always ask whether appetites should be indulged. Our rational brains can tell us how to get rich, but we can always ask whether money is a worthy end. The problem of ultimate ends is insoluble, in Tillich's view, because as John Stuart Mill observed, they are not amenable to proof. Tillich says that we are driven to religion, the solver of insoluble problems, because it gives us ethics by fiat. We must believe in the divine because we cannot bear to exist without some exogenous source of meaning and purpose.

An immensely practical by-product of ethics is that it regulates social behavior. The ethical aspect is particularly well developed in religions that grew out of the world's major civilizations, whose size and complexity demanded that people learn an ideology and behavioral norms at the conscious level. The code of Hammurabi, the Mosaic law it inspired, the teachings of Confucius, and Hindu dharma fall within this category. The two great functions of culture are therefore unified in religion: the management of stress and the management of society.

Stress-management mechanisms take many forms across cultures. In addition to a staggering variety of religions, a rich mythical literature, and a vast repertoire of rituals, cultures may rely on loyalty to the extended family; group solidarity and communitarian values; superstition; friendship and relationships of mutual obligation; stoicism and self-denial; fatalism; purity or cleanliness standards; meditation; exercise regimens; absorption in music and art; humor; festivals and revelry; and altered states of consciousness induced by trances, drugs or ritual. A key mechanism for Western culture is universalizing rationality, which is a precondition for science, the basis for technology, which in turn provides security and predictability by allowing Westerners to restructure the secular world around them. Every culture finds its own way, and a number of the specific mechanisms are discussed in these pages.

Notes for Chapter 8

1. *Stress* can refer either to the cause of the stress or its effect on the body; here the latter sense is intended.

2. Edward T. Hall, *The Hidden Dimension,* Doubleday (New York, 1966).

3. Clyde Kluckhohn and Dorothea Leighton, *The Navaho,* Harvard University Press (Cambridge, Mass., 1974, orig. published 1946).

4. Ibid., 229–30.

5. Ibid., 242.

6. Ibid., 233.

7. Thomas E. Mails, *The Cherokee People,* Marlowe and Company (New York, 1996).

8. "Broomsticks and Dollars," *Economist* 334 (no. 7901, 1995): 54.

9. Trish Hall, "There in the Crystal Ball," *New York Times* (April 29, 1992), sec. C, p. 1, col. 4; J. Peder Zane, "You Are Going to Go on a Long Trip . . . ," *New York Times* (September 11, 1994), sec. 4, p. 2, col. 1.

10. Victor Navasky, "The Demons of Salem, With Us Still," *New York Times* (September 8, 1996), sec. 2, p. 37, col. 1.

9 China

After coteaching a workshop in Beijing, I had several days of spare time before my next engagement in Hong Kong. I took the opportunity to explore part of China by rail. Train tickets can be hard to come by, but I had made advance reservations for "soft bed" tickets with the Chinese Foreign Travel Bureau. I could have saved money by traveling "hard seat" or "hard bed," and I would have experienced the travel class used by the mass of ordinary people in China. But I was afraid I would not have the endurance for a long trip. Lower-class cars are notoriously overbooked, there is no air conditioning, and the heat was already unbearable that summer. There were reports that people in Shanghai were dropping dead from heat exhaustion. Besides, my Chinese friends would be horrified to learn I had traveled less than first class. (I have difficulty getting them to tell me where to rent a bicycle, since an honored guest should ride in cars.) I was not sorry I took the easier path. Simply waiting a couple of hours in the sweltering Beijing train station was so oppressive that I required three days to rehydrate.

My first stop was Qufu, a small city in Shandong Province south of Beijing—small by Chinese standards at any rate, having a population of some 600,000. Qufu is the ancestral home of the Kǒng family, whose most famous member is Kǒng Fū-Zǐ, or Master Kǒng. He was a minor politician who lived in the sixth century B.C.E., but since his lifetime he has doubtless influenced more lives than any other human being. The Jesuits who first translated his teachings into Latin called him "Confucius."

I told the tourist bureau in town that I wanted to learn about Confucian philosophy and asked if I could hire an English-speaking guide. I mentioned that I was a philosopher myself—which is no lie, as I once earned a Ph.D. in philosophy—and would prefer an expert on the subject. I was provided a graduate in Confucian philosophy from Qufu Normal University, which unsurprisingly is distinguished by its philosophy department. The guide's English was not a lot better than my rudimentary Chinese, but we got along famously. In fact, he showed up at my hotel the next morning, his day off, to give me a second day of instruction free. It was not often he had so eager a student from the West. I returned the favor with a gift, a calculator for his daughter, who was good at mathematics. Exchange of favors and gifts is a very important tradition in China, even older than Confucius.

The guide's discourse was so interesting that I almost forgot about the heat. Confucius suffered a midlife crisis, I was told. He left his bourgeois home and family to do basically what I was doing at the moment. He traveled around China, found out who the knowledgeable people were in each town, and learned from them. This sort of peripatetic behavior was not unknown in the later Chou dynasty, when scholars would go from city to city seeking employment as tutors to privileged children or advisors to governments. Confucius might be described as such a scholar, but with a remarkable bent for lifetime learning.

On the second day the guide insisted that I visit the ruins of the Duke of Zhou's residence. He had brought his bicycle but rented a pedicab for me. The uphill trip to the duke's house promised to be strenuous, and the guide began to haggle with the cyclist. He was bargaining on my behalf and would not be so unhospitable as to settle for a high price. It is important to honor one's guest even in small matters, for to do less not only is loss of face but also is scarcely civilized. He offered the driver 8 RMB (that is, 8 *kuài rénmínbì*, or eight units of the People's Currency), but the driver, nervously eyeing the oversized foreigner, wanted more. Seeing my host in a bind, I stepped in and offered the cyclist 10 RMB, whereupon he gave me an enthusiastic thumbs-up (a common gesture in much of the world), and we were off.

I soon learned why the Duke of Zhou warranted the climb. As we enjoyed the hilltop breeze, the guide told me that the duke was Master Kong's model for the ideal ruler. He ruled not by force but by example, by exhibiting good character, by embodying the essence of Chinese civilization in his conduct and leadership. At the time, however, no one had articulated exactly what this essence is. Huston Smith, the student of world religions, tells us that Confucius' great contribution was to do just this: he brought Chinese civilization to self-consciousness. Confucius lived during that remarkable period when civilizations seemed to become self-aware through their great interpreters: Socrates for Greeks, Zoroaster for Persians, Gautama Siddharta (founder of Buddhism) for Indians, and Confucius for Chinese. The Confucian analysis of Chinese culture is a good place to start on our journey toward understanding China and why it is so different from the West.

Why China Is So Different

It is said that, for a Westerner, India seems totally alien on first impression but actually has many cultural ties with the West. China, on the other hand, seems not so different but, in time, is found to be totally alien. The most important difference between Western and Confucian culture is that the West relies on internalized universalizing rationality, while China does not. The

West is rule based, as defined in Chapter 7, and China is relationship based. This difference permeates every aspect of life and can be frustrating and demoralizing for a visitor who does not understand its origins.

China's relationship-oriented sensibility is captured in two Confucian principles: maintain harmony with family and associates, and show proper deference to superiors. Harmony is preserved through respect and sensitivity for the feelings of others, rather than by observing abstract rules or fairness or efficiency—that is, by appealing to rationality—as in the West. To be the subject of criticism or to be caught in an error is like having a smudge on one's face; it is embarrassing and demeaning, or as the Chinese say, it is "loss of face." In a Confucian culture, no action is undertaken, and no word spoken, without first calculating the effect on face. In the West people may become hurt or angry over their differences but, if all goes well, can eventually resolve them by appeal to principles of efficiency or fairness. In China there is no such appeal, and it is important not to give offense in the first place. Even direct eye contact is traditionally avoided, as it may be considered a provocation. Naturally, either the Eastern or the Western mechanism can break down, opening the door to hostility.

Submerging differences does not abolish them, and at some point there must be a resolution. The Confucian solution is to defer to one's superiors, who include one's elders, one's husband, one's boss, and ultimately one's ancestors. It is little surprise that Chinese are characterized by high power distance, a trait to which they must cling tenaciously, because it is a foundation of social cohesion. This leaves open the question as to how authorities can command obedience, and Confucius proposed an answer. When I tell my management students that the most effective leadership quality is good character, they roll their eyes at such naïveté, but I got the idea from Master Kong.

An elder in authority can govern relations among people who belong to a single family, business firm, or governmental agency, but associates over which there is no common direct authority require some alternate mechanism. In China it is the institution of *guānxì*, which is the Mandarin Chinese word for "connection" or "relationship." *Guānxì* is the practice of accumulating debts by doing favors for others. It may begin by presenting small gifts or taking someone out to dinner and progresses to making concessions in a business deal, securing a license or permit, getting a job for one's son, and so forth. A personal bond is therefore cemented by mutual obligation. To Western sensibilities this may seem crass and manipulative, at least when described so bluntly, and the exchange of favors tends to be regarded as bribery. It is certainly not bribery, because it is not quid pro quo. Favors maintain the relationship in general, rather than repaying a specific debt or greasing the palm for a specific dispensation. In fact, *guānxì* may seem crass to Westerners precisely because we try to understand it in terms of personal incentive. The Chinese people honor *guānxì* obligations for the same reason people eat dinner from plates rather than directly off the table. Yes, there is a certain practicality in the use of plates, but we use them because it is the civilized thing to do. *Guānxì* is practical and can be justified on this basis, but more fundamentally it is a mark of civilization. A person who reneges on his or her *guānxì* obligations is regarded as not only immoral but also scarcely human. This is one reason Chinese have traditionally seen Westerners as barbarians.

Whatever one may think of *guānxì,* it is essential to getting anything done in China. On a personal level it is not unlike friendship in the Western sense and can lead to satisfying lifetime relationships. Also, an exchange of favors is practiced among friends in much of the world, including the West, although it may not serve the central cultural function it does in China.

Chinese culture may appear on its surface not so unlike the West because it, too, is a complex and urbanized civilization. Indeed, it is ironic that Westerners refer to China as a "developing" country. It is developing, all right, and has been doing so for five thousand years. The Roman republic was a primitive settlement when China was training its bureaucrats in a university and using civil service examinations to measure their qualifications. The world had yet to hear of Julius Caesar when China was building complex irrigation systems, canals with locks, ships with steering oars, and the "Ten Thousand *Li* Wall," or Great Wall, which is even today one of the world's greatest artifacts. Chinese developed gunpowder, paper, and the compass long before Europeans appropriated these key technologies of colonial expansion. China suffered some setbacks in its encounter with Western colonialism, but it remains the world's most enduring and most populous civilization. Aside from its own record of cultural achievement, it does rather well at Western-style development. It constructs modern urban centers dominated by skyscrapers, for instance at Shenzhen and Shanghai's Pudong district, where it maintains a low crime rate that is the envy of Western cities. It surrounds its cities with superhighways that compare with any in the world. It has achieved double-digit rates of economic growth that have rarely occurred anywhere in the West. It is therefore not surprising that Western visitors might not initially sense the vast cultural gulf between themselves and China.

China and "Development"

My next stop after Qufu was Shanghai, where I changed trains. I did not linger more than a day or two, since I had taught there in the past and was familiar with much of the city. My main goal was to find air-conditioned space, which I initially located in the new subway system. I sympathized with the mob at every subway entrance, who had gathered, not to ride the train, but to feel the cool air from underground. Obviously not everyone enjoys an air-conditioned apartment, but air conditioners have thankfully become common in Chinese cities. Chinese invariably use the Japanese-made "split" air conditioners, rather than the noisy and obtrusive window units that for some reason remain popular in the United States. It is interesting how purely engineering decisions are so often culturally based. I once recommended split air conditioners to a university committee in the United States that was seeking to reduce the noise level in summer classrooms. The engineers on the committee rejected my idea without ever giving a clear explanation. As best I could determine, the ultimate reason is that, well, we use window units in this country.

Shanghai is a showcase city, proof that China can match or exceed Western urban development. It is surrounded by superhighways and affluent suburbs, even if the suburban dwellings are three-story structures with ceramic walls and blue picture windows rather than American ranch-style homes. Expensive Western designer clothes are de rigeur. Weddings are thoroughly Western, with white gowns and rice and all the rest, and the divorce rate is fashionably high; one of my students told me that a divorce can be obtained for $10 (U.S.). I have heard Shanghai women talk proudly of their househusbands who take care of the kids. There is a youth orientation that must surely disturb Confucius' eternal sleep. People say that companies lay off older workers in order to hire young college graduates, and that those who remain are subordinated to the new upstarts; both practices should be unthinkable in China. One must of course bear in mind that Shanghai has long been the least Chinese of Chinese cities; its residents themselves refer to Shanghai as the "New York of China." Yet Chinese want desperately to belong to the club of First World nations, and Shanghai is their membership application.

The Chinese are proudest of the Pudong New Area, just across the Huangpu River from the Bund, Shanghai's famous downtown promenade. In 1990 the area was mostly farmland. A decade later it was a cluster of shiny new skyscrapers, flanked by the appropriately hideous Oriental Pearl TV tower. British, French, and Italian architects were consulted in the design of a carefully planned infrastructure. The Pudong "information port" complex provides state-of-the-art telecommunications. By the end of 1998, more than eighty multinational corporations had opened branches in Pudong.[1] But the main point of Pudong is the skyscrapers, which look so Western and so developed. Some traces of the old China remain, however, in Pudong's tallest building, the eighty-eight-floor Jin Mao tower. In Chinese superstition, the number 8 symbolizes wealth.

Judging from my friends and acquaintances, many Chinese seem to have bought into the Western concept of development. This is a little surprising, given Chinese cultural pride. Perhaps more than any other country, China sees itself as a distinct *culture* rather than a nation or an ethnic group. It has a strong national government today, but its cultural unity survived for centuries when it was, not a nation at all, but a collection of warring states. Its ethnic makeup is overwhelmingly Han Chinese, but this seems less important than its common civilization. Its name for itself is *Zhōngguó* (central kingdom), which refers to an oasis of civilization surrounded by uncivilized hoards, not least the barbaric Western colonial powers that forced a destructive narcotic trade on the country during the nineteenth-century Opium Wars. The Chinese government continues to resist Western cultural pollution, albeit with limited success. For years it kept Western popular media at bay, finally acquiescing to Hong Kong–based cable TV and its motley entertainment in order to distribute its own government-controlled channels. It issues cultural standards for advertising, even if they have no influence on media content that originates elsewhere.

Despite its immense cultural pride, China plays the development game by Western rules. Everyone talks about Shenzhen, for example, the brand-new city just inside the mainland, hugging the border with Hong Kong and the New Territories. Shenzhen is about as culturally rich as an exit on the New Jersey Turnpike, but it boasts the all-important skyscrapers. People flock across the checkpoint from Hong Kong ostensibly to take advantage of low prices, but the city's popularity has deeper roots. Everyone knows that in Shenzhen the skyscrapers rose without a hint of the colonial involvement that taints Hong Kong's achievement. It is proof of Chinese "development."

The automobile plays a similar role. On my last trip to Chengdu, I was taken for a ride on one of the new superhighways in the area. The broad expanse of asphalt was nearly deserted, but the government will fix this with its policy of encouraging automobile use.[2] Someone bragged to me that gasoline prices in China are as cheap as in the United States, in order to encourage more driving. Westerners are all too familiar with the problems of an automotive society, but Chinese welcome the cars. A friend of mine pointed with disdain to a bicycle parking lot in downtown Chengdu, grumbling that those things are a nuisance in traffic and consume too much space in parking lots. The development imperative is so strong that no one pauses to consider that automobiles consume far more space and cause more congestion than bicycles. Unfortunately, the government's pro-automobile policy is working all too well in urban areas. Several cities, including Chengdu, have reached the point of Bangkokian gridlock. On one occasion I had to abandon car and driver and hire a pedicab in order to deliver a talk on time. The problem is obvious enough, but the "obvious" solution is the American one of increasing the carrying capacity of streets and highways rather than investing in public transportation. I have no idea what China will do if its 1.3 billion people become as addicted to driving as Americans. But for the time being, the automobile is a symbol of Western-style development and receives top priority.

The headlong rush toward urban development carries other costs. Personally, I miss the fascinating street life that has vanished from some cities in only the last three or four years. Foot massage, haircuts, and ear cleanings with Q-tips were available on the sidewalk. Vendors carried on their bicycles a hundred little bamboo cages, each with a chirping cricket inside to keep one company. My favorite were the entrepreneurs who set up shop on the curb with a hand pump, tube of glue, and rubber patches for flat bicycle tires. Even the colorful outdoor meat and vegetable markets are fast disappearing. Yet Chinese seem to be about as nostalgic for these things as Americans were for dung in the streets when automobiles replaced the horse and buggy.

The Western pizzazz of Chinese cities can again mask the gulf between East and West. A city can look as modern and technological as any Western metropolis, but skyscrapers and technology exist in China for a very different reason than they exist in the West. Chinese indulge in Western-style development because of cultural pride. They will be second to none, even as measured by alien standards. The West, on the other hand, developed science and technology because it desperately needs them. Far from being optional frills, they give Westerners some assurance that they have control over their fate. When disease or other misfortune strikes, Westerners are less prepared to rely on family support, as even the nuclear family has largely disintegrated. Many receive no succor from a religion they no longer take seriously. Instead they turn to technology: to the healing power of modern medicine for personal illness, and the technical fixes of science and engineering for social problems. The sleek glass and steel of a sky-scraper represent an orderly and engineered environment, nature tamed and bent to human will, an assurance that everything is under control. Chinese obtain security in other ways. They rely on rock-solid family loyalty, superstition, and religion. Western technology has its advantages, but ultimately the Chinese can take it or leave it.

Family

My train rolled out of Shanghai toward Guangdong Province and the Cantonese-speaking region of China. As the terrain grew hilly and the climate wetter, flat fields gave way to terraced rice paddies. I watched peasants in conical hats working the rice crop, bent over in the hot mud under a blazing midday sun. I had nothing but admiration for their industry. As the train wound its way south, evidence of flooding, China's ancient scourge, came into view. I recalled seeing the swollen rivers from the air as I flew over the area a few days earlier—a privileged perspective that most of the affected population would never experience. Floods in China are deadly as well as devastating, since there may be no ready means of evacuation when the rivers rise.

Rural life today is bearable, due in part to Deng Xiaoping's agricultural reforms of the 1970s, but it remains difficult and monotonous. I reflected on the countless peasants who over the ages had endured the grueling work of survival, the uncertainties of disease and weather. Toughened by centuries of struggle, these peasants, the bedrock of Chinese culture, have evolved a Chinese strategy for coping with life. Family, superstition, and religion have already been mentioned as elements of it. Other elements include exercise regimens, holistic medicine, and a certain sense of fun (see table 9.1).

The first and last line of defense against life's contingencies is the family. It is not a warm, intimate kind of family but an extended family based on authority. Parents and grandparents dote on the little ones, but only while they are little. My Chinese students tell me of a somewhat distant relationship to their elders that is based on duty and obedience. Even older brothers and sisters must be respected, a fact reflected by the language itself, as in many family-oriented cultures. Mandarin Chinese distinguishes big brother (*gēge*) from little brother (*dìdi*) and big sister (*jiějie*) from little sister (*mèimei*).

TABLE 9.1
Stress-Management Mechanisms in China

Mechanism	Contribution to Stress Management
Loyalty to extended family	Disciplined economic unit; old-age security; jobs for children
Guānxì	Help in time of need
Superstition, including temple rites, numerology, *fēng shuǐ*	Sense of control over one's fate
Religion (Buddhism, Taoism)	Assurance; predictability of ritual; coherent interpretation of life
Exercise regimens, including chi gong (*qìgōng*), tai chi (*tàijíquán*), *fǎlún gōng*	Control of one's mental states despite chaotic surroundings
Traditional holistic medicine	Control of one's fate through healthy lifestyle
Diversions (e.g., humor as amusement, games, eating)	Relief from monotony of everyday life

(Kinship names seem to have been invented by little kids; my favorite is the term for the maternal grandmother, *lǎolao*, literally "old-old.") Although the eldest brother carries a good deal of authority, Chinese do not normally practice primogeniture, according to which he would inherit the entire family farm or business. As a result, Chinese family businesses often dissolve upon the death of the patriarch rather than survive across generations.

The authoritarian family provides security in several ways. When it comes to economic survival, the family is a well-disciplined little army whose efficiency provides some degree of control over its fate. Whether it be a family farm or a family business, the patriarch in charge can command and coordinate his troops to wrest a living from the surroundings. The family provides security in old age, due to the never-ending obligation of offspring to honor and support their parents and grandparents. It provides some degree of security to children, who can expect their elders to connect with relatives to find a good job for them. Nepotism therefore remains an inevitable feature of Chinese hiring practices. Even ancestors can supply protection, and many Chinese renew proper relationships with the departed during the massive New Year celebration. The extended family combines with *guānxì* to cement business relationships, since a trust relationship with an individual traditionally implies a trust relationship with his or her entire family. In old times this provided an important boost to national commerce, since it allowed one to do business with family members scattered across great distances. The negative side of this arrangement is that a single family member's misdeeds could disgrace an entire family and bring them to economic ruin, an old theme in Chinese literature. Family and clan connections remain important today, particularly as a conduit of investment capital from overseas Chinese.

The persistence of family loyalty among expatriate Chinese confirms the pivotal role of family in Chinese culture. It resists even the disintegrative forces of the United States, where second-generation Chinese adolescents obey their parents and pursue careers chosen for them. Ancestor worship remains strong in some communities, where Chinese Americans seek out cemetery land with good *fēng shuǐ* characteristics and honor their departed ancestors with burnt sacrifices of food, money, and mobile phones.

China's one-child policy is said to threaten the traditional role of family by supplanting yesterday's obedient children with today's "little emperors." People talk about yuppie parents in Shanghai who hover over their ten-year-olds, dress them in the finest fashions, fatten them with hamburgers and French fries, tie their shoes, and even wipe their bottoms. In reality, the one-child policy is closer to a two-child quasi policy. The Western media like to paint horrible pictures of forced sterilization and the like, and such things have occurred, as they did in the United States during the eugenics movement of the early twentieth century. Yet the Chinese government works overwhelmingly through moral suasion and economic incentives, not compulsion. The incentives themselves recognize many exceptions, such as for parents who are themselves only children, and guidelines are more lax for rural families and ethnic minorities. The incentives are unevenly administered and in many areas seem to be fading out. The Chinese government estimates a fertility rate of 1.26 children per urban family and 2.8 per rural family in the mid-1990s,[3] and the U.S. Embassy provides a comparable estimate of 2.1 children per family overall.[4] There is no denying that the fertility rate has dropped precipitously since the 1960s, but this could be primarily the result of China's phenomenal economic growth: a *quadrupling* of gross domestic product in two decades (probably an exaggeration but impressive nonetheless). It is well known that fertility tends to decline as affluence grows. My acquaintances from Shanghai minimize the government's role by pointing out that modern urban families prefer small families no less in China than in Europe and North America. The "little emperor" phenomenon, to the extent that it exists, may be as much a product of modern urban lifestyle in general as family-size incentives in particular. Casual observation suggests that some parents are indeed spoiling their children, but it is too early to estimate the cultural impact of this behavior.

Superstition

Superstition is remarkably strong in China, in the most Westernized cities as well as in the countryside. It remains a coping mechanism for people of all walks of life. By *superstition* I mean "practices that are undertaken to improve one's lot but have no justification in Western science." Superstitions also tend to be fragmentary and seemingly unrelated, rather than corollaries of a single body of thought or myth. Thus, the Taoist philosophy would not be superstition, even though it has no foundation in Western science.

Superstition can be seen everywhere. The incense spirals that hang from the temple ceiling spell good fortune if they burn to the end without going out. The worshiper shakes a can of numbered sticks, and the one that falls out corresponds to a fortune provided by the priest. Good fortunes can be more expensive; on one occasion I was asked to contribute 5 RMB to the temple for my good fortune, when a bad one would have cost only 1 RMB. Superstition is visible on automobile license plates and in telephone numbers. Hong Kong residents bid astronomical sums (I am told as much as $1 million, HK) for plates that bear lucky numbers, such as 8 for wealth or 9 for longevity. It is said that 168, 289, 518, and so on, are good sequences to have in one's address or telephone number. Mobile phone customers in

Taiwan reportedly must pay a premium to get favorable phone numbers, perhaps over $1,000 (U.S.) for one that contains 888. The number 4 is unlucky because it sounds like the word for death in Cantonese. I have seen hotels that please both Chinese and Westerners by omitting all floor numbers containing a 4, as well as the thirteenth floor. It can be a bit confusing, but numerology in China dates back at least to the *I Ching*, written three thousand years ago.

There is much more. No one wants to receive a clock as a gift, because it is an omen of death. At dinner, no one inserts chopsticks upright in the rice bowl, because it reminds one of incense sticks used in temple death rites. The red decorations and clothing used during the New Year celebration reflect the fact that red is a lucky color. *Baqua* (octagonal) mirrors placed over a building's entrance improve the *qì* (flow of energy) inside, repel negative influences, and lead to a more harmonious life. These are part of the Chinese rules for design, known as *fēng shuǐ*, which have become rather well known in the West. Literally "wind and water," *fēng shuǐ* originally referred to guidelines for locating tombs—in a spot with a good breeze, overlooking water. Today the most modern Chinese buildings and interiors are designed in close consultation with a *fēng shuǐ* master. The practice can result in striking architecture as well as a harmonious environment, an excellent example being the recently constructed Hong Kong University of Science and Technology. Situated on a beautiful site overlooking Clearwater Bay, the buildings seem designed solely for aesthetic effect but in reality are minutely shaped by the strictures of *fēng shuǐ*. The school was built by superstition in another sense as well, as it was financed with gambling revenues raised by the Hong Kong Jockey Club. No one bets more enthusiastically on the horses than the citizens of Hong Kong, and one can only imagine the numerological calculations that go into choosing the lucky horse on its lucky day.

Westerners are sometimes a little surprised that so many sophisticated, urbanized Chinese embrace superstition with such unashamed gusto. Yet Chinese superstition has seen growing popularity in the West, particularly *fēng shuǐ*. One way to observe this is to note the many *fēng shuǐ* associations and organizations, which as Fukuyama points out (see Chapter 3), is the way Westerners do things. There are a Feng Shui Association (U.K.), an American Feng Shui Institute, an International Feng Shui Guild (U.S.A. and U.K.), a Feng Shui Research Center (Canada), a Feng Shui Network (Australia), plus countless *fēng shuǐ* Web sites, training programs, magazines, and emporia. Equally popular in Europe and North America are the ancient Chinese exercise regimens of tai chi (*tàijíquán*) and chi gong (*qìgōng*), which are perhaps too systematic to qualify as superstition but are scarcely verified by Western science (more on these shortly).

There is a second reason that Westerners should not find Chinese superstition so alien. In many cases the individual psychology of appealing to superstition is not so different from that of appealing to a scientifically correct method. This is not to say that there is no distinction between superstition and Western science. The latter is based on controlled experimentation, which until recently was unknown in China, and science purports to explain how things work through a verifiable natural mechanism. Yet when I take two aspirin, I have not the foggiest idea of what mechanism allows them to relieve my headache, nor of what controlled studies may have been undertaken to show that they work. In fact, I find that my headache goes away only about half the time, and when it does go away I suspect it may have done so without the aspirin. I therefore take aspirin without having seen any scientific or even personal evidence that it works. I rely on it presumably because people say it works, or because it is the way one deals with headaches in my culture. I see very little difference between this, on the level of individual psychology, and mounting a *baqua* mirror (which, incidentally, has been called "the aspirin of *fēng shuǐ*"). One can extend this argument to much of science-based technology. Many who watch TV in Europe and North America have no clue about what makes the picture appear on the screen. One can tell them about cathode-ray tubes and florescence, but would it be less meaningful to them if one attributed the picture to yin and yang and the flow of *qì?*

One can debate about whether traditional Chinese medicine is superstition, especially since no one knows how much of it might someday be supported by Western science. Nonetheless, there is much to be learned about Chinese stress management by examining this ancient art. Chinese practice both Western and traditional medicine, and the upper class in fact shifted almost entirely to Western medicine in the early twentieth century. Mao Tse-tung later encouraged efforts to blend the two traditions, and today it is not unusual for people to hedge their bets by getting both Western and traditional health care. Westerners, being the universalizing rationalists they are, tend to stick to one approach, but Chinese have no problem with eclecticism. For similar reasons they are free to take a holistic approach to healing. Western physicians tend to acknowledge only those phenomena that fit into a single, logically consistent conceptual framework: the one they learned in medical school. Most focus on purely physiological ailments, and even then specialize in a single aspect of the body. Chinese physicians regard health as encompassing one's mental and moral state as well as the physical body, with emphasis on lifestyle and prevention. Western medicine is beginning to understand the value of a holistic approach, even if it has made little progress in this direction to date.

Chinese medicine has another aspect, however, that its Western counterpart finds more difficult to swallow. Many of its treatments and diagnostic
procedures seem to be based on pseudoscience. Perhaps the best known is
acupuncture, in which very thin needles are carefully placed so as to cure
disease or relieve pain. Skeptics who have seen acupuncturists successfully
anesthetize patients for surgery have no choice but to take the art seriously,
but they cannot accept the underlying theory. Acupuncture is said to work
because it redirects or regulates the flow of *qì* through a network of 365
meridians in the body. *Qì* is a form of energy that gives life to an organism
(literally, it means "air" or "breath"). It is somewhat reminiscent of the
concept of negative entropy in the Western science of thermodynamics, but
it corresponds to no single Western concept and cannot be measured or detected by scientific instruments. Likewise, the meridians correspond to no
observable anatomical structure.

The fine art of massage is likewise concerned with redirecting *qì*, rather
than with relaxing muscles as in the Western variety. In addition to physical
therapy, there is a vast pharmacopoeia of herbs and other remedies, some
of which may strike a Westerner as positively medieval: dried scorpions,
geckos, deer antlers, and snake gallbladders. To be sure, Western science has
learned to value traditional remedies, and gene prospectors scour the earth
in search of useful DNA material. Yet Chinese physicians prescribe their
regimens on the basis of whether they increase or reduce *qì* in a certain
organ, regulate the amount of "heat" in the body, and so forth.

Diagnostic methods seem equally suspect to the Western mind. According to David Eisenberg, the first medical exchange student from the United
States to China, a Chinese physician can recognize forty or more kinds of
pulse.[5] The pulse is as important for diagnosis as X-rays and ultrasounds,
and a physician may spend several minutes reading a patient's pulse at various points on the wrist. The physician is trained to identify more than a
hundred colors and textures on the tongue, each of which has medical significance. In one case Eisenberg reports, a patient with a duodenal ulcer
was examined. His tongue was slightly large and pale, with teeth indenta-
tions, indicating a deficiency of heat in the spleen. (The spleen and liver
seem to receive a great deal of attention across cultures, perhaps because
they are such distinctive-looking organs.) The spleen problem was identified as the cause of the ulcer, and treatment was therefore focused on this
organ, not the ulcer itself.

The two main differences between Chinese and Western medicine are
clear in these examples. It was only natural for the West, steeped in its
understanding of the world as a secular realm suitable for human manipulation, to develop the practice of controlled experimentation. Chinese
remedies are based on centuries of observation, but even today there are

few controlled experiments to distinguish the wheat from the chaff. A subtler difference between East and West is that, although both ground their medical practice in an underlying mechanism, the West insists that its mechanism be independently verifiable. One must be able to dissect a cadaver and find the meridians. If the spleen is at fault, one must be able to observe the offending pathology in the spleen itself, and to trace a verifiable causal path between it and the duodenum. This principle may be relaxed at the far reaches of scientific theory, such as in the theory of quarks, but this is perhaps only because elementary particle theory is as much an indication of the breakdown of Western science as its success.

It is therefore inaccurate to refer to Chinese medicine as pseudoscience, because it does not purport to be science in the Western sense. It is empirical but views twenty centuries of experience as better evidence than controlled experiment. It sees no point in trying to observe an underlying mechanism, because it makes no reductive claims. There was never any suggestion in the first place that one could dissect a body and find meridians; the sole claim is that the theory of *qì* and all the rest results in successful medical practice. Few deny that some success has in fact been achieved. Patients regularly report cures for fibrous tumors, back pain, irritable bowel syndrome, and other chronic conditions that resist Western treatment. Granted, Chinese medicine could probably benefit from controlled experimentation. Yet its lack of interest in verifying the underlying mechanism is a distinctive trait that may allow it to outperform Western medicine in some areas. Acupuncturists, for example, can apparently discover regularities in the nervous system that do not correspond to the physical layout of nerves and are therefore less obvious to a reductive science. The holistic approach likewise allows Chinese physicians to harness the power of the mind for healing. Some Western physicians may dismiss this as a placebo effect, but in so doing only concede its reality.

Superstition may have limited value as a stress-management tool for Western visitors who cannot believe in it. Even if using *baqua* mirrors is psychologically similar to using aspirin, one must be culturally conditioned to accept the practice. On the other hand, Chinese medicine and such exercise regimens as tai chi and chi gong have attracted many foreign devotees. At any rate, they are unlikely to be harmful, certainly less so than Western tranquilizers and marathon races.

Religion

This and the previous section attempt to distinguish religion from superstition, but in China one fades into the other. The quest for good luck has been a central part of Chinese religion from the beginning. Relics from the first Chinese dynasty, the Shang (which began thirty-six centuries ago), include oracle bones that were heated to determine from the resulting cracks whether one could expect good fortune.[6] The fortune sticks in today's Buddhist temple are precisely analogous.

China's Mahayana Buddhism is of course an import from India, but it is the most widely practiced faith in China today. It is also very much customized to the Chinese point of view. The best-known indigenous religions, using *religions* in a broad sense, are Confucianism and Taoism (pronounced *dow-ism*), which both arose in the sixth century B.C.E. Confucianism is an ethical philosophy rather than a religion with rites and temples. Taoism supports priests, temples, and monasteries, and is practiced to some extent. Many attend Taoist funerals, rural people participate in magic ceremonies and sorcery based on its principles, and millions adhere to exercise regimens with Taoist roots. Taoism's greatest influence, however, is perhaps through a philosophy that continues to inform much in Chinese culture. Confucianism is likewise very much alive. Communist ideology initially opposed it as feudal and counterrevolutionary, but it has been rehabilitated to some extent, and I am told that President Jiang Zemin frequently quotes the sage. Indeed, Jiang visited the tomb of Confucius, with much fanfare, only a few days before I did.

Confucianism and Taoism correspond to the "inner" and "outer" approaches to stress management distinguished at the end of Chapter 7. Confucianism gets life under control by building an orderly society, and Taoism primarily by withdrawing from society and aligning one's inner life with the underlying order of the universe.[7] In fact, Confucianism is so concerned with social norms that it cannot provide the existential comfort many people expect from religion and is generally supplemented by a more personal faith, such as Taoism or Buddhism. While universalizing Westerners view religions as radio buttons—one must be selected to the exclusion of others—Chinese have no problem with playing two stations at once.

Taoism is said to have been founded by Lao Tzu, whose name is given various romanizations (e.g., Lao Tse, Lao Tze). The name is Lǎo Zǐ in the modern Pinyin spelling and means "Old Master," where *old* is a common title of respect. It is not certain that Lao Tzu existed, and no one really knows who wrote the famous text of Taoism, *Tao Te Ching*. In modern spelling it is *Dào Dé Jīng* (literally, "The Way-of-Virtue Classic"). The "way" (*dào*) that gives Taoism its name refers to the underlying order and unity of the cosmos, thus revealing the mystical character of the faith. It is by following this way that human beings can put themselves in harmony with the universe and lead a more natural and happier life. The true nature of *dào* transcends intellectual categories and is therefore ineffable, but it can be apprehended intuitively if one is pointed in the right direction, for instance by studying the *Tao Te Ching*. The concepts of yin and yang, which actually predated Taoism, play a central role both in the ancient texts and in today's understanding of the faith. Literally "shade and sun," they represent the feminine and masculine principles whose interplay shapes the world we experience. They correspond, for example, to the cold and heat that, in Chinese medical theory, must be balanced in the body to obtain good health. An important lesson is that yin and yang never exist in isolation, since one is always mingled with the other, and it is in fact this admixture that gives the world its motive force, or *qì*. This is the meaning of the famous yin yang symbol, which is a round field with a white portion and a black portion, showing a black dot inside the white area and a white dot inside the black area. Again there is a rough parallel with Western thermodynamics, in which the uneven distribution of energy into hot and cold regions creates negative entropy and makes organized motion possible as energy flows from hot to cold.

The philosophy of Taoism perhaps receives its most widespread application in such exercise regimens as tai chi and chi gong. Each morning countless Chinese appear in urban parks and rural fields to practice these disciplines in every kind of weather. Adults of all ages participate, although the old seem particularly devoted. Tai chi, sometimes called "tai chi chuan," derives from the Chinese *tàijíquán,* which means something like "very extreme boxing" or "extreme ultimate boxing." Chi gong is from the Chinese *qìgōng,* where *qì* is the concept discussed earlier and *gōng* means "achievement," "effort," or "skill." Thus the "chi" (*jí*) in *tai chi* has no connection with "chi" (*qì*) in *chi gong*. Both regimens involve concentration, slow and deliberate movements of the body, efforts to maintain balance and locate one's "center," and management of one's *qì*. The general idea is that by training the body in certain ways, the lessons will rub off on the mind and the whole of life. Thus, by maintaining balance, one maintains health, since health is essentially a balance of yin and yang. By learning to focus intently on the body, one learns meditative skills in general. By finding one's center of gravity, one finds an existential center that provides security in an unstable environment, thus controlling stress.

Similar ideas occur in other advanced meditative traditions, such as yoga. All of these regimens are ancient responses to the problem of self-consciousness, which induces stress by making one aware of the future and of one's lack of control over it (see Chapter 8). It is no surprise that they are apparently as old as the civilizations that gave rise to them, since the advent of civilization and its complex lifestyles probably enhanced the level of self-consciousness and therefore the need for resources to deal with it. The meditative arts deal with stress by inculcating a mental discipline that allows one to take control of one's inner life, no matter what uncertainties the world may present. They improve health even today by reducing anxiety, which helps one to escape the physical and mental pathologies it induces.

A politically charged exercise regimen receiving much attention worldwide is *fǎlún gōng* (law-wheel exercise), also called *fǎlún dàfǎ* (grand law-wheel method), which might be described as a mixture of Buddhism and chi gong. I will not broach the issue as to whether *fǎlún gōng* is a religious cult, but the Chinese government regards it as a security threat and outlawed the practice in 1999 following a demonstration by 10,000 adherents in Beijing. The government's fear may be partly based on China's experience with the Tai Ping rebellion in the mid–nineteenth century. Led by quasi-Christian Hong Xiuquan, it inspired a bloody civil war that was finally suppressed by the Qing dynasty. *Fǎlún gōng* was founded in 1992 by Li Hongzhi, who at this writing lives in New York state. I am by no means prepared to give a definitive interpretation of the practice, but my understanding is that when one performs the exercises, a law wheel (*fǎlún*) appears in one's abdomen. The law wheel rotates in a manner that is sympathetic with the cosmos, which puts one in harmony with the universe and improves one's life in various ways. I have seen claims that 70 million people in China are at least occasional practitioners, as well as 30 million elsewhere, even though it is risky to practice the art openly in China and Singapore (it is legal in Hong Kong). My impression is that educated Chinese tend to regard *fǎlún gōng* as a cult for unsophisticated people, much as Pentecostalism is regarded in the United States. In any event, its followers insist that their movement is not a religion and has no political ambitions, even if its members form a rather tightly organized network. My personal view is that it is similar to a revitalization cult (see Chapter 3) and represents a reaction against the rapid social change experienced by both domestic and overseas Chinese.

Buddhism developed in China over a period of several centuries, beginning in 67 C.E. when a Han emperor received a delegation of Buddhists to his court. Buddhism is a profoundly mystical faith, but its Chinese manifestation is more concerned with the practical. Worshipers in search of good fortune come to the temple to pray, burn incense, and deliver offerings of fruit or flowers. The temple also conducts funeral services, which in China may be Buddhist, Taoist, or a mixture of the two. The funeral typically involves chants and burnt offerings of paper money and other goods that may be useful to the departed. The money may not be real currency, but specially prepared slips with inscriptions and perhaps inlaid gold or silver. The color of mourning is white, which explains why on other occasions gifts of white flowers are inappropriate.

Buddhist temples and monasteries are ubiquitous in China, even if jittery governments have always regarded them as slightly subversive. Buddhists were tolerated in earlier times because they made themselves useful, building hospitals and orphanages, and operating pawn shops that provided banking services until the middle of the last century. To this day some run guesthouses, although one should not expect five-star accommodations. The government shut down many temples and monasteries during the cultural revolution of the 1960s but reversed its policy in recent decades.

Diversions

Chinese are a fun-loving people who take delight in the small diversions of everyday life. The Chinese sense of humor is based on amusement with something out of the ordinary, rather than jokes as in the West (see Chapter 7), and amusement is not hard to find. Visitors discover this quickly, since they provide some of the best opportunities for the locals to entertain themselves. At one point the government published a pamphlet, "How to Be Nice to Visitors," in order to discourage people from staring and asking personal questions. Since the curious are particularly intrigued by hairy arms and big breasts, clothing that conceals the same can be recommended. There is not much Westerners can do, however, about their famous "big noses" (dà bízi).

Chinese love games and puzzles, mahjong perhaps being the most popular. It is a sophisticated and addictive board game that uses tiles, although one should beware of variations in the rules between one region and another. When street life was more interesting, one could see games in progress everywhere, although perhaps less often in workaholic Guangdong Province. Mathematical brain teasers are also an old tradition. Popular sports include soccer, basketball, kite flying, and of course table tennis. On a Beijing summer evening one can see total strangers (particularly older people) gather spontaneously to dance in a circle, perhaps to the accompaniment of drums. The frivolity continues for five or ten minutes, whereupon the dancers disperse and go about their business. As much as any American or European, Chinese also love tourism, which no doubt appeals because it exposes them to something different. Popular venues include such obvious ones as the Great Wall, Beijing, and the terra-cotta warriors of Xi'an, but also such spots (if I may mention some I have visited) as the Buddha and nature park at Leshan; Emei Shan, a mountain with a Buddhist monastery on top; the waterworks at Dujiangyan, which some consider more impressive than the Great Wall; and above all, the restaurants of Guangzhou.

This brings me to the chief of diversions: eating. Chinese are immensely proud of their cuisine and will settle for little else when abroad. Its range and scope are beyond reckoning; I would not be surprised to learn that there are more dishes than characters in the language (more than 50,000, with roughly 3,500 in common use). Chinese in fact seem almost as interested in novelty as taste; some delicacies strike me as being impossible for anyone to enjoy. Visitors should be forewarned that food on the mainland can be very different from "Chinese" food elsewhere. Chinese restaurateurs abroad seek to please customers and cater to their tastes no matter how prosaic they may be. The Chinese themselves, as they are fond of saying, eat everything that flies except airplanes, and everything in the sea except ships. The flavors can be strange and hard on the digestion. Almost all Chinese seem to like Cantonese cuisine best, on the excuse that the ingredients are absolutely fresh, whence the pilgrimages to Guangzhou. If I may offer my humble opinion, water-based Cantonese cooking leeches out almost all the flavor and quickly becomes monotonous. From my perspective, Chinese culinary heaven lies in Sichuan Province, not necessarily in such overspiced meals as hot pot, but in the preparation of tasty vegetables. I consumed my best Chinese meal ever in a small rural establishment near Emei Shan.

Given the central role of eating, it is important to know something about table manners. The first rule is to have fun. Since eating is the primary diversion, one should make the most of it. Second, one should feel free to eat as much as one's alimentary system can handle. Practically no Chinese outside of McDonald's-infested areas are overweight. One should bear in mind, however, that the host will inevitably order too much food, since it is an embarrassment to have no leftovers. It is no insult simply to stop when one has had enough. Rule number three: don't ask what you are eating. It is sometimes best not to know. The fourth rule is to avoid becoming too proficient at chopsticks before going to China. Dinner companions derive great delight from watching visitors fumble with them, and it is fun for the visitor, too.

Chinese of course eat in polychronic fashion by sharing a number of dishes. One retrieves small portions from the lazy susan or serving dishes with one's own chopsticks, unless common chopsticks are provided with the dishes. Most of the dishes are eaten in no particular order, although one should save room for items that are brought out in the latter part of the meal. The soup is normally served after the meal is well underway, and such staples as rice may be served at the end or not at all. It is perfectly all right to ask the waiter for rice at an earlier point. The meal is accompanied by tea and perhaps wine and beer, or by sweet drinks that may be considered lowbrow in Europe or North America. Sweet, white Chinese wine complements the cuisine nicely, although trendy diners have taken to dry French wine, an abomination with Chinese food. Before taking the first drink, it is wise to wait to see if someone offers a toast. In a more formal setting there may be several toasts, and they may resume later in the meal. One should allow the host or waiters to refill one's glass or teacup and should in general allow others to sense one's needs rather than ask (except when there is no other way they could know). Guests should not be offended if the host places food on their plates with his or her own chopsticks, as this is a gesture of friendship. When in doubt about how to eat an unfamiliar dish, it is obviously best to watch the others, but unfortunately the guest is often expected to sample each item first. In such cases the solution is simply to ask how to eat it. The others will be delighted, not offended, by the ignorant visitor. Remember, the aim is to have fun. Australians and some North Americans who blow their noses at the table should suppress this habit while in China. Yet it is perfectly acceptable to use a toothpick at the end of the meal, if one covers one's mouth with the other hand.

Practical Matters

Perhaps the best way to elaborate further on the Chinese cultural system is to be very practical, as the Chinese themselves are said to be. One who plans a professional trip to China should start developing relationships at home. On arrival in China, it is best to be already acquainted with one's coworkers there, or with persons who know them. If the proper contacts cannot be made in one's own country, another option is to work through consultants or other professionals in Hong Kong. The ideal is to identify people who are older, due to the Chinese respect for age, and who have experience with the system on the mainland.

Dress in China is highly variable. Hong Kong and Shanghai are fashion conscious and Beijing is somewhat formal, but many professionals dress casually (e.g., shirt and slacks). Guangzhou and western cities seem to be the most casual, but when in doubt one should ask a Chinese contact about attire. Some professional women, particularly in Shanghai, follow Western fashions and wear slacks, but it is best to start more conservatively.

Chinese are sexually conservative. Revealing outfits are inappropriate outside a few Westernized enclaves. It is best not to touch another person, except for handshakes, and a man should not shake hands with a woman unless she offers her hand first. Sexual jokes or innuendo, or even asking about someone's girlfriend or boyfriend, can be deeply offensive, particularly to women. Lovers normally do not demonstrate their affection in public (although they may have public arguments!). Kissing in particular is traditionally considered disgusting, as it suggests cannibalism.

Chinese culture is basically polychronic, but meetings usually start on time, and one should arrive promptly. The main difference between Western and Chinese time consciousness is scale. During a recent crisis situation between China and Taiwan, an interviewer on the U.S. Public Broadcasting

System's *News Hour with Jim Lehrer* asked a guest whether China might attack Taiwan in the near term. The China expert responded that they might very well do so. Slightly startled, the interviewer asked what the Chinese might mean by *the near term*. "Within fifty years," was the response. This expansive view of time plays a role in negotiation. It is best to humor the Chinese preference for long-range planning, even when it seems unrealistic. There is likewise no sense of urgency in concluding a deal, the primary reason being that there is really no discrete "deal," or contract in the Western sense, but an ongoing relationship. A common error, in Korea and Japan as well as China, is for visitors to mention their departure date or company deadline, which only puts them at a disadvantage. The Asian hosts have no deadline and may simply withhold concessions until the last minute, when they know their guests must cave in to get their "deal."

As already noted, Chinese culture is characterized by high power distance, and this fact will be evident in meetings. On one occasion, while helping to run a seminar for executives of a Chinese electrical firm in Guangzhou, I asked for their opinions on a few matters. Everyone remained silent until the top executive spoke up, whereupon the others agreed with him. The lesser executives always rose when their boss entered the room, and they took care to tell me in his presence about how hard he worked for the firm. Afterward the top executive proudly presented me a copy of the handbook he had written for his managers, which bore the English title "The Moulding of the Soul" but was written in Chinese. It contained a number of quotations from famous historical figures about leadership and life in general. Part of a boss's task is to be a mentor as well as a boss, and providing a philosophical guidebook is an ancient means of fulfilling this role. Thus Chairman Mao's "little red book" was inspired much less by Karl Marx than by ancient Chinese tradition. One's Chinese hosts will instinctively look for a similar authority figure on the visiting team, and it is important to let them know who it is. Even if decision making in the team is democratic, a leader should be singled out who can speak for the group. This person can indicate his or her status by entering the room first.

As is well known, business card rituals are important in Asia, and China is no exception. A business card should clearly show one's title and position, in English on one side and Chinese on the other. It should indicate any college degrees, particularly if from a Western institution, as Western degrees carry considerable prestige. The visitor should present his or her card first, held between thumbs and forefingers of both hands with the Chinese-language side oriented toward the recipient. The visitor receives the host's card in the same manner and treats it with respect, meaning that he or she studies it for a moment rather than stuffing it in a pocket. It is common practice to place cards on the table or desk at which one sits during the meeting, perhaps aligned with their owners across the table.

Humility is a traditional Confucian value, and visitors should avoid the sort of aggressiveness associated, for instance, with U.S. business people. Rather than burst into the room with loud greetings and viselike handshakes, one should speak in quiet, confident tones and avoid excessive eye contact, particularly with individuals of higher rank than oneself. Although handshakes have become common, perhaps with a slight bowing of the head to signal respect, they are not a way of demonstrating physical strength. Masculine virtue is identified with poise and self-control rather than displays of machismo. Modesty rather than braggadocio inspires respect for the visitor, as social relations are based on maintaining harmony. It is perfectly acceptable to drop names, however. Some observers mistakenly assumed that the Asian political contributors who spent the night in Bill Clinton's White House were interested in influencing U.S. government policy. In reality they craved a signed photograph of themselves and the American President to display on their office wall, along with the opportunity to drop the most impressive name of the day.

Chinese often impress Westerners as evasive, but the impression is created by a relatively high-context culture in which overly direct communication is avoided. It may be best not to press immediately for clarification. As in many polite societies, there is a strong reluctance to say no outright, or in general to say what the other party does not want to hear. Such remarks as "We will think about it" often signal bad news. On the other hand, Chinese may ask repeated questions, perhaps to test one's veracity by noting whether the answer is always the same. They are said to be masters of the soft sell and the hard buy.

Asian cultures run on the masculine side, and drinking and smoking are often expected. One colleague told me that he used to smoke without inhaling in business meetings. Actually it is all right to demur if one avoids the appearance of rejection by affirming one's Chinese associates and their culture in other ways. As for drinking, one can bear in mind that waiters fill empty glasses, not full ones.

Much is said in Western business literature about tough Chinese negotiators and their militaristic thinking. Australian businessmen are fond of reading Sun Tzu's *The Art of War* in order to understand the Chinese strategic mind. Chinese negotiators are said to use a large team and drag out the process indefinitely, so as to wear down their opponents. They constantly keep one on the defensive with lavish entertainment interspersed with probing questions. They take advantage of cultural ignorance by saying that such and such is the norm in China. They may orchestrate the whole affair merely to extract information about one's company and technology rather than to make a deal. Yet they are suspicious of their opponent's motives and may bluntly state what those motives appear to be in order to observe the reaction.

The impression given in Western business literature is one of ruthless Chinese warriors versus well-intentioned Western business people. It is generated by the fact that the two sides come to the negotiating table with different worldviews inside their heads. Westerners assume that negotiation is a poker game in which one can bluff and posture but must play by the rules. This kind of internalized, universal code of behavior is an absurdity to the Chinese mind. For Chinese, as for many people in the world, the other party is either friend or foe, and there is no neutral ground in between. If a friend, there is little need for formal negotiation in the sense in which, say, Western labor and management bargain across the table. The parties will develop their mutual enterprise gradually as they get to know each other. If the enemy, however, then the business at hand is war—with no Geneva Convention. The Chinese will win, as they are on their home turf.

Chinese are uncomfortable with negotiation precisely because, in their lexicon, it is confrontation. Confrontation is disruptive rather than constructive as in the West, because it causes loss of face and upsets all-important harmony among associates. Chinese prefer to seek common interests by pursuing a relationship. The relationship will flourish if there is opportunity for mutual benefit, and will lapse if not. The Western conception of business, in which the parties hammer out a fixed contract and execute it without modification, is totally wrongheaded in this context. It is true that Chinese make deals and sign contracts every day, but they do so partly in deference to Western custom, and the whole affair remains grounded in mutual trust relationships. For this reason the contracts tend to be vague and are always subject to renegotiation the next day. Westerners may feel the need for legal enforcement, but it is as unnecessary as it is impractical. If one has the proper relationship with Chinese counterparts, their word is their bond. Remarkably, however, many Western professionals continue to enter China with Anglo-Saxon notions of contract law firmly fixed in their minds, and they too often end up casualties of war.

The language barrier is substantial, as the Chinese language seems to employ entirely different neural processes than Western languages. The main barrier, however, is not so much the difficulty of the language as the fact that it is a high-context language in a high-context culture. It is terse and suggestive, rather than explicit and logically connected as are Western languages. It is wise to have a fluent speaker of the appropriate Chinese dialect on one's team, since some interpreters in China are as inept as others are proficient. One can minimize misunderstanding by providing Chinese-language copies of proposals as well as a glossary of technical terms. (The written Chinese language is fairly standard around the world.) Proposals should be phrased clearly and repeatedly, as the Chinese may not admit that they fail to understand, to avoid loss of face. In the long run, however, the language is less important than Westerners think, since mutual agreement is grounded in the relationship rather than in verbal formulations.

Decision making in China is slow and cautious, since no one wants to be responsible for a mistake. In fact, it may be impossible to tell who is making the decisions. The process may take months or even years. In addition, approvals may be necessary at several government levels, depending on the size of the deal. Bureaucrats may repeatedly ask for changes in the agreement, weakening one's position each time. The rule of survival in a bureaucracy, after all, is to make one's signature a requirement for as many permits and licenses as possible, even if they have little relevance to one's office. The bureaucrats may therefore know little about the business at hand. The only way for Westerners to stay sane in this environment is to view it with a certain amount of detachment, as though they were anthropologists observing the scene, rather than fume about its inefficiency.

China has a reputation for corruption, yet bribery and corruption are often illegal. The central government has no more taste for graft than Western moralists, if only because corruption dissipates its power. It is not unusual for offenders to be lined up and shot. The primary reason bribery corrupts the system, however, is that it shortcuts *guānxi*. A complex civilization cannot operate, in the long term, through transient liaisons based on payoffs. Only stable, long-term relationships provide the predictability needed to plan and carry out complex projects, particularly in the private sector. *Guānxi* serves this function because it is not based on quid pro quo, takes time to build, and lasts a lifetime if properly maintained. Foreigners should therefore rely on *guānxi* and avoid bribery whenever possible. Those who indulge in making side payments risk developing a bad reputation, and unsavory characters may descend on them. It is more effective, not to mention safer, to maintain an aura of incorruptibility and accomplish things through relationships cultivated over the long term. The situation is somewhat different in Korea and some other parts of Asia, where side payments may be routine and even functional. Yet even there it is best to let local associates take care of things whenever possible.

The Western media have made much of the problem of piracy and enforcement of intellectual property rights in China. The problem is real enough, as one can, for instance, buy pirated copies of CDs on the street only a few days after they are released in the West. It is not uncommon for pirates to take their camcorders into cinemas and record the movie from the big screen, complete with audience noise. However, the popular notion that Chinese are culturally incapable of recognizing or understanding intellectual property is nonsense. The one time that the West recognizes a cultural angle, it gets it wrong. China developed a sophisticated system of property rights more than two thousand years ago and is no less capable of recognizing intellectual property than Western countries, where enforcement is a recent development in any case. One should bear in mind that Charles Dickens complained bitterly about piracy of his works in the United States scarcely a century ago. The United States strengthened (perhaps overstrengthened) intellectual property laws and enforcement when the business community insisted on it. The Chinese government will do the same when and if it sees fit. In the meantime, the best course one can take is to register patents, copyrights, and trademarks immediately with the Chinese government and hope that it enforces the law.

Nepotism is ubiquitous in hiring and is not as inefficient as it may seem to Westerners. Incompetent workers may be taken on, but the boss is aware of their incompetence and in general knows the strengths and weaknesses of employees who are members of the family. He can therefore match their assignments with their abilities. He can also command greater loyalty, and perhaps extract greater effort, through his authority as a family patriarch than he would have over an employee who is not kin—just the opposite of the West, where the boss may be tempted to go easy on a family member. In any event, nepotism will always be a feature of Chinese employment because of the fundamental role of family in the culture.

Since the culture is based on high power distance, the boss is expected to take charge and exercise authority. It is permissible to deal sternly with employees when the occasion demands it, but at the same time, the boss should respect an employee's "face." The balance is struck on the basis of the employee's rank and the extent to which he or she has already lost face due to inept performance. Bonus plans and the like are common and can be effective, as Chinese respond well to personal incentives.

China has a masculine culture in several senses: competition is accepted (particularly in Cantonese-speaking regions), men are expected to be tough, women normally defer to men, and martial arts are valued. Yet women are by no means shut out of professional life. Many occupy highly placed jobs in the public sector, as dictated by Communist ideology, and it is not uncommon to find middle-aged women occupying important positions in family firms, including that of owner. A female professional from abroad can usually function effectively if her associates make it clear that she has authority, for instance by deferring to her in the presence of their Chinese counterparts.

A final piece of advice to visitors is to know something about China. One should learn about its history and geography, and try to observe the practices of good etiquette described here. It is wise to use at least a few words of the language (a brief tutorial follows). Chinese are not offended by ignorant visitors—only convinced that they are uncivilized.

Returning to the Chinese reputation for practicality, some Western visitors to the country have expressed to me a certain disappointment. Their image before arriving was of a vast, inscrutable place, and yet on arrival nothing could be more earthbound. Every thought and action seems directly tied to some practical purpose. Perhaps that is why all those Chinese college students in the United States seem to major in business or engineering, as opposed to art or literature. Their parents are telling them to be practical. Is there no room for imagination in China, for flights of fancy and innovation, for deeply probing a subject for its own sake? Even the temples seem mundane, as worshipers light an incense coil in the hope of getting a better job. The facts, however, refute any impression that China lacks depth or imagination. Chinese not only developed a rich literary and artistic tradition, but they were also innovative enough to invent paper on which to record it. The very script in which the language is written is an art form. They were first to make gunpowder, but the Europeans were the ones who used it for something so practical as guns; Chinese were more interested in fanciful pyrotechnics. History, in the Chinese mind, is a vast hall of wonders, rather than a dusty warehouse of facts and dates. Chinese mythology spins countless tales of ghosts, animals, spirits, and gods with human personalities. If one is looking for something supremely impractical, one can consider the equivalent of $1.5 billion (U.S.) sunk in the construction of the Ming Tombs. Perhaps the deeper reason for Western disappointment is that China has not a trace of the romanticism that so thoroughly shapes the Western perspective on the world.

Politics and Government

Westerners nod with approval as governments around the world take on the trappings of democracy, but they frown at Chinese insistence on authoritarian government. They too often forget, however, that parliaments and constitutions do not a democracy make. In most cases the ancient mechanisms of cronyism, family connection, and side payments continue to run governments that look democratic on the surface. Democratic window dressing may even disrupt good government if it is sufficiently foreign to the culture. China is likewise undemocratic but has the cultural integrity not to pretend otherwise. Its government has been based on respect for authority since long before Confucius pointed out as much, and it will continue in this vein no matter how much Westerners may rail against it. Even supposing that democracy made sense for Chinese culture, and it almost certainly does not, introducing a parliament and prime minister would not democratize the government.

I am speaking of democracy in the full and literal sense of the word: a government in which the people rule and therefore take responsibility for themselves. To allude to Abraham Lincoln's formulation, it is government "of and by the people" as well as "for the people". This means in part that people must somehow come to an agreement as to how the government will be run. The rule-based culture and institutions that support this process in modern Europe and North America required at least a thousand years to develop. They cannot be grafted onto a different cultural system by scheduling an internationally supervised election. Democracy is often conceived in an attenuated sense, however, as a government that keeps people reasonably content, but the people themselves are not active in civic matters. They may protest and demonstrate when things go wrong, but they do not maintain a day-to-day, grassroots involvement. If this is what democracy is, then some rough approximation of it may be possible in China if, for example, rulers exhibit the Confucian virtues.

The popular Chinese understanding of democracy is in fact attenuated. A "democratic" government provides services but otherwise leaves one alone to go about one's business. Its police do not harass, and its officials do not require bribes. It may even allow one to move to Shanghai or Hong Kong whenever one wants (a policy, incidentally, that would transform these cities to something resembling Mexico City, where mass migration from the hinterland is legal). This is obviously not everyone's view, but it is my impression of the general attitude. So when Chinese students demonstrate for democracy in the streets of Beijing, they do not necessarily have in mind a Lincolnesque society in which people take responsibility for their own welfare.

Chinese also have their own interpretation of human rights, another concept the West wishes to export. One hears the opinion that the West cares about human rights when its own interests are at stake but forgets about them when ethnic Chinese are attacked and driven from their homes in Indonesia. Many Chinese are skeptical as to whether Western talk of human rights is more than empty rhetoric, although it must be said that some admire and even idealize Western political ideology.

A political system can work only if it takes advantage of preexisting cultural mechanisms for social cohesion. China's mechanism has for millennia been Confucian respect for authority, and any viable government must rely on obedience. An authoritarian government also has certain advantages. While democratic governments may enact uncoordinated and even

contradictory policies to please various interests, an authoritarian government at its best can implement the coherent vision of a benevolent leader,
such as Deng Xiaoping's agricultural reforms. It can accomplish much in a
short time, simply by giving the order, such as a nationwide system of superhighways, a Shenzhen or Pudong Area, or a Great Wall. An obvious disadvantage of authority is that it can oppress; it can go awry and wreak
enormous destruction before it is checked, as during the cultural revolution
of the 1960s. It can become paranoid and suppress freedom of thought.
China is a risky place to voice dissenting opinions, and government censors
nervously block Web sites they view as objectionable. A third liability is
that authoritarian government can be unpredictable. Information in
high–power distance societies flows upward, not downward, and few outside the Chinese inner circle truly understand what it is up to. This unpredictability is perhaps the greatest liability to foreign organizations at the
moment. Stability could evaporate overnight if the government cracks
down on some group, invades Taiwan, or exacerbates the already high level
of discontent in rural areas. I never try to predict what the government may
do tomorrow, and I put little stock in anyone who does.

Despite the impression that Western media may create, most Chinese
outside Beijing have little interest in political ideology or international relations. Foreign journalists who hang around Beijing may be misled on this
point, due to the political bent of its population. For instance, news coverage of the U.S. spy plane incident near the island of Hainan in April 2001
might have given the impression that the entire Chinese population was in
an uproar and could be hostile to visitors from the United States. In fact,
the average Chinese associates Hainan with delicious shrimp rather than an
international incident. Many will volunteer political opinions if asked,
such as the common view that there is too much freedom in the West, or
that the Dalai Lama is evil and deserves to be exiled from Tibet. But the
vast majority are gracious and hospitable to visitors regardless of what
kind of mess the politicians may be creating at the moment. Cantonese-
speaking Chinese are particularly apathetic about politics, their passion
being business and profit. An acquaintance in Beijing told me a little story
that illustrates this point. (He had lived several years in Canada, where he
picked up the Western ironic sense of humor.) He took a vacation in
Guangzhou to sample the restaurants and decided to make a side trip to
Hsiang-shan County. He wanted to visit the birthplace of Sun Yat-sen,
the famous leader of the Chinese Nationalist Party (*Guómíndǎng*) of
the early twentieth century. His driver, however, was perplexed about
why one would want to waste time on such an excursion. "Why do
you care about Sun Yat-sen?" he asked. "Did his family give you money or
something?"

Language

Chinese comprises several languages, some of which are mutually unintelligible when spoken. The Chinese people nonetheless view Chinese as a single language with dialects, presumably because they identify themselves as belonging to a single culture. Minority groups within China speak Turkic, Mongolian, Tibetan, Thai, and other languages.

The linguistic situation is very different in the north than in the south. Essentially all Chinese-speaking people north of the Yangtze River use mutually intelligible variations of Mandarin Chinese (*Guānhuà*). The same is true in the southwest provinces of Guizhou and Yunnan. Mandarin Chinese is historically the dialect spoken by the mandarins (courtiers) of Beijing, and it became the *lingua franca* for governmental affairs about five hundred years ago. Before that time, classical literary Chinese was regarded as the standard, but it became impractical as the contemporary dialects diverged from it. Today Mandarin is the official "common language" (*Pǔtōnghuà*) or "national language" (*Guóyǔ*) of China. Southern China, by contrast, is a patchwork of dissimilar dialects, perhaps because the hilly terrain once made travel and linguistic diffusion more difficult. The most important southern dialect is Cantonese (*Yuè*), spoken in Hong Kong, most of Guangdong and Guangxi Provinces, and in many overseas Chinese communities. In particular, nearly everyone in the city of Guangzhou speaks Cantonese, although many residents of nearby Shenzhen are migrants from the north and speak Mandarin. Foreign business people sometimes learn Cantonese because its speakers are prominent in commerce and may speak little or no Mandarin. Shanghaiese (*Wú*) is spoken around Shanghai and in Zhejiang Province to the south. More people speak it than Cantonese, but there is no particular reason for foreigners to learn it, since many residents of Shanghai speak Mandarin as well. Table 9.2 lists the other principal dialects in China.

The choice of Mandarin as the official language was a slow and fitful process that dates back to the founding of the Chinese republic in 1912, with the official pronouncement finally coming in 1956.[8] Foreigners who wish to study Chinese are normally advised to learn Mandarin. This is certainly wise if one intends to live or work outside of Cantonese-speaking regions at least part of the time. However, if one anticipates residence exclusively in Hong Kong or Guangzhou, for example, the choice is not so obvious. All Chinese are technically required to study Mandarin, but everyone seems to exaggerate the number of Cantonese speakers who know it. A foreigner living in Hong Kong or Guangzhou will hear constant Cantonese and precious little Mandarin day in and day out, and it is no fun to study a language one never hears. A counterargument is that Cantonese is devilishly

TABLE 9.2
Principal Chinese Dialects

Language Group	Primarily Spoken In
Mandarin (Pŭtōnghuà)	Provinces north of Yangtze River, Guizhou and Yunnan Provinces
Shanghaiese (Wú)	Shanghai area, Zhejiang Province
Cantonese (Yuè)	Hong Kong, Guangdong, and Guangxi Provinces; overseas communities
Xiāng	Hunan Province
Northern, Southern Mĭn	Fujian Province, Hainan Island, Taiwan (Taiwanese)
Hakka	North of Guangzhou, parts of Taiwan, and so on
Gàn	Jiangxi Province

Dialects are arranged in order of the number of speakers within China, and areas in which they are primarily spoken.
Source: Ramsey, page 5.

hard to learn, partly due to its complicated system of nine "tones" (vocal inflections), compared to four in Mandarin. Even native Mandarin speakers have difficulty with Cantonese and seem rarely to learn it.

The written Chinese language is fairly standard worldwide, although Cantonese newspapers may contain characters that are unfamiliar to readers from other parts of the country. Various systems have been devised for writing Chinese in Roman letters, but the official romanization in China is the Pinyin system for writing Mandarin Chinese, adopted in 1958. The most popular word processors accept text in the form of Pinyin and print the document in Chinese characters. When a Pinyin word corresponds to more than one character, the user is given a list to choose from. All foreigners should learn how to pronounce Pinyin, if only to be able to say names correctly. Pinyin spellings are chosen to be as readable by English speakers as possible, but since Chinese contains some sounds that do not occur in English, one must learn several exceptions (see table 9.3). Each Chinese character corresponds to a syllable in Pinyin. When two or more characters constitute a word or common phrase, it is common to run the corresponding Pinyin syllables together into a single word, although there is no well-defined rule for this. Each syllable consists of an "initial" (a consonant, including *y* or *w*) and a "final" (a vowel). One should not be surprised if some Chinese, particularly around Beijing, introduce what sounds like a deep-throated North American *r* (the retroflex *r*) into some syllables.

Mandarin Chinese has four tones, which are ways of inflecting a vowel sound. The tones cannot be ignored because they change the meaning

TABLE 9.3
Spellings that Sound Different in Pinyin than in English

Pinyin Spelling	Sound (Varies by Region)
Consonants (Initials)	
c	Somewhere between *t* in *bit* and *ts* in *bits* (for me, this is the most difficult)
q	Like *ch* in *cheese,* but with the tip of the tongue against the back of the lower teeth
x	Like *sh* in *sheep,* but with the tip of the tongue against the back of the lower teeth
zh	Like *j* in *jade,* but with the tongue further back
Vowels (Finals)	
ai	Like *i* in *like*
ao	Like *ow* in *how*
a	Like *a* in *hat*
ang	Like *on* in *bond*
e	Like *u* in *fur*
ei	Like *ay* in *say*
eng	Like *un* in *hunger*
er	At the beginning of a syllable, like *ar* in *bar*
i	Like *ee* in *see* after most consonants, but like *i* in *bit* pronounced with rounded lips after *c, ch, r, s, sh, z, zh*. In the latter case, one should retain the mouth position of the consonant while pronouncing a short *i*. Letter *i* is like *y* when it occurs before a vowel and is replaced by *y* when also the first letter in a syllable. The initial *y* tends to be silent before *i*.
o	Like *o* in *hot*
ong	Like *un* in *hung*
ou	Like *o* in *hope*
u	Like *oo* in *loop.* Letter *u* is like *w* when it occurs before a vowel and is replaced by *w* when it is also the first letter in a syllable.
ui	Somewhere between *wai* in *waist* and *wee* in *sweet*
ü	Like the German *ü*
y	See *i* above

entirely. For example, the spelling *ma* can be written with four tones: *mā*, *má*, *mǎ*, *mà*, or with no tone mark at all. *Mā* (mother) is pronounced with a somewhat high, even pitch. *Má* (as in *má jiāng*, the popular game mahjong) is pronounced with a rising tone, much like a question in English. *Mǎ* (horse) is pronounced with a falling and then a rising tone. *Mà* (to curse) is pronounced with a falling tone and sounds something like an order that is barked to a military squad. Without a tone, *ma* is placed at the end of a sentence to indicate that one is asking a question. The best way to hear tones is to listen to the official news anchors in Beijing, who are trained to speak precisely. Tones may not be audible in ordinary conversation among native speakers, but they are nonetheless present in some residual form. To be understood, beginners must carefully pronounce the tones even if it sounds a little silly. They will become more natural with time.

It is not as difficult to learn rudimentary Chinese as one might think. The grammar is simple and logical, there are no tenses or genders, and words are never inflected, even for plurals (although one must learn the "counting words," such as the word *kuài* in 8 *kuài rénmínbì*). The tones give words a songlike quality that helps cement them in memory. One can go a certain distance without learning characters, and some books are even published in Pinyin. After a while, however, the words begin to run together, because the same Pinyin syllable with the same tones can represent several characters with different meanings. There are remarkably few distinct sounds in Mandarin Chinese. Native Chinese speakers do not get confused because they have associated words with characters since early childhood. Any reasonably systematic study of Chinese should probably include memorization of characters and the proper procedure for writing them; the strokes are drawn in a certain order. I will not pretend that general reading ability is anything less than a monumental challenge for adults to acquire, however. To take a typical example, one of my MBA students (in his twenties) spent three summers, five days a week, several hours a day studying intensive Chinese. At this point he traveled to Taiwan on assignment and could read the newspaper with some difficulty. A year later he was again assigned to Taiwan, and he found he could no longer get through a news article.

The first phrases one should learn are *nǐ hǎo* (hello; literally, "you well"), *qǐng nǐ* (please), and *xiè xie* (thank you). Chinese like to repeat words, and one who is really grateful can say, "*xiè xie xiè xie.*" One can ask, "*Nǐ hǎo ma*" (How are you?), to which the response is *hěn hǎo xiè xie* (very well, thank you). Chinese like to use an adverb rather than "to be" before a predicate adjective, so that one would idiomatically say, "*Wǒ hěn gāoxìng jiàndào nǐ*" (I very pleased to meet you) rather than "*Wǒ shì gāoxìng jiàndào nǐ*" (I am pleased to meet you). The phrase from old Charlie Chan movies, "Long time, no see," is an almost literal translation of the

Chinese greeting *hǎo jiǔ bù jiàn* (very long, no meet). "Good morning" is *zǎoshàng hǎo* (or simply *zǎo*), "good evening" is *wǎnshàng hǎo,* and "good-bye" is *zàijiàn.* Visitors in need of assistance can address someone on the street by saying, *"Duìbùqǐ"* (Excuse me . . .), followed by the universal question *nǐ shūo Yīngyǔ ma* (do you speak English?); one should not pronounce the first *y* in *Yīngyǔ.* As for the response, it is wise to be prepared for one of the most uttered phrases of the Chinese language: *méiyǒu.* Literally it means "don't have," but it conveys something between "I can't help you" and "get lost." I was told that Western expatriates in Beijing at one point got so tired of hearing the phrase that they began wearing T-shirts with *méiyǒu* written across the front.

Chinese names consist of the family name followed by one or two given names, the latter written as one word in Pinyin. Thus, Wang Lin is Mr. Wang, or Wáng xiānsheng in Chinese. The titles Mr. (*xiānsheng*), Mrs. (*nüshì*), and Miss (*xiǎojie*) are less common on the mainland than elsewhere. An older Mr. Wang can be addressed as Lǎo Wáng (Old Wang) and a younger Mr. Wang as Xiǎo Wáng (Young Wang). Common titles include Wáng jīnglǐ (Manager Wang), Wáng jiàoshòu (Professor Wang), and Wáng lǎoshī (Teacher Wang). When interacting with Westerners, Chinese often reverse their names to conform to the Western convention, so that Wang Lin might present an English-language business card bearing the name Lin Wang. It is often impossible to know whether the names have been reversed, unless the surname is easily recognizable. The following twenty surnames, listed in order of frequency, are said to account for about half the population of China: Zhang, Wang, Li, Zhao, Chen, Yang, Wu, Liu, Huang, Zhou, Xu, Zhu, Lin, Sun, Ma, Gao, Hu, Zheng, Guo, and Xiao. Since either Wang or Lin could plausibly be a surname, it is advisable to refer to Wang Lin (or Lin Wang) by his full name, as indicated on his card, until the issue is clarified.

I have a pet proposal that school children around the world be taught some Chinese characters, while they are young enough to absorb them with minimal effort. This would admit them to literacy in the world's most widely read language and open the door to an advanced civilization that, if history is any guide, will outlast all the others.

Notes for Chapter 9

1. Available: http://pudong.shanghaichina.org/.
2. *People's Daily,* July 18, 2001.
3. *Family Planning in China,* Information Office of the State Council of the People's Republic of China (Beijing, August 1995).

4. "China's One Child Policy, Two Child Reality," report from the U.S. Embassy (Beijing, October 1997).

5. "Medicine in a Mind/Body Culture," in Bill Moyers, *Healing and the Mind,* Doubleday (New York, 1993).

6. "China," in Geoffrey Parrinder, ed., *World Religions: From Ancient History to the Present,* Facts on File Publications (New York, 1971).

7. Herbert Stroup, *Founders of Living Religions,* Westminster Press (Philadelphia, 1974).

8. S. Robert Ramsey, *The Languages of China,* Princeton University Press (Princeton, N.J., 1989), 5.

10 *India*

In India, they do not cut the grass. There are exceptions, as for example when one occasionally sees cattle drawing an antique mower across temple grounds. But it is nothing like the situation on a street where I used to live in the United States. The neighbors would look askance at me whenever the grass in my front yard got ankle high. The people across the street not only trimmed their lawn as closely as a golf green but also brought out a broom to sweep away any debris.

Small things in a strange culture can provide clues to large mechanisms that operate beneath the surface. The key to is distinguish the important details from trivia, which is particularly difficult for Western visitors in India. Everything is so different that everything seems important. When I first arrived on this alien planet, the shock began the moment I emerged from the Air India plane. I was hit by a blast of steam that literally took my breath. The first rain of the monsoon season had just fallen on the parched earth after weeks of relentless dry heat, instantly turning into hot vapor. I wondered what I had got myself into, but this was only the beginning. Upon hiring a cab, I found myself in streets clogged with every imaginable vehicle, ranging from shiny Mercedes sedans to smoke-spewing auto-rickshaws to inhumanly crowded buses, all making their way with ceaseless honking of horns through herds of animals and hoards of humanity. At every pause in the traffic, children thrust begging hands through the taxi windows and demanded alms. Dapper and suave bureaucrats, laborers in tattered shirts, jeweled matrons in colorful saris, itinerant holy men, foreign backpackers carrying huge wads of cash, and homeless mothers with baby at breast mingled in the crowds. Squalid shanties and foul-smelling open sewers surrounded high-rise luxury apartment buildings. Areas that should have been sidewalks were impassable, clogged with weeds, fruit stalls, vendors of tempting home-cooked food, families living in cardboard boxes, and reputable physicians offering medical care and drugs, the last more than a little reminiscent of Lucy's psychiatrist stand in the *Peanuts* comic strip. When my host later asked me about my first impression of India, I could only tell him the truth: everything was so new and so overwhelming that I could not take it all in. He understood what I meant.

The exotic sensations of India provide an unforgettable experience for the visitor, but many of them are unimportant culturally. Take the food, for example. The flavors are intense and the spices strong, particularly in southern India. I have put mango pickles into my mouth that could just as well have been live electric wires. But Indian food is spicy because spices were traditionally necessary to preserve it in the hot climate, not because spiciness has a functional role in the culture.

Failure to cut the grass, however, says something profound about India. It is difficult to distill this fact from the chaos and contradiction of everyday experience, but Indians themselves have isolated the essence beneath the confusion. In fact, a core premise of the Hindu worldview is that there is a unity that underlies the bewildering diversity of the phenomenal world. India, which may be the world's most highly intellectual culture, has developed a sophisticated philosophy around this premise. So why do people fail to cut the grass? It is not because Indians are lazy or sloppy, even if some are. It may be partly because there is little grass to cut during the long dry season. But the main reason is that the world around us is God, and God does not require routine maintenance.

I begin with an explanation of the Hindu worldview because it is the key to everything else. There are many religious philosophies in India, but Hinduism is the most widely practiced faith, and its perspective most deeply influences the culture. In discussing rarefied Eastern philosophies, however, I do not want to suggest that everyday Indians sit around contemplating philosophical abstractions, any more than everyday Westerners think about theoretical physics, however much its philosophy shapes their lives. Nearly all Indians occupy their time in very practical pursuits, as they struggle for survival in a land where poverty oppresses most and threatens all. Nonetheless, their everyday life reflects at every turn the Hindu perspective.

The Hindu Worldview

Hindu philosophy and religion show some striking parallels with Western thought, as well as a fundamental difference. The parallels may result from common roots. Although Indian culture traces back at least four thousand years to the Indus Valley or Harappan civilization, Hinduism is primarily the legacy of chariot-riding Aryans who entered the subcontinent about 1500 B.C.E. Historian John Keay tells us that the word *Aryan* is of uncertain and variable meaning through the ages, but it is related to *Iran* and presumably refers to people from that part of the world.[1] They left a body of literature that remains the foundation of Hindu thinking: four Vedas, or religious poems; the philosophical Upanishads; the popular stories of the *Ramayana;* and the massive epic *Mahabharata,* fifteen times longer than the Christian Bible. The *Mahabharata* contains the famous *Bhagavad Gita* (Song of God).

A clue to the Western connection lies in the classical Sanskrit language that dates back to the Vedic era. William Jones noted in 1785 that Sanskrit is closely related to Greek and other Western languages. He suggested the possibility of an Indo-European mother tongue, no longer in existence, that is the ultimate ancestor of Greek, Sanskrit, and Hindi as well as the Romance and Germanic languages of Europe.[2] Hindus and Greeks may therefore have common ancestors, which could explain some of the parallels between them. The most important parallel for present purposes is a common reliance on reason. Both traditions developed advanced philosophies that explored many of the same topics, such as mathematics, formal logic, ethics, the mind-body problem, and the immortality of the soul. It is the pivotal role of universalizing rationality in both cultures that brings Indian culture much closer to the West than, say, Chinese culture.

There is, however, a fundamental difference, and it makes all the difference. The Greeks alone developed the idea of a secular world that operates according to a mechanism without spiritual influence. They explained nature as arising wholly from the interplay of a few physical elements, such as earth, air, fire, and water—a kind of reductionism that still forms the basis of Western science. As early as the sixth century B.C.E., the philosopher Thales was already suggesting that a single element, in his estimation water, is the basis for all of nature. It is interesting that these early philosophers clung to a certain pantheism despite their materialistic account. Thales' successor Anaximander, for example, described this single underlying substance as somehow divine. By the fourth century B.C.E., however, Democritus had proposed a purely secular world made of atoms, or indivisible particles. He suggested that the physical shape of atoms could determine all the sensible properties of matter. This idea of the secular in nature was reinforced by Judaism's idea of the secular in history, which reached the Hellenistic world through Christianity. A transcendent God sits above the secular world and allows human beings below to shape events and create history. Thus the Greeks gave Westerners the intellectual wherewithal to manipulate the world for their own purposes, and Christianity gave them permission to do so. The eventual result was technology, on which the West came increasingly to rely.

The Hindu worldview is precisely the opposite. It is thoroughly pantheistic. Far from sitting above nature, God is identical with nature. Rather than consist of inert matter, the world is infused with divine consciousness. While Westerners typically see consciousness as an epiphenomenon of some complex mechanism, such as a brain or a computer, Eastern philosophy sees it as an attribute of all matter. Mind and body are the same substance, seen as it were from different angles. When looking from outside, one sees a body and a brain; while looking from the inside, one sees consciousness.

This dual-aspect theory has surfaced in Western thought, for instance in the writings of the seventeenth-century thinker Baruch Spinoza, but it remains a distinctly minority opinion.

If India's rationalistic philosophy is to perform its stress-management function, however, it must find order and predictability in the chaos and confusion that surround us. Westerners accomplish this by seeking a mechanism in nature, and using it as a basis for imposing order on their environment through technology. Eastern thought takes a different approach. Rather than interpret the world as a complex reality that flows from simple laws, it postulates a simple reality that appears complex due to the confused way we perceive it. We view the universe as through a kaleidoscope that splinters and fragments the underlying wholeness. The Upanishads call his wholeness, among other things, Brahman. Even the gods, such as Vishnu, Shiva, Krishna, and some 330 million others (yes, 330 million, according to scripture), are manifestations, or avatars, of Brahman. Consciousness appears to us to be fragmented into millions of individual minds, but these are actually flickers of consciousness in a single mind, just as a single lamp may cast many patches of light. The center of consciousness is Atman (spirit). The word *atman* derives from an Indo-European word for "breath" or "air" (as in *atmosphere*), just as *spirit* derives from the Latin for "breath." Atman and Brahman are not distinct substances, however, because Atman is Brahman "seen from the inside." They are two aspects of the same unified reality.

The emphasis on the oneness of all things makes Hinduism a mystical faith. Mysticism suggests something magic or supernatural to Western ears, but this is a misunderstanding. The very distinction of natural from supernatural is a Western concoction, since it presupposes a secular mechanism that can at times be overridden by an external agent. Far from recognizing the supernatural, mysticism provides insight into the natural. It is motivated by what Western philosophy has called the "principle of sufficient reason," which states that nothing can exist unless there is some reason that justifies why it rather than something else should exist. This principle is difficult to sustain in the West's pluralistic world of objects located in space and time. Even if one can explain how their current configuration is the necessary result of their positions and velocities a moment ago, it is much harder to explain how the whole process got started, and why it started in one particular configuration rather than another. The rationalist philosopher and mathematician Gottfried Wilhelm von Leibniz was driven to supposing that objects ("monads") exist only in time, not in space, in order to reduce the arbitrariness of nature by reducing the number of degrees of freedom. The Eastern solution is to remove *all* degrees of freedom by supposing that there is no plurality, and therefore no arbitrariness. There is only a single undifferentiated entity: Brahman-Atman. The world can be explained because in this simple monism there is essentially nothing to explain.

This leaves the problem of how to account for the messy perceived world around us. Western science attempts to make perception part of the reality it perceives and to explain it the same way. If the room looks blurry to me, it is because of the way light is refracted in my eyes. The operation of my near-sighted eyes is explained by the same physical laws as the room they observe. The Eastern view is totally different. What we call "perception" is confused thinking about reality, rather than a relationship between perceiver and object. (A similar idea can be found in the writings of René Descartes and other Western rationalists.) While Western science strives in vain for a unified field theory or a "theory of everything" that wraps all phenomena in a single, consistent system, Hinduism recognizes the impossibility of this project. It responds to a confused and multifaceted phenomenal world with a confused and multifaceted faith. It proposes no creed, no underlying principle from which one can derive its sprawling mythology, riddled as it is with variations and contradictions. To make things worse, its various doctrines come in different levels of sophistication to suit a bewildering diversity of people, from rural peasants to ascetic monks to urbane Ph.D.s.

Hinduism offers salvation from the exigencies of life by counseling mental discipline. One trains oneself to set aside the confusion of appearances and to view life sub specie aeternitatis. This is the ultimate goal of the regimen called *yoga,* which is a Sanskrit word for "connection" or "yoke," referring to the fact that one is connected to the underlying reality. An important tool of yoga is meditation, which helps one learn to control the contents of one's mind. Meditation may connote to Westerners a relaxation technique or simply a way to space out, but it is much more than this. Mathematicians who concentrate intensely on solving a problem are closer to effective meditation than many yoga initiates who focus on their breathing and sit in various positions. Indeed, I do not personally know of any Indians who practice yoga, aside from some elements of traditional Ayurvedic medicine. Mental discipline generally takes the more practical form of rigorous education. Children are admonished to take their lessons seriously, and the competition to get into good schools and colleges is intense. This is partly because people are desperate to get ahead in a country with limited resources, but it is their choice to compete on the basis of academic prowess. They so choose because it suits their method of coping. Rather than control their environment in Western fashion, Indians try to control the way they think about the environment, and rigorous study is one way to accomplish this.

Most Indians remain tethered to the phenomenal world, however, and it is only natural for their rationalistic culture to seek a law that governs it.

This is the law of karma (*karman* is Sanskrit for "action"). It is not a closed, consistent system like relativity theory or quantum electrodynamics. It is as confused and incomplete as the quasi-reality with which it deals. The best-known aspect is the doctrine of reincarnation, which attempts to explain why some people are born as wealthy Brahmins and others as poor out-castes, seemingly through no merit or fault of their own. It is a matter of cause and effect. Events set in motion in a prior life determine one's fate in the present life. Before scoffing at the notion of transmigration of souls, Westerners might consider that Socrates took it very seriously—one of the many parallels between classical Greek and Indian thought. In Plato's dialog *Meno,* Socrates coaxes a proof of the Pythagorean theorem (or a special case of it) from Meno's slave boy in order to demonstrate that he learned it in a previous life. The doctrine also has a more sophisticated form, namely the mystical idea that all souls are manifestations of a single world soul and therefore exist independently of any individual body. This is an idea one should not reject before thinking about it for twenty or thirty years. Karma and reincarnation admittedly provide a less than satisfying expla-nation for injustice, and they may counsel complacency in the face of poverty. The main point of karma, however, is not so much its precise doc-trine as its determination to make some kind of sense of the human condi-tion as we perceive it.

Westerners see the world as a secular realm that must be structured and maintained. The land must be bulldozed, the streets laid out in a grid, the buses dispatched according to schedule, and of course the grass cut. In Hinduism the world as we know it is our finite way of apprehending God, or Brahman. We do not maintain the world; it maintains us. This is why India, to Western eyes, seems to be falling apart. The power system fails, the telephone service is unreliable, the water is unsafe to drink, broken headlights are seldom replaced, and weeds grow on the golf course. It is not that Indians are incapable of order, system, and technology. Their mental discipline is well suited to advanced technology, as one can confirm by walking into any Silicon Valley laboratory and noting the number of Indian scientists at work. It is just that Indians have evolved coping mechanisms that do not require them to structure their environment.

Religions

India possesses the world's state of the art in religion, much as the West possesses the state of the art in technology. Working in India without knowledge of its religions is like working in the United States without knowing how to surf the Web.

More than 80 percent of Indians are Hindus, even if not all practice the faith in an overt way. Many bring offerings regularly to the temple and participate in ceremonies, while others acknowledge the Hindu worldview in their general philosophy of life. It is impossible to summarize the beliefs, rituals, or mythology associated with Hinduism as one might do with Islam or Christianity, since as already noted the unsystematic nature of the faith is part of its essence. One can, however, mention some of the more popular gods and practices. The chief gods are the four-headed Brahma, the Creator; the many-armed Vishnu, the Preserver; and Shiva, the Destroyer. They have female counterparts: Saraswati, Lakshmi, and Devi, respectively. A very popular god is the elephant-headed Ganesha, the remover of obstacles, of which there are many in India. These gods can appear in countless forms or avatars. Some of the best known are Lord Rama, hero of the *Ramayana,* and Krishna the playboy, both associated with Vishnu. The vast pantheon makes the faith meaningful and intelligible for ordinary people who are not ready for a more abstract interpretation. While Christianity may suffer a schism between a fundamentalist wing that interprets the scripture literally and a liberal wing that aims for a more sophisticated reading, Hinduism recognizes from the start that the faith must adapt itself to all stages of intellect and maturity.

The basic Hindu ceremony is the *puja,* which may take place in a temple or at an altar at home. It includes a mantra, or sacred recitation, and possibly a mandala, which is a sacred pattern that symbolizes some deeper aspect of the universe. There may also be music, flowers or fruits, and offerings of fire or expensive gifts. People ask me why Indian women wear a dot (*bindi*) on their foreheads and whether it is a caste indicator. Actually it is related to the *puja,* since one traditionally places a red dot on the forehead at the close of the ceremony. Married women also place the red dye in the parting of their hair, a practice that seems to be more common in the north. In recent times the *bindi* has become more adornment than religious symbol and may be worn in fashion-coordinated colors. Widows are not supposed to wear a *bindi* but may do so anyway.

The ancient literature of Hinduism remains a living aspect of the faith. If Hollywood movies and TV shows can be viewed as myth in some sense, their counterparts in India are often myth in a literal sense. Stories from the *Ramayana* and *Mahabharata* are perennial favorites in the entertainment media. A televised serialization of the *Ramayana* so mesmerized the country that everything came to a stop during the Sunday morning broadcasts.[3] Hinduism reflects the symbolic nature of Indian culture, which can be bewildering for visitors accustomed to the strongly image-based culture of the West. A visit to the holy river Ganga (Ganges) drives this home. Pilgrims flock to bathe and defecate in its polluted waters. Crematoria line the banks so that the ashes of the departed may be cast into the river. Families who cannot afford cremation may simply throw the body into the water, and it is not uncommon to see bloated corpses floating downstream. This is not a scene for a picture postcard, but it is the symbolism that matters, not the appearance. Appearances are merely figments of our own confused thinking, while symbols connect us with ultimate reality. Westerners such as myself who do not grasp the symbolism can take comfort in the fact that there are more things in heaven and earth than are dreamt of in our philosophy.

Hindus are sexually conservative. In 1996 protesters in the streets of Bangalore demonstrated against a Miss World pageant, some with self-immolation. An article I read in the Western press described this as a feminist protest against the swimsuit competition, but it was primarily a protest by religious conservatives, many of whom have no more affection for feminism than commercialized sex. While Christianity may view sex as dirty and a transmitter of original sin, Hinduism sees it as holy. It would be difficult to imagine erotic scenes on the walls of a mosque or Protestant church, but Hindu temples are often adorned with voluptuous nudes. The god Shiva is often represented by a lingam, or phallic symbol, and the god Krishna is known for stealing the clothes of young girls while they bathe. (The idea that sex is holy also occurs in Plato's dialogue *Symposium*, but this attitude disappeared with the arrival of Christianity.) Due to its sacred status, sex must not be treated casually, least of all commercialized in a beauty contest. There is no nudity in Indian movies and only a little in the way of kissing. The conservatism extends to everyday life. Outside the context of the family, men and women do not touch each other, although in Westernized circles a handshake may be appropriate if the woman offers her hand, and in some parts of India a woman may touch a man's arm during conversation. Sexual topics are unmentionable in mixed company and tend to be embarrassing in unmixed company. Some girls in Westernized enclaves may wear tight jeans, but by and large the attire for both men and women is unrevealing.

My Western students ask about Hinduism's sacred cows and its vegetarianism. I tell them that it is unclear why they should not eat dogs, but the Hindu proscription against eating beef is entirely practical. A dead cow supplies beef for a few days, but a live cow converts grass, agricultural waste, and street garbage to milk and butter for years. Its dung provides fertilizer, building material, and fuel in a land practically denuded of trees. Marvin Harris argues that the sacred cow is in fact an ecological measure that became enshrined as a religious precept.[4] As for vegetarianism, it is not a Hindu principle, although the Jains have inspired many Hindus to forswear meat.

The Jains are few in number, perhaps three or four million, but large in influence. They are famous for their thoroughgoing respect for life. They not only reject meat and leather products but also avoid agricultural occupations, which may harm worms or other creatures in the earth. Jainist monks are known for breathing and drinking through gauze so as not to ingest small organisms, and one order of monks go naked to avoid crushing tiny insects in their clothes. Most Jains are merchants or money lenders but may gravitate toward a monastic life as they get older. Jains have made important contributions to India's intellectual life, having invented the idea of zero as a placeholder in about the fifth century C.E. (simultaneously with the Maya of Mexico), and having made early advances in formal logic.

Sikhism was founded by Guru Nānak (1469–1539), partly in order to rise above the animosity between Hindu and Muslim. Ironically, Sikhs have been locked in bitter conflict with Muslims in their Punjabi homeland for centuries. The teaching of the faith was developed by a series of ten gurus, beginning with Nānak and finally recorded in a holy book, the *Guru Granth,* which is kept in the inner sanctum of a Sikh temple (*gurudwara*). Sikhs are recognizable by their distinctive turbans, which cover their neatly combed uncut hair, as well as their steel bracelets. Orthodox Sikhs do not use surnames, but men call themselves *Singh* and women call themselves *Kaur.* Sikhs do not smoke or drink alcohol, and many avoid beef. Any meat they do eat must be slaughtered in a ritually correct manner. Sikhs suffered persecution in the bloody riots following Prime Minister Indira Gandhi's assassination by a Sikh bodyguard in 1984.

This is a good point to pause and explain the institution of the guru, who is an intellectual and spiritual leader in an intellectual and spiritual culture. There is no precise parallel in the monochronic West, because a guru is expected to demonstrate wisdom across many aspects of life, not just in one specialized area. Teachers and professors are viewed as gurus and are highly respected on that basis. Indians who study in the United States are sometimes surprised and disappointed that their professors are not gurus but claim expertise only in a narrow field.

Zoroastrianism, the religion of ancient Persia, has almost vanished from the earth, but it is still practiced by the tiny Parsi community in Mumbai (Bombay) and thereabouts. The prophet Zoroaster was one of the most influential figures of world history, because he helped to formulate the very concept of world history. His vision of a cosmic conflict between good and evil leads to the idea that events can progress toward a conclusion rather than simply repeat a cycle. The Persian emperor Cyrus the Great brought Zoroastrianism to Babylon, where it influenced the Jewish people in exile. They further developed the idea of secular history and progress, which through Christianity became a foundation of Western culture. The Tata family, who bear perhaps the most famous name in Indian commerce and industry, are Parsis.

Islam came to India by way of Muslim invaders in the north (primarily Moghuls) and Muslim traders in the south. They left an indelible impression in both regions but particularly in the north. The incomparable Taj Mahal in Agra, imperial capital at the time, was built by the Turkish-speaking Moghul emperor Shah Jehan as a tomb for his wife. The Moghul empire had broken up by the mid–eighteenth century, but Muslims still constitute more than a tenth of the Indian population. Communal strife between Muslim and Hindu remains an unfortunate fact of life.

Christianity has existed in India since the earliest days of the faith. Christians make up 2 or 3 percent of the Indian population, including a quarter of Kerala state and a third of Goa, a former Portuguese colony. Roman Catholic schools make an important contribution to the educational system throughout India.

Buddhism is India's signal contribution to world spirituality. It stands to Hinduism much as Christianity stands to Judaism. In both cases a spiritual leader isolated what is universal in an ethnic religion and made it accessible to the world at large. They did so primarily by trimming away the excesses of the old faith and going back to the basics. Jesus Christ tempered the legalism and guilt of rule-based Judaism with a message of love and forgiveness. Siddharta Gautama sidestepped the hair-splitting intellectualism of Hinduism by describing a spiritual journey all could understand and undertake. Salvation is an important theme in both faiths. Christianity recognizes that people inevitably depart from God's law and make a mess of their lives, but it gives them a chance for a new beginning if they renounce their old ways. In the language of the faith, people can be saved from their sin if they repent and are "born again." Buddhism recognizes that suffering is inevitable in this life but provides an opportunity to escape it by recognizing the unreality of the world around us. Since desire binds us to this world of illusion, we must learn to renounce desire by following an eightfold path to enlightenment or nirvana.

According to tradition, Prince Gautama was born about 560 B.C.E. into a wealthy Nepalese family. His parents raised him in the confines of a luxurious palace occupied by young and beautiful people who never spoke of misfortune, death, or illness. Soon after becoming a father, however, Gautama convinced his driver to take him for an excursion out into the real world. (There is something about becoming a parent that brings one back to reality.) He saw a man debilitated by old age and another person ravaged by disease. He finally saw a corpse and realized, to his horror, that this is the fate of us all. Unable to deal with this, he left his young family and wandered for six years in search of an answer to suffering. Finally, while sitting under a *bodhi* tree (also known as a banyan or *bo* tree), the answer came to him and he became Buddha, the Enlightened One.

Buddhism, like Christianity, was seen as a threat by the religious establishment in its country of origin but has flourished elsewhere. Today Mahayana Buddhism is the dominant faith in China, Japan, Korea, Mongolia, and Vietnam, while Theravada Buddhism prevails in Cambodia, Laos, Myanmar (Burma), Sri Lanka, and Thailand. Since the 1950s B. R. Ambedkar, a spokesman for untouchables in India, has attracted a sizable number of them to Buddhism, but aside from these there are few Buddhists in India itself. Theravada Buddhism, which spread largely through the efforts of the Indian emperor Asoka, emphasizes the monastic life. Those who do not actually become monks are expected to strive for some degree of monastic discipline and support monasteries. In some areas, such as Sri Lanka and Myanmar, boys may be expected to spend some time in a monastery.[5] Mahayana, or "large vehicle," Buddhism is so called because it believes laypeople can fully participate in the faith, no less than monks. Its ideal is the bodhisattva, or saint, who stops short of nirvana to continue participating in this life and assist others on the way to enlightenment. The Japanese variety of Mahayana Buddhism is Zen, which exhibits some of the austerity of the Theravada lifestyle.

Buddhism, like Hinduism, is a deeply symbolic faith. A good illustration is the proliferation of Buddha statues throughout Asia. Raised in a Western visual culture, I was for years unable to see the point of so many Buddhas, many of which are very similar to one another. I was looking at them as I might look at a Monet or a Renoir, and the comparison was not favorable. I eventually realized that the Buddhas are symbols, not images. Every Buddha (the word is from the Sanskrit for "light") is like a flashlight sending up a beam of light, that is to say, a ray of consciousness emanating from Atman. Thousands of Buddhas scattered round the earth remind us that it is not an inert, meaningless hunk of rock and dirt. The world is infused with intelligence and therefore meaning.

Society

Indian society is based on coexistence rather than organization. Whereas Germany or Denmark may require a highly structured society in order to maintain its highly structured environment, India has no such need. The country tolerates a staggering variety of lifestyles, prompting comparisons with the United States. It is relatively easy for foreigners to blend in, despite the high-context culture.

Two mechanisms allow this highly disparate society to hang together. One is that every Indian has a well-defined place in it, a place that confers certain privileges and restrictions. Just as visitors to the West have the illusion of freedom because they do not experience the guilt internalized by Westerners, so Westerners have the illusion of freedom in India. They are not bound by social convention because they fit into no particular slot, while Indians are very much tied to their family and social background.

Caste is only a part of this picture. To begin with, there is no caste "system" in India, because there is no system of any kind in India. The word *caste* translates the Sanskrit word for "color" (*varna*), because higher castes were originally associated with light-skinned Aryans. Color still correlates somewhat with caste, but it is an unreliable indicator. The traditional castes are the Brahmins (priests and teachers), Kshatriyas (soldiers), Vaisyas (merchants and farmers), and Sudras (laborers and servants). Things are not as simple as this, however. Caste interacts with hereditary communities (*jatis*), which correspond roughly to occupations, ethnic/linguistic groups, and religious sects. By one count, there are 4,635 *jatis* in India, many of which constantly rise and fall in status.[6] Hindu *jatis* can be often regarded as subcastes, since most of them fall entirely into one caste or another. Some 134 *jatis*, however, consist of untouchables (*dalits*), who are outcastes assigned such dirty work as collecting garbage and cleaning out pit toilets by hand. *Jatis* might be roughly compared with such groups in the United States as plumbers, dock workers, public school teachers, Puerto Ricans, and even Boston Brahmins, except that it is easier to escape one's background in the United States than in India.

The law forbids discrimination on the basis of caste and *jati* distinctions, but they still play a role, particularly in rural areas. Indians with whom I have talked differ considerably on their importance. I think all would agree that they still affect one's social duty, or dharma, such as one's duty to relatives and what sort of person one can marry. There may be a fine division of labor in the workplace, since those with reputable backgrounds may consider themselves above such menial duties as filing documents, making copies, or even carrying their own briefcases. Nepotism and favoritism are always at the center of hiring, since the employer has a duty to his family, *jati*, or caste. In an effort to assist untouchables and members of lower castes, the law recognizes six "backward" castes and classes, also known as "scheduled" castes, and allocates to each a certain quota of government jobs and seats in universities. Since about 52 percent of the population belong to lower castes or are outcastes (75 percent in southern India), politicians take advantage of quotas to win votes from the scheduled castes. However, the benefit to untouchables remains limited, as they fill only about 10 percent of governmental jobs.[7] I believe it is almost impossible for foreigners to understand castes and *jatis*, not only because there are so many of them but also because their social implications are unpredictable. In my experience, at least, it has not been necessary to understand them—only to realize that they exist. In my view a much more important "caste" is the upper stratum of Westernized elites, some of whom speak only English even though they are native to India. Many live in a sheltered world and may know scarcely more about the culture around them than foreign visitors.

A second mechanism that supports Indian society is networking. Indians are the world's consummate networkers, because it is essentially the only way to get things done. A successful Indian spends a lifetime building and maintaining a vast network of extended relatives, friends, and acquaintances. When I visit with an Indian colleague, more often than not the first half hour of conversation consists of an update on who is doing what. Many of the contacts are maintained by E-mail, which is a godsend to Indian culture. Whether in India or abroad, Indians do nothing without pulling strings. One who needs a visa contacts a distant relative employed by the consulate. One who books a seat on a flight calls up a friend or relative at the airport, if possible, to make sure the seat stays booked. (It is not unusual for reserved seats on Indian Airlines to vanish due to VIP travelers or other contingencies, although the recent appearance of competition on domestic routes has resulted in somewhat better service.) In general, one who needs anything, whether it be a hotel room or a job, works through connections.

Indian networks are global in scope, which is one reason Indians are the accomplished travelers they are. They feel at home almost anywhere, partly because they have contacts almost everywhere. A second reason, already discussed, is that Indians have disciplined themselves not to rely on their environment for support. They are as comfortable in a strange airport as in their hometown. Travel is tiring but is accompanied by very little of the stress that inflicts those who rely on organized or familiar surroundings. For similar reasons, Indians can thrive as immigrants in almost any country where the winters are mild, ranging from South Africa to Australia to Malaysia.

Networking may be the primary reason that, even today, nearly all Indian marriages are arranged. The union must certainly consider the caste and *jati* of the partners, but equally important is the fact that a marriage joins two family networks. Such networks are a necessity of life in India and cannot be left to the vagaries of young love. The elaborate wedding, lasting hours or even days, reflects the social importance of the event. Friends and relatives converge on the ceremony from locations foreign and domestic. The wedding not only cements new connections but also provides guests an opportunity to renew old ones. Banners are suspended across the street to announce the event, musicians are hired, and a wedding procession may tie up traffic. At some point the beleaguered couple find themselves on a platform at the front of the room, surrounded by relatives who are seemingly there to prevent them from escaping. The climax is a rather brief ceremony in which the bride and groom circle a sacred fire seven times. The bride's family is supposed to provide a dowry, which can be substantial. At times the groom's family may demand a larger dowry after the wedding, resulting in an ugly scene.[8]

A particularly important function of networking is political stability. India's democracy, by far the world's largest, seems periodically on the brink of collapse, whether it be due to constitutional crisis or communal (i.e., religious) riots. Yet the typical crisis seems to cool off after a few weeks, with civil government intact, although political consequences may ensue. This is largely because personal and family connections reinforce the social fabric like a network of nylon cords. Violence in the streets is frightening when it occurs, but it generally subsides without rupturing the fabric. Life for most Indians is the monotony of a grinding poverty, and many crave some temporary release, perhaps in the form of street demonstrations. The riots eventually end as the demonstrators become emotionally drained. The nylon cords of the power structure weather the uprising, and life returns more or less to normal.

Stability also derives from conservatism in public affairs. No Indian with influence is going to take political action that endangers his or her hard-won network of connections, which means that change usually occurs slowly. (An exception is the economic reform of 1991.) When Prime Minister Atal Bihari Vajpayee and his Bharatiya Janata Party (BJP) came into power in 1998 on a rather alarming Hindu nationalist platform, Indians told me not to worry, because the nationalist rhetoric was only for mass consumption. They were right in the sense that mostly the same networks continued to operate after the shift in power. Some of Vajpayee's rhetoric, however, has become policy. His nuclear weapons program, for example, is wildly popular with his Hindu supporters but poses substantial risk to the nation.

Strife between Hindu and Muslim represents the most serious challenge to Indian stability. The dismantling of colonial British rule in 1947 lifted the lid on communal violence. Muhammad Ali Jinnah and his Muslim League pushed for the partition of the Indian subcontinent into a Muslim and a Hindu state. They feared that without British protection, Muslims could not be secure in a single Hindu-dominated country. India's first prime minister, Jawaharlal Nehru, although a strong supporter of a unified secular India, was obliged to go along. The result was a secular but truncated India and the new Muslim-dominated state of Pakistan, consisting of the northwestern and northeastern wings of colonial India. The name of the new country reflected its multiethnic makeup: P for Punjabi, A for Afghan, and K for Kashmiri. The suffix *stan* derives from the Farsi word for "land" and is related to the English *stay*. (The eastern part of Pakistan became Bangladesh, Land of Bengal, in 1971.) Shortly after the partition, some 20 million Muslims and Hindus fled their homes, and perhaps half a million were killed in riots. Not even Mohandas Gandhi's hunger strikes could calm the violence for long. Both Pakistan and modern India began their existence with crippled economies and bitter memories. The enmity of this period persists in periodic conflict between the two countries, as well as communal violence in India, which is home to nearly as many Muslims as is Pakistan.

A story from my experience will illustrate this and other aspects of Indian life, including its unpredictability. I happened to be working in India when, in 1992, radical Hindus demolished the deteriorating mosque in the northern Indian town of Ayodhya, in order to clear the way for a Hindu temple. Their grievance was that the mosque sat on the birthplace of Lord Rama. Nationwide rioting over the next several weeks posed what was probably the greatest threat to India's secular government since 1947. The eventual political fallout was the 1996 defeat of the venerable Congress Party. This was the party that gave birth to modern India under Gandhi's leadership and sponsored the Nehru dynasty of prime ministers: Nehru himself, his daughter Indira Gandhi, her son Rajiv Gandhi, and Rajiv's Italian widow Sonia Gandhi (who has not served as prime minister but is head of the party).[9] The victory went to Prime Minister Vajpayee and the BJP, which played a role in the mosque's destruction. At this writing the Ayodhya situation remains a powder keg.

Each morning during the period of riots I read in the newspaper how many had been shot by the local police on the previous day. The national death toll climbed into the thousands. There was talk of a *bandh* (general strike), and a number of strikes did occur. I smelled the smoke from burning buildings in riot areas, where for several days the police conducted "flag marches" to intimidate troublemakers, following an old British practice. Curfews were placed on much of the city, and I was careful about where I went shopping. By taking common-sense precautions, I was safe, but I could not use E-mail to reassure my family back home. At that time all E-mails from India passed through a single workstation in the Air India building in Mumbai. A bomb had exploded in the building and knocked out the power to the workstation.

Eventually my work was finished and it was time for me to leave India. But this required that I make my way to some city with international airline connections. The pilots were on strike at Indian Airlines, the only domestic carrier at that time. The government tried to resume air service by borrowing some Uzbekistani pilots and aircraft, which were idle due to the state of

Uzbekistan's economy. They gave up on that idea when the Uzbekistani planes began to crash upon takeoff. Trains were still being stopped by mobs, and automobile travel was even riskier. So my boss solved the problem the Indian way, by networking. He arranged for me to give a talk at the Ministry of Defense in New Delhi. This enabled me to get a VIP seat on the one remaining daily flight out of town. After giving the talk in New Delhi, I could catch an Air India flight out of the country.

The driver who met me at the airport in Delhi happened to mention that I was giving two talks that day, not one as I expected. In the afternoon I would give my prepared talk on reasoning in expert systems to a technical audience. But that morning I would give a general talk to an audience of high-ranking Defense Ministry officials. This would occur within the hour, and my mind began to race as I wondered what I would talk about. Upon arriving at the Ministry, I was ushered through security and immediately into a room containing a very long conference table. Fifty or sixty important-looking people filled the seats, except a few near the front. Suddenly everyone rose, and a few people walked in and took the seats nearest the head of the table, where I was hurriedly pulling out nontechnical transparencies I might use in the talk. Someone mentioned they were the top brass in the Ministry. As I began my speech, the microphone started to sputter, and a technician hovered below me to work on it during my entire presentation. It was clearly an occasion that called for yogic powers of concentration. I have no idea what I said in my speech, but I doubt it had much to do with their work. Nonetheless, the audience took an interest and responded with a number of astute questions. I was never more appreciative of the Indian intellectual bent.

Immediately after the talk I was taken next door into an office filled with military generals. They offered me a cup of tea and politely asked me how they could defend India from Pakistan. I am not sure what my boss told the Ministry about my background, but there was simply nothing I could say. When I apologized for my ignorance of military matters, the generals graciously changed the subject and released me after some cordial conversation. I glanced at my watch. The day was not even half over.

The Economy

Telephone service is a metaphor for the Indian economy. For decades it was notoriously unreliable. The grassroots social organization necessary to install copper wire in every building, and link it to switching systems, is not part of Indian culture. I recall watching a technician work on a hopelessly tangled mass of wires overhead and telling myself it was no wonder that I could not get my calls through. However, when Rajiv Gandhi arranged for the installation of satellite hookups, it became easier to make international calls than in parts of the United States. High-end technology is often easy to install in a country whose social organization is not amenable to older technology. Local telephone service remained poor for some time, but mobile phones are now proliferating. Again, high-end technology comes to the rescue. A few technical experts can manufacture pocket phones and install antennas to do a job that once required maintenance of a vast network.

The experience with phone service suggests a general strategy for the Indian economy. Rather than follow the traditional path of development through conventional industries and eventually to a high-end information economy, start at the high end. Skip over the industries that require social infrastructure India does not possess, and focus on the knowledge-intensive activities that can exploit India's intellectual capital. This approach was not followed until recently. Beginning with the Industrial Policy Resolution of 1956, India originally adopted a socialist plan for its economy. Heavy and strategic industries were controlled by the government, and foreign investment strictly regulated. This policy was doomed from the start. Socialism, a Western idea, requires a high degree of social organization that is possible in secular Sweden but makes no sense in pantheistic India. To make matters worse, well-connected individuals constantly abused the government's licensing power to favor themselves and exclude everyone else, particularly the poor. Change finally came in 1991, following a foreign exchange crisis, when Prime Minister P. V. Narasimha Rao oversaw a sweeping liberalization known as the New Industrial Policy. The rupee was placed on the world currency market, capital markets were created and opened to foreign investors, tariffs were reduced, and private ventures were granted entry to almost every industry. Many problems remained, since the reforms did not so much install a good system as get rid of a bad one. Nonetheless, they opened the door to a high-end strategy. The most glamorous manifestation of such a strategy is Bangalore's world-class software industry. Software development takes full advantage of India's tendency toward rigorous intellectual discipline. For eight hours a day programmers escape the chaos of the streets outside and immerse themselves in a neat, clean world of the mind. The many arms of Vishnu could not have designed an occupation more ideally suited to the culture.

The information economy taps India's reservoir of cerebral talent, and yet it requires minimal infrastructure and social organization (aside from a reliable power supply!). Favorable intellectual property law is clearly central to this strategy, and Indian business people tend to have strong opinions on the subject. It is a risky strategy in that there is little precedent elsewhere. Economic development almost always begins with the agricultural sector.

India's agriculture, although it feeds the country and embodies a good deal of ecological wisdom, remains technologically primitive and provides a meager existence to most farmers. One might also fear that a high-end strategy may serve the educated elite but continue to leave the masses behind. Yet even this is not obvious. The Simputer project, for example, has developed an inexpensive handheld computer that links with satellites to bring the information infrastructure to poor villages.[10] Perhaps this is the first step in reconceiving information technology in a way that benefits the whole of Indian society.

There are factors in India's favor other than its intellectual talents. Business and trade are inescapably global, and Indians are perfectly positioned for international business. They are urbane and well traveled, and they speak fluent English. As mentioned earlier, they are globally well connected and are as comfortable in a strange environment as at home. One commentator lists several reasons why India may provide Westerners with a more attractive investment opportunity than, say, China:

- It has a history of cooperation with foreign firms.
- It provides higher returns.
- It has a more developed legal system.
- It has a more developed financial sector.
- It has an established entrepreneurial class that understands modern business concepts and ethics, and therefore provides greater opportunities for fruitful partnerships.
- Much skilled manpower is available.
- English is widely spoken.[11]

The theme behind several of these points is that India is culturally closer to the West than China, not only because of British influence but ultimately because India and the West share a grounding in rationality.

Serious liabilities of the Indian situation include religious conflict and social barriers to advancement. The former results in political instability, which discourages investment, and the latter deprives India of a vast pool of talent. Indian culture will probably always require stratification in some form, although it may be consistent with limited social mobility based on examinations, which already occurs to some extent. Another barrier is that women have family duties, particularly to in-laws, that often prevent them from taking a job. This limits the participation of half the population in the workplace. On the other hand, it is not necessarily employers who limit the opportunities of women. They are commonly accepted as equals once they arrive at the workplace, but social obligations may prevent them from getting there. A final liability is that certain parts of the infrastructure admit no obvious high-end substitute for social organization. The most obvious case is transportation, since Indian roads are poorly maintained and dangerous, and the extensive railroads bequeathed by the British are slow and unreliable. The lack of dependable electric power obliges many industries and private homes to install expensive backup generators. Health care adequately serves only the wealthy. Behind it all is a national bureaucracy that moves at glacial speed.

Getting Things Done

The Indian bureaucracy is indeed a place where time stands still. The British set it up, as Indians like to point out, but in the Indian context it quickly became a sprawling polychronic organization where personalities and connections are far more important than tasks and functions. At times it can be remarkably corrupt. In his excellent book *Chasing the Monsoon,* Alexander Frater tells of an appropriation of money that was approved in New Delhi to upgrade the sewers of Kolkata (Calcutta).[12] As the money worked its way down through the system to Kolkata, bureaucrats at every level took a cut of the action. By the time the appropriation reached its destination, nothing was left. I myself have heard similar anecdotes.

The best way to get anything done in the bureaucracy, or anywhere else, is to work through connections. These are often based on the extended family and in-laws, on professional relationships, or a chaining together of the two. One reason foreign business people commonly set up joint ventures in India, despite the pitfalls, is to tap into a network of connections. Businesses that go it alone can work through a professional go-between, such as the Federation of Indian Chambers of Commerce and Industries (FICCI), a well-established bank, a foreign consulting firm with branches in India, or the U.S.-India Business Council.[13]

India can be a land of frustration. Some readers may have lived through the exasperation of hiring a contractor to install a new kitchen in one's home. Workers show up when they feel like it, needed fixtures are out of stock, mistakes must be reworked, and a two-week job takes six months. If this experience is multiplied by a factor of four or five, one has some idea of what it is like to operate in India. Watching a project take shape is like watching a tree grow. It is best not to think about how long it takes. This again is not because Indians are lazy or sloppy, even if some are. It is because the culture accommodates stress-management needs in other ways than providing an orderly environment.

The best way to deal with frustration is to exercise patience and persistence. Americans, raised in a land of consumerism, generally respond to delays by getting huffy and demanding service. This is precisely the wrong approach. The more demanding one gets, the more the bureaucrats dig in.

One must be patient but persistent. Keep coming back, keep explaining what you need, always politely but insistently. If one person offers no help, try someone else. Indians are very good at this sort of thing, and it is instructive to observe them in action. Imitating them may require yoga-like mental discipline and detachment, but this is what India is all about.

An alternative method of getting things done is to make side payments. There are actually two kinds of side payments in India, which are sometimes difficult to distinguish. One is the facilitating payment, which is a small amount of cash collected by functionaries for routine service. I have been told that even postal clerks may ask for a side payment when they sell stamps, although this has never happened to me. Government and other employees say they rely on these payments to supplement an inadequate salary, and in any case they think they deserve the money. It is essentially a method of self-financing the bureaucracy, which has historically been used in the West as well. It was standard procedure in the Roman Empire, for example. Facilitating payments are capriciously and unevenly collected, but they are more of an irritation than a serious corruption. Indians do not necessarily see them as unethical, since they can be viewed as a minor income-leveling device.

A far more insidious practice is the payment of large bribes or kickbacks to influence a decision or policy. One hears widely differing accounts of their prevalence, although such public scandals as the 1995 "Hawala" affair, in which a businessman kept a diary of more than $30 million (U.S.) in bribes to government officials, reassure us that corruption is alive and well. Foreign business also has a soiled record, as represented by alleged Enron payments to Indian officials in the 1990s to push through a power plant in Dabhol that would have substantially raised electricity rates. Enron also reportedly tried to pay an Indian journalist $1 million (U.S.) a year to silence his criticism.[14] Despite such incidents, Douglas Bullis offers the opinion that India relies less on bribery and kickbacks than does most of Asia.[15] In any event, Indians regard influence-purchasing bribes as unequivocally wrong, however common they may be, and one should feel no compunction to "go along" with the culture by paying them. No essential Indian cultural practice rests on this kind of bribery. Most seasoned business people advise that foreigners should never pay bribes, because once the honey jar is opened, the flies start to buzz. Since payments to government officials are illegal, one should never mention bribery in E-mail or written documents, even if there is no intention to engage in it. One may have no control over what one's Indian associates are doing, but it is good policy to work with associates who belong to prominent families or well-connected companies, so that bribery is unnecessary.

Much of what one achieves in India is arranged through negotiation. One can expect Indian negotiators to be astute and on top of all the details. They have weathered countless grueling examinations in their school careers and know what it means to be prepared. Indians who want to get ahead are sometimes prone to flattery and obsequiousness, and these may surface in negotiations. Be warned that behind the pleasant exterior lies a savvy camel trader. In general, however, Indian professionals tend to operate in the same conceptual universe as Westerners, partly because they have absorbed considerable Western influence. They understand Western concepts of accounting, efficiency, and the bottom line. They are comfortable with spreadsheets and other computer-based tools for management. Although they live in a high-context culture, they draw up careful and detailed contracts. They take advantage of a sophisticated albeit sluggish court system. They are interested in technology and innovation. Unlike most Asians, they view professional life basically as an endeavor to accomplish specific tasks in a rational way rather than a world of personal relationships, although relationships play an important role as a source of connections. Relationships are also a source of mutual trust, as they are elsewhere in Asia, but this role is secondary in India and operates in a specifically Indian way. The trust relationship is based primarily on dharma or culturally based obligations to relatives, rather than on a history of mutual favors as in Chinese *guānxì,* or on long-term camaraderie as in Japanese old-boy relationships.

Intellectual property rights are flagrantly violated in India, particularly in entertainment media and software. I have heard Indians mutter that although their compatriots may sell pirated CDs, this only compensates for international intellectual property conventions that are stacked against developing nations. Whatever the case, the Indian situation is changing rapidly. Changes made in 1994–95 to India's copyright law made it one of the world's strictest with respect to software. Indians are well aware that if they are to excel in intellectual property, they must have a well-developed legal environment in which to regulate it. Foreigners concerned about intellectual property rights should stay abreast of these developments and take advantage of them.

Managing Stress

Indians cope primarily on the basis of their distinctive worldview. Students of yoga and meditation may find themselves somewhat better prepared for India, even if much practice and discipline are required to absorb a perspective that Indians take for granted. I find it useful simply to practice being patient before going to India, perhaps while stuck in a traffic jam or waiting in a long checkout line. I mentally back away from the situation and think about something other than what I want to get done. This simple maneuver is actually a small step toward nirvana. I can hone similar skills when dealing with sluggish bureaucracies or surly clerks. This not only prepares me for travel but also lowers my blood pressure while at home. One must not expect immediate results, however. As with any skill, practice, practice, practice is necessary.

The Indian strategy of networking can also be put to good use, and it can start long before one leaves home. Professional business in India is usually initiated through Indians abroad, who can provide a starting point for one's Rolodex. Almost any person of Indian ancestry, anywhere in the world, has active contacts in the home country.

Another strategy is to follow the Indian practice of hiring servants who can invest time in overcoming the many obstacles of daily life. They can be full-time, live-in servants or part-timers. I have never availed myself of this option, and I cannot provide pointers on finding and supervising domestic help. There is definitely an art to it, and one should seek the assistance and advice of Indian friends before taking the plunge.

The key to stress management is to train oneself not to rely on the physical environment for comfort, convenience, or anything else. Many Westerners, for example, are accustomed to convenience at every turn. They can drop into a fast-food place for a quick meal, or stop by the supermarket to pick up something for the microwave. They can go anywhere they want with reasonable safety by hopping in the car. They take for granted such things as potable water at the tap, a telephone that works, air conditioning, and power that rarely goes out. Westerners have these conveniences because they need them. In India, they must try to overcome this need. Rather than fret over the lack of infrastructure, they must transform their perspective on life.

Several of India's stress-management techniques (listed in table 10.1) are available to outsiders, such as networking, rationality, and temporary

TABLE 10.1
Stress-Management Mechanisms in India

Mechanism	Contribution to Stress Management
Pantheistic worldview	Ability to rise above chaos and uncertainty of the phenomenal world; cultivation of patience and mental discipline; lack of reliance on one's surroundings
Rationality	Mental discipline that takes the form of intellectual development, which provides a sense of control and has become economically beneficial
Religion (primarily Hinduism, Jainism, Sikhism, Islam, Christianity, Parsi)	Assurance; coherent worldview; predictability of ritual
Networking; family	Ability to get things done; help in time of need
Mythic tales; music and dance; movies	Momentary escape from harsh reality

escape through music or literature. Religious visitors should feel free to practice their faith as well. The pantheistic approach to life, however, may require a much more fundamental adaptation.

Languages

The Indian government recognizes fourteen official Indian languages: Assamese, Bengali, Gujarati, Hindi, Kashmiri, Marathi, Malayalam, Oriya, Punjabi, Sanskrit, Sindhi, Tamil, Telagu, and Urdu. At least ten additional languages are each spoken by more than a million people. English is also recognized as an official language, is widely spoken, and is the medium of business and higher education. Many Indians are remarkably fluent in English, more so than many native English speakers. Others speak the language with idiosyncratic diction and syntax as well as an accent, although I have never had real problems with comprehension, except when listening to announcements in the airport. I often cannot tell whether the announcer is speaking in English or Hindi. In fact, it is common in northern India for people to speak "Hinglish," randomly combining words from both languages. This occurs even on TV and in advertisements.

India is the only country in which I have worked without trying to learn a local language, aside from countries whose native tongue is English. This was partly because of the prevalence of English in India, and partly because I spent most of my time in southern India, where Hindi is not often spoken or well received. Hindi is ordinarily the obvious language to learn, certainly in the north, where it is widely used and mixed with English. Southerners, however, speak such languages as Kannada, Malayalam, Tamil, and Telagu, which are non-Indo-European and difficult for Westerners to learn, partly because some of the sounds are indistinguishable to Western ears. It is not unusual, however, for educated Indians to speak several local languages, having learned them from servants when they were children.

Two words that all foreigners must learn right away are *lakh* and *crore*. A *lakh* is 100,000, and a *crore* is 10 million. These words are invariably used to count rupees, or anything else that comes in large numbers.

Etiquette and Lifestyle

Professional meetings in India are normally informal, except perhaps at high levels. Indians tend to be cordial and easy to get along with. They are comfortable with foreigners, particularly Westerners. There are usually no elaborate courtesies or formalities to observe. It suffices to exercise ordinary politeness and consideration for others. Indians are expert hosts and know how to smooth over any awkwardness on the part of visitors. (Formalities may be observed in settings where foreigners are unlikely to be present. For example, one's Indian counterparts probably show respect to their parents by kneeling to touch their feet on every visit home.)

The standard professional attire for men is a white long-sleeved shirt and tie with slacks, although it is extremely common to skip the tie or wear other colors. Short sleeves are rarely worn, and short pants never, even in the hottest weather. This is partly due to a natural inclination to modesty, and partly because the temperature often rises above human body temperature. On such occasions long sleeves and long pants help insulate one from the heat. A coat may be worn by highly ranked officials, in formal situations, or when it is chilly. The smart-looking Nehru shirt is also popular, particularly for older men, although a foreigner would look a bit ridiculous in one of these.

The sari (also *sadi*) and other traditional garments remain the norm for Indian women. This is presumably because they indicate a woman's social status, and perhaps because they are also quite practical and comfortable. The sari, for example, is a one-size-fits-all garment, although I understand that Brahmin women wear saris that contain more cloth. The Punjabi outfit, with its loose pants, seems to be popular because it strikes a compromise between a Western and Indian look. Foreign women generally wear what they would wear at work back home. It is never appropriate to wear a revealing outfit, such as a sleeveless or low-cut blouse, shorts, or a short skirt. Foreign women should not try to don Indian garb. An interesting contrast with Western tastes is that fat is fashionable in India, at least traditionally. The sari seems designed to reveal an ample midriff.

Indian names have something in common with castes and *jatis:* they are essentially impossible for foreigners to understand. Some Indians list their given name before their surname, Western-style. Others, particularly in the south, use their village name as their first name, their father's given name as their middle name, and their given name last. The first two names may be written as initials. Or the first name may be the father's name. Still others have a surname that indicates a title or membership in a certain caste; their fellow Indians can decipher the code. Sikh men usually take the surname Singh, but not all Singhs are Sikhs. Married women often adopt their husband's surname. Titles of respect are used with the given name; some of my students from India call me Professor John. Indian names can also be quite long or difficult to pronounce. The key is to break them down into parts, which frequently refer to gods or goddesses. Indians are good natured about their long names and very often adopt nicknames to make things easier. If one is not sure what to call another, it is perfectly all right to ask.

Indians love to entertain and are accomplished at the art. Visitors will almost certainty be invited to dinner parties at private homes. One should not be surprised if the guests include high-ranking government officials, diplomats, or even movie stars. It is imperative to arrive at least a half hour late, and some of the guests may show up two or three hours later, perhaps after making appearances at another party or two. Standard procedure is to drink and converse until about 11 p.m., begin the meal, and say good-bye very soon thereafter. The meal itself may be buffet style or a sit-down dinner. I make it a practice to eat snacks before going to a party, so I do not faint from hunger. One need not fear an evening of inane chitchat. Indians are engaging conversationalists, and many are widely traveled and widely read. The conversation may delve into such substantive issues as political theory or even philosophy, on which one can generally feel free to express one's views. Enjoy it. If the topic of India and its problems comes up, however, it is best for visitors to listen in silence. Indians do not consider foreigners qualified to hold forth on the Indian situation, and they are usually right.

The late dinner hour may be due to the fact that no one wants to start cooking until well after dark, when some of the daytime heat has dissipated. It is well worth the wait. Partaking of home-cooked Indian fare is one of the great pleasures of this life. Servants and female family members hover over the guest, offering irresistible second and third helpings. One should note that although some Indian dishes are "hot," as they are reputed to be, many are only intensely flavored. If in distress, one should reach for the yogurt, which has a protective quality. It is important to resist the temptation to overeat, because the spices place a burden on the alimentary system. It is one thing to dine occasionally in an Indian restaurant back home, and quite another to sustain an exotic diet three meals a day. It is a good idea for newcomers to eat bland meals whenever possible to give their systems a rest.

My favorite dish is the southern Indian lunch, a vegetarian *thali* (Hindi for "plate"). It is served on a round stainless-steel platter with a rim, with several round steel containers of scrumptious vegetables and *raita* (seasoned yogurt with cucumber, etc.) arranged around the periphery of the plate. Rice is piled in the middle. On the side is a huge *dosai* (crepe) and two steel bowls for the *sambhar* and *rasam* dips. There may be sweets for dessert, but this and most Indian meals end with a handful of anise-flavored fennel seeds (*saunf*). The proper way to eat *thali* is with one's fingers, and water and towel are provided both before and after the meal. One scoops up vegetable and rice with fingertips and thumb to make a bite-sized morsel. As at any meal, one should never use the left hand, which is considered unclean. Since foreigners tend to make a mess, they may be provided utensils, or everyone may use them in the presence of a guest so as not to appear Third Worldish to Western eyes. This is vegetarian fare at its finest. In much of the West, cooks seem to regard vegetables as vitamin pills and make them even less enjoyable to ingest. Being a vegetarian in India, however, is no sacrifice whatever.

Indian arts and theater reflect the diversity of the nation. One can experience Shakespeare and Shaw as well as a number of repertories in indigenous languages. Music and dance are a functional part of traditional life and ritual, as Marxist critics of Western art like to recommend, and outsiders cannot fully appreciate them. The best dance companies, however, put on performances that are skilled enough to transcend some of the cultural boundaries. The squeaky singers of Indian popular music can become tiresome, but the nation's classical music is complex and highly developed. It is also quite popular in its own right, particularly in the south. It is often said that music is the universal language, a very Western remark, even though this is totally untrue. Indian classical music is unintelligible to the uninitiated ear. Yet after sufficient study and listening, Westerners, particularly those with musical training, can come to understand some aspects of the music, just as they can grasp some aspects of Indian culture in general. One must start by realizing that Indian classical music is primarily about rhythm, which is much more complex than Western rhythms and based on mathematical relationships, as befits an intellectual culture. Also, it has not a trace of romanticism, which Westerners will miss. The music is to a large extent improvised and has been aptly compared with American jazz. It is played according to one or another classical form that dictates the overall structure and meter. A common pattern is a theme and variations that gradually increase in force and complexity until reaching a climax at the end. The rhythms often accompany familiar tunes, and some members of the audience may quietly hum along. Listeners may also tap their fingers in a certain way, which is not only good etiquette but also, if they know how to do it, indicates a sophisticated appreciation of the music.

We can be thankful that a nation of a billion people prefer their own cinema to Hollywood. The Indian movie industry is said to produce more films than the American one, a fact I have never been able to confirm but that seems plausible. In a land centered on family and religion, it is no surprise that most Indian movies deal with family conflict and resolution, or stories from the religious epics. There are countless Romeo and Juliet stories, which invariably contain an otherworldly scene in which the boy and girl sing to each other. In recent years, violent gang movies have also begun to appear. The situations and plotlines of Indian films are unrealistic, but this is the point. They provide escape for masses of people who will see quite enough reality when they leave the theater.

This brings me back to the inescapable fact that countless Indians do not enjoy the lifestyle I have described here. The poverty is massive, and visitors are confronted with it every day. They see it in the streets, and as if this were not enough, they are hounded by beggars. Many respond to the situation by giving alms, which is entirely appropriate if one knows the etiquette of almsgiving. Nothing should be offered until one is about to leave the scene, to avoid being mobbed. It is also important to give the right amount, which one can discern by carefully watching the behavior of Indian companions. The proliferation of beggars is evidence many Indians give them money. One may complain that generosity only perpetuates beggary, but no one has pointed out to me a realistic alternative for these people.

For many outsiders, including myself, the juxtaposition of affluence and extreme poverty is the most difficult aspect of India to deal with. This may say as much about the Western guilt complex as about the Indian situation, but in any event it is a burden that constantly weighs upon one's mind. Some may view middle-class Indians as callous for tolerating such misery in plain view. I have no easy answer to this challenge, except to observe that many Indians work tirelessly to better the lot of the poor, karma notwithstanding. There is also a deeper issue at stake. As the Buddha taught, suffering and sorrow are the essence of life as we know it. Indians do not kid themselves about this. They know at some level that whether one lives in a Delhi slum or a Beverly Hills estate, suffering and death are inevitable. Attempts to keep them out of sight accomplish nothing but denial. Technical fixes ultimately fail. The harsh and visible realities of India force this truth upon us. We are compelled to deal with life authentically, as Siddharta Gautama did twenty-five centuries ago.

Notes for Chapter 10

1. John Keay, *India: A History,* Atlantic Monthly Press (New York, 2000), 19–21.

2. Ibid., 20.

3. Gitanjali Kolanad, *Culture Shock: India,* Graphic Arts Publishing Company (Portland, Oreg., 2000), 57.

4. Marvin Harris, *Cows, Pigs, Wars and Witches: The Riddles of Culture,* Vintage Books (New York, 1989, orig. published 1974).

5. David A. Rausch and Carl H. Voss, *World Religions: Our Quest for Meaning,* Fortress Press (Minneapolis, 1989), 77.

6. Manoj Joshi, *Passport India,* World Trade Press (San Rafael, Calif., 1997).

7. Douglas Bullis, *Doing Business in Today's India,* Quorum Books (Westport, Conn., 1998), 22–23.

8. Kolanad, pages 88–89.

9. The name Gandhi reflects Indira's marriage to the distinguished statesman Feroze Gandhi, who was unrelated to Mohandas Gandhi.

10. Available: http://www.simputer.org.

11. Joshi, 52.

12. Alexander Frater, *Chasing the Monsoon*, Knopf (New York, 1991).

13. Joshi, 53–54.

14. CBS News, 60 *Minutes* (April 14, 2002).

15. Bullis, 209.

11 The West

For the last half millennium or so, human history has increasingly assumed the character of an encounter between the West and the rest of the world. Western adventurism began with the Greek and Roman empires but took on new dimensions during the sixteenth-century colonization of the Americas. It reached China and Japan by the nineteenth century and today envelops the globe. There is scarcely a person in the world whose life is not profoundly affected by Western political, cultural, and economic influences. In a real sense it is impossible to understand the current state of any culture without understanding its infiltration by the West.

The West is an awkward term, and I wish there were another. My students ask, west of what? Perhaps west of Istanbul, at least historically, since Western cultures originated in Europe. Chapter 1 defines the West to include Europe's cultural offspring, such as Australia, Canada, New Zealand, and the United States. Western cultures obviously exhibit enormous variety, but a major thesis of this book is that they have something in common. They share a cluster of mutually supporting traits that center around universalizing rationality. The pattern is perhaps less clear in portions of the West that are heavily influenced by adjacent cultures, such as parts of southern and eastern Europe. It is weak in some social strata and nearly absent in some ethnic subcultures. Nonetheless, there is a strong common thread that ties all Western cultures together. Naturally many individuals do not fit the pattern, but as Chapters 4 and 7 explain, the primary aim of cultural analysis is to describe the structural traits of a culture viewed as a system, not the personalities within it. The present chapter attempts to sketch the historical sources of the West's distinctive traits and to explain how they interacted to create a civilization that, for better or worse, drives world history today.

Origins

Western culture resulted from the merger of two great cultural streams: the rationalistic tradition of the classical Hellenistic world and the Judeo-Christian religious heritage. Ancient Greece anticipated the West's reliance on reason, and Judaism provided through Christianity a religious foundation for its secularism. The resulting civilization germinated in the soil of Etruscan, Celtic, Nordic, and other early cultures of the European continent.

I say much about Western rationality, but this in no way implies that the West has reached a higher level of intellectual achievement than other cultures. All advanced civilizations have spawned intellectual elites, and it is unnecessary for present purposes to decide who is more advanced than whom and who borrowed from whom. I suggest only that universalizing rationality is more important for getting ordinary folks through the day in the West than elsewhere. Its rational-technological approach is perhaps most evident in a personal crisis. A cancer victim, for example— particularly one in a more affluent class—is likely to become a walking encyclopedia of diagnostic tests, chemotherapies, and well-regarded oncologists. To be sure, people in many cultures call on some kind of medical technology for relief, such as herbal medicine, massage, or purification. The Western difference is not only a greater reliance on technique but also its purely secular nature and its grounding in a universal, reductive science.

A similar approach extends to all areas of life. If oil reserves run low, the response is to research alternative fuels and develop more efficient transport, rather than to change lifestyles. If the economy is stagnant, complex macroeconomic equilibration models are formulated and then solved by computers. An enormous infrastructure of scientists and laboratories is built to support such efforts. The West has become more adept at applying science and technology than other cultures, not because its population has a higher average IQ, but because it clings to them for salvation. Chapter 6 observed that Westerners enhance their sense of security by engineering their environment, and by measuring and structuring time, thereby producing the world's only truly monochronic societies. Order, reason, and technology stand between the Westerner and despair.

This characteristic is rooted in twenty-five centuries of cultural history. The West is not what it is because it has technology. It has technology because of what it is: a culture that derives assurance from its analytical approach to nature and secular worldview. The West's love affair with secular and universal science traces to the natural philosophers of ancient Greece, as briefly recounted in the previous chapter. The Greeks increasingly saw the world as a mechanism that mortals can comprehend by virtue of their rational faculty. Reason is not only our window on the universe, but it constitutes the very essence of humanity and is therefore our primary and most characteristic tool for coping. The identification of humanity with its rational faculty has persisted in the West through the ages, as witnessed by Descartes' famous cogito and today's metaphysical concern that computers that "think" well enough may someday be regarded as human. Western literature acknowledges the centrality of reason in some of its earliest expressions. As Sophocles has Haimon say in the ancient Greek tragedy *Antigone*, "The gods implant reason in men, the highest of all things that we call our own."

The universe is not only an intelligible mechanism but also one that mortals can manipulate. This secularism, which opened the door to technology, did not flower until the Renaissance but is implicit in the Judeo-Christian worldview. Judaism itself may owe much to Egyptian and Mesopotamian influence. The descendants of Abraham were exposed to both civilizations over a period of several centuries and, due to a strong sense of nationhood and historical continuity, sufficiently preserved elements of both to bring them together in a creative alchemy. A nascent form of monotheism in Egyptian theology combined with the Sumerian idea of law to form, gradually, the notion of a transcendent deity, Jahweh, who is both Creator and Lawgiver. Jahweh was originally Abraham's household god. But since Jahweh is moral judge, then to the extent that morality is universal, Jahweh must be a God for the entire universe. Conversely, to the extent that Jahweh is the One God, morality must be universal. Monotheism and the universality of morals therefore tend to reinforce each other.

This partially accounts for the universalizing morality of the West and Islam, one of the most distinctive and some would say the most exasperating traits of the two cultures. A universalizing society can be expected to proselytize infidels or send colonial missionaries to convert pagans—or in recent times to dispatch neoclassical economists from the World Bank, or management consultants to teach Western business practices. In fact, a missionary appeared as early as the Old Testament and Koranic figure of Jonah,[1] whom God sent abroad to the great city of Nineveh. Jonah was to warn its inhabitants to repent from their wicked and violent ways, lest they be overthrown by an enemy. When Jonah refused to go, he ended up in the belly of the famous whale.

Jonah's Hebrew culture believed that Nineveh's behavior was its business because the laws of Jahweh are universal. Today, a universalizing culture can be expected to shake its finger at societies that are insufficiently environmentalist, feminist, or human rights oriented, or if Islam is shaking the finger, too feminist and too fixated on rights and freedom at the expense of faith and family values. Note how the West tends to assume that its own concerns of the moment should be everyone's concerns. After populating four continents with abandon (Europe, North America, South America, Australia), Westerners eventually sensed the danger of overpopulation. At this point they began to chide other nations about high growth rates that they themselves were quite content to produce in earlier years. After their industrial economy despoiled and polluted the earth to an extent unprecedented in world history, Westerners finally became environmentally aware and promptly advised "developing" nations to give environmental-ism top priority. A similar history characterizes worker rights. Only in the last few decades have Westerners developed a feminist perspective, but when they finally did so they lost little time turning their gaze on the rest of the world, urging governments to drop everything else until they implement women's rights.

The West does at least impose on itself many of the same universal oblig-ations it assigns to others. The much-discussed American ethicist Peter Singer argues that Westerners have the same obligation to save anonymous children in Somalia as they would to save a drowning child 20 feet away.[2] His view is not eccentric, since Western nations dispatch foreign aid, as well as their own sons and daughters in uniform, for humanitarian purposes.

A closer look at the story of Jonah reveals a second fundamental West-ern trait. When God sent him on a mission to correct Nineveh's wicked ways, Jonah not only balked, but he got on board a ship headed in the op-posite direction. Obviously troubled, he confided to the sailors that he was fleeing God's command and could become a liability for them. Before long a fierce gale arose and nearly capsized the ship, and the crew began to ask why this fate had befallen them. The Hebrew text says that they cast lots to learn who was responsible, and the lot fell upon Jonah. Jonah reiterated his confession and urged the sailors to throw him overboard and save them-selves. Reluctantly they obliged, the storm subsided, and Jonah was swal-lowed by the whale, allowing him to survive in an air pocket inside the animal. The lesson of this story is that Jonah was tortured by guilt, not shame. He confessed his transgression to the sailors before they even sus-pected him. He was running from himself and his guilty conscience, not from the censure of others. As Chapter 7 notes, Western cultures rely to a great degree on guilt to enforce an internalized code of behavior, and Jonah symbolizes the guilt complex Westerners must endure.

Another key development in religious consciousness was to occur, how-ever, before the embryonic Judaic faith was brought to term. It is symbol-ized by the story of the burning bush. As it is told in the Hebrew scripture, Moses came upon a bush that was aflame but was somehow not consumed. He demanded that the spirit within the fire give its name.[3] The request was perhaps based on the traditional belief, common around the world, that calling a thing by its name gives one some power over it. The principle sur-vives to this day in the Roman Catholic practice of exorcism (literally, the "calling out" of a spirit by name), and even in the fact that salespeople are taught to call their customers by name as often as possible. The spirit in the bush, however, refused to divulge its name, saying only something to the effect that "I am Who I am" (Exodus 3:14). This is the origin of the term *Jahweh,* which is the result of adding certain vowel marks to the Hebrew consonants that spell the words from the bush. In Semitic languages, only consonants are written as letters; diacritical marks indicate the vowels.

Scholars differ over the interpretation of God's response, but it can be read as heralding the birth of secularism. God must refuse to identify Himself, since otherwise Moses could control nature by invoking a spirit by name, as peoples had done for ages. The God of the Hebrews is not a spirit that indwells nature, but a transcendent Creator and Judge. The pantheism of Hindu philosophy is ruled out. Nature is disenchanted and left to the devices of humankind. This clears the way for something new under the sun: the possibility of controlling and manipulating nature as a mechanism on the human level. In a very real sense, Calcutta and Copenhagen are like different planets because Moses saw a burning bush.

Christianity was the agent that brought Jewish secularism to the West. It began as a sect of Judaism that adapted itself to the Hellenistic world. It passed along Judaism's moral universalism, which reinforced Greek scientific universalism, but it performed an even more distinctive service: because it took spiritual forces out of the world around us, it cleared the way for Greek rationality to manipulate as well as to understand nature.

Again, the development of manipulative science was gradual. The classical world, as represented by Aristotle, recognized four *aitia* (types of scientific explanation): material, formal, teleological, and efficient "causation." Over the centuries scientific explanation has become virtually synonymous with the last, which is causation in the familiar sense of cause and effect. It is the most conducive to manipulating nature, because one can control the effect by controlling the cause. The other types of explanation are equally legitimate, and something very like teleological explanation has recently appeared in ecological science. Yet the Western technological imperative has kept the efficient cause in the forefront.

A problem with secularism is that it leaves the world disenchanted, a lump of dead matter, aside from living organisms whose possibility has always puzzled Westerners. Individual human beings become lonely islands of consciousness surrounded by forces of nature. A romantic reaction eventually developed, encompassing both the cult of the individual and the reinvestment of meaning in a sublime natural world. The West's environmentalism and wilderness values, its fascination with animals and the natural environment, and its anthropomorphism toward pets of little practical value are all manifestations of romanticism. The tourist industry around the world has learned to offer affluent Western tourists nature parks and game preserves, and eco-tourism has exploded in popularity. Countless Western TV shows focus on animal behavior, scenic landscapes, and natural science. There is a craving for outdoor recreation in wilderness areas, including fishing and hunting for food one does not need. People journey to campgrounds just to live in a tent and cook over a fire, activity that most of the world would judge insane when one has a comfortable home with a gas range. I asked my students to note which professors took their classes outdoors during beautiful spring weather. Although our faculty is highly multicultural, I predicted that every group sitting on the grass would be instructed by a Westerner. So far there have been no counterexamples.

The Jewish View of History

Another symbolic legacy of the burning bush is the Jewish conception of history, which the West has inherited. It is the view that history is in fact historical. It is a story with a beginning, middle, and end, rather than, say, an endless cycle that ultimately goes nowhere. God can act in history, but since human beings are given a good deal of control over the secular realm, they become part of an epic drama whose script they themselves help to write. This idea, as noted earlier, may have originated from exposure to Zoroastrianism during the Jewish exile in Babylon.

The historical drama assumes central importance in Jewish consciousness. Their deliverance from Egypt, their sojourn in the wilderness, their exile in Babylon become parts of a moral saga that explains their purpose on Earth. Recent events in the Middle East may strike outsiders as merely the ebb and flow of political fortune, but they take on cosmic significance for both Palestinians and Jews. An outcome seen as fulfillment, such as the establishment of an ethnic homeland, gives meaning to their history and therefore to life itself. However a historical narrative without culmination reduces their existence to pointlessness and absurdity, like that of the characters in Samuel Beckett's *Waiting for Godot*. This perspective may help explain some of the intransigence of factions in the Middle East.

The Jewish sense of history lays the foundation for the Western idea of progress, which is the view that history can, if properly managed, advance toward a more desirable state of affairs. This view is echoed again and again in Western philosophies, ranging from Hegel's historical dialectic to Teilhard de Chardin's Omega Point. The idea that history is moving toward socialism (Marx), democratic capitalism (Fukuyama),[4] or some other kind of higher state profoundly shaped events of the last century. It lies behind the assumption that nations ascend a single developmental ladder. Westerners who travel abroad, however, should be prepared for a view of history as static or beyond significant human control.

The Jewish interpretation of history gives rise to a distinctive stress-control mechanism that sheds further light on recent events in the Middle East. Since history is partially given over to human control, we cannot rely entirely on divine intervention for security. At some point we must take charge and redirect history. This leads to a radical activism that is characteristic of the region, symbolized by the famous 1976 Israeli raid on Entebbe. Hijackers forced an Air France jet to land at the Ugandan city and threatened to start killing Israeli hostages on board. The Israeli government responded by immediately dispatching a risky but successful commando raid across a 2,000-mile distance. Decisive action of this kind, successful or not, relieves stress. Some Israelis told me recently that they rarely felt more secure than when Iraqi-launched Scud missiles were falling on their country during the 1991 Gulf War. The reason, they said, is that the population was totally mobilized during this period. Authorities were passing out gas masks, civilians were huddled in shelters, and soldiers filled the streets. Because people were taking action, they felt more in control.

Westerners inherited the action-oriented approach, but they typically combine it with technological restructuring of the environment, which provides assurance even when no action is being taken. This avoids a difficulty with a purely action-based response, namely, that there may not be any immediate steps one can take in a given situation. One may respond impetuously simply to relieve the stress. The recent threat posed by Palestinian suicide bombers, for example, put Israelis in the highly stressful position of simply waiting for the next attack. Since the stress could be relieved only by immediate and decisive action, Israel launched preemptive military operations against Palestinians. Without taking a position on the political issues of the region, one can observe that these operations were perhaps temporarily reassuring to Israelis but may in fact exacerbate the situation in the long run.

More generally, the action-oriented approach to stress relief may reinforce the cycle of violence in the Middle East. Every lull in the unrest can generate stress so severe that someone feels compelled to take action to relieve it, thus recharging the cycle. As peace is more nearly achieved, it becomes more difficult to maintain.

Max Weber and the West

The German sociologist Max Weber (1864–1920) is one of the most astute analysts of Western culture on record. He recognized the central role of rationality in the West and identified cultural factors behind the rise of Western capitalism. His account of the latter is found in his celebrated book *The Protestant Ethic and the Spirit of Capitalism*, which is by far his best-known contribution, even if it is perhaps less convincing than his treatment of Western rationality.

I happened to visit the small, quiet German city of Augsburg while it was celebrating its founding by Caesar Augustus 2,000 years earlier in 5 B.C.E. The city was of little historical consequence until something of global significance began to occur there in the last quarter of its long life. As much as any spot in the world, Augsburg can claim to be the birthplace of Western-style capitalism. By the fifteenth century, industries were raising private capital to finance mining, textile, banking, and other enterprises in Augsburg as well as Nuremberg, Antwerp, Venice, and other European cities. Such wealthy Augsburg families as the Fuggers even financed the Habsburg government of the day, in exchange for precious metals from imperial mines. One of Augsburg's most successful products was fustian, a fabric of blended cotton and flax. It was produced by small-town weavers in a putting-out system that characterized much of early European industry.[5]

The historical significance of Augsburg leads us to Weber's fundamental question about capitalism. Why did the multinational, wealth-generating behemoth that so dominates the world today begin in Augsburg and thereabouts? Why not Shanghai or Jakarta? Weber recognized economic and historical factors, but he thought there must be a cultural reason that industrial capitalism arose and continued to prosper in the heart of Europe.

Fukuyama, as we saw in Chapter 3, offers an explanation based on spontaneous sociability. The rule-based culture of Europe, when freed from the yoke of an authoritarian government, permitted a high-trust culture to flourish. This led to the formation of voluntary associations and in particular the accumulation of capital through private corporations. Fukuyama's explanation is a plausible one for later times, but in its early days Augsburgian industry was financed primarily through loans from family members, much as is done in China today, rather than through joint stock ownership—even if in keeping with a rule-based system, family investors would file their claims in bankruptcy court along with everyone else if the firm went under. Fukuyama might respond that Augsburg's early merchant capitalism would in retrospect be no more remarkable than that of Mogadishu or Tashkent if the great European corporations had not followed. Yet Weber believed another factor was at work even before the rise of corporations: the Protestant work ethic.

Weber's specific explanation is admittedly a bit strained. He pointed to John Calvin's Protestant theology, which has been well received in some of the most enthusiastically capitalist societies. According to the Calvinist doctrine of predestination, God chooses in advance who will be saved from eternal damnation. Weber's theory, in a nutshell, is that Protestants are uneasy about their salvation and look for signs that they are among the elect. Since earthly prosperity is taken as a positive sign, Protestants work hard to succeed and thus reassure themselves.

Weber is right to emphasize the historical importance of Calvinist thinking, but he assigns an implausibly pivotal role to a particular theological doctrine. Calvin himself apparently did not regard predestination as central to his theology, even if some of his followers gave it greater weight. Yet in a larger sense Weber shows considerable insight. If our analysis of Western culture is correct, he is right to view the work ethic as a stress-relief mechanism. While some Protestants may have worked hard at various times to assure themselves of their election, there is no doubt that many more worked hard, and continue to do so, to bring their environment under control. By keeping the house clean, the fields mown, and the factory in repair, one lives in an orderly and predictable environment. The work itself gives one the sense of taking charge of the situation and doing something about one's problems. It may also actually help to solve the problems. Calvinism may of course reinforce the work ethic, and historian James G. Leyburn provides an amusing piece of evidence that it can even create work-oriented values. He finds that the Scots, so reputed for discipline and hard work, were at one time remarkably unclean, undisciplined, and even cheerful. This state of affairs ended abruptly in the late sixteenth century, when Scots adopted the Calvinist Presbyterian faith, a stern work ethic, and a dour disposition.[6]

Calvin's personal situation seems to encourage an interpretation of his theology as recommending stress relief through effort and discipline. Biographers tell us he described himself as an anxious and insecure man, but he compensated with stern self-control.[7] Although passionate within, he could project a cool and forbidding exterior, rarely using even a first-person pronoun. He obliged his fellow citizens of Geneva to learn similar self-discipline by convincing the town council to enact strict ecclesiastical law. Calvin was no doubt less demanding than the Taliban regime in Afghanistan, but he mandated religious education for children and imposed measures against dancing, drinking, and swearing, much to the irritation of the townspeople. Behind this behavior is Calvinism's theological emphasis on the concept of sanctification, which is the struggle for perfection in this life. Rather than write off the world as beyond redemption, believers are admonished to fight against sin in themselves and against evil in the world around them. In other words, the Calvinist always has work to do. Yet despite the Scottish example, in most cases it is perhaps unlikely that Calvinism itself introduced a work ethic. It is more plausible that it simply resonated in Western societies already disposed to find salvation in work. The work ethic is cultural in origin, as Weber suggests, but perhaps not specifically Calvinist.

Weber is in top form in his analysis of Western rationality. His treatment is both detailed and comprehensive, ranging widely enough to find a central role for rationality even in Western music. In a little-known book on this topic he traces the development of Western musical theory and points out the importance of form and structure.[8] Chapter 6 has already remarked the distinctive nature of Western music as a harmonious blend of rigorous intellect and romantic sentiment, reflecting the Apollonian/Dionysian dialectic in Western culture generally. There is much to be said for the idea that its music is one of the West's most distinctive and admirable contributions to the world. However, it may be fully intelligible only to those who develop a romantic consciousness.

One of Weber's major contributions is his analysis of rationality in the Western-style monochronic bureaucracy (see Chapter 2). The boxes on the organizational chart are determined by subtasks—purchasing, operations, marketing—rather than personalities who happened to accumulate power. Eventually every nook and cranny of the organization reflects the logic of the task, and the organization begins to have a life of its own. This was exemplified in the 1970s by a division of the U.S. Department of Energy, for which I did some consulting work. This division maintained a mathematical model written for the Project Independence Energy System (PIES). The division's organizational chart was identical to the logical flowchart of the computer program that implemented the PIES model. Weber could scarcely ask for a more graphic illustration of his theory. Furthermore, it is not difficult to predict what would happen if the computer program lost its usefulness: the organization would continue to use it, at least for a time, because its very structure and existence are defined by it.

Weber foresaw that the rationalization of bureaucracy would alienate individuals, who find themselves pulled in different directions by organizations that are wrapped up in their own objectives. While at work, I might be part of a large corporation that demands complete allegiance to its profit-maximization goals. When I become ill I am enmeshed in a complex health care establishment in which the patient seems to serve the needs of the system rather than vice versa. Even when I go to church, I may find a hierarchical organization imposing still another set of values. Weber predicted that people would take refuge in art that emphasizes the nonrational and the irrational. He was remarkably prescient, given the character of modern art, and the fact that art museums in Europe have in some ways become the sanctuaries that cathedrals once were. This is where people spend their Sundays, standing reverently before inscrutable objects almost as before an altar. Ironically, cathedrals are maintained by the state largely because of their value as art museums. The religious establishment they represent, in the meantime, attracts minimal interest. Weber would have predicted as much, given its association with a state bureaucracy.

This phenomenon has taken a different twist in the United States, where religious organizations have no connection with the state and tend to be less bureaucratic than in Europe. The United States is far more religious than other Western nations, and the fastest-growing sects are conservative, Protestant evangelical movements. Theologian Harvey Cox suggests that members of these sects find in them a way to resist oppressive bureaucracies. These people associate rationality itself with the intellectual elite, and the rationalized government and corporate bureaucracies they control. They therefore swell the ranks of anti-intellectual Pentecostal sects, while the more reasoned mainline denominations lose members, and those members who remain eschew any discussion of theology.[9]

Weber also predicted, incorrectly this time, that capitalism would gradually lose its appeal. He thought that as corporations grow larger and more bureaucratic, business would forfeit its sense of adventure. The great appeal of capitalism, Weber suggested, is not the opportunity to get rich, but the challenge of entrepreneurship. It gives an individual an opportunity to embark on the heroic voyage of building a business from scratch, like a modern-day Ulysses. This sort of heroism is impossible in the bowels of a large bureaucracy. Entrepreneurs with whom I have discussed the issue agree wholeheartedly that they seek adventure rather than money. Yet capitalism has not lost its appeal and in fact seems to be taking over much of the world, perhaps in part because entrepreneurship remains a major part of the business sector. Even in the more mature capitalist economies, entrepreneurial firms continue to generate most of the new jobs and many product innovations.

Universalism

Western culture is universalizing as well as rationalistic. It is a culture in which people adhere to beliefs and norms they take to be universally valid. They expect other cultures to accept these beliefs and norms as well. Something similar to this idea has appeared for some time in the cross-cultural management literature, which commonly distinguishes universalist from particularist cultures. Fons Trompenaars, for example, develops the universalist/particularist distinction as one between (a) primary concern for universal rules and (b) primary concern for the people involved in a particular situation.[10] He describes a scenario in which, say, I am riding in a car driven by a close friend. The car hits a pedestrian while exceeding the speed limit. The driver's lawyer says that my friend will be spared serious consequences if I will testify that his speed was within the limit. People in universalist cultures tend to say that I should tell the truth in court, while particularist cultures emphasize loyalty to my friend. More generally, universalist cultures focus on rules rather than relationships, emphasize legal contracts, stick to an agreement once it is made, and believe that "there is only one truth or reality," as opposed to "several perspectives on reality relative to each participant."[11] Adapting definitions of Charles Hampden-Turner,[12] Trompenaars describes a universalist culture as one in which people "apply rules and procedures universally to ensure equity and consistency," and a particularist as one in which people "encourage flexibility by adapting to particular situations," although in practice these two approaches often occur in some combination, perhaps giving one more weight than the other.

The universalist culture described by these authors is, as I interpret it, both rule based and universalizing in the senses used here. These two concepts should be distinguished, because the one refers to how behavior is regulated, and the other to what sort of beliefs and norms people accept. A rule-based culture, as defined in Chapter 7, regulates behavior by teaching adherence to rules rather than through direct personal supervision. A universalizing culture is one in which people recognize universally valid beliefs and values. Thus, a rule-based culture would have me tell the truth in traffic court because I should obey society's rules, whereas a universalizing culture might have me tell the truth because there is a universally valid moral principle at stake. Rule-based cultures are, to my knowledge, always universalizing, because the two tendencies naturally support each other. They are also always Western.

Trompenaars cites data that seem to confirm the universalizing and rule-based character of Western nations. He recorded, for example, the percentage of survey respondents who would have me tell the truth in traffic court. Among a sample of 38 nations, the 16 with the highest percentages are Western nations, ranging from 72 percent for Belgium to 96 percent for Canada. The bottom 7 are all non-Western nations, ranging from 26 percent for South Korea to 56 percent for Hong Kong (then a British colony). The middle 15 include 5 Western nations in southern and eastern Europe. In another scenario, I am a restaurant critic and dine at a good friend's new restaurant, which I find to be of really poor quality. What percentage of survey respondents would have me tell the truth in my newspaper column? The results are somewhat more complicated this time, but 11 of the 15 countries with the highest percentages (ranging from 64 percent to 91 percent) are Western nations, while only 3 of those with the lowest 15 percentages (ranging from 17 percent to 56 percent) are Western. In a third scenario, I am conversing with a good friend whose business will be ruined unless I give her confidential information I just learned in a competitor's board meeting. Presumably more people in a universalizing and rule-based culture would have me hold my tongue. The results here are still more nuanced, with 11 of the top 15 percentages obtained in Western countries, and 7 of the bottom 15 obtained in Western countries (all 7 in southern and eastern Europe).[13] Survey results of this kind can be suggestive, but they require as much interpretation as the culture itself. Responses to the first scenario, for example, are complicated by the fact that perjuring oneself in court is generally a crime, which one may be reluctant to commit on fear of being caught. Surveys are best treated as one cultural phenomenon among many others.

Surveys also fail to reveal the functional role of a cultural trait. Why are Western countries universalizing? I suggest it is because they rely fundamentally on rationality, and reason is by definition universal. Westerners expect people worldwide to be convinced by a logical argument, since logic is universal. They in fact characteristically use logic as a means of persuasion, an approach that can fail miserably in Latin American or Asian cultures.

Universalizing rationality is indispensable to the West because it is the basis for both stress management and rule-governed behavior. It is needed for stress management because Westerners control their environment through technology, which rests on science, which in turn presupposes the possibility of universal laws in nature. Universalizing rationality also gives legitimacy to rules of conduct that are expected to apply universally, enforced to a large extent by guilt feelings. People in the United States, for example, often report that they dutifully stop for a traffic signal even when there are no other vehicles or pedestrians in sight. This same universalism, in its purest form, implies that there is only one legitimate way to live and therefore only one legitimate culture, aside from such surface differences as language and cuisine, a culture realized more adequately by the "developed" nations.

There are several ironies in the Western approach to dealing with stress. The scientific worldview that rejects myth supplies myth. The secularity that permits Westerners to manipulate nature leads them to romanticize nature. Most importantly, the universalizing rationality that compels them to deny fundamental cultural differences marks the most fundamental difference between their culture and others.

The Western Cultural Nexus

Western culture is characterized by a cluster of traits that center around universalism and support one another much as the organisms of an ecosystem. As stated in Chapter 1, these traits include our sense of time, the way we process information, our faith in reason, our reliance on technology, our belief in progress, our egalitarianism, our secularism, our romanticism, our neglect of courtesy, our missionary impulse, our exploitation of nature, our expansionism and colonialism, our respect for law, our guilt complex, our fascination with natural science, our mechanisms for dealing with stress, and even our peculiar sense of humor.

We are now in a position to explain how these traits relate to one another and to universalism. Figure 11.1 is an attempt to diagram these relationships. The two great historical sources of Western culture appear in the shaded boxes: Judeo-Christian monotheism, which gave us the concept of a transcendent God who is a universal moral judge, and classical Greek

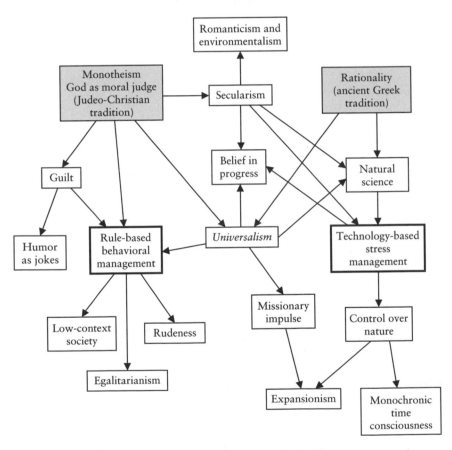

FIGURE 11.1. The Western Cultural Nexus. The shaded boxes represent the historical sources of Western culture. The boxes with heavy borders represent two primary functions of culture: (1) to regulate how people live with each other, and (2) to enable people to cope with the stress of existence.

rationality. Both of these support universalism, since a single divine Law-giver implies universality of morals, and the rational analysis of nature im-plies universality of natural law. The rest of the diagram divides into three regions. The top region depicts the role of secularism, the lower left region explains the regulation of society, and the lower right region describes stress management.

Secularism is a corollary of God's transcendence, symbolized by the burn-ing bush. It gives humans permission to analyze and manipulate nature without trespassing on divine territory. It therefore makes Western science culturally possible, as well as technology, which is the basis for stress man-agement in the West. Since humans are given dominion over the secular realm, historical progress becomes possible, and with it the idea that nations are more or less advanced along the road to improvement. Technology en-hances optimism about the possibility of progress, and universalism dictates that there is but one developmental path that is appropriate for all nations. The disenchantment of nature implicit in secularism generates a romantic reaction, which gives rise to the West's distinctive style of music and art and a reverence for nature that coexists with its brutal exploitation.

Turning to the lower left portion of the diagram, the West is a rule-based society in which compliance depends partly on guilt, which in turn is grounded in Judeo-Christian moral law. Universalism reinforces the belief that everyone should obey the law. A rule-based mechanism is compatible with a low-context society, whence the transparency and free flow of infor-mation that mark Western business and literature. Since rule-governed individuals are directed primarily by internalized norms, Western society is characterized by low power distance and egalitarianism. On the other hand, courtesy does not play the integrative role it does in relationship-based societies, and everyday rudeness is compatible with the culture. Finally, the Western guilt complex provides some consolation by cultivating a sense of humor that appreciates jokes.

The lower right portion of the diagram begins with science and technol-ogy as the primary means of stress management. Technology enables West-erners to control their environment, which leads to the exploitation of nature and a tendency to extend control to surrounding regions, perhaps through colonialism. Western expansionism is reinforced by its missionary impulse, which is grounded in the belief that all nations should advance along the same universally valid developmental path.

There are secondary connections that, for simplicity, are omitted from the diagram. For instance, guilt helps to enforce monochronic time consciousness by motivating people to be on time. Universalism supports egalitarianism, because it insists that rules be applied equally to all. Rude-ness is possible in part because technology rather than personal connection bears the lion's share of stress management. Greek natural philosophy entails secularism, and yet the arrow is omitted, since a rationalistic approach to life need not imply secularism, as illustrated by India.

Western cultures may view their norms and values as universal, but they form a tiny sample of some five thousand highly diverse cultures worldwide. Each culture has a logic and legitimacy of its own, as represented by its "ecosystem," that is, its nexus of mutually supporting institutions, beliefs, and practices that enable people to live with one another and with the stress of self-conscious existence. When getting to know an unfamiliar culture, it is wise to try to understand how it accomplishes these two great tasks. Many things happen in a given culture, but only some of them are culturally important: the ones that play a functional role in the system. Visitors are not likely to be able to do things, or persuade others to do things, that interfere with the working of the cultural ecosystem. On the other hand, projects or activities that mesh with the system, and that attempt to change only culturally unimportant behaviors, have a better chance of success.

Notes for Chapter 11

1. Jonah's story is told in the Old Testament book of Jonah and is alluded to in the Koran 37:139–148.

2. Peter Singer, "Famine, Affluence and Morality" (1972), reprinted in Peter Singer, *Writings on an Ethical Life,* Ecco Press (New York, 2000), 105–17.

3. A similar story appears in the Koran 20:9–51, but without the matter of the name.

4. Francis Fukuyama, *The End of History and the Last Man,* Free Press (New York, 1992).

5. Mark Häberlein, "Economic Policy, State Finance, and the Development of Merchant Capitalism in Upper Germany, c. 1500–1620," workshop on Entrepreneurship and Institutional Context in a Comparative Perspective, Netherlands Graduate School for Economic and Social History (Catholic University of Nijmegen, Netherlands, May 2002).

6. James G. Leyburn, *The Scotch-Irish,* University of North Carolina Press (Chapel Hill, N.C., 1962).

7. For example, Bernard Cottret, *Calvin: A Biography,* translated by M. Wallace McDonald, William B. Eerdmans Publishing Company (1995).

8. Max Weber, *The Rational and Social Foundations of Music,* translated by Don Martindale, Johannes Riedel, and Gertrude Neuwirth, Southern Illinois University Press (Carbondale, Ill., 1958).

9. Harvey Cox, *The Secular City: Urbanization and Secularization in Theological Perspective,* Macmillan (New York, 1965); also, *Religion in the Secular City: Toward a Postmodern Theology,* Simon and Schuster (New York, 1984).

10. Fons Trompenaars, *Riding the Waves of Culture,* Irwin Professional Publishing (Chicago, 1994).

11. Ibid., 49.

12. Charles Hampden-Turner, *Charting the Corporate Mind: Graphic Solutions to Business Conflicts,* Free Press (New York, 1990).

13. Trompenaars, 37ff.

12 _Turkey and Islam_

The driver knocked on my apartment door at four o'clock in the morning, rather than at six as I had expected. My work in Ankara was complete, and I was catching a plane for Stockholm. It was not easy to get my rudimentary Turkish working at that hour, but I finally understood the driver's explanation of why an early departure was essential. It was the weekend between July and August, when July vacations end and August vacations begin in Europe, and travelers jam the airports. I was aware of this but had casually decided that non-European Ankara would not be affected, a foolish conclusion since so many Turks live in Europe and spend their vacations back home with the family.

My driver's wisdom became evident as we approached Esenboğa Airport, which was deluged with traffic. I had to exit the car at some distance from the terminal and make my way to the entrance. Unfortunately, the X-ray machine was just inside the door, which caused a mass of people to accumulate outside as they waited to get through security screening. There was only a narrow space between the building and a roadway clogged with vehicles, and the press of bodies became almost violent. I felt myself being shoved left and right, back and forth, with little control over what was happening. Finally I felt a hard push, tripped over someone's luggage, and went sprawling. I expected to hear exclamations of surprise and annoyance from bystanders as I fell into them. Instead, a dozen hands instantly reached out. They broke my fall and firmly restored me to my standing position. I looked around to see the various dark-haired, mustachioed men who had instinctively come to my aid. Delighted and grateful, I could only say, "_Teşekkür ederim!_" (Thank you!).

It quickly dawned on me that this little incident was a metaphor for Turkey. Ever since Mustafa Kemal Atatürk founded the modern Turkish state in 1923, the country has aspired, with only partial success, to Westernize itself. Its economy has never reached the Western standard that the European Union seems to require for membership (at least from a state with a Muslim population), and its infrastructure has yet to achieve anything like Germanic efficiency—even if much of the German infrastructure was built by Turks. All of this is no doubt a blessing, because it has permitted Turkey to remain Turkey. It remains a land of warm-hearted people, of supportive male comradeship, and of unexcelled hospitality to visitors, even one who is by all appearances a Christian infidel. The airport design is inefficient, but the people are ready to reach out to a stranger in trouble.

Nationalism

To my knowledge, Turks are the most nationalistic people on earth. Most people, it is true, define their identity in part by identifying with their state or ethnic group, but Turks do so with the greatest gusto. All thoughts and feelings pass through an "I am Turkish" filter. This became evident to me right away when I began teaching a cross-cultural management class in Ankara. Each time we began to discuss a country, my students would concentrate on one task to the exclusion of all others: determining what is wrong with that country, and why Turkey is better (except in the case of Italy, a country that Turks seem to admire). The habit seemed unbreakable. I finally warned the students that, when they made their presentations, I did not want to hear one word of evaluation about the country they were discussing. I told them that any company that sent them abroad on business would expect them to spend their time making money rather than refining their likes and dislikes. The students did their best, but many were not up to the task.

My classroom experience notwithstanding, Turkish nationalism is not a virulent sort directed against other nations; rather, it serves internal purposes, primarily to unify the Turkish people and provide them mutual support. This function is clearest when Turks live abroad. It is easy to find expatriate Turks in an organization, no matter how large or decentralized it may be, because one need only identify one Turk. He or she will have sought out all the others and will be able to tick them off by name. Camaraderie between Turks may prompt Europeans and North Americans to suspect them of bending the rules for each other, but this is not necessarily the case. Turkish expatriates often take special pains to avoid the appearance of cronyism. An Islamic sense of justice, along with a national tendency to look West as much as East, equip many professionals to operate in a Western rule-based environment. The main reason for associating with other Turks is to experience the support and reassurance of national solidarity.

Turkish nationalism seems to be a response to a national identity crisis, which may be inevitable in Anatolia, the Asian part of Turkey that constitutes almost all of the country. Peoples have competed for space in Anatolia since the very beginnings of civilization, and it is difficult for any one nation to claim a historical right to the land, even if this does not stop the Turks from trying. Although their roots lie deep in central and even eastern Asia,

Turks cite the earliest possible date for their arrival in Anatolia in order to establish their right of ownership. I have seen dates ranging from 1000 B.C.E. to 100 C.E., with the earliest ones inevitably appearing in Turkish sources. When the Turks did arrive, however, they mingled with any number of peoples, with the result that it is impossible to trace a single cultural history for the Turkish population today. Subpopulations range from dark-skinned people of Arab ancestry to light-skinned Circassians (Caucasian Muslims). Most are happy to call themselves Turks, but not all. For instance, the 12 million Kurds who live in Turkey, primarily in the southeast, have been at odds with the Turkish government over the right to maintain their culture and language.

A related source of Turkey's identity crisis is the mixing of Mediterranean cultures that has been going on for ages. Turks love to contrast themselves with the Greeks, for example, but I have heard Turks admit, in moments of honesty, their many cultural similarities with their archrivals. This was impressed upon me when I stayed in a guesthouse at Boğaziçi University overlooking the scenic and fast-flowing Bosphorus. The university is named for the famous strait, which the Turks call "Boğaziçi" (pronounced *bo-ah'-zi-chi,* it is from the Turkish for "throat"). An elaborate wedding party took place in a courtyard below my window one night, and the ear-pounding amplified music ruled out all activity except to watch the proceedings. Judging by the food, drink, dances, and music, I could just as well have been in Athens. The national drink of Greece, ouzo, is essentially the national drink of Turkey: raki (pronounced *rah-kuh*). Both are clear, anise-flavored aperitifs that turn white when diluted with water. Greek coffee is similar to Turkish coffee—thick, and drunk slowly from a small cup, with care not to imbibe the grounds at the bottom. People drink it sweet (*şekerli,* "with sugar"), medium sweet (*orta*), or without sugar (*şekersiz*). Even the famous Greek gyro has a Turkish equivalent, *döner kebap* (which has several variations); both *gyro* and *döner* come respectively from the Greek and Turkish words for "rotate," since the meat is roasted on a rotating vertical spit. With parallels such as these, the only tip-off that I was in Istanbul rather than Athens was the Muslim garb of some of the women. The parallels concern surface features that, as I never tire of saying, are only incidental to what a culture is really all about. But Turks, like most people, identify their culture with surface matters and therefore might take pains to distinguish themselves from all-too-similar Mediterranean neighbors.

A third possible source of an identity crisis is the fact that Turkey straddles East and West, both geographically and culturally. The Boğaziçi is the boundary between Europe and Asia, with Istanbul lying on one side and most of Turkey on the other. Although the Turkic peoples are Asian in origin, they have had considerable involvement in European affairs, far too much in the opinion of Europeans. For centuries the Ottoman Empire (named for the Turkish Osmanlı family) occupied parts of Europe, even to the gates of Vienna. The empire finally expired in the aftermath of World War I, when Mustafa Kemal Atatürk negotiated the establishment of modern Turkey, Türkiye, in the 1923 Treaty of Lausanne. From the start Atatürk strove to build ties with Europe. He ordered that school children be taught to write in Roman script rather than the old Arabic script (Turkish is related to neither Arabic nor Latin languages but can be spelled phonetically in either script). He replaced Muslim authorities with a European-style secular state. He even outlawed the fez, the Ottoman hat that Europeans had associated with Muslim domination. He gave women political rights and recommended that they no longer cover their faces.

If Mustafa Kemal Atatürk intensified Turkey's identity crisis with a schizophrenia of East and West, he also supplied a remedy. Turkish nationalism is the legacy of his strong leadership and legendary accomplishments. The sobriquet Kemal, bestowed by one of his early teachers, means "perfection." The name Atatürk, "father Turk," was given to him by the Turkish National Assembly shortly after its constitution, whereupon the rest of the nation adopted the Western practice of using surnames. He almost single-handedly built the modern Turkish nation on the ashes of the old Ottoman Empire through shrewd negotiations with European powers and effective statecraft at home. He transformed the image of ordinary Turks from that of backcountry hicks to leaders of a new nation and even reformed the Turkish language, replacing the antique and Arabized Ottoman dialect with the language of the common people.

Remarkable as Atatürk was as an individual, he succeeded because his culture supplied a role for him to step into. Turkey's type of high–power distance society, which is not unusual in the Middle East, places power in legendary figures whose superior abilities inspire devotion and admiration. They must begin with intellectual and leadership talent, and initially distinguish themselves by some accomplishment. In Atatürk's case it was his World War I defense of the Turkish homeland as commanding officer at Gallipoli in 1915. Preferably, a Turkish leader should have genuine interest in the welfare of his followers as well as his personal success. At some point, legends, possibly quite far-fetched, began to accumulate and cement his reputation as a worthy leader. Atatürk fit this mold perfectly. Someone told me, for example, that he had supernatural ability to predict the future.

Though a textbook example of a high–power distance mechanism that works, Atatürk's legacy has not been all roses. Extremists fought in the streets in the 1970s. Islamic fundamentalists reacted in the 1990s against the legacy of Atatürk's secularism, and the government responded harshly.

For instance Turkish women who make a point of wearing the Muslim head scarf in Europe find it sometimes prohibited in their homeland. It is banned in certain universities and public places because the government sees it as threatening the secular state. In May 1999 duly elected deputy Merve Kavakçı was removed from the Grand National Assembly for wearing the scarf. Turks also complain about weak political leaders. The last decade has seen no fewer than five prime ministers: Süleyman Demirel (who served a decade earlier as well), Tansu Çiller (Turkey's only female prime minister), Mesut Yılmaz (who served two nonconsecutive terms), Necmettin Erbakan (who represents the fundamentalist wing), Bülent Ecevit, and the current office holder Tayyip Erdoğan. Demirel also served a seven-year non-renewable term as president, followed by the current president Ahmet Necdet Sezer. All of these politicians have received strong criticism, but in fairness one must recognize that it is difficult to operate in the shadow of Atatürk, not to mention alongside a powerful military establishment whose generals form a kind of apostolic succession from the great leader.

Another problem for Turkey is the status of the Kurds, a people without a country who have lived in what are now Iran, Iraq, Syria, and Turkey for thousands of years. Atatürk's solution was to declare that the Kurds living in Turkey shall be Turks in every way, a hard-line policy that has only recently softened somewhat. The Kurdish language was officially banned until 1991, a ruling enforced in part by sending Kurdish children to large boarding schools where they had to speak Turkish. The Turkish government has shut down Kurdish political parties and imprisoned Kurdish politicians on charges of advocating separation from Turkey. The government reportedly pays "village guards" in Kurdish towns to keep out the militant Kurdistan Workers Party (PKK). Villages are said to be caught in a bind between Turkish military threats to raze the village if they cooperate with the PKK, and harsh PKK reprisals if they do not cooperate.

The Kurdish problem is of the utmost practical importance for Turkey, for two reasons. One is that it complicates Turkey's petition to enter the European Union. Finger-wagging Europeans cite human rights violations as good reason to keep Turkey out, while Turks respond that Europeans use this as an excuse to discriminate against a Muslim country. There is in fact strong anti-Turkish sentiment in Europe, dating back to the Ottoman occupation. The bitterness of the recent Balkan struggles is rooted in resentment of the Ottomans, as is the neo-Nazi anti-immigrant movement headed by Jörg Heider in Austria. Muslims claim that until recently, even clocks and watches in European advertisements were set to the time of day of the Ottoman surrender. Even if human rights issues are a mere excuse for exclusion, however, they are a convincing excuse that can keep Turkey out of the European Union.

A second reason is that Kurdish terrorism can be deadly for the all-important tourism industry. Depressed and demoralized by their cold, dreary climes, Europeans will go almost anywhere for a taste of warm sunshine, sandy beach, and turquoise waters (*turquoise,* meaning "Turkish," is the label the French gave to the translucent blue waters off Turkey). A mere breath of possible danger, however, spoils the vacation, and the beach crowds at Izmir and Antalya vanish. This was the situation while I was living in Ankara. The Kurdish activist Abdullah "Apo" Öcalan (pronounced *er-ja-lon*) had been apprehended by Israelis in Nairobi and returned somehow to Turkey, where he was accused of treason and causing 30,000 deaths. He was tried and sentenced to death, whereupon his followers threatened violence against tourists if the sentence were carried out. The tourist industry went through the floor. Some colleagues and I took this opportunity to visit the striking Cappadocia area, south of Ankara, where we were the only guests in our hotel and explored the historical sites without the usual crowds. As it happened little violence ensued, as Öcalan's sentence must be approved by Parliament, which at this writing awaits a ruling from the European Court of Human Rights before acting on the matter. This is as much a concession to European sensibilities as to economics, since EU officials look disapprovingly upon the death penalty, which has not been used in Turkey since 1984. Meanwhile, Turks accused European newspapers of using old file photos of bomb damage to create the impression that Turkey was rife with violence during this period. I cannot confirm this, but conversations with Europeans convinced me that Turkey was more peaceful than they suspected. Whatever the case, the tourists stayed away.

Despite its problems, Turkey can legitimately claim to be an anchor of stability in a troubled region. Many Muslims, reportedly including President Purvez Musharraf of Pakistan, look to it as an example of how to coexist with the West. Turkey's international role is likely to grow further as it develops relations with Turkic states that have come out from under the Soviet yoke: Azerbaijan, Kazakhstan, Kyrgyzstan, Turkmenistan, and Uzbekistan. In fact, few in the West realize the extent of Turkic peoples. They originated somewhere in Asia and migrated more or less westward, leaving a trail of their kinsmen across much of the continent. They played a major role in Asian history; even India's Taj Mahal was built by a Turkic Mogul king, Shah Jehan. Today Turks identify not only with the Turkish states but also with Balkars, Bashkirs, Chuvash, Karachai, Crimean Tatars, and Tuvans in Russia; Gagauz in Moldova; the Turkic population of Xinjiang Province in China; and of course the Turkish Cypriots, on whose behalf Turkey intervened militarily in 1974. (Turks claim to be related to Hungarians, no doubt hoping to strengthen their ties with Europe, but this is unlikely, even if some Turkish words can be found in the Hungarian language.) Turkey itself is the westernmost outpost of this great expanse of peoples and, despite its peripheral location, is becoming its cultural and economic hub.

Avoiding Stress in Turkey

Turkey's nationalism is itself a stress-management device. It is easier to face the uncertainties of life if people do it together, whether as a family, a group of friends, a village, an ethnic group, or a nation. The extended family is central in much of the world. We have seen the key role of friendship in Mexico (see Chapter 5), and it, too, is a worldwide strategy that occurs in various forms. The village is a fundamental support unit in much of Africa. Given sufficient solidarity, an entire ethnic group or nation state can provide significant support. We have seen this at work in Denmark (see Chapter 6). Japan, and of course Turkey, are also examples.

Even more crucial than nationalism, however, is the Turkish style of friendship. I will focus on male friendship, since I know much more about it than female friendship. Middle Eastern cultures are strongly masculine in Hofstede's sense, and the sexes tend to frequent different circles, even in relatively Westernized Turkey. Perhaps the most important quality of Turkish male camaraderie is that men level with one another. It is OK to admit to friendly coworkers that one has indigestion every night or trouble with the kids. For me it was a refreshing contrast with many relationships in the United States. The primary cultural function of friendship is to provide mutual support, and a competitive relationship works against this. Friendship becomes deeper over time, and old comrades can be seen walking hand in hand, a practice that may signal a homosexual relationship in the West, but far from it in Turkey.

Men often gather over tea to discuss things. Most people picture Turks as drinking coffee and raki, and many do, but tea is most often the everyday beverage. While I was teaching in Ankara, every day at noon the faculty belonging to one of the departments would gather in the lounge on my floor of the building. The professors ate their bag lunches and conversed for an hour over tea. The tea was readily available, since the university employs full-time tea brewers for the academic buildings. A small kitchen next to the lounge was devoted to this purpose, and it gave me an opportunity to listen in on the conversation while refilling my teacup. The contrast with academic life in the United States was remarkable on three counts. First, no U.S. university would hire someone for so civilized a task as making tea. Second, no group of U.S. professors I have ever met would find time to meet every day at lunch. Third, most U.S. academics would find the concept of noncompetitive conversation unfathomable. I am reminded of a wonderful scene in David Lodge's novel *Changing Places*.[1] A British visitor tried to teach the game Humility to a group of literature professors in California. The idea of the game is to mention important works of literature one has *not* read. The Californians did their best to play the game but kept mentioning obscure and impressive works they *had* read. They simply could not grasp the concept. In a wry coda to the story, one professor finally got the idea and blurted out that he had not read *Hamlet*. This admission eventually led to his dismissal from the university.

The lunchtime group of professors in Ankara knew how to play Humility. The conversation was noncompetitive. Usually they talked about what all Middle Easterners talk about: ethnic politics. I read somewhere that, according to recent research, this kind of support group can substantially improve one's health by reducing stress. In Turkey such groups are a way of life. They can be seen in restaurants or coffee shops, or wherever little knots of men gather. Friendship is an important component of business relationships, too. It may not be a requirement for doing business, as in Mexico, but a business relationship works best when it evolves into friendship. The honesty that is so important to Turkish friendship is an obvious aid to business: it leads to honest dealing.

Turkish hospitality is a form of friendship directed at visitors and is shown in a thousand small ways. When I went to the landlord's office periodically to pay my rent, I was always greeted by two or three employees who, seeing that a foreigner was present, would say, "Welcome! Welcome!" (in English) as I came in. I would walk down the hall to pay my bill and return a few minutes later, whereupon the same group would repeat, "Welcome! Welcome!" as I left. I suppose if hospitable people wish to learn a single word of English, *welcome* is a good choice. On a few occasions I went into the city via the *dolmuş*, which is a passenger minivan and quite handy. Each *dolmuş* follows a fixed route but will stop at any point along the route where a passenger waves it down. I was slow to understand the fare system, however, and I would sometimes underpay the driver or fail to have the right change. On such occasions the driver, seeing that I was a foreigner, would smile and wave his hand, indicating that what I gave him was close enough. Can one imagine a Pittsburgh bus driver doing the same for a visiting Turk? While in Istanbul on one occasion, I decided to become a tourist for a day and arranged to join a tour group to see the city. The tourist trade was so depressed, due to the threat of terrorism, that the morning part of the excursion was canceled. Nonetheless, the owner of the touring company drove out to pick me up, bought two tickets on a boat plying the Bosphorus, and gave me a personal tour of the sights. Afterward he gave me his mobile phone number and told me to call him if he could be of any assistance while I was in Istanbul. He meant it, too.

Religion plays a stress-management role in Turkey, as in much of the world. Nearly everyone in the country professes Islam, although the faith is practiced with a certain amount of moderation. Muhammed's injunction against alcoholic beverages seems to have little effect on consumption of raki and Türk Tuborg beer. The month of fasting (Ramadan) is recognized to some extent, but most urban dwellers do not fast or close their shops. The Koran proscribes food, drink, and sex from first light (when one can distinguish a white and black thread) until nighttime. This is interpreted as applying to tobacco as well, which presents difficulties for the many Turks with a smoking habit. Ramadan in Turkey ends with the three-day celebration Şeker Bayramı (sugar holiday) or Ramazan Bayramı (Ramadan holiday). During this period people like to visit relatives and may present gifts of candy. Although Turks are not as overt in their practice of Islam as some Middle Easterners, there is no denying that they subscribe to the basic philosophy of the faith, and that it is an indelible part of their ethnic consciousness. Some Turks, particularly in rural areas, observe its rituals devotedly, even if others never darken the door of a mosque. Not even the great secularist Atatürk was able to outlaw the Muslim practice of praying five times a day. An analysis of the basic philosophy of Islam, and how it deals with stress and uncertainty, is attempted in a subsequent section.

Table 12.1 summarizes Turkish stress-management mechanisms. The first of these, Turkish nationalism, is unavailable to visitors. The third, the practice of Islam, is available only to Muslims. One of course may draw upon one's own religion, but it is unwise to practice it in a way that calls attention to oneself. This leaves friendship. The best way to avoid stress and flourish in Turkey is to learn the Turkish art of friendship, accept the generous hospitality, drink tea, and enjoy.

TABLE 12.1
Stress-Management Mechanisms in Turkey

Mechanism	Contribution to Stress Management
Nationalism	Identity; mutual support at home or abroad
Friendship, camaraderie, hospitality	Trust relationships; support groups, help in time of need
Islam	Assurance; coherent worldview; sense that events are under control from above; predictability of observances (e.g., Ramadan)

Language

This is a good point to say something about the Turkish language, so that the reader can practice saying the Turkish words that come up in the discussion. Turks are quite forgiving if foreigners mispronounce things, even their names, but they are delighted and impressed if someone takes the trouble to get it right.

Turkish is a grammarian's dream, because it is an almost perfect language. After Atatürk romanized the alphabet, the Turkish Language Society (later the Turkish Linguistic Association) oversaw a remarkable reform of syntax and vocabulary. Words are spelled exactly as they sound, and the grammatical rules, although complex (there are so many tenses that I lost count), operate with the consistency of mathematics. Thankfully, there are no genders. To be honest, I did encounter one irregularity at breakfast. To order orange juice I had to say, "*Lütfen portakal sulu,*" which literally means "Please, orange water." The grammatically correct phrase should be *lütfen portakal susu.* "Water" is *su,* but because *portakal* is an attributive noun rather than an adjective, *su* takes a suffix and becomes *susu.* However, Turks seem to believe that *susu* sounds silly and prefer to say *sulu.* This is the only exception to the rules I know.

Turkish pronunciation is not that far from English, once one learns a few tricks. The vowels *e* and *i* are just like a short *e* and *i* in English (as in *bet* or *bit*). The *e* never takes a neutral sound, so that President Sezer's name is pronounced *sez-zehr,* not *sezzr.* The *a* and *u* take slightly longer sounds (roughly as in *hall* and *push*). The sounds *ö* and *ü* are as in German (roughly as in *worm* and *mute*), *ey* is as in *hey!,* and *ay* as the *i* in *hide.* Turkish is the only language I know that does not require one to dot all the *i*'s, because there is an *ı* without a dot. It sounds like a neutral *e,* and this is why *raki* (spelled *rakı* in Turkish) is pronounced *rah-kuh.* To avoid ambiguity, dotted *i*'s require a dot when capitalized, as in *İzmir* (Izmir). There are a few odd consonants, too. The letter *ş* sounds like *sh,* and *ç* is *ch.* Most confusing to English speakers is *c,* which comes across as *j.* The letter *ğ* can be treated as silent.

Turkish is an agglutinating language, meaning that suffixes can pile up at the end of a word. The stem for "speak" is *konuş-,* and "I speak Turkish" is written by attaching a tense indicator and the pronoun to the end of the verb: *Türkçe konuşuyorum.* "I don't speak Turkish" is written by squeezing an extra suffix in the middle: *Türkçe konuşumuyorum.* Word order in Turkish is something like the reverse Polish notation used by some calculators. It is supremely logical but difficult to get used to. Basically the words occur in opposite order as in English. For example, "I speak Turkish a little" comes out *Biras Türkçe konuşuyorum* (a little Turkish speak I). The most distinctive characteristic of Turkish is vowel harmony, which is a real blast for beginners. Consider the questions:

İngiliz misiniz?	Are you English?
Türk müsünüz?	Are you Turkish?
Alman mısınız?	Are you German?
Mutlu musunuz?	Are you happy?

Vowels in the second word change to harmonize with the last vowel in the first word. Another difficulty for English speakers is that there are precious few words in common between the two languages. I can think of one off-hand: *tişört* (t-shirt).

The Turkish language is designed for courtesy. One often hears *efendim* (madam or sir), *lütfen* (please), and *teşekkür ederim* (thanks), to which the response is *bir şey değil* (it's nothing). I like the popular and thoroughly Turkish word *buyurun,* which means something like "at your service." Greetings include *merhaba* and *selam* (hello), both modified from the Arabic, as well as *nasılsınız* (how are you?), *günaydın* (good morning), *iyi günler* (literally, "good days"), and *iyi akşamlar* ("good evening"). To welcome someone, say, "*Hoş geldiniz,*" to which the response is *hoş bulduk. Affedersiniz* is "I beg your pardon." When leaving, say, "*Görüşürüz*" (See you later), and the host may respond, "*Güle! Güle!*" (Smiles! Smiles!).

First Meeting

The most difficult part of a meeting in Turkey is getting there—if one drives an automobile. Perfectly sane Turkish men revert to crazed adolescents when behind the wheel. Drivers dart back and forth so that one must often slam on the brakes to avoid a collision. They pull out from the intersection before the light changes. To discourage this, some intersections are equipped with signs that flash a countdown to the signal change. This is supposed to convince drivers to wait a few more seconds, but it does not seem to work. In Turkey, defensive driving is not just a good habit; it is the only way to get there alive. My solution is to take a taxi or *dolmuş.* As one who gives advice on how to avoid stress in a foreign country, I would look pretty silly renting a car in Ankara or Istanbul. It is a good idea to allow for traffic delays. Turkey is a polychronic country, but meetings are normally punctual. The polychronicity is evidenced by a tendency toward multitasking and by organizations that are managed from the top (see Chapter 2).

Dress for a business or professional meeting is formal: a dark business suit, shiny shoes, and an expensive watch. A three-piece suit for men is not too much. The dress code may apply even in the heat of summer. One should greet the host with a hearty Western-style handshake. It is essential to show that one enjoys the host's company, whether or not the business at hand is interesting. The visitor should demonstrate genuine interest in the other's welfare by inquiring about how things are going, whether that deal went through the other day, or whether the kids like their new school. If one person is of higher rank, he will normally initiate such questions. Turkey is a high–power distance culture, and proper deference should be rendered to superiors. In some contexts subordinates keep their suit jackets buttoned in the presence of the boss. Supervisors can be gruff with subordinates and may bark orders. Whatever the difference in rank, however, Turks interact as human beings first and functionaries second. The chitchat does not continue as long as in Latin America, but longer than in Europe or North America. Smoking is very common, although Turks are beginning to ask if they may smoke before lighting up.

Turkish hospitality being what it is, visitors are normally invited to a restaurant or a private home for meals. If visiting a home it is appropriate to bring a gift, such as candy or a picture book. Turkish food is quite tasty and surprisingly underrepresented among restaurants around the world. I ate probably the best lunch of my life one day at a restaurant in Ankara (but sadly I cannot recall the name of the dish). A full dinner always begins with a large array of *mezeler* (starters), which in my view are the highlight of the meal. One must take care to save room for later courses. Popular cold *mezeler* include *kavun* (melon), *yeşil* (greens), *cacık* (cucumber in yogurt), *karides* (prawn), a spicy dish called *acılı,* and especially *patlıcan* (eggplant). Hot *mezeler* include *midye tava* (fried mussels) and *kalamar* (calamari). The most famous *meze* is *imam bayıldı,* which literally means "the priest fainted." It is an oily stuffed eggplant that reputedly so impressed an imam that he swooned with delight. The main course is commonly some kind of *kebap* (roast meat), such as *şiş kebap* (meat roasted on skewers) or *köfte* (meatballs). Meat is often served in a spicy tomato sauce. A very Turkish and delicious dessert is a *muhallebi* (pudding) made with tiny pieces of chicken. A more rudimentary meal may consist simply of *döner kebap,* French fries, and a dry salad made of shredded lettuce and carrot.

This being the Middle East, conversation will sooner or later drift to politics and ethnic groups. The political discussion can be interesting at times. Middle Easterners see levels of intrigue in every event and show remarkable ingenuity in imagining ulterior motives. I can sympathize with North American and European officials who attempt political negotiations in the

Middle East. It must be like a Little Leaguer stepping into Yankee Stadium. The ethnic topics are more troublesome, however. Turks love to talk about the Greeks, the Germans, the neo-Nazis, and the Armenians. Turks can cite occasions centuries ago on which the Greeks invaded this town or that, as though it were yesterday. The only option for visitors is to listen quietly, even if this can become tedious. A particularly sensitive topic is the treatment of Armenians under the Ottoman Empire, and people on both sides can become surprisingly emotional about a situation that occurred long before they were born. The Kurds may not even be mentioned in front of visitors, since feelings on this matter are intense. Again, visitors must stay out of these discussions. They can try to change the subject, but the relief will be momentary, as the conversation will drift back to the usual topics. One can get a sense of how deeply ingrained is the Middle Eastern habit of viewing the world through an ethnic lens.

Down the Road

Turkish organizations appear Western on the surface, but most are typical of polychronic, high–power distance cultures. The boss is often reluctant to delegate authority and may have his fingers in many details of the operation. There are rules and regulations, but personal relationships are always important. Leadership qualities are equally important. Visitors who find themselves in a leadership position should firmly take charge. Decisions should be made by the boss, not by committee. Employees may want to come in and negotiate their position, their salary, or their assignments. Negotiation is social glue in Turkey, and the boss should listen to their point of view and take it seriously. However, after due consideration the boss must make a firm decision and explain why it is fair.

Turkey has a masculine culture in which competition is acceptable and men are almost always in charge (except that female administrators are common in education). Tansu Çiller is an exception to the rule. It is true that women often get advanced degrees and hold some kinds of professional (as opposed to managerial) positions in a ratio not much different from that of Europe. I got the impression, however, that the traditional family with male breadwinner and housewife is more common in urban Turkey than in the West. This is probably due not to Islamic strictures but to the masculine culture. Rural communities reflect Islamic traditions more strongly. Another sign of the masculine culture is the enormous prestige of the military, although Atatürk's aura also helps. All young men are required to serve in the military, although as in nearly all countries there are ways for the privileged to minimize or escape their duty.

The best way to succeed in Turkey is to build friendships over time. The first rule for a healthy relationship is honesty, since friendship cannot play its supportive role in Turkey unless friends level with each other. Turks are alert for signs of dishonesty. They sometimes test acquaintances by giving them a chance to tell a fib that they can apparently get away with. As in employee relations, there is a sense of fairness, much as in the West. A proposal will be judged not only according to whether it is practical or profitable but also by whether it is basically fair to both parties. Roger Fisher and William Ury, in their small book *Getting to Yes,* recommend that negotiators appeal to principle in order to persuade the opposite side.[2] A certain amount of this is good advice in most Islamic countries as well as in the West. The question of negotiation is examined more closely in the next section.

Turkish professionals tend to be acquainted with both Western and Turkish ways. As mentioned earlier, they are sensitive to issues of cronyism and corruption. Some try conscientiously to avoid them, but this can be difficult in a Turkish environment. A striking example was the 1999 attempted suicide of Hikmet Ulugbay, then Minister of State for the Economy, all the more striking because the Koran is widely interpreted as prohibiting suicide. He apparently allowed confidential documents concerning negotiations with the International Monetary Fund to leak to the media, which affected financial markets. I was told that Ulugbay enjoyed a reputation of doing his best to play it clean and might well have been upset by this lapse. If so conscientious an official as Ulugbay failed to play by the rules, one can assume that many others also fail. Turkey is a relationship-based society at heart, and no edict from Mustafa Kemal Atatürk could have changed this.

As often happens when rule- and relationship-based behaviors mingle, no one system works very well, and corruption sets in. Bribery is common, whether it be on the level of traffic tickets or political deals. In fact, a 2001 survey found that police officers and members of Parliament are the least-trusted groups in Turkey.[3] (Unsurprisingly, the most trusted organization is the military.) The same survey revealed that about half of the respondents, who were a cross-section of Turks rather than specifically government officials or business people, admitted to paying at least one bribe in the previous two years. A typical bribe runs (U.S.) $25 for traffic police, $50 for primary and secondary schools, $63 for tax inspectors, $97 for public hospitals, $98 for registry of deeds, $113 for municipal governments, $130 for non-traffic police, $260 for law courts, and $280 for customs. (This is based on a conversion rate of 600,000 Turkish lira per U.S. dollar, the approximate rate in April 2000.) In about half the cases, bribes are paid to obtain services to which one is already entitled, and in the other half they yield special favors. It is characteristic of Turkey's East/West schizophrenia that a Western-style analysis of bribery would be forthcoming in a country where at least half the population pays bribes!

Corruption can be merely irritating, or it can lead to tragedy. One morning I peered out of my window as I rode the Ankara Express, a shiny white train that makes the overnight trip between Ankara and Istanbul. The train passed through the working-class city of Izmit, which sits on top of the north Anatolian fault system, and I watched the prefabricated apartment buildings pass by the window. They consisted basically of concrete floor slabs supported by prefab walls. It occurred to me that a modest tremor could collapse these buildings like a house of cards, and residents would be crushed between the floor slabs. Less than three weeks later I picked up a newspaper and learned, to my horror, that this nightmarish vision had come true. By one account, 18,000 people perished when a magnitude 7.4 earthquake struck Izmit in the early morning hours of August 17, 1999. Everyone was indoors asleep. How could the buildings be so deadly, given that Turkey has modern standards for construction in an earthquake zone? It is common knowledge that building inspectors look the other way when properly compensated, especially in poor and working-class areas. Presumably many of the residents of Izmit would not have been able to afford their apartments if they had been built to code. I was later told that at least half the buildings in earthquake-prone Turkey are *kaçak* (not up to standards).

Negotiation

Few visitors escape Turkey without a visit to the carpet shop. It is a worthwhile experience because it says more than one might think about Turkish culture. Upon entering, the customers are offered tea or coffee and a seat on one of the benches surrounding the carpet display floor. Westerners may be uneasy about accepting refreshments, but there is no need to worry. This is Turkey, where hospitality is simply part of being human. The visitor would do well to loosen up and enjoy a small, clear glass vial of tea, perhaps sweetened with a sugar cube. The glass should be held by the rim at the top to avoid burning one's fingers. Employees will begin unrolling carpets as the salesman explains the various types of carpets and how they are made. Some shops even demonstrate the art by allowing customers to watch poorly paid country girls at their task, laboring perhaps months on a single carpet. They work only a few hours a day, since the stitching is maddeningly tedious, and mistakes can ruin a carpet—although an expert can often spot them in carpets that look fine to the average person.

The assistants roll out carpet after carpet, possibility accumulating a 6-inch stack on the floor. By accepting refreshments and watching such a lengthy demonstration, the visitor incurs no obligation to buy. In fact, the salesman may warn tourists not to buy a carpet unless they know what they are doing. The merchants naturally prefer to make a sale, but in any event they enjoy showing off these masterpieces and explaining the significance of their designs. They are truly beautiful, and the wise visitor will relax and enjoy the experience.

When the show is over, a customer may express interest in one of the carpets. At this point the showman walks out of the room, and the negotiators walk in. This is the Middle East, where negotiation is a skill roughly on the level of brain surgery. It is also sport. On one occasion I watched a three-hour negotiation over a $40 (U.S.) *kilim* (small rug). (Unfortunately, most carpets are far more expensive than this.) The rug was hardly worth the effort, but the fun of negotiating was. A group of customers and salesmen gathered to observe. One can see the same phenomenon in any Middle Eastern bazaar, where a crowd may coalesce when a good bargaining session gets started. Negotiation is a unifying activity in the Middle East, much as sports is in the United States, where one can talk about last night's game with any stranger. A carpet shop is the big leagues, however, and Turks usually advise visitors to leave the negotiation to a Turkish friend.

Westerners are often uncomfortable with the idea of negotiating a price. They call it "haggling," which suggests an unpleasant altercation. Some automobile dealers in the United States have attracted additional customers by setting a fixed price rather than putting them through the dreaded negotiation session with a shifty salesman. Negotiation need not be viewed as a struggle, however, because in essence it is information exchange. It is useful to analyze this process, because Westerners often fail to understand what is happening in a negotiation session that takes place elsewhere in the world.

To simplify matters, we can assume that the seller begins with a minimum price in mind, and the buyer with a maximum price. The aim of price negotiation is to determine whether the former is less than or equal to the latter, and if so, to agree upon a selling price between the two. The simplest approach is for the seller to announce his minimum price at the outset, and for the buyer to announce her maximum. This makes it obvious whether a deal is possible, but it does not resolve the issue as to what the selling price will actually be. The seller wants to sell at the buyer's maximum, and the buyer wants to buy at the seller's minimum. Unless these two numbers are identical, there is no agreement.

This is where culture comes in. Either party wants to obtain information about the other's limit without revealing too much about one's own, and culture determines how this is done. Generally there is a series of offers,

alternating between seller and buyer, that begin rather far apart and gradually move toward the middle. As the offers begin to converge, the seller's
offer may move below the buyer's maximum, and the buyer's offer may
move above the seller's minimum. Once both occur, a deal is possible. Otherwise the negotiations eventually break off, and the customer perhaps considers another carpet. If negotiation continues, the offers continue until
they converge at a selling price on which the parties agree.

A difficulty with this procedure is that both parties will wish to revise
their previous offer only slightly, since to do so reveals less information
about one's own maximum or minimum price. In theory the negotiation
could go on interminably. Fortunately, cultures have evolved various
signaling conventions that speed up the process (not too much, however, as
negotiation has social functions other than commerce). In essence, the
signals tell the buyer that she can increase her offer a certain amount without sacrificing anything, because the seller would never agree to a lower
price anyway. They provide similar information to the seller, and the negotiation can make some progress. Signals take many forms. The initial offer
may provide a rough clue as to the size of the final offer, as may the rate at
which the offers increase or decrease. Ancillary remarks and gestures can
also convey information, such as comments and questions on the quality of
the goods, sighs and grimaces, and walking out of the shop. It may appear
that many of these "signals" are actually bluffs, such as walking out of the
shop when one really wants the carpet (which incidentally can be effective
in Turkey if business is slow; the merchant may chase the customer to her
car with a better offer). Actually the comments and bluffs are made in conventional ways and therefore convey information, much as playing a certain card or bidding a certain suit conveys information in a game of bridge.
An experienced negotiator knows the conventions and how to draw infer-
ences from plays. Amateurs lose this game because they reveal information
without obtaining any. It is all quite complex, and the conventions depend
on the setting and the type of goods as well as the surrounding culture. This
is why the carpet purchase is best left to a knowledgeable Turk.

The most popular signaling mechanism in Western culture is a price tag,
which may seem the most efficient of all. One need only look at the price
and decide immediately whether to buy. Why is this rational approach not
used worldwide? Perhaps because some countries are less economically
advanced? This question deserves close analysis, because again Westerners
tend to misread the nature of non-Western negotiation.

While a price tag may be a convenient device for the buyer, it is a major
problem for the seller, who must determine what price to charge without knowing anything about the buyer. This appears idiotic to a Middle

Eastern merchant, who will naturally present high bids to ignorant tourists and low ones to savvy locals. There is no reason such a merchant would even consider advertising a fixed price. (Shopkeepers in tourist areas may put tags on their merchandise, but they do not show real prices. They bear ridiculously high figures designed to confuse tourists.) Then why do Western merchants use price tags, despite their disadvantages? Perhaps they are an obvious approach for someone who lives in a low-context, rule-based culture, where information is transmitted explicitly rather than implicitly through cultural interaction (see Chapter 2).

Once prices become public, the classical arguments of Western economics take effect. The same product cannot sell at two different prices, because no customer would pay the higher price when a lower one is available. The price of a given item must therefore reach the same equilibrium level in every shop that is easily reached by the same group of consumers. The onus is on the merchant to learn what this equilibrium level is, for if the price is too high, no one will buy, and if it is too low, profit is sacrificed. In a high-context culture such as that of most of the Middle East, everything is different. The price of an item does not exist until someone buys it. There can be no equilibrium price, and the Western economic arguments break down.

One can now examine the "rationality" of negotiation versus fixed prices. Western economists argue that the equilibrium price is not only rational but also optimal in a particular sense. The argument goes like this. When the seller sells an item, he generally sells it for more than his minimum price. He comes out ahead in some sense, and the amount by which he comes out ahead is the "producer surplus." When the buyer buys an item, her "consumer surplus" is the difference between her maximum price and the amount paid. The equilibrium price of classical economics is "optimal" in the sense that it maximizes surplus summed over all producers and all consumers. It maximizes the total amount by which buyers and sellers come out ahead. As it turns out, this is the price at which supply and demand are equal: the price at which the number of buyers who want the item equals the number of sellers who want to sell it.

The problem with the optimality argument is that it presupposes a fixed, advertised price. This is a constraint that actually makes the sum of producer surplus and consumer surplus smaller than it would be otherwise. To see this, suppose that the fixed-price system is suddenly replaced by a system of traditional negotiation. We can make two observations. First, negotiation can clearly generate a producer and consumer surplus that is no less than before. Every purchase that occurred under the price tag system can still occur, because if nothing else the parties could agree on the old advertised price. It is greater than the seller's minimum and less than the buyer's maximum, since otherwise there would have been no transaction. It is true that the actual negotiated price may differ from the old advertised price, but in this case one party's increase in surplus is exactly offset by the other's decrease in surplus, and overall surplus remains the same. Second, the negotiation system allows transactions to occur that would not occur under the price tag system. Suppose, for example, that a buyer finds the tag price too high. If there is an opportunity for negotiation, the seller may let the item go for a lower price that is still above his minimum in order to make a sale. Similarly, a seller may find the tag price too low but sell the item to a rich buyer who is willing to pay more, but still less than the buyer's maximum. In this way negotiation allows additional transactions to take place and therefore results in more producer and consumer surplus. It also allows more buyers to acquire the goods they want and more sellers to clean out their inventory.

In this sense, at least, traditional negotiation is more efficient than the fixed-price system. Yet in another sense it is less efficient. If customers negotiated the price of everything they purchased in a supermarket, the checkout queues would be much worse than they are now. In a word, traditional negotiation allows more people to get what they want, but fixed prices save time. The fixed-price system seems clearly superior for a consumer-oriented society in which people make hundreds of transactions a day (reserving negotiation for major items like real estate), while the negotiation system seems superior for economies in which there are fewer consumer transactions. Perhaps the West developed its consumer orientation in part because its low-context culture allowed a fixed-price system to evolve.

In general, a low-context culture seems more suited to a society with complex technology-based systems, whereas a high-context culture is better suited to a society with complex cultural norms and values. One provides instant communication and a house full of consumer goods but leaves people wondering what it is all for. One is slow and inefficient but wraps its participants in a rich system of meaning. Can we say that one is more "rational" or more "advanced" than the other?

Islam

Islam provides rock-solid security in a treacherous world. It has many parallels with Protestant Christianity, and one cannot help recalling Martin Luther's famous Reformation hymn, *Ein Feste Burg Ist Unser Gott (A Mighty Fortress Is Our God)*. For Muslims, Allah is the mighty fortress, the one immovable point in a shifting and unpredictable world. Muhammad the Prophet (may peace be upon him) founded Islam in seventh-century Mecca, which makes it the youngest of the world's great religions. He traveled in the Levant, where he came to admire the monotheism of Judaism and Christianity. He believed that the Arab peoples should embrace monotheism as well, but in a refined form that superceded all the religions of the day.

Islam provides security through its austere and serene simplicity, reflecting the desert landscape from which it sprang. The entire faith is summed up in the two assertions that constitute the *Shahadah* (declaration of faith): *La ilaha illa'Llah; Muhammadun rasulu'Llah* (There is no god but [the] God; Muhammad is God's Prophet). All essentials follow from this. The first statement expresses the uncompromising monotheism of Islam. The only god is *the* God (*al-Llah,* Allah in English). This was a major departure from the prevailing religion in Mecca, which recognized 364 gods, one for every day of the year. Allah is also God of all peoples, whether they recognize it or not, whence the universalizing character of Islam. God is not divisible into a trinity, as in the Christian faith, because only an indivisible God can have the stainless-steel solidity that Allah provides. Once one begins to analyze God, to raise questions and develop various concepts of God, cracks begin to appear in the divine edifice, and absolute security begins to crumble. The existence and nature of Allah can only be revealed, not deduced. The nature of this revelation is given in the second part of the *Shahadah*: Allah is revealed through Muhammad, who was inspired to recite the Koran (*Qur'an*) to his followers; *Qur'an* is from the Arabic for "dictation" or "recitation."

The Koran instructs human beings in how to relate to Allah. The core of Islam is submission and obedience to God, which is roughly the meaning of *Islam* in Arabic; one who submits is a Muslim. In addition there are specific duties. First and foremost is the duty to profess one's faith in Allah by repeating the *Shahadah*. Many Muslims recite it daily, and some endeavor to make these their last words on earth. The second duty is prayer (*salat*) five times daily at dawn, at noon, in late afternoon, at dusk, and before retiring. Human beings are thrust into a secular world in which they are tested for righteousness. Because they are weak, however, they will go astray unless they reach up to Allah for help. It is through regular prayer that the certainty and stability of Allah become available to human beings. Anyone who has visited an Islamic city will remember with awe the cacophony of prayer calls periodically broadcast from minarets. Muslims at prayer normally spread out a rug and prostrate themselves facing Mecca, although I have heard Muslims in Europe mutter their prayers while riding a bicycle in a southeasterly direction. The most familiar prayer is the opening chapter of the Koran, which a billion Muslims worldwide have committed to memory. The translation of A. J. Arberry follows:[4]

> In the name of God, the Merciful, the Compassionate, Praise
> belongs to God, the Lord of all Being,
> the All-merciful, the All-compassionate,
>   the Master of the Day of Doom,
> Thee only we serve; to Thee alone we pray for succor.
>   Guide us in the straight path,
> The path of those whom Thou hast blessed,
> not of those against whom Thou art wrathful,
>   nor of those who are astray.

The third duty of Muslims is fasting (*siyam*) during Ramadan, the ninth month of the Muslim lunar calendar. The obligation applies only to adults, and those who are ill or otherwise indisposed can postpone the fast or replace it by almsgiving. During Ramadan, non-Muslims should take care not to eat or drink in the presence of colleagues who may be fasting. Almsgiving (*zakat*) is the fourth duty. Giving to the poor is not an act of charity, but justice. Islam inherits the strong justice tradition of Judaism and recognizes that the widow and the orphan are disadvantaged through no fault of their own. Wealth must be redistributed to correct the injustice we see around us. A common practice is to give 2.5 percent of one's income annually. The fifth duty is to make a pilgrimage (*hajj*) to Mecca at least once in one's lifetime, if able. It is scarcely an exaggeration to suggest that if a Muslim of limited means were offered the fulfillment of one wish, that wish would likely be a trip to Mecca. Pilgrims walk seven times around the *Kaaba*, a small cubical structure containing a black meteorite that was already a focus of devotion when Muhammad was growing up in Mecca. A spiritual highlight of the pilgrimage is that rich and poor become equal by wearing the same simple garb and blending into the mass of worshipers. An exception is the VIP treatment given the Saudi royal family, which offends the sense of justice of some Muslims who know about the practice.

These five duties are the five "pillars" of Islam. There are also six "pillars of the faith" that summarize the Islamic creed: belief in Allah, angels, divine revelation, prophets that speak for Allah, the hereafter, and predestination by Allah. Valid revelations include the Psalms of David, the Torah of Moses, the Gospel of Jesus, and of course the Koran as dictated by Muhammad. All of these persons are regarded as legitimate prophets, as are Adam, Noah, Abraham, Ishmael, Isaac, Jacob, Aaron, and Solomon, who are recognized in the Jewish tradition, and the New Testament figure John the Baptizer. Revelations prior to the Koran are seen as having transcription errors and subject to misinterpretation by their recipients. Muhammad is the final prophet, and the Koran the final and complete revelation.

The idea of predestination deserves special attention, since Westerners may find it an obvious and sometimes irritating feature of Islamic societies, particularly in Africa and the Middle East. One of the most repeated phrases in these regions is *inshallah* (God wills it). When things go wrong or get bogged down, people may respond with fatalistic *inshallah*s, rather than taking initiative and getting things done as impatient Westerners would have it. Yet fatalism serves much the same purpose in Islam as the notion of individual initiative and responsibility do in the West, particularly in the United States. Individual initiative is based on the assumption that defeat or calamity can be avoided if one takes responsibility for oneself. Automobile accidents, for example, kill some 40,000 people in the United States each year. One might ask how drivers can so casually get behind the wheel of so dangerous a vehicle. Perhaps it is because Americans have convinced themselves that they are individually in control. After all, one has one's hands on the wheel and one can drive defensively. People who die on the road are drunk, aggressive, sleepy, or otherwise irresponsible. (No one seems to think about cases in which the irresponsible driver is the *other* party in a two-car accident.) After the 2001 terrorist attacks on the United States, many travelers chose to drive rather than fly, even though driving is five or six times more likely to result in a fatality. Why? Perhaps because individuals have no control over what happens to the aircraft. One must simply sit there and perish, and so the anxiety level is higher. In the Middle East one's fate is more readily seen to be the will of Allah rather than the outcome of personal behavior. This likewise provides a sense of control, because *Someone* is in control, Someone to whom one can pray for intervention, who has some ultimate purpose in earthly events, and who is always there to welcome us into heaven. By all earthly appearances, Arabs and Westerners are both wrong. Our fate appears to be out of anyone's control, but we cannot accept this. The worst nightmare is a world full of senseless, random events. I am reminded of a friend who apparently dozed off momentarily on the highway and slammed into the rear of a bus that had stopped to pick up a passenger. He was killed instantly. This is the kind of meaningless fate no one wants to think about, and Arabs and Westerners have different ways of diverting attention from it. Westerners who become impatient with *inshallah*s might reflect on this.

In addition to the Koran, Muslims recognize the collection of writings known as the Hadith, which is seen as being consistent with the views of Muhammad but having less status than the Koran. It contains much of the basis for Islamic law (*shari'ah*), which is a key element of Islam due to the involvement of clerics in temporal government. Many of the tensions in Islam today trace to this temporal aspect of the faith. For example, the worldwide schism between Sunni and Shi'ite Muslims stems from a dispute over who should inherit political power or religious authority. The Shia Ali (Party of Ali) believe that leadership positions should be conferred on descendants of Ali, Muhammad's cousin and son-in-law, while the larger Sunni sect holds that succession need not be hereditary. The two sects recognize different writings as composing the Hadith.

The most talked-about worldly aspect of Islam, however, is jihad. The word has a sinister connotation in the West, much as the word *crusade* (from the Latin for "cross") does in the Islamic world. Muslims correctly point out that *jihad* need not refer to a "holy war," just as the Billy Graham "crusades" in the West do not involve military action. Literally, *jihad* is an "effort" or "struggle." On the other hand, the Koran identifies warfare as one type of jihad (the "lesser" jihad) and commands Muslims to convert infidels by force if necessary (9:29). Historians tell us that military jihads were an important part of early Islam, just as the Crusades were for Christians. It was a military jihad under Muhammad's command that made Mecca the holy city of Islam in 630 C.E., and within four years his followers had united all of the Bedouins of Arabia by the sword. The Bedouins formed a holy army that moved out across the Levant and North Africa. It is sometimes claimed that conversion to Islam was often left to individual choice, in part because Muslims honor the prophets of Judaism and Christianity. Whatever the case, warfare is historically an important component of jihad and remains so for the radical element of Islam today. The Western counterpart of jihad, however, is not so much the Crusades as colonialism, which often involved the force of arms. Both jihad and colonialism reflect the universalizing tendencies of the respective religions.

The Hadith and other worldly aspects of Islam may threaten its unity and simplicity, but the essentials have changed little during its fourteen centuries of existence. Freethinking and liberal theology are much less tolerated than in Judaism or Christianity. Westerners may see this as a weakness, presumably because it makes it difficult for Islam to keep up with the times. Yet Muslims can respond that a simple and unchanging faith is exactly what modernism needs. The Western world is a bewildering kaleidoscope of lifestyles, ideas, technology, and cults that have no coherence or ultimate meaning. Skepticism, pluralism, and constant change have corroded its religious foundations, leaving people without moorings. Obsession with sex, dependence on drugs, addiction to inane entertainment, and neglect of family are symptoms of the malaise. The answer to this complexity is not an equally complex postmodern religion that does not know what it believes, still less a godless existence. The answer, in the Islamic view, is the eternal simplicity of Allah.

The anachronism that Westerners see in Islam is due not so much to the immutability of its basic doctrines as to its epistemology. Since conservative

Islam invests ultimate authority solely in the holy scripture, there can be no independent basis for reconsidering even the less-important details. No latter-day prophet, no vision, no chain of reasoning, and no wisdom gained from experience can serve as a corrective. Muhammad's views toward women were progressive in his day, for example, but once they were recorded, there was no easy possibility of further progress. The same problem occurs in fundamentalist Christianity or in any faith that places ultimate authority in the written Word of God.

In the meantime, Westerners should take care to understand accurately what is in fact written in the holy book of Islam. The Koran is not easy reading for Westerners, partly due to the difficulty of translating Arabic, and the illogical arrangement of material. Aside from the opening chapter, or sura, the chapters are arranged in order of decreasing length. A remarkable amount of misinformation circulates about the Koran, not only in the West but also in the Islamic world due to the confusion of Koranic authority and local custom. Perhaps it is useful to set a few things straight on the rights of women in particular, since there is much misunderstanding in this area: (a) The Koran does not forbid women from working or getting an education. On the contrary, it protects the right of women to earn wages (4:32), inherit wealth (4:7), collect a dowry (4:4), and retain control over all of these. Muhammad was a manager in his wife's business. Today women play a role in the business sector even in conservative Saudi Arabia, where many earn advanced degrees; (b) The Koran is widely interpreted as saying that a man can divorce his wife by uttering "I divorce you" three times (2:229–30). It is more plausibly read as saying that a husband and wife cannot remarry if they have been divorced three times (unless the wife marries and divorces another man). In general, the Koran enumerates a number of rights that women have in family situations. It is also common in the Islamic world for women to keep their family name when they marry, a development that occurred only recently in the West; (c) The Koran suggests that a man can have up to four wives at one time if he can treat them equally (4:3), but it elsewhere says that it is impossible to treat multiple wives equally (4:129); (d) The Koran requires that women cover their bosoms, not their faces (24:31); and (e) The Koran does not forbid women to drive an automobile or fly an airplane.

Islam's strict monotheism provides assurance to a billion souls, but not all Muslims have found it adequate. By the eleventh century a yearning had arisen for a less formal and more mystical approach to faith. Led by Abu-Hamid Muhammad al-Ghazzali, an Islamic movement known as "Sufism" (from the Arabic for "wool wearers") developed a monastic lifestyle with an emphasis on asceticism and achieving union with God. One group of monks, the dervishes, enter a state of ecstasy through such practices as whirling and howling. Sufis have produced a rich religious literature, including the thirteenth-century poetry of Jalal-ud-Din Rumi. Sufi pantheism is diametrically opposed to Islamic theology, but Sufis nonetheless revere the Koran and have exerted a corrective influence on the formality of mainline Islam.

Parallels with Protestant Christianity

Islam is not as alien to the West as it may seem. There are close parallels between the conservative side of the faith and the fundamentalist wing of Protestant Christianity. Fundamentalists are more sedate in worship and emphasize a literal reading of the Bible. The well-known preacher Jerry Falwell is a fundamentalist, for example, while Jimmy Swaggert is a Pentecostal.

The resemblance begins with Martin Luther's emphasis on holy scripture as a foundation for faith, rather than the pronouncements of the Church hierarchy. His main protest was against the corruption of some Church officials, but by calling into question the authority of post-Biblical Church tradition, Luther opened the door to a fundamentalism that invests ultimate authority in canonical scripture. Conservative Islam not only has a similar view of scripture, but the holy books of the two faiths substantially overlap. Even the Annunciation of Jesus's birth to Mary appears in the Koran. In addition, the stern prohibitions of Islam are mirrored by similar strictures in Protestantism. If conservative Muslims must forswear alcohol, girly magazines, and premarital sex, conservative Christians must do likewise. Guilt is important in both groups, and self-esteem requires that people occupy the moral high ground and display a certain amount of self-righteousness, even if this requires implausible rationalization.

Given these parallels, it is ironic that many Muslims seem to be unaware of the existence of Protestant Christianity. Muslims in the Middle East tend to identify Christianity with the Orthodox churches that are prevalent in that region. They frown upon the icons that adorn church interiors, since Islam strictly condemns any representation of the divine as idolatry. Perhaps Muslims would take a different attitude toward a Christian sect whose lifestyle, and church interiors for that matter, are as austere as any Muslim's.

A particularly close parallel between Protestantism and Islam is the emphasis on ritual purity. Protestantism gave rise to the Puritan lifestyle, which insists that cleanliness is next to Godliness. It does not recognize unclean foods as Islam does, since the New Testament rejects Jewish dietary laws, but it emphasizes wholesome living, a clean body and tidy home, and abstinence from premarital sex and profane language. Language may not seem a matter of cleanliness, but recall that one traditional punishment for obscene talk was washing out the offender's mouth with soap. Cleanliness deals with stress by giving one some means of protecting oneself from harm. Guilt becomes part of the mechanism for enforcing clean living, because feeling guilty is related to feeling dirty. In recent years Puritanism has evolved away from sex taboos toward a preoccupation with avoiding germs, eliminating mouth and body odor, exercise, avoiding tobacco, using politically correct language, and eating natural foods.

Islam has a comparable focus on cleanliness. Unclean foods are similar to those of Judaism: pork is *haram* (forbidden), as is blood and the flesh of animals improperly slaughtered. In addition, alcohol is prohibited, along with drugs that fog the mind (e.g., narcotics). Muslims must wash them-selves before prayer and in general practice good hygiene. Various tradi-tions require men and women to clip their nails, pull their armpit hair, and shave their pubic hair. As in many cultures, menstruating women are considered unclean, and there are restrictions on their behavior.

A final parallel with Christian fundamentalism is a common emphasis on ideology and legalism, which again traces to placing all authority in scrip-ture. There is a tendency to build a thought system and to engage in "proof texting," or citing chapter and verse from the holy book to settle any dispute that may come up. Fundamentalism, whether it be religious funda-mentalism, doctrinaire Marxism, or right-wing ideology, feels a need to derive all of life from an unquestioned set of principles, even when there are gaps in the logic. This is a Herculean task, and fundamentalists may invest enormous energy in maintaining and implementing their thought system. Since there can be no independent corrective to their deductions—since the heart cannot temper the mind—extremism and terrorism may result.

It is unclear that Islam, any more than Protestant Christianity, must in-vest *sole* authority in scripture in order to maintain the faith. In any event, history teaches that Islam need not embrace a fundamentalism that retards cultural and economic development. Medieval Islam grounded one of the world's most affluent civilizations. Islamic scholars of this period, for example, were among the best in the world, particularly in science and mathematics. One could write volumes on the contributions of medieval Islam to Western science and letters. To take just one illustration, com-puter scientists who write algorithms pay homage to Al-Khwarizmi, the great ninth-century Islamic mathematician (*algorithm,* originally *algorism,* derives from his name). Mathematicians and engineers who use algebra are indebted to his treatise *Kitab al-Jabr wal-Muqabala,* or *Al-Jabr* for short. Al-Khwarizmi lived in Baghdad, which at that time was one of the commercial and intellectual capitals of the world.

Conflict with the West

Despite the past achievements of the Islamic world, today it sees itself as besieged. It is subservient to a global economic system that it views as favoring Western interests. It feels compelled to play by Western rules or suffer economic decline. Perhaps even more distressing than external pressures is the poverty that persists in most Islamic countries. The spectacle of wealthy business people watching CNN in lavish Cairo apartments, while children outside dig through garbage dumps, profoundly insults the Koranic sense of justice. Islam feels humiliated, and Western domination provides a ready explanation for its predicament. Resentment against Western powers, particularly the United States, has grown since the rise of globalization.

A number of alternate explanations have been offered for anti-Western sentiments. Muslims themselves most often cite U.S. support of Israel in its conflict with Palestinians. Cultural memory of the Crusades, as well as the presence of the U.S. military in Saudi Arabia, stir resentment. Since Islam and the West are the world's two most strongly universalizing cultures, they become locked in self-righteous condemnation of each other, one preaching women's rights and democracy while the other extols family values and religious devotion. These are all factors, but there is something else at stake. Even Islam's quarrel with the West derives from something still more basic: discontent with its own leaders. Too many of the elite have turned their gaze to the West and abandoned their responsibilities at home. They speak English, send their children to American universities, and make alliances with Western interests. Although Westernization of elites is a worldwide phenomenon, Islamic societies see it as particularly corrupting, because it distracts the privileged from a Koranic duty to do justice and succor the poor. The Islamic world therefore views the West as contributing to its own injustice and poverty and unleashes its wrath accordingly.

Poverty is not the only factor, as demonstrated by anti-Western sentiment in wealthy Kuwait. Nonetheless, resentment is stronger and more violent in countries with large numbers of poor. A compounding factor is that it is often safer for Muslims to protest against foreign powers than against their own governments, which may have little tolerance for internal dissent. The U.S. government exacerbates the situation by supporting pro-Western potentates, such as President Hosni Mubarak in Egypt and the former Shah Reza Pahlavi in Iran. It does not help that the Egyptian elite benefit from massive American foreign aid, a legacy of the Camp David peace agreement between Israel's Manachem Begin and former Egyptian President Anwar Sadat, who was later assassinated by Egyptian terrorists to avenge his accommodation with the West. Well aware of opposition to its pro-Western stance, the present government permits anti-American vitriol in the media as an escape valve. In similar fashion, the conservative House of Saud compromises with the West while tolerating and even supporting the fundamentalist Wahhabi wing of Islam, which schools children worldwide with an anti-Western bias.

The long-term solution would seem to be a recrudescence of Islamic civilization, which in some senses is already underway. There is every reason to assume that Islam can provide the foundation for a tolerant and prosperous culture today, as it has done in the past. It will not be a clone of Western culture, however. Governments may be less like Western democracies with their deal making among self-interested factions and more like an Arab kingdom in which every citizen traditionally has the right to an audience with a local sheik, whose Koranic duty is to mete out justice and consider the welfare of the whole. Popular media may remain under the influence of a culture that expects it to inculcate moral values, rather than be turned over to business interests that prosper by appealing to one's basest instincts. Men and women may enjoy the rights and privileges endowed by the Koran, but within the constraints of their traditional family roles. Again we are reminded that cultural development can proceed in many directions, not only the one that the Western mind takes to be self-evident. Perhaps the first step toward a renewed Islamic civilization is to turn off the Western TV set.

Notes for Chapter 12

1. *Changing Places: A Tale of Two Campuses,* Penguin Books (New York, 1995).

2. Roger Fisher and William Ury, *Getting to Yes,* Penguin Books (New York, 1991).

3. Fikret Adaman, Ali Çarkoğlu, and Burhan Şenatalar, "Corruption in Turkey: Results of Diagnostic Household Survey," February 2001. Available: http://econ.boun.edu.tr/staff/adaman/research/Corruption.PDF.

4. A. J. Arberry, trans., *The Koran Interpreted,* Simon and Schuster (New York, 1955). Islam maintains that all translations of the Koran are, properly speaking, interpretations, since the Arabic text is untranslatable.

13   Zimbabwe

I had been teaching a short time in Zimbabwe when a colleague suggested that I accompany him on a trip to a remote rural area. His task was to deliver some materials to a farmer who was involved in agricultural experiments. Some of the country people may not speak English, he pointed out, and it would be a chance for me to work on my Shona language skills.

We drove south into a semiarid region known for its baobab trees, which have been described as both upside-down and inside-out. The branches resemble roots on a tree whose branches are buried underground. Nutrients rise through the interior of the tree rather than through the bark, allowing local people to strip off the external layer for utilitarian purposes without harming the tree. For long stretches the only buildings in sight were little round *mamusha* (plural of *kumusha*) with conical thatched roofs, the traditional Shona dwelling, and school buildings. The latter are part of President Robert Mugabe's successful effort to raise literacy rates in both urban and rural areas. Driving was relatively easy, as the British colonial administration left the country with a respectable infrastructure, including good roads, and the mild, dry climate of the Zimbabwe plateau does not rapidly erode the pavement. However, there were no electricity or telephone wires to be seen. We carried a spare gasoline tank in the back of the car, as petrol stations can be a hundred miles apart, and even those few may close unpredictably.

As we approached our destination, we left the highway and immediately encountered some women and children walking alongside the road. The Shona and many other African peoples believe in sharing, and motorists in particular are expected to make good use of empty seats in the car. Hitchhikers can sometimes be dangerous, but the women and children were harmless enough, and so we stopped and let them pile into the back. I started the conversation with the Shona greeting ritual: "*Maswera sei?*" (How is your day?) One of them replied with the usual formula, "*Ndiswera maswerawo*" (My day is good if yours is). It is a remarkable response. The very language of greeting reflects the deepest foundation of Shona culture, a characteristic that is nearly incomprehensible to Western individualism. One person's pain is everyone's pain, and one person's joy is everyone's joy. The community is a single human organism.

The greeting ritual normally continues with such remarks as *Hwakadii hupenyu?* (How is the family?) *Hupenyu hwakanaka* (the family is fine).

Kwakadii kumusha? (How are things at home?) *Kumusha kwakanaka* (things are fine at home). My companion urged me, however, to ask how many of the children attended school, since it is customary to give school children ball-point pens, which they often cannot afford to buy. He kept a cache of them in the glove box. *"Vangani vana vanoenda kuchikoro?"* I went on to apologize for my speech, explaining that I was only learning the language and was not very good yet. *"Ndiri kudzidzira kutaura chiShona, ase handinyadzi kugona chiShona."* At this point one of the ladies broke into perfect Oxfordian English: "On the contrary, sir, you are rather good for a beginner."

Our aim was to confer with the village chief, who lived in a small frame house among a cluster of *mamusha*. When we arrived several kids gathered around us as others hid bashfully behind the house. They knelt and clapped their hands when we passed out ball-point pens, demonstrating the traditional way that women and children express their appreciation. The chief had been listening to news from the outside world on his battery-powered radio, and he was eager to discuss the latest developments in agricultural economics. He, too, spoke English, but it was difficult to follow—not due to his accent, but due to his liberal use of economic jargon. He spoke of exchange rates, balance of payments, and so forth, with a level of sophistication that is rare in national capitals and astonishing in an area that is several hours' drive from the nearest telephone. All the while he interspersed his peroration with smiles and laughter, at times literally slapping his knee with delight. I had never heard the dismal science discussed with such mirth. One might have thought he had drunk a bit much of the local maize beer, but he was only displaying a signature characteristic of the Shona culture: their love of laughter.

Already I was being exposed to several key traits of Shona culture: their emphasis on courtesy, their identification with the community, their high level of literacy, and their reliance on humor and amusement to get them through the day.

African Cultures

Much of the world tends to view Africa as a unit. In the 1960s the United States employed an "ambassador to Africa," who resided in Nairobi (the capital of Africa?). In reality Africa is a vast area supporting vastly different peoples. Libyans and Botswanans provide no hint that they might inhabit the same continent. Many outsiders distinguish Muslim North Africa from subsaharan Africa, but not even this is correct, since there is a Muslim population in Tanzania and a Christian population in Egypt. The very size of the continent tends to be underestimated. We know intellectually that most map projections shrink equatorial land masses, but they influence our thinking nonetheless. The coast of Mozambique alone, for example, is longer than the east coast of the United States stretching from Boston to Miami, although it appears much shorter on most maps. I often show my classes the Peters projection in order to correct these misperceptions.

Our best evidence indicates that Africa is the cradle of humankind. The continent not only contains the earliest traces of Homo sapiens, which are at least 200,000 years old, but here alone can one trace the early evolution of such hominid species as *homo australopithecus, homo habilis,* and *homo erectus.* Africans invented human culture, and for eons theirs were the only cultures. The Nile valley produced one of the world's earliest farming regions, and later one of the world's first civilizations.

Due to its remoteness and difficult climate, central Africa was largely insulated from outside influences until the late nineteenth century. Northern Africa and coastal regions, however, have interacted with Middle Eastern and Mediterranean cultures for millennia. Christianity spread along the Mediterranean coast and up the Nile valley by the sixth century. Muslim armies invaded Egypt in 642 and occupied North Africa to Gibraltar within seventy years. Within a few centuries, Muslim traders operating across the Sahara and in the Indian Ocean had brought the Islamic faith to parts of West Africa and halfway down the east coast. The Portuguese inaugurated European colonialism in the late fifteenth century. They quickly began using black slaves, purchased from West African chiefs, on the colonial sugar plantations of Principe and São Tomé. By the eighteenth century the trans-Atlantic slave trade reached a peak of some 100,000 captives per year, shipped across the ocean under almost unimaginably wretched conditions. In the nineteenth century Great Britain, which by that time accounted for about half the slave trade, became the first major power to abolish it, and other European states followed suit. This ironically led to the last great surge of African colonialism, since Europeans reasoned that if they were to benefit from African commerce in a more legitimate fashion, they had better establish a presence there. Colonial powers carved up the remainder of the continent in the late nineteenth century.[1] One of the new colonies was Southern Rhodesia, precursor of today's Zimbabwe.

Zimbabwe and Its Origins

Unlike many African countries, Zimbabwe is dominated by a single ethnic group. The Shona people make up about 71 percent of the population. Although European colonial powers drew national boundaries with little regard to ethnic homelands, Zimbabwe was lucky enough to avoid much of the ethnic fragmentation that afflicts so many countries. The population is by no means entirely homogeneous, however, since the Ndebele people in the southwest represent a significant minority, accounting for 16 percent of the total. In recognition of ethnic minorities, the government has promoted English, rather than Shona, as the official language and has achieved about 85 percent English-language literacy. This is despite the fact that native English speakers represent less than 1 percent of the population, and many of these are leaving the country due to recent seizures of their farmland. I focus on the Shona people partly because of their numerical dominance, and partly due to my ignorance of the Ndebele culture; I lived in Mutare, whose population is almost entirely Shona.

The name *Zimbabwe* dates back to the 1950s, when the native populations of southern African colonies began to reject their colonial names, at least unofficially. Northern Rhodesians called their land "Zambia," an abbreviation of Zambezia. Nyasaland became Malawi, after a seventeenth-century empire in the area. Southern Rhodesians adopted the name *Zimbabwe*, which derives from the Shona words *dzimba dzamabwe*, or "stone buildings." Historically, a *zimbabwe* is a royal residence or palace, a number of which were built by Shona rulers in roughly the fourteenth and fifteenth centuries C.E.[2] The most impressive of these was the Great Zimbabwe, a large compound whose ruins I made a point to visit. At one time white residents of the country widely believed that outsiders must have built the Great Zimbabwe, on the theory that Africans are not capable of such a structure. Ian Smith's regime, the last white government in Rhodesia, passed a law forbidding any archaeologist to publish a different opinion, whereupon the country's archaeologists moved to South Africa. The Shona people typically have not, however, expressed their aspirations through physical architecture. According to historian David Beach, they "put their greatest efforts into the creation of a complex set of political, religious and social relationships that rarely left material traces."[3]

The Shona people migrated to the Zimbabwean plateau at least as early as 900 C.E., most likely from the coastal area that is now Mozambique.[4] The Ndebele apparently descend from Nguni people of South Africa and established a nineteenth-century kingdom north of present-day Pretoria. In the late 1800s Cecil Rhodes' British South Africa Company colonized what is now Zimbabwe in the name of the British crown. Rhodes and his agents salivated over the ancient gold mines of the Rozvi and Mutapa empires. They were disappointed to find the mines exhausted, however, and so they took land instead, primarily from the Ndebele and Shona. Eventually white settlers owned one-third of the colony, reserving for themselves the best land.

By the 1960s the United Kingdom was resigned to granting independence to its African colonies. Malawi and Zambia received statehood, but Prime Minister Ian Smith of Southern Rhodesia was a step ahead of the British. Supported by a small minority of the white population, in 1965 he unilaterally declared independence in order to preserve white rule of the country, resulting in the 1970 establishment of a new republic of Rhodesia. This galvanized the determination of the two main opposition groups to install black rule. Joshua Nkomo's ZAPU (Zimbabwe African People's Union) was largely Ndebele, and Ndabaningi Sithole's ZANU (Zimbabwe African National Union) was primarily Shona. They began with isolated of acts of sabotage and gradually escalated violent resistance against Smith's regime.[5] It is characteristic of the region that unrest builds very slowly but inevitably, a phenomenon that is repeating itself in Zimbabwe as I write this. By the late 1970s ZANU was gaining the upper hand, partly because it was able to use Mozambique as a base for raids. When walking near the Mozambique border, I was careful to stay on the road, to avoid land mines that were planted in that era to keep the rebels out. Under pressure from the resistance and at the insistence of Henry Kissinger, Smith finally agreed to majority rule in Zimbabwe. Free elections were held in 1980, with the victory going to Robert Mugabe, a leader in the ZANU resistance. Over the next few years Mugabe crushed opposition in ZAPU and the Ndebele minority, and consolidated his power. Even in recent years, opposition leaders have died in suspicious auto accidents. Mugabe and his ZANU-PF (PF for Patriotic Front) still ruled the country as of early 2003.

The Post-Colonial Situation

One can get a glimpse of Shona culture by noting that Ian Smith continues to live in Zimbabwe and is often seen around the capital city of Harare. He owns a farm in Shurugwe, although it is apparently on the list of those the government has decided to confiscate. The octogenarian has written columns for Harare newspapers and vehemently defends his record. Given the misery and oppression he visited upon black Zimbabweans, he might seem a likely target for a lynch mob, and yet he receives a certain amount of respect as a venerable leader. This remarkable phenomenon is due in part to the tendency of the Shona to forgive and forget. They prefer to move on rather than hold a grudge, except where traditional ethnic rivalries are involved. I recall that when U.S. President Bill Clinton toured Africa, he made it a point in some of his speeches to apologize to Africans for the American slave trade. I was not on the scene, but I can imagine African audiences listening politely to comments that must have seemed totally irrelevant to their concerns. Clinton's remarks were less an apology to Africa than an attempt at absolution for his own country, which still struggles with guilt over chattel slavery. Africans have long since moved beyond the issue.

Some may interpret the Ian Smith phenomenon and similar situations as "reverse racism," but this is again a mistake. It is true that white visitors to Africa are sometimes ushered through customs or other formalities when black travelers are detained. I experienced something like this myself when I went shopping. It is common for shops to post a guard at the door to check receipts as customers leave, as a deterrent against shoplifting. I always had my receipt ready, but without exception the guard waved me through without checking. He did not do so because I am white, however. He did so because my race and age were tip-offs that I was probably someone rich and important, and should therefore be shown deference. Any rich person is by definition a leader, for reasons I will discuss shortly. Since white visitors from abroad are usually rich by local standards, they often receive special treatment that might give the impression of reverse racism. But Zimbabweans do not share the West's conception of race, still less its preoccupation with the subject. They give respect where respect is due, and as an elder statesman and former ruler of the country, Ian Smith deserves some degree of respect whatever his opinions or race.

Another misconception regarding the post-colonial situation surrounds Mugabe's recent expulsion of white commercial farmers from their lands. It is easy for Westerners to see the matter as one of racial conflict: whites confiscated the best farmland during the colonial era, and whites still hold on to large tracts of this land. Black Zimbabweans resent this and clamor for land reform. This is in fact the sort of rhetoric that Mugabe uses to explain his actions, perhaps in expectation that it will resonate in the Western media. As it happens, race plays almost no role in the situation. There is no denying the rapacity of the colonial land grab, but few black Zimbabweans hold this against the current white landowners. They prefer to forgive and forget. They regard whites as an ethnic group with some very queer characteristics, but as useful to have around due to their managerial skills. Their somewhat distant and impersonal nature seems to equip them to make objective decisions. Their disbelief in witchcraft makes them less susceptible to its influence. Aside from their economic role, whites do not seem to interest Zimbabweans. The Shona almost never mention whites in their literature, despite their overbearing role in the nation's history. A good example is the epic poem *Soko Risina Musoro* written by resistance hero and lawyer Herbert W. Chitepo, which is often assigned reading in schools. Although Chitepo defined himself largely through his legal opposition to the white regime and died from a bomb blast one morning when he turned the ignition key of his automobile, he never alludes to Westerners in his best-known work.

As for the white population, they prefer to lie low and stay out of trouble, much like the ethnic Chinese in Malaysia, who play a parallel role in that country. The colonial settlers, or "Rhodies," commonly exhibited the racist attitudes of that era, but it is widely recognized that nearly all such people left the country after independence. The white population today is less than one-fifth of its 1980 level. They see themselves as patriotic Zimbabweans who were performing a valuable service, namely, generating about 40 percent of the country's export trade. Yet they do not regard themselves as missionaries in a heathen land. They are a bit irritated by Western backpackers who come to Africa for the "Third World experience" and refer to them as "TWGs" (Third World groupies).

The seizure of white-owned farms has a very different etiology than racial conflict or resentment of colonialism. Since the beginning of his administration, Mugabe has been dogged by the question of the war veterans, who expect some reward for their sacrifice. According to one story in circulation, which I cannot confirm, Mugabe was reluctant to follow the usual African practice of hiring them as police, since they had become hardened to violence and would make for an oppressive police force. Instead Mugabe gave them pensions and hired civilians as police, some of whom do have remarkably sweet dispositions. It appears, however, that he stopped paying stipends to the veterans after two years.[6] The issue reemerged in 1997, when veterans agitated for benefits with strong public support. Mugabe promised benefits and land, but it was unclear how he could afford to keep his promise.

In the meantime Mugabe was facing a second crisis. In the early years he strongly championed English-language literacy and achieved nearly universal education. School children diligently studied their lessons in the expectation that when they graduated from high school their lives would change. In the late 1990s these students in fact began to graduate, whereupon they found a disintegrating economy rather than attractive new jobs that would take advantage of their education. The economic woes have several causes. The unrest of the 1980s got things off to a bad start. In the late 1980s Mugabe appealed to the World Bank and International Monetary Fund, which encouraged the government to sell part of its grain reserve to generate foreign exchange.[7] The timing was unfortunate, as the most severe drought in memory hit southern Africa in 1991. It killed countless farm animals and drove many rural people to the cities, where some resorted to a life of crime for survival. Even today Harare streets are unsafe, day or night. In more recent years the AIDS pandemic has exacted a terrible toll in both human and economic terms. There are stories that employers sometimes hire three men to fill one position, because two are expected to die soon.

Mugabe's land seizure was apparently designed to kill two birds with one stone. He would give war veterans parcels of white-owned land rather than pensions he could not afford. The prospect of land reform would restore his popularity among a disillusioned population—a pipe dream, since Zimbabweans are more interested in a healthy economy than land reform. At first he more or less invited veterans to begin seizing farms. Some of them obliged, resulting in several deaths and much destruction. Many of these "veterans," incidentally, are hangers-on who are veterans of nothing but vagrancy and crime. In recent months Mugabe has stepped up the seizures, threatening landowners with prison or worse if they refuse to leave. The economic impact promises to be a disaster, since confiscated farms have so far sat idle. Thousands of agricultural jobs are disappearing from a land where a single employee typically supports a large extended family, and farm production is dropping precipitously.

Zimbabweans see their slide into disaster as inevitable. As mentioned in the previous chapter, many people outside the West do not conceive history as a process subject to human control.

Kunzi Munhu Vamwe

This traditional saying captures the soul of Shona culture. The best rendering I can give for the aphorism is, "To be human is to be named by others." It expresses the idea that human existence does not occur on an individual level. Humanity is shared by the community, and one partakes of humanity when recognized by the community. This has very practical consequences. When walking down the hall, I made it a point to greet each person I saw, even those I had greeted several times earlier in the day. To fail to acknowledge another person is pathological, like failing to acknowledge a part of oneself. When I walked into a shop, I took time to exchange pleasantries with the clerk. When making a presentation, I was careful to recognize people in the audience by name for their role in the enterprise under discussion. One of the many errors committed by pharmaceutical corporations when they tried to address the AIDS problem in southern Africa was to ignore local officials. This behavior not only bruised egos but also violated basic cultural norms. As a teacher, I was expected to relate to every student in a personal, albeit authoritative, manner. Shortly after my first class I had lunch with colleagues, who pointed out a couple of my students as they walked by our table. When I confessed I did not yet know their names, one of the professors remarked, "Just like you Americans. You care nothing for your students."

A vivid illustration of community occurred in one of my classes. A student from Sierra Leone learned, several weeks after the fact (due to poor communications), that his mother had died in that country's civil war. She had been undergoing treatment in a hospital when armed militants drove off the doctors and nurses, leaving many patients to die in their beds. This student was scheduled to make a presentation in my class, but I suggested to him beforehand that we should postpone it until he felt more like concentrating on his work. He insisted on going ahead with the presentation, for a reason that my students in the United States may find difficult to believe: he so valued his education that he would not allow a single opportunity for learning to slip by. (On more than one occasion students came to my class sweating from malarial fever, so as not to miss a word of instruction.) The class rallied around the bereaved student and offered encouragement, despite the ethnic differences between himself and the others, differences that can be very potent in Africa. Unfortunately he lost his composure during the presentation and was obliged to cut it short. His fellow students not only comforted him, but the following day one of his classmates stood up and asked to make a statement. He apologized to me, the professor, for the student's poor performance and explained the reason for it. I reassured the class that I was well aware of the reason and would certainly give the student a second chance when he felt up to it.

Mutual support is economic as well as emotional. The ancient system of reciprocity, which has characterized many traditional cultures, allows one who is less fortunate to "borrow" tools or other items from those more fortunate. The favor is returned when fortunes are reversed, although no strict accounting is kept. Something like this system still operates in Shona culture. I happened to meet a Canadian journalist of African ancestry who had been working in Africa for several months. She had obviously come to Africa in search of her roots, and she was disillusioned. This business of African generosity, she told me, is a fraud. It is all based on self-interest. For example, she had recently interviewed some villagers who had pooled their meager resources to send a young man to college. The only reason a family would contribute to this effort, she insisted, was that next time one of their own children may benefit. It was purely a matter of self-interest. Why else would they do it? It was clear to me that in the journalist's worldview, nothing was allowed to count as adequate explanation of behavior except self-interest. Her conclusion that self-interest was behind everything was therefore unsurprising. The fact is, however, that self-interest (in the sense of the individual self) is not at work here. It is the interest of the community, which can benefit by educating its young people. This might be called "self-interest" of a sort, but only if the self is identified with the community.

The communitarian viewpoint combines with the "big man" system of leadership (see Chapter 3) to impose a form of noblesse oblige on persons of wealth and status. Leaders typically receive and retain their status through their generosity to others, and those who possess wealth are expected to assume this kind of leadership. Western tourists sometimes get a taste of this system when they make acquaintance with a guide or driver in Zimbabwe. The Zimbabwean asks for the tourist's address back home, so that he or she can write a letter. A few weeks later the letter arrives. It tells a heartbreaking tale of family misfortune, all of it doubtless true and unexaggerated, and asks the recipient for money. Westerners tend to be a little shocked by what appears to be a crass solicitation, but in Shona culture it is entirely proper, even obligatory. Foreign tourists are viewed as having a leadership role because of their wealth. There is no shame or loss of pride in asking for a handout that is genuinely needed, and in any event, the supplicants would literally give the shirts off their backs if the tables were turned. This fact is illustrated by the story with which I began this book.

The Shona system of sharing sustains the community through thick and thin. Good jobs are scarce, but those who have them support a large extended family, perhaps in addition to live-in maids and security guards. When misfortune strikes, there is no insurance, but one can go to the boss or village chief for help. Any manager or supervisor can therefore expect frequent requests for money or special favors. It is impossible to meet all such requests and unwise to try, but it is imperative to respond to some of them. It is one of the duties that come with authority. One must use one's best judgment in meting out favors, honoring the requests that are legitimate, urgent, and reasonable. Several of my students, for example, asked me to give them a laptop computer. Their requests were perhaps encouraged by the fact that I had given them textbooks, whose price was far beyond their means. I had to explain that laptop computers are more expensive than textbooks, and it was a major investment even to buy one for myself. However, I offered to teach them how to use a computer and in the end gave private lessons in Excel spreadsheets to all of my beginning students. Fortunately the university provided a public-use computer lab in which they could practice their skills.

The ethic of sharing operates even at the national level. Partly at the request of the South African Development Community, in the 1980s Zimbabwe sold much of its reserve grain at low prices (through aid agencies) to famine-stricken Malawi, Mozambique, and even Ethiopia. These acts of generosity helped to deplete the national grain reserve prior to the 1991 drought.[8] The same value system leads Zimbabweans to accept aid as readily as they give it. In fact, the African viewpoint interacts in a curious way with the very different values of Western donor nations. Westerners who believe in individual self-reliance nonetheless feel a duty to make charitable contributions, while Africans who totally reject individualism accept the aid without shame or loss of self-respect. The resulting dynamic tends to reinforce the very sort of African dependence that Westerners cannot respect.

An important byproduct of the communitarian viewpoint is Zimbabwe's "feminine" culture. It is not feminine in the sense that men and women have equal status, since men are unquestionably in charge. It is feminine in the sense that competition is seriously discouraged, for the obvious reason that it undermines the kind of cooperation and sharing that sustains the culture. In my operations management course I asked student teams to analyze a local manufacturing or service operation and present their conclusions to the class. One of the teams chose to study the Mutare post office. For their presentation they converted the classroom into an elaborate mockup of the post office, in order to demonstrate how it processes mail. When I walked into the room and saw their handiwork, I knew immediately there would be trouble. The students had gotten carried away in their enthusiasm and forgot how their classmates would react. As the class arrived they displayed what I call the "African frown," an unmistakable signal of disapproval. They saw this group as trying to outdo the others with their elaborate demonstration. Upon seeing the hostile stares from classmates, one of the presenting students apologized to the class. They were only trying to illustrate the points in their presentation, she explained, and there was no intent to surpass the other presentations.

Zimbabwe's ancient system of sharing, reciprocity, and accountable leadership has substantially deteriorated in the urban centers, and no one is more aware of it than Zimbabweans. They constantly complain, both privately and in newspaper columns, about village leaders who seek their fortunes in the city and forget about their obligations to the folks back home. Too many urbanized young people get caught up in night life and neglect their families. The big-man system has degenerated into political patronage that further enriches a few well-heeled cronies rather than redistributes resources to the needy. The generosities to villagers that once kept a leader in power have become bribes reluctantly paid to officials who keep him in business. The rampant corruption that outsiders see in Zimbabwe and other African countries is indeed corruption, but it is not corruption of Western-style transparency. It is corruption of a redistributive system that helped to sustain humanity's oldest cultures for a quarter of a million years. The root of the corruption is an economic system that disrupts traditional relationships. It removes people from their village context and employs them on commercial farms, in city shops, and in government offices. The new economy has its advantages, but Western agents installed it and

Zimbabweans embraced it with little thought as to how the ancient cultural fabric could be rewoven to fit the new lifestyle.

Managing Stress

Occasionally I come across a true story that provides a better textbook illustration than anyone could invent. I heard such a story from a young American couple who were teaching in Zimbabwe on a Fulbright scholarship. One day they went for a drive in the isolated but scenic Honde Valley at the eastern edge of the country. It is one my own favorite places in Zimbabwe, since the culture here seems less disturbed and more authentically Shona than in many areas. As the car descended into the valley along the steep and curvy access road, two women at roadside waved it down. One of them was obviously in the late stages of labor, and the Americans assumed they wanted transport to the clinic. It turned out that they wanted to visit a woman who served as a kind of village shaman, so that she could bless the newborn according to local traditions, but as it happened she lived next door to the clinic. One of the Americans told me with some satisfaction about how his wife hurriedly drove the ladies toward the clinic, while he sat in the backseat and timed uterine contractions by his watch. They arrived on time, and the baby was successfully delivered, albeit under the shaman's supervision rather than the clinic's.

The irony in this little story is multilayered. First is the obvious fact that the baby will come when it comes, regardless of how accurately one might clock the mother's biological functions. There is also the notion that these young Americans could offer assistance in the birthing process to Africans who have been delivering babies for at least 200,000 years, and who probably invented the human species for that matter. The deeper lesson, however, is the juxtaposition inside one automobile of two utterly different stress-management tools that nonetheless serve the same purpose. The Americans are comforted by medical science and technology. It gives them a sense of having some control over the situation. If not, why did they bother to take useless measurements? The Shona are comforted by the ministrations of a shaman, even if they, too, have limited effect, albeit perhaps more than a wristwatch.

The point is not that Western medical technology has no objective consequences. Clearly it can work miracles, and I myself am a beneficiary. The point is that it serves a stress-management function that relies partly on its efficacy but also on its ability to put things in a reassuring context. It interprets natural phenomena within a worldview that sees them as subject to human manipulation, based on one's understanding of the mechanism that underlies them. This worldview can provide comfort even when the technology itself has nothing to offer. The Shona likewise interpret their lives as under control, even if it is not direct human control. Their worldview sees events as influenced by spiritual forces, which can be brokered by someone sufficiently skilled in the art. In both cases people are reassured by a myth, not in the Western sense of a falsehood, but in the sense of an integrative story that seems to explain our fate and bring it under some semblance of control.

The commonly quoted statistic is that about half of Zimbabweans practice Christianity and half practice an indigenous faith, although Christianity is often mixed with elements of local religion. One can also see groups of white-clad Seventh-Day Adventists. The primary indigenous religion is the centuries-old *Mwari* cult, which emphasizes ancestor worship and the Voice of Mwari, a cave-dwelling oracle that has given advice at critical historical junctures. My impression is that most people believe in witches, and mining crews sometimes refuse to show up for work when they believe a spell has been cast.

When Zimbabweans do adopt a Christian faith, they tend to be enthusiastic about it. They have little interest in those aspects of Christianity that deal with guilt and justification by faith, but they seem to take naturally to the Protestant vision of Jesus Christ as a personal savior, perhaps because it meshes with the traditional Shona belief that individuals have a personal relationship with the spirit world. Visitors can get some idea of the flexibility of the Christian faith by attending church services in both white and Shona churches, even if the latter are likely to be conducted in the Shona language. They should not be surprised if the Shona preacher spots them in the congregation and asks them (in English) to stand up, introduce themselves, and perhaps lead the congregation in a prayer.

Myth and religion are only two of the Shona's stress-management mechanisms (see table 13.1). Their group solidarity, already described, is equally central. Living among the Shona was for me something like soaking in a warm bath. Their skills at mutual support and empathy are well honed, and I recall wondering whether I could bear to return to a world of obnoxious Westerners. This is not to say everything is peaches and cream. Superiors can be gruff with subordinates, and subordinates can organize to oppose their superiors. Feuds and family grievances can complicate life, and those who infringe against custom can be severely censured. All smiles disappear when ethnic rivalries enter the picture. Yet through it all the communal impulse is strong and reassuring.

The Shona love of laughter and amusement, which I described in Chapter 7, is another coping strategy. Music plays a similar role by providing temporary escape from life's cares. In fact, I know of no place where

TABLE 13.1
Stress-Management Mechanisms in Zimbabwe

Mechanism	Contribution to Stress Management
Group solidarity and communitarian values	Mutual support and concern; sharing of resources; help in time of need
Myth and religion, including indigenous faiths (e.g., *Mwari* cult), Christianity, and syncretism	Assurance; coherent worldview; sense that events are under control; personal relationship with the spirit world
Elaborate ritual	Predictability; everyday life invested with meaning
Music and the arts	Return to childhood; temporary escape from self-consciousness
Amusement and laughter	Diversion from burdens of everyday life

music plays a more fundamental cultural role than in parts of Africa. To begin with, everyone sings. Musical performance is not limited to those who have what Westerners call "musical talent." The songs are easy to learn and stick in one's memory, much like an advertising jingle. They have a childlike quality and bear only superficial resemblance to African American music, particularly the North American variety, which is very adult and heavy with the burden of slavery. In fact, the Africans I knew had little interest in such idioms as blues, jazz, and hip-hop, as illustrated by a little anecdote. I got permission to practice an hour a day on the university's only keyboard instrument, a small electric piano that was kept in the auditorium. Often students would come to the auditorium to study before class, and I decided to conduct an experiment. On some days I would play Western classical music (Mozart or whatever), which seemed to interest the students in the room, to the point that some would walk up and ask me about it. On other days I played blues, perhaps songs by Billie Holliday, who in my opinion is one of the greatest blues musicians of all time. The students ignored the music completely. They showed equal disdain for gangster rap, despite some U.S.-based efforts to market it in the area. I should acknowledge, however, that the musical scene is different in the larger cities, where there is more exposure to Western media. Young people love the loud music in discos, and there is a good deal of interaction between performers in Africa and elsewhere in the world.

Authentic African music has a definite cultural function. Its childlike songs return one to childhood. The conscious mind is switched off, and with it the stress of self-awareness. Every Saturday morning, people would gather at about nine o'clock to sing in two buildings near my apartment. One was a church, and one a public hall. They sang for hours from memory, taking cues from a leader who sang in counterpoint with the choir—a style that has survived in some American gospel music. Drums or other percussive instruments might accompany the singers. I often found excuses to walk by in order to hear the beautiful sounds emanating from the two buildings. Many songs were sung in harmony, a technique that Africans learned from Western missionaries but execute in a particularly striking manner. They sing pure intervals rather than the tempered intervals of the Western diatonic scale, and the effect is enhanced by the open vowels typical of Shona and other Bantu languages. The purpose of the music, however, is not performance but deliverance from the cares of the day. While singing, one is almost in a trance, which is itself an escape from the self-consciousness found in many parts of the world.

I do not mean to suggest that African music is always simplistic, since it can be remarkably complex. I once accompanied some colleagues, including some Westerners, to a marimba concert. The marimba is not a specifically Shona instrument, and in fact its origins are obscure. The best-known traditional Shona instrument is the *mbira* (thumb piano). Marimba playing, however, was revived in Bulawayo in the 1960s and has become quite popular in Zimbabwe. At the concert, eight or ten musicians played as many marimbas of different sizes. The individual parts, always played from memory, were rhythmically complex and blended to form an intricate texture. Only with intense concentration could one comprehend the music. Most of my colleagues, conditioned by the simple rhythms of the West, found it inaccessible.

The arts in general form an integral part of Shona life. Women often sew their own clothes, using patterns and colors that to my eye are almost always attractive and tasteful. Rural *mamusha* are commonly adorned with mural paintings. Shona sculpture is well known in Europe and North America. One cannot say that colonialism was totally without salutary influence, if only because Europeans induced the Shona to take up sculpture. It is a thoroughly grassroots activity, practiced by countless talented amateurs, perhaps with hopes of selling their work to tourists. It is interesting that the original human cultures, those that have had the longest period to evolve and adapt themselves to human needs, give the arts a central role in everyday life.

Ritual also receives strong emphasis. The best illustration I can provide came from close at hand, the university graduation ceremony. One must bear in mind that the university's tuition cost, though small in absolute terms, imposes an onerous burden on most students. I was almost incredulous when I learned that a large fraction of this cost goes toward the purchase of a graduation robe. The culminating ritual is no less important than this. Ceremonies in general, academic or otherwise, tend to be frequent, long, and attended in elaborate costume.

Two items that do not appear in the Shona's repertory of coping mechanisms are Western-style organization and time consciousness. While I was living in Mutare, the city decided to put on a parade and other festivities to celebrate the centennial anniversary of its founding. The parade was scheduled to start Friday afternoon. I went downtown at the appointed time, but as I half-expected, nothing was going on. I came back Saturday morning and found a crowd milling around, but no parade. The procession finally got under way Saturday afternoon. To the Shona mind, it is the same parade whether it starts at five o'clock Friday or five o'clock Saturday. It only makes sense to start it when everyone is ready.

Every month I went downtown to pay my electric bill. This required standing in a long, slow-moving line at the utility office. All payments were in cash, and each day the clerk would start the day with no change in the cash box. Naturally most of the customers did not carry the exact change, and they got into a lengthy negotiation with the clerk about how this matter would be resolved. In my case the clerk, after some discussion, allowed me to pay a little less if I promised to make up the difference next month. I naturally saw this procedure as maddeningly inefficient, but my Shona neighbors seemed to have no complaints. Perhaps from their point of view it provided an opportunity to give every customer some personal attention. If the process had been efficient, it would have had no redeeming value whatever.

The Shona Language

Shona, *chiShona* to its speakers, belongs to the Bantu family of languages. Nearly one-third of Africans speak a Bantu language as their native tongue. If one imagines a line stretching from Cameroon in the east to Kenya in the west, Bantu languages are spoken in every country on and below this line, and they include such well-known languages as Swahili and Zulu. The word *Bantu* comes from the root *ntu* (*nhu* in Shona), which means "human." It refers to itself simply as the language of humans.

There is no real need for visitors to learn Shona, due to the high degree of English-language literacy in Zimbabwe. However, it is interesting and fun to study, and I found it useful for conversing with the ladies who go door to door selling fresh vegetables. I was able to keep my kitchen well stocked without too many tiring walks to the grocery and street markets downtown. One must be aware of the many dialects, however. On one occasion I tried out my Shona in a shop that was 20 or 30 miles from Mutare. The clerks grasped not a single word, but a couple of customers understood me and repeated my request to the clerks in a manner they could comprehend. It was a difference of dialect.

Constructing a grammatically correct sentence in Shona requires roughly the same intellectual effort as integration by parts in calculus. There are some twenty-one noun classes, for example. Words throughout a sentence must be inflected to agree with the noun class of the subject, often in a way to produce alliteration. For example, the earlier question *Vangani vana vanoenda kuchikoro?* (How many children go to school?) has *vana* (children) as its subject. *Vana* belongs to noun class two, which usually involves people words in the plural. This generates the prefix *va-* that is attached to two other words of the sentence. The last word, *kuchikoro,* means "to school," where *school (koro)* is a class-seven noun and therefore takes the prefix *chi.* Many Shona surnames begin with *Mu-* because words that refer to a person in the singular take this prefix.

Another complication is that pronouns, as well as verbs, reflect tense. The present-tense pronoun for *I* is *ndi,* while the past-tense version is *nda.* Beginning with the stem *dya* for "eat," one says *Ndinodya* to mean "I eat," and *Ndadya* to mean "I ate." The *no* syllable in *Ndinodya* makes the present tense indicative. The progressive tense is indicated by *ri,* as in the construction *Ndiri kudya* (I am eating), where *ku-* indicates the infinitive form of the verb.

It gets worse. To add "not" to a sentence, everything must change. For example, *Ndinoda nyama* means "I like meat," while *Handidi nyama* means "I don't like meat." How did this happen? The prefix *ha-* provides the negative sense. The indicative syllable *no* is dropped in the negative, and the verb stem *da* changes spelling to *di* because it is monosyllabic. Incidentally, the phrases *Ndinoda* and *Handidi* are useful while shopping, since they also mean "I want" and "I don't want," as in *Ndinoda iyi here* (I want this one).

Some useful expressions are *mangwanani* (good morning), *masikati* (good afternoon), and *manheru* (good evening). "Hello" is *mhoroi* when speaking to several persons or to one person with respect; *mhoro* is the familiar form. One can also greet another by saying, "*Kwaziwai.*" *Ndatenda* is "thank you" (literally, "I thanked you"). *Chisarai* is "good-bye."

Mr. Svosve is referred to as VaSvosve, and Mrs. Marufu as Amai Marufu. If Abisai is Mrs. Marufu's firstborn, one can address her as Mai Abisai, Mother of Abisai. If one is speaking English, however, the titles *Mr.* and *Mrs.* are appropriate (Mrs. is simply a title of respect and need not imply that the woman is married). Women, particularly in rural areas, will sometime refer to a white man as *baas,* an Afrikaans word from South Africa that means what it sounds like. Shona men often use English given names, which sometime refer to qualities or emotions, even negative ones. A columnist in one of the Harare newspapers is named Hatred. Women tend to use either an English or a Shona given name. One of my students, for example, was named Patience, while another was named Vimbai, which is Shona for "patience." I detected no desire to express cultural pride by rejecting English names, partly because the Shona do not hold a grudge against the English, and partly because they do not seem to feel a need to assert their own culture.

I enjoy the onomatopoeia in Shona. A "small child" is *mwana,* which sounds to me like the child's first word. A "dog" is an *imbwa* whose bark is presumably *bwa, bwa!* My favorite is the word for "motorcycle," *mudhudhudhu,* which people pronounce with an absolutely straight face.

Practical Matters

Professional dress in Zimbabwe is formal. Men wear a business suit, perhaps with vest. The wristwatch and other jewelry are items people notice. Women should avoid slacks and wear a conservative dress or skirt and blouse. Introductions and other formalities tend to be more or less in the British style. Although the indigenous culture is very much a high-context one, educated Zimbabweans adopt a certain amount of Western directness in a professional setting. They seem to be truly bicultural, moving effortlessly from one culture to the other as easily as they switch between English and their native language, apparently without any conscious awareness of the shift. Negotiations with outsiders therefore tend to be logic based, resting on facts and argument, as in the West, rather than personal relationships as in the much of the East. It is acceptable to challenge or contradict another's viewpoint on rational grounds. One must be aware, however, that the indigenous culture lies just beneath the surface. Any issue that is felt deeply enough to tap into this subterranean layer is ultimately resolved according to local norms. This can be puzzling to a visitor who hears people saying reasonable things by Western standards but finds the ultimate decision incomprehensible.

Leaders should be both authoritarian and accountable. African cultures are characterized by high power distance, and persons in charge are expected to give firm orders. The boss should remain aloof, rather than "pitch in" and help the staff with their tasks, even in an emergency. Attempts to descend to the level of subordinates not only erodes respect for the boss but also encroaches upon their turf. When I first arrived at the university I visited the campus bookstore to find out what kinds of books were available for the students. The store manager, who knew I was on the faculty, immediately approached me to ask what business I might have in the bookstore. When I saw the manager's African frown, I realized, too late, that I had violated her territory. As a faculty member, I should have inquired with the manager about what I wanted to know, and let her do the legwork in the bookstore.

The flip side of authority is accountability. In Zimbabwe, as in much of the world, the traditional means for accountability have been supplanted by the trappings of Western democracy, which are likely to be dysfunctional in a country without the cultural resources to support them. The ancient big-man system, which once helped to keep leaders in check, has been thoroughly corrupted. Nonetheless, Zimbabweans have found a Western medium of redress that can work for them at least to some extent: the labor union. Workers who would be very reluctant to confront the boss individually have no hesitation to organize and send a representative to negotiate with the leadership. On the second day of the semester, for example, one of my students stood up to announce to me that his classmates had chosen him as class president. I soon realized that the term *class president* is a euphemism for a student representative who would negotiate with me over their concerns. I was a little surprised that students normally so deferential would be assertive on this point, but the communitarian mentality of the culture seems to lead naturally to collective bargaining. Strikes are common in Zimbabwe, not only student strikes over tuition cost but also labor strikes over wages. Before Mugabe's breakup of the commercial farms, for example, agricultural employees would stop work on a fairly regular basis to protest the declining value of their wages due to inflation. Before traveling to Harare, I had to find out whether picket lines were blocking the highway on that particular day.

Collective bargaining is an imperfect mechanism for Zimbabwe, but there are reasons to take the process seriously. It responds to an ancient cultural need for accountable leadership. It is one way the boss can learn about problems or grievances that subordinates would not mention in ordinary conversation. The first issue that my class president brought to me concerned the textbooks I had contributed to the school. The dean of the management faculty had told the students they could only keep the texts for the duration of the course, because he wanted to lend them to future students. My students, however, wanted permanent possession of their texts so they could refer to them while on the job. I thought the dean made the right choice, but I sympathized with the students' desire to learn. I told them that the books now belonged to the university and were no longer under my control, but I would take their case to the dean. He struggled with the issue and talked with some of the students, but he ultimately denied their request on grounds they understood perfectly—they must share with others. This little episode could provide a rough blueprint for how accountability can work in post-colonial Zimbabwe. Subordinates who must defer as individuals speak through their collectives, and the boss justifies his or her decisions in a way that respects local norms. The whole affair is regulated by a culturally sanctioned balance of power: the authority of superiors over individuals versus the authority of collectives to challenge their superiors.

Zimbabwe is by and large a man's world, even if women hold responsible positions in some areas, such as education. One can get a vivid impression of the role of women by visiting a rural community. If invited to a meal, male visitors will find themselves eating with the men only. The women literally bring them dinner on their knees, as it is good etiquette for women to remain at a lower level than men. In fact, male visitors should avoid sitting unless asked to do so, as women in the room may feel obliged to kneel. The women and children eat the leftovers after the men have finished. Women are also responsible for cultivating the fields, often with infants carried on their backs in blankets. Such practices are not found in the cities, but they nonetheless symbolize the traditional Shona conception of how the sexes should relate. As for Shona men, they tend to speak in sotto voce, sometimes barely audible, as if to show their self-confidence. If one has unquestioned authority, there is no need to raise one's voice.

On the other hand, much about the current role of women in Zimbabwe is far from traditional. The status of women in precolonial times was recognized in the institution of bride price, which is a payment that suitors must make to the bride's family for the privilege of marriage. Partly for this reason, girls were closely protected, but by no means oppressed; many seem to have been pampered. Women could accumulate wealth and in a few cases become rulers. Prostitution and sexually transmitted diseases were rare until colonial powers introduced migrant labor. This system limited women's choices, but men were no less constrained, since many could not afford the privilege of marriage.[9]

Whatever their own practices may be, Zimbabweans understand that foreigners have different customs and adapt to them. Western women should be able to operate effectively in professional circles, even if they may attract unwanted attention on the street.

Bribery is rampant in Zimbabwe, as in much of Africa, and it is thoroughly dysfunctional. Zimbabweans detest the practice even more than Western critics, as became evident in a workshop I conducted for Mutare businessmen. I did not plan to spend much time on the subject of bribery, since it was a given in Zimbabwe, and I thought that not much could be achieved by talking about it. The workshop participants, however, would not let me get away from the topic. They insisted that bribery is a scourge on the country and must somehow be eradicated. They were sensitive to the fine distinction between a gift of appreciation and a bribe. Too often, they said, a gift is presented after the fact, but the recipient expected it all along as quid pro quo. They recommended that companies permit only gifts that bear the company logo. I could not tell them how to eradicate bribery, nor do I know now. But I can assure visitors that they should feel absolutely no obligation to accede to the practice on the ground that it is "accepted" or "business as usual," but should resist it whenever possible. The German policy of allowing their companies to write off bribes as a cost of doing business, for example, may appear sophisticated and worldly-wise, but the Africans I know see it as doing no favor for their countries. They point out that bribery requires two parties, and multinational corporations can do their part to avoid becoming one of them. They can, for example, deal with people who have much to gain from the company's legitimate activities, such as sourcing from local suppliers or increased tax receipts. It is naturally helpful when the corporation has enough clout to secure the necessary permits and contracts without resorting to bribes. It is possible in several countries for an Exxon or a Siemens to remain aloof from corruption while smaller companies are obliged to play the game.

Americans who disapprove of the African ethical situation, incidentally, might be interested to learn that the negative judgment is mutual. When I was in Mutare, TV sets were blessedly rare, but remarkably many middle-class people found one on which to watch a certain new series religiously. The show had apparently failed in the United States and was shipped off to the Third World market. Like many Hollywood productions, it was full of sex, violence, and family breakdown. Several Zimbabweans approached me to express their outrage over the immorality they saw on the screen, particularly the shocking disrespect for parents. They seem to pity me for having to live in so depraved an environment. When they asked me how they could get this trash removed from their airwaves, I told them, "Don't watch it." But they naturally could not resist the show.

Zimbabwe is a strongly polychronic country in which deadlines and schedules are not taken very seriously. Visitors may arrive two or three days late, shipments may be delayed, meetings may start late and run long, and buses may not stick to any particular timetable. One can see groups of people waiting interminably for "chicken buses," so called because of the farm animals often carried in cages atop the bus. The common phrase *just now* indicates the polychronic nature of the country. When people say something will happen "just now," they mean it will happen sooner or later, but definitely not now.

In the way of cuisine, one has an unenviable choice between British and Shona fare. The Shona staple is *sadza,* which the British call "mealy meal porridge." A mealy is an ear of corn (maize), and mealy meal is cornmeal. *Sadza* is something like thick grits, and people eat it day in and day out. It is often consumed with gravy or meat (*sadza ne nyama*), or even more commonly with hot sauce. I found *sadza* tolerable at first and wondered why foreigners always complained about it. I even ordered it at a restaurant once, which provided the waiters a good laugh. My opinion of the sticky substance soon changed, however. My going-away lunch at the college cafeteria was *sadza* and tripe, which I had to force down. I could not even drown it in a decent cup of coffee, since "coffee" in Zimbabwe is almost all chicory. My solution to the culinary situation was to cook fresh vegetables at home and complement them with the imported British tea available in the grocery, which is quite good.

Development and Foreign Involvement

Zimbabwe is one of those countries called "developing." A more accurate description is that it is caught between two worlds. The traditional culture and economy have been substantially dismantled, but a modern Western-style economy has been only partially installed, and neither functions as it should. The dominant Western view continues to be that the latter process should be carried to completion, even though countries that provide the world's success stories for Western-style development, such as Singapore, South Korea, and Japan, have borrowed Western ideas but have built their economies solidly on the strengths of their own culture.

This raises the question as to how Zimbabwe can best build a consumer economy, if that is what it wants, upon its own cultural foundations. Robert Mugabe's initial approach was to install some variety of socialism, perhaps because its emphasis on communal action appears to harmonize with Africa's communitarian values. Yet the level of organization required by socialism seems as ill-suited for Africa as for India, and Mugabe never got far with it. Zimbabwe has achieved some important successes under his government, including a high literacy rate and a productive agricultural sector. The British-installed infrastructure, including roads, electric power, and water supply, is still in place. Yet industrial development has been limited, even in recent years when Mugabe shed some of his ideology and began to court multinational corporations. People told me that interested corporations encounter endless bureaucratic obstacles and eventually give up, despite Mugabe's assurances that they are welcome.

Zimbabweans see considerable promise in their game parks, which take advantage of the Westerner's fascination with animals. On one occasion I was convinced to visit a wildlife refuge, where tourists are advised to congregate at a certain spot at a certain time. As it turned out, this was feeding time for the animals, and they dutifully showed up for their dinner. The African caretakers watched with some bemusement as the tourists enthusiastically snapped photos of animal species they can equally well photograph back home in the local zoo. (I felt distinctly out of place, as I never carry a camera on any of my travels.) Zimbabweans find the tourists puzzling but their wallets very interesting. The money spent on a safari expedition can rival the annual budget of a small Zimbabwean city. Yet it is unclear that tourism alone can support a consumer economy.

The issue again arises as to what role, if any, Western ideas and assistance should play in African development. Zimbabweans have reason to be wary, as they have seen aid attempts that are almost humorous in their ineptness. On one occasion a Scandinavian organization decided to address the HIV pandemic in Zimbabwe. They showed up on the campus where I taught, with a film that demonstrated how homosexuals can practice safe sex. Evidently the Scandinavians were unaware that homosexual behavior is almost unknown in Zimbabwe. The students found the film to be incomprehensible and were no doubt confirmed in their judgment that Westerners are odd people indeed. On another occasion a well-meaning church group shipped several large crates of toilet articles to the university, apparently under the misapprehension that such items are unavailable in Zimbabwe. When customs officials examined the crates, they imposed a 100 percent duty, on the ground that all of the articles are marketed in the country. The university was obliged to sell them at full price in the campus bookstore, in order to raise enough cash to pay the duty.

I attempted to address the Western role when I taught an MBA course on operations management. I began by telling my African students that efficient operations are an essential element of wealth creation. One country can learn from another in this area, I explained, but only by adapting the lessons to its own culture. I spent a good deal of time discussing Japanese manufacturing techniques, for example, pointing out how they revolutionized manufacturing in the United States and contributed much to U.S. prosperity. It was a revelation to my African students (indeed, to my American students) that the world's superpower could learn so much from a smaller country, but I went on to observe that the United States did not achieve this prosperity by importing Japanese culture. Rather, it adapted Japanese ideas to U.S. culture. I told the students that, in similar fashion, they may learn some useful lessons from the American textbook I brought them, but the lessons must be adapted to the situation in their own countries. It was their responsibility as managers to help find a distinctively African approach. They understood me perfectly and seemed quite serious about taking on this challenge.

There was one culturally based belief I contested, however. This is the view, widely held around the world, that enterprises should be organized to provide as many jobs as possible, whether they be in the manufacturing or service sector. Factories in particular should not be too efficient, since efficiency reduces the number of jobs available. I insisted that a successful consumer economy is built by achieving maximum efficiency in the manufacturing sector and providing jobs in the service sector. This strategy works because manufacturing is, by its very nature, susceptible to enormous efficiency improvements, whereas services generally are not. It therefore makes sense to create wealth where it can best be created, and to use the surplus to provide jobs in a sector that will never be very productive anyway.

I honestly do not know how a consumer economy should be built in an African context, again supposing that this is desirable, but I have no doubt that my African students and thousands like them can find a way. I am troubled, however, by a tendency of Zimbabweans to underestimate their cultural heritage. I heard Shona businessmen and clergy make remarks to the effect that they should reject their local practices in favor of Western values. This self-effacing attitude stands in the way of building a future for the country on its own cultural foundations, which in my view is the only strategy that can succeed in the long term.

A Culture of Sustainability

African cultures are all about sustainability. If it were otherwise, we would not exist, since African cultures were the only game in town for untold ages. They bore full responsibility for the survival of Homo sapiens. Sustainability has been very much on Western minds in recent years, as well it might be. A few back-of-the-envelope calculations should convince anyone that our planet cannot long endure the globalization of Western-style growth and resource consumption. It is conceivable that African cultures, today regarded as primitive and dysfunctional, may soon teach lessons in long-term survival.

There are of course many African cultures, and they are in constant evolution. Archaeological and other evidence suggests that the continent has been a constantly shifting mosaic of peoples, nations, and empires for millennia. Yet many of these cultures share characteristics that favor sustainability. As Marvin Harris points out, their devotion to ethnic territorial conflict can permit regeneration of land and wildlife in contested areas where people are afraid to settle. Totemism, still part of African culture, has long regulated hunting as well as intermarriage. I generally avoid direct questions of this sort, but on one occasion I asked some students at lunch to tell me about their totems. They were happy to oblige. Some of the totems were animals and others body parts (e.g., leg, arm, head). The body-part totems seem to regulate only intermarriage, since one traditionally should not marry a person with the same totem. The animal totems, however, have a clear ecological purpose, since there may be a taboo against eating one's totem animal.

Ethnic conflict has clearly lost any positive value, even if it tragically persists worldwide with greater intensity than ever. Totemism, however, can still play a role and seems to be reflected in vegetarianism. Other African cultural traits have an even clearer relevance to the modern world. Rugged individualism perhaps made sense for Vikings, Celts, or Pashtun in a sparsely populated region, but a crowded world requires a more communitarian view. Westerners see themselves as solving the problem of community by adjusting incentives so as to induce self-interested individuals to act in a socially responsible fashion. This piece of ideology allows Westerners to regard themselves as individualists, but it is unrealistic. Aside from the impossibly of fine-tuning incentives in this way, people will administer the incentives honestly only if they have already learned, through conscience and guilt, to consider the collective interest. African culture addresses the same concern, albeit through a relationship-based rather than a rule-based mechanism, and in a more thoroughgoing way. It literally identifies individual welfare with collective welfare. This is not the West's totalitarian collectivism of the twentieth century, which represented a grossly primitive and distorted understanding of the concept, even if it did reflect a vague realization that untempered individualism can no longer succeed. It is a collectivism that holds leaders accountable but cares as much about one's neighbors as oneself. The West cannot and should not import African culture wholesale for its communitarian values, any more than it can or should import Japanese culture for its productive efficiency. Yet the West can perhaps learn some lessons from more experienced peoples. It should give us pause that the world's oldest cultures evolved a radically communitarian approach in their struggle for long-term survival.

African cultures have perfected the art of mutual empathy and support, in the context of not only the extended family but also the entire community. Westerners get a taste of this during times of war or crisis, but normally they face the world alone, or at best with the aid of a nuclear family (perhaps fractured by divorce), or one of the countless support groups that are improvised in an attempt to compensate for the culture's lack of community. They end up relying heavily on the assurances of technology to deal with medical or emotional problems, legal intervention to resolve conflicts in the family and on the job, and social welfare systems to deal with famine or crisis. All of these institutions are necessary and serve legitimate purposes, but as the world becomes more complex they can be strained beyond their capacity to respond.

Africans recognize the importance of long-term sustainability. Their communitarian approach satisfies the basic human need for support and assurance. They have learned to find satisfaction in social institutions rather than profligate resource consumption. They incorporate the arts into daily life, recognizing their centrality to human existence. They, the world's original people, have much to teach their cultural offspring.

Notes for Chapter 13

1. Kevin Shillington, *History of Africa,* rev. ed., St. Martin's Press (New York, 1995).

2. Ibid., 149.

3. David Beach, *The Shona and Their Neighbors,* Blackwell (Oxford, 1994), 64.

4. Ibid., 40ff.

5. Peter Godwin's book *Mukiwa: A White Boy in Africa* (*Mukiwa* is Shona for "white boy") vividly documents this period and its aftermath (HarperCollins [New York, 1997]).

6. Martin Meredith, *Our Votes, Our Guns: Robert Mugabe and the Tragedy of Zimbabwe,* PublicAffairs (New York, 2002), 83–84.

7. Michael H. Glantz, Michele Betsill, and Kristine Crandall, *Food Security in Southern Africa: Assessing the Use and Value of ENSO Information,* National Center for Atmospheric Research (Boulder, Colo., 1997).

8. Ibid., sec. 4.2.

9. Beach, 52–54.

14 *Cross-Cultural Ethics*

An American businessman on assignment in Taiwan meets with representatives of a potential supplier. After they depart, the businessman notices that one of them left a briefcase. On opening the case to learn the identity of the owner, he finds it stuffed with cash.

A marketing executive for a European medical supply house is relocated to India. Part of her task is to oversee the sale and distribution of ultrasound machines, which are popular in poor rural villages. After some inquiry she learns that the machines are often used to identify the sex of unborn babies. When the baby is female, the mother's pregnancy is aborted.

A German executive has patiently negotiated a joint venture with a Chinese pharmaceutical company. At last the project has reached the point where a headquarters can be set up in Shanghai, to be jointly administered by the two partners. In the course of discussions the top Chinese negotiator proposes a roster of top executives, who happen to include his son, son-in-law, and nephew.

An Australian accounting firm wishes to set up operations in South Korea, due to that country's interest in Western-style accounting. There have been delays, however, in obtaining the necessary government permits. A Korean consultant offers to facilitate matters. His approach is to meet with government regulators and hand them white envelopes—containing money.

A team of French negotiators has worked hard to iron out a deal to provide satellite TV feeds to an Egyptian media company. When the contract is finally drawn up, the French notice that it explicitly provides for kickbacks to the negotiators on both teams.

A recent Saudi immigrant to New York lands a job at a top Madison Avenue advertising firm. Her first client is an upscale fashion house and, as luck would have it, the client wishes to market a new line of very revealing swimwear. Her task is to oversee the artwork and layout for a series of advertisements in a major fashion magazine.

Quando a Roma Vai, Fa Come Vedrai

When in Rome, do as the Romans do. Professionals who work across cultures must constantly struggle over whether to heed this old Italian proverb. The dilemma affects travelers from all cultures, since all travelers encounter unfamiliar customs and expectations. Cross-cultural differences are particularly problematic, however, for the universalism of the West and Islam. They raise the possibility that ethical principles are contextually dependent rather than absolute. The aim of this chapter is to determine whether and how a universalizing culture can deal with the challenge of ethical relativism, and in particular how it might resolve the dilemmas posed above.

Discussions about ethical relativism tend to produce a quagmire of confusion. To think clearly about the topic, it is useful to make some distinctions. There are three distinct concepts that commonly go under the label *relativism*.

- *Contextualism* allows for different obligations in different cultural contexts but allows for the possibility that they flow from the same universal principles. Cronyism and nepotism, for example, may be wrong if one's culture is built on transparency but acceptable if it is a relationship-based culture. The underlying principle, perhaps, is that one should support the cultural system on which one relies. Contextualism is therefore not really a form of relativism, since it does not rule out absolutes.
- *Ethical relativism*, properly understood, claims that fundamentally incompatible ethical principles rule in different cultures. For instance, Western individualism leads to such ideas as equality and human rights, whereas Hindu pantheism recognizes the connectedness of all beings and permits a stratified society based on karma. The opposite of ethical relativism is ethical universalism, which holds that world cultures ultimately agree on basic values.
- *Metaethical relativism* states that value statements are inherently relational, much like *warm* and *cold*. If a resident of Anchorage says 10 degrees Celsius is warm and a resident of Chennai says it is cold, they do not really disagree, because their judgments are made in relation to the prevailing climate. In similar fashion, a value statement is always made *relative to some context,* such as a particular culture. When a Londoner insists that people should pay their taxes, and a Roman says they should not if they can get away with it, metaethical relativism does not see the two as disagreeing with each other. This sort of relativism is called "metaethical" because the field of metaethics analyzes what ethical assertions mean, as opposed to normative ethics, which investigates which ones are true.

These three theories differ in kind as well as content. Contextualism is a *normative* theory, ethical relativism is a *descriptive* theory, and metaethical relativism is a *linguistic* theory. Contextualism is normative in the sense that it makes claims about what is right or wrong. It states that one type of conduct is ethical in one place and another type is ethical in another place.

Ethical relativism is difficult to read as a normative theory, however, because it would affirm contradictory views, such as Western individualism and Hindu pantheism. It is best understood as describing the values that are in fact held by Westerners and Hindus. It states a sociological or anthropological thesis rather than a normative one. Finally, metaethical relativism is a linguistic theory because it analyzes the semantics of value statements in a particular way, without deciding which statements are true.

Contextualism may provide universalists a way to deal with cultural difference. It says that although divergent practices may make one feel uncomfortable, many of them can be seen to be acceptable when the context is properly considered. For example, one might say that cronyism is inappropriate in Scandinavia because it undermines a rule-oriented system based on transparency, but it is proper in Malaysia because, there, it is the glue that holds society together. The underlying obligation is to conduct oneself in such a way as to support the culture in which one works, rather than undermine it. This approach can in fact go a long way toward a culturally sensitive understanding of corruption and is developed first in the following discussion. It is further questioned, however, whether all value differences can be explained away in this fashion, that is, whether ethical universalism is true.

Contextualism is most satisfying for universalists if ethical universalism is in fact correct. If the world's value systems are ultimately congruent, then visitors can blend in abroad without violating their basic principles. This does not mean that they should always do as the Romans do, since Romans may sometimes act unethically by their own standards. At the very least, they park illegally. But outsiders can adopt fundamental Roman values with integrity. If ethical relativism is true, however, universalists are put into a difficult position. They must ultimately reject most of the world's value systems. They must subject themselves to charges of arrogance and self-righteousness because they refuse to adjust to local norms, or else they must sacrifice their integrity and suffer the guilt that results.

Ethical relativism also forces universalists to abandon their fondly held belief that everyone is basically the same inside. In the West one hears statements to the effect that the world's ethical systems converge at the top. The greatest prophets and philosophers—Confucius, Lao Tzu, Moses, Jesus, Gautama Siddharta, Muhammad—ultimately deliver a similar message. The Golden Rule, which requires people to treat others as they would be treated themselves, occurs in various forms in the Christian New Testament, Judaism's Jerusalem Talmud, the analects of Confucius, the *Mahabharata* of Hinduism, and even the sacred writings of Zoroastrianism. Roman Catholic theologian Hans Küng has attracted widespread attention with his call for a global ethic based on common themes across world religions.[1] He sees the identification of common ethical ground as essential for working out a new world order that can deal with the forces of globalization. Westerners want to see the universality of values affirmed across cultures. Similarly, Muslims see the values taught in the Koran as valid for all peoples.

The West and Islam therefore have a considerable stake in refuting ethical relativism. The issue is a difficult one and cannot be addressed until universal ethical systems are examined in detail, so as to understand exactly in what sense they claim to be universal. This is attempted for Western ethics in the second and third sections to follow.

Metaethical relativism is the easiest theory to dispense with, since it is clearly inadequate. Some Westerners in liberal circles may seem to profess something very like metaethical relativism, but they do not mean it. These same relativists are likely to condemn censorship, worker exploitation, and oppression of women wherever it occurs. Not only is it practically impossible to find anyone who professes metaethical relativism in any coherent fashion, it has absurd consequences. It implies that a Muslim fundamentalist and a Unitarian liberal cannot disagree. Any impression that they disagree is based on a grammatical mistake, namely, a failure to recognize the relational character of ethical predicates. This is nonsense. One cannot avoid the conflicts among world value systems by defining them out of existence.

Corruption

Corruption exists around the world, but different systems are corrupted in different ways. What is nepotism or cronyism in Europe may be mainstream and functional behavior in China. What is a routine lawsuit in the United States may be destructive antisocial behavior in Japan.

Corruption can be understood as a practice that either (a) undermines a functioning system, or (b) represents a system out of control. Chinese *guānxì*, for example, provides stable and trusting relationships that are an important basis for trade and negotiation. Often, however, people try to create an obligation quickly by offering or demanding a bribe. A system based on this kind of quid pro quo would lack the stability that is necessary for a complex civilization. Bribery therefore undermines the system and is a form of corruption in China.

Bribery is corrupting in the West for a very different reason. Since Western culture is rule based, the stability of society rests largely on the perception that the rules are fair and are justly enforced. People trust one another to the extent they do because it is assumed that most people play by the rules. If people bypass the rules in exchange for bribes, however, the perception of legitimacy vanishes, trust evaporates, and the society is in danger of disintegration. Again bribery undermines and therefore corrupts.

Bribery can be corrupting even where it is business as usual. It is common enough in China, and as noted in the previous chapter, it is ubiquitous in much of Africa, where it is thoroughly dysfunctional. In some settings, however, a certain amount of bribery can be constructive. South Korean businesses routinely make side payments to government officials (often through third parties) in order to obtain permits and the like. The payments represent an investment in a relationship with a government official. These investments provide incentives for business people to follow governmental regulations, because no one wants to sacrifice a costly relationship. Thus, by accepting bribes, government officials gain some control over the country. The practice seems to work so long as it remains limited, which perhaps explains why one can lose face by being exposed in bribery. Ironically, officials have been known to bribe news reporters to keep quiet about the officials' bribery.[2] Excessive bribery would be corrupting, because it would represent a system out of control.

Another system out of control is legalism in the United States. Although the U.S. rule of law is fundamental, people commonly file nuisance lawsuits that have little or no legal merit. The defendant will pay off to settle the case and avoid further legal expenses. One who suffers a mishap may instinctively sue anyone in sight, as though an accident is by definition somebody else's fault. These practices are no less corrupting than bribery in China and at least as prevalent.

Lawsuits are corrupting in Japan, not because they represent a legitimate practice out of control, but because they undermine a system based on courtesy, deference, and group harmony. If an airliner crashes, the rift between the airline and the victim's family is addressed with a personal apology from the CEO, rather than a lawsuit. If the CEO has been replaced in the meantime, his successor makes the apology, even though he had nothing to do with the crash. The idea is to restore harmony, not to acknowledge guilt.

Cronyism can likewise be corrupting or constructive, depending on the context. A classic example is the purchasing agent. In a rule-based country, the agent is supposed to look at bids, investigate suppliers, and choose the best deal. The system is based on transparency. Annual reports, accounting statements, and the like are expected to reveal the facts about the supplier. If the purchaser favors an old friend instead, the system is undermined. The purchaser is said to have a conflict of interest, because his company's interests and his friend's interest may not coincide.

In relationship-based systems, business is based on trust between individuals, which may be built over a long period. Transparency is unnecessary, because the purchaser trusts his friends not to sabotage a valuable relationship with dishonesty or poor products. Far from undermining the system, cronyism makes it work. Because it is in the company's interest for purchasers to deal with trusted suppliers, there is no conflict of interest.

It is commonly believed in the West and elsewhere that even if a relationship-based system legitimizes cronyism in some sense, it is nonetheless inferior to the West's rule-based system, and cronyism should be resisted for this reason. Rule-based systems are presumably superior because they are more efficient and create more wealth. Rule-based transparency tends to be more efficient in the short run, but in the long run it is less stable. Transparency works very well while it lasts but is vulnerable to loss of public trust, a lesson taught by recent business scandals in the United States, while relationship-based economies have sustained great civilizations for thousands of years. Aside from the questions of efficiency, however, it is unclear why one is ethically obligated to resist participation in a less-efficient system. Should one refuse to buy handwoven rugs at a county fair because factories could have made them more cheaply?

Nepotism is standard practice in much of the world. Western business partners may be expected to hire relatives of the local boss, a practice that can have advantages. Some relatives may be incompetent, but in any case the boss knows their strengths and weaknesses better than those of other employees, and can assign them duties accordingly. This is possible because employees are more likely to be managed directly by the boss than assigned to a fixed job description. Also, in some cultures an older relative tends to carry great authority. This can enable the boss to obtain a level of effort and devotion that would not be forthcoming from more competent but unrelated employees. It is just the opposite in the West, where the boss tends to go easy on relatives. The main reason for nepotism, however, is the pivotal role of the family in providing security. Elders rely on their children to support them in old age, and children rely on their elders to get them jobs.

Contextualism can therefore provide a useful approach to understanding corruption, if one assumes a basic obligation to support the system that allows a culture to survive and flourish. Since corruptive behaviors depend on what cultural system is being corrupted, one would naturally expect them to vary around the world. Again, one should not necessarily do as the Romans do, since Romans may break their own rules. One should not necessarily pay bribes in a country where bribery is common, since that country may operate in spite of bribery rather than because of it. One is obligated to engage in the sort of conduct in which people in general must engage to keep the system running.

One can of course question the principle that underlies the contextual approach to corruption. Should one support just any cultural system one happens to find oneself in? What if it is not working well in the first place? There in fact seem to be cultures that are dysfunctional in some sense, perhaps due to famine, ethnic conflict, revolution, or excessive outside interference. One thinks of Chechnya, East Timor, Myanmar, North Korea, Russia, Sierra Leone, Somalia, South Africa, and Ulster as places where most people would say the system is broken. Perhaps the underlying principle should ask one to support a *functional* culture, which presumably is a culture that has reached some kind of equilibrium without the stress of famine, conflict, or outside interference. If a country is dysfunctional, contextualism alone may not provide clear guidance.

This analysis is of some value, and it is helpful to me personally. Unfortunately, however, even a functional culture may rely on institutions of which people often disapprove, such as racial or sexual inequality. This takes us back to the question of ethical relativism: is it possible to reconcile, say, radical inequality with Western values if the context is properly taken into account? This issue is probed later in this discussion, but in the meantime it is clear that one cannot make blanket statements about what constitutes corruption and when it is wrong. Westerners in particular must realize that cronyism, nepotism, and even bribery are not necessarily corrupting, while their own accepted practices may be harmful to another culture. When working in an unfamiliar country, one must learn as much as possible about the cultural system that sustains it and make judgments on that basis.

Western Ethics: Utilitarianism

Western philosophers and theologians ranging from Socrates to Schleiermacher have developed subtle and sophisticated ethical theories over the past twenty-five centuries. Two of the most characteristic are utilitarian and Kantian ethics, otherwise known as consequentialist and deontological ethics. Both systems ground ethical obligation in logical consistency by arguing that consistency alone requires people to do certain things. Since logic is universal, the resulting ethical systems are viewed as universally binding, regardless of one's history or culture. These systems are more sophisticated than most everyday ethical reasoning, but they can be viewed as rational reconstructions that capture much of the essence of Western ethics.

Utilitarianism states that one should act so as to maximize utility across the general population, where *utility* might be defined as "happiness or some other desirable condition." The best way to understand utilitarianism is to recall the situation it originally tried to address, namely, the criminal justice system of eighteenth-century England. At the time, punishment was based on the ancient idea of retribution, or literally, paying back. The state should exact revenge on the criminal. Jeremy Bentham, however, believed that criminal justice should be rooted in reason rather than primal emotion. Policies should be dispassionately designed to maximize the overall welfare of society. Criminal penalties in particular should aim to deter crime rather than make the criminal suffer.

The underlying ethical philosophy is that one should make up one's mind what is good (well-being, happiness, etc.) and try to maximize it, without being distracted by such concerns as a desire for retribution. It is difficult to quantify such things as happiness or pleasure, but it is nonetheless possible to have more or less of them; eating filet mignon is more pleasurable than eating moldy bread. Utilitarians simply tell us to bring about more good rather than less. Admittedly, they differ on what kind of good should be maximized. Bentham equated utility with pleasure and disutility with pain (hedonistic utilitarianism), while John Stuart Mill suggested that some pleasures are better than others. But the main point is that one should be *consistent* by deciding what is important and sticking to it. Utilitarianism, conceived as a principle of consistency, does not tell one exactly what to do. It places formal restrictions on one's pattern of conduct.

Utilitarianism can be counterintuitive when used as a guide for individual actions. For example, it might instruct me not to bother with such obligations as voting. One vote makes but an infinitesimal difference to the success of democracy, and it is inconvenient for me to travel to the polls. Unless I take pleasure in the act of voting, which we may suppose I do not, the utilitarian choice is to stay home. This seems unfair, however, since if others take the trouble to vote and uphold a democratic system from which I benefit, I should do my part. Utilitarianism can avoid this sort of counterexample by restricting itself to policy issues for governments or organizations, which were after all its original application. (This approach is similar to what is historically known as "rule utilitarianism.") If, for example, there is to be a law requiring people to vote, as in Australia, utilitarianism can help shape the law so as to maximize benefit. The law would define which eligible voters are required to vote in terms of general characteristics rather than specific individuals. It might, for example, exempt those who are ill or residing abroad. Although overall utility might increase if I am exempted individually, an exemption of everyone for whom voting is merely inconvenient and unenjoyable would reduce utility. It is difficult to specify exactly what is meant by a "general characteristic," but presumably it is a characteristic that has a bearing on the net utility of voting. Thus, a voting law should not exempt a person with my name or living at my address, since these characteristics have no causal influence on the cost I would incur or the benefit I would create by voting.

It is important to note that a utilitarian policy is not necessarily an instruction for individuals, because it ignores the status quo. Suppose that organized crime has taken over the country. Few people vote anymore because voters are attacked by the mob. The utilitarian policy would be for people in general to defy the mob and vote en masse, but this is relevant only if someone is in a position to make and enforce such a policy. It would be futile and risky for me to follow the policy as an individual, and I am not required to do so.

A weakness of utilitarianism, even when applied to policy decisions, is its treatment of distributive justice. It is true that utilitarianism provides for some degree of justice by giving everyone's utility equal weight. One cannot (arbitrarily) favor members of the upper class or of a certain race, for instance. But utilitarian calculations may nonetheless endorse a highly unequal and apparently unjust distribution of utility. They may determine that the well-born should receive the lion's share of resources because they are best equipped to use them productively. Bentham's response to this objection is that utilitarianism is biased toward equality due to the principle of decreasing marginal utility. As one acquires more resources, utility rises at a decreasing rate. A fixed amount of resources may therefore bring more utility when they are distributed widely rather than concentrated in a few individuals. This may be true in general, but it is easily conceivable that overall utility might be maximized by repealing taxes on the wealthy, paying astronomical salaries to chief executives, abolishing the minimum wage, and so forth. It is an old issue in political economy: the poor suffer in an inequitable system, but some say that inequality leads to a more productive economy that creates greater aggregate utility. When it does, utilitarianism supports inequality. Even if one grants that this is sometimes a just solution, it is unlikely to be just in every conceivable case, which means that something is missing from utilitarianism.

Western Ethics: Kant

Kantian ethics addresses the two main deficiencies of utilitarianism by addressing the obligations of individuals and taking justice explicitly into account. This deontological (or duty-oriented) approach to ethics was articulated by the eighteenth-century German philosopher Immanuel Kant. He began with the simple premise that one should always act for a reason. There should be something that one takes to justify the action. For example, if I choose not to vote, there must be some reason I so choose. Perhaps it is because voting is inconvenient.

Kant obtained enormous leverage from this seemingly innocuous assumption. He pointed out that I must regard my reason for not voting as a reason for anyone's not voting. I might protest that my reason does not work for people who enjoy voting. Then I really have two reasons for not voting: it is inconvenient, and I do not enjoy it. If these are really my reasons, then I am committed to saying that they are reasons for anyone else.

So far there is nothing wrong with my decision not to vote. But suppose there is another reason involved in my choice, which there very likely is: most others will vote even if I do not, and democracy will be preserved. If it were otherwise, I would be first in line at the polls. So part of my reason for not voting is the assumption that although most eligible voters have these same reasons not to vote, most of them will vote nonetheless. I accept these reasons as good enough for me, but I am unwilling to let them be good reasons for others. This is irrational and inconsistent. If these are good reasons for me, I must regard them as good reasons for anyone. This is sometimes called the "generalization test," although it is really a rationality test. For Kant, failure of the generalization test is the tip-off that my intention is immoral. Kantian ethics, like utilitarianism, is at root a call to rationality and consistency.

If I live in a failed democracy ruled by organized crime, the Kantian obligation is likewise reasonable. There is no inconsistency in staying home from the polls because voting is dangerous and futile. Nothing about my rationale presupposes that others will vote despite the danger and futility of doing so. I therefore have no obligation to vote.

The free-rider principle is a special case of the generalization test. When I enjoy the benefits of democracy but refuse to vote, I am a free rider on a system supported by others. To take another example, suppose that a student cheats on an examination in order to improve his grade and career prospects. Yet cheating can improve his career prospects only if most people are honest enough for grades to be meaningful. So the dishonest student is a free rider. He allows others to support a grading system from which he benefits, but he refuses to pay his freight by behaving honestly. This behavior is immoral on Kantian grounds because of inconsistency in the cheater's reasons for cheating. Among his reasons is the assumption that other students will not cheat, even though they have the same reasons to cheat. The cheater accepts these reasons as sufficient to justify his own dishonesty but is unwilling to let them justify the dishonesty of others. This is irrational and inconsistent and therefore immoral.

The free-rider principle provides some justification for the contextualism cited earlier. Outsiders can benefit from working in a country only if most people support its practices, just as a cheater can cheat only because most people support the system. One can therefore find Kantian inconsistency in outsiders who refuse to adapt to customs that undergird a society on which their activities depend. They can avoid inconsistency only by conforming or withdrawing from the country. The latter option may be exercised if visitors find the country's practices fundamentally irreconcilable with their values.

Kant tried to summarize his view in a categorical imperative, which instructs one to act only according to a maxim that one can at the same time will to become universal law. For Kant, acting according to a maxim is acting for reasons; my maxim for voting is "don't vote if it is inconvenient and unenjoyable, and most eligible voters will vote even though it is usually inconvenient." By willing my maxim to be universal law, I recognize that if my reasons justify the action in my case, they justify the action in anyone's case. In other words, ethical action is rule based, since it is governed by rules or maxims that are seen as applying to all agents.

The philosopher John Rawls proposed a vivid way of understanding the universality of reasons.[3] In his view, one must make ethical decisions behind a "veil of ignorance" as to one's position in life. The student who is tempted to cheat must make this decision *without knowing who he is*. He could be himself, his employer, the instructor, or another student. He will find out who he is only after he makes the decision. His reasons must be sufficient for his choice no matter who he turns out to be, which is again is the heart and soul of Kantian ethics. This does not mean that one should figure the probabilities and maximize the expected outcome. A business executive, for example, might decide it is a good bet to lay off some older workers to make a company more profitable. This would be a disaster for her if she were one of the workers terminated, but there is a much greater chance she would be someone who benefits from the layoff. She is willing to take her chances. Rawls says this is not enough. She must construct a justification for the layoff that she would find equally convincing if she were transported into the body of one of the redundant workers. Kantian ethics clearly implies a radical egalitarianism.

This whole affair is based on the premise that anyone who acts must act according to reasons that are taken to justify the action. Why is this so? Because, in the Western mind, it is the only way to distinguish free action from mere behavior. It is the only way to solve the problem of freedom and determinism: the problem of explaining how free action can be possible when it is causally determined. If a mosquito bites me, this is mere behavior. I do not judge the mosquito morally, because it did not "freely choose" to bite. The bite was merely the result of chemical reactions in the mosquito's body. Yet human actions are also the result of chemical reactions. The difference is that one can give two kinds of "reason" for many human actions. One kind of reason is a cause, such as the chemistry of one's body. The other kind of reason is the agent's rationale for the action. For Kant, behavior is free action *when it can be reasonably explained as based on reasons derived from conscious deliberation.* It makes no sense to say that the mosquito bit because it thought to itself, "I will bite that human in order to obtain nourishment." However, it is often very reasonable to explain human actions in this way.

Free agency is not so much an objective property of an event as its susceptibility to a certain kind of explanation. In principle the behavior of computers, robots, or beings from Mars could someday be more easily explained as resulting from conscious deliberation rather than from an algorithm or alien chemistry. Kantian ethics is therefore universal in the highest degree. It can impose duties on and to any sufficiently complex creature in any culture or on any planet.

Ethical Relativism

I recently led a discussion about ethics with a group of business students, and the question of the free-rider principle came up. I told them about some transit systems in Europe that operate on the honor system. All riders are expected to buy a ticket or a pass, but no one checks to make sure they do so. In reality there are spot checks, but to clarify the example, I asked the students to assume that there is no risk of being caught. I then asked them to tell me whether it is ethical to ride without a ticket and become, literally, a free rider on the system.

The Western students sensed that there is something wrong about being a free rider, even if they were equivocal about affirming a principle that might impose unwelcome obligations on them. Two Chinese students, however, spoke without hesitation. Of course it is all right to ride without a ticket. If the government did not want free riders, it should have designed a better system.

It is not surprising that an authoritarian culture would place primary responsibility on the authorities rather than ordinary individuals. The more interesting question is how Chinese might deal with what Westerners see as the inconsistency inherent in being a free rider. I did not rehearse Kant's argument with this group, but if I had, would it have convinced the Chinese students?

The answer, I believe, is yes and no. The Chinese students could say, yes, Kantian justice principles can be derived from consistency arguments, but no, we are not interested in this particular kind of consistency. There are more important things in life. (Socrates noted that the one position a philosopher can never refute is lack of interest.) The problem with Westerners, the Chinese might say, is that they care too much about universal principles and too little about what really matters. They talk loftily about preserving human rights and the environment in some distant country, but they have little concern for the feelings of people in the same room. Courtesy, respect, and saving face are alien concepts. Westerners divorce their spouses, abandon their elders to institutions, and provide weak discipline for their children. No ethical norm is more important than caring for the human beings around one, and yet Westerners get so caught up in legalistic abstractions that they forget the fundamentals.

Many such Confucian values as consideration for others and care for one's family can perhaps be derived from Kantian arguments, and the fact that Westerners misapply their justice principles does not show the principles are wrong. Yet the question remains: can Chinese, or anyone else, legitimately reject the Kantian consistency arguments as binding on their action? It seems not, so long as the Kantian theory of agency is accepted. Agents are bound by the categorical imperative so long as (a) they are regarded as morally autonomous individuals, (b) agency is understood as free action, and (c) free action is distinguished from mere behavior by virtue of being rule based and explicable as the outcome of ratiocination. Yet the notion that human beings are autonomous moral agents is a Western concoction, a product of a worldview in which humans are lonely individuals in a secular world. Islam, which likewise recognizes secularity, adopts a similar view of moral agency. It does not have to be this way. The locus of human existence may reside in the community rather than the individual, as in the African tradition. Individual human beings may be manifestations of a single consciousness, as in mystical thought. Human beings may not be defined by their rational faculties and may share a close kinship with other creatures, as in many traditional cultures. Only certain authoritarian figures may possess significant autonomy, as in Confucian cultures, while most people surrender the greater part of their autonomy to elders, rulers, and ancestors. Not even a Chinese emperor is conceived as a being that makes ruled-based judgments, since the problem of freedom and determinism does not arise in the Chinese worldview, as it does in Western secularism. In each of these cases, ethics depends on one's understanding of human nature, and that understanding varies enormously across cultures.

I cannot say that divergent worldviews actually stand in contradiction to each other. If the postmodernist view is correct (see Chapter 4), there may be alternate interpretations of life that are equally legitimate but admit no direct comparison, because neither can be fully understood in terms of the other. I therefore cannot endorse an ethical relativism that sees ethical systems as strictly incompatible. Yet they are fundamentally different, because they flow from radically different conceptions of human nature. I see no possibility that one can be derived from another, or that all can be derived from a global ethic.

The divergence of worldviews need not imply, however, that the world's peoples cannot live together. We are all brothers and sisters, even if we must recognize that brothers and sisters can be very different. Perhaps radically different value systems cannot coexist in a single society, just as two ecosystems cannot thrive on the same land. Yet there is by definition less interaction between societies than within a society (see Chapter 4). It should be possible for radically different cultures to prosper in coexisting societies, just as a forest can grow next to an ocean. One key to coexistence would seem to be a willingness for each society to understand, respect, and make accommodation to the culture and worldview of their neighbors.

Tanti Paesi, Tanti Costumi

So many countries, so many customs. The vignettes at the beginning of this chapter illustrate some of the variety of ethical norms. They provide an opportunity to investigate whether the concept of contextualism is adequate to allow ethical universalists to operate across cultures.

Perhaps the easiest case to deal with is the German encounter with Chinese nepotism. As already noted, family solidarity is one of the foundations of this ancient civilization. By observing local custom, the German firm helps to sustain the system with which it is doing business. In a contextualist view, it would be wrong to do otherwise. If the Chinese executives wish to locate their relatives in Germany, however, that is another matter, since nepotism is inimical to the German rule-based system. In either case, one should act so as to support the system on which one relies. Contextualism seems to resolve the Germans' dilemma, since there is no apparent conflict of fundamental principle.

The South Korean scenario appears to be similar. It was suggested earlier that, up to a point, side payments play a constructive role in Korea. If this is true, then the Australians could argue on the basis of contextualism that it is permissible to allow the Korean consultant to adhere to his country's custom on the visitors' behalf.

When the U.S. businessman discovered a briefcase full of money (an actual incident), he was confronted with one of the easier dilemmas in the Taiwanese environment: they are offering a bribe rather than demanding one. He can ask a trusted subordinate to return the case to the Taiwanese representative who left it. The representative's superior, who undoubtedly approved the bribe, should be sent a vaguely-worded letter or email informing him that this particular dispensation will not be necessary. Otherwise the representative could keep the money for himself without informing his superior. A more difficult conundrum presents itself when visitors are compelled to pay bribes to get much of anything done, a situation that may be more prevalent in some industries than in others. I have no reason to believe that bribery is any less corrupting in Taiwan than in mainland China. Transparency International's 2002 *Bribe Payers' Index,* which is based on interviews with experienced business people, suggests that Taiwanese are actually slightly less prone to bribe foreigners than are mainland Chinese.[4] Both the Chinese and Taiwanese systems are based on *guānxi* and are undermined by bribery. It is perfectly all right to give and accept gifts, when those gifts reinforce a long-term relationship rather than reward a particular action. It is true that *guānxi* practices are sometimes hard to distinguish from bribery, and this is probably why bribery is so common in Confucian countries. It easy to slip from one into the other, just as it is easy for people in the United States to slide from constructive lawsuits into a litigiousness that undermines the system. Yet this is all the more reason to resist bribery and avoid contributing to an inherent weakness in the Confucian system.

The U.S. Foreign Corrupt Practices Act may have a role in such cases, because it forbids U.S. citizens from bribing government officials. This law has been internationally criticized as a typical example of U.S. arrogance and self-righteousness, but in most cases it only forbids what is already illegal in the host country. Taiwan's anticorruption statute, for example, prohibits bribery of Taiwanese government officials. In fact, Taiwan recently amended its law to prohibit Taiwanese nationals from bribing government officials abroad.[5] If U.S. law displays arrogance, one must say the same of Taiwanese law. In any event, critics of Puritanical attitudes in the United States can take comfort in the fact that Transparency International ranks U.S. nationals about halfway down the bribery scale. When working abroad, they resort to bribes far more often than Australians, Canadians, and many western Europeans, and only a little less often than Malaysians.[6]

The Egyptian scenario illustrates how cultural practices can mix, sometimes in strange ways. Kickbacks are a firmly established tradition in Arab lands, while written contracts are part of an imported Western system in which kickbacks are unsavory. Ironically, the kickbacks can end up in the text of a contract. When practices mix in this fashion, it can be very difficult to tell what actually makes the system work, and therefore difficult to determine one's contextual obligations.

The case of the Indian ultrasound market is quite difficult. It is clearly inadequate to say simply that abortion for female birth control is part of the local culture and outsiders have no business passing judgment. I agree that few of us are qualified to pass judgment on someone else's culture, but we must evaluate our own actions. In this case, Westerners already disagree profoundly on the morality of abortion, so that much turns on one's position on this issue. The European marketing manager in this scenario may see abortion as tantamount to murder, presumably due to her philosophy of human nature. In this case contextualism provides no consolation, and she must consider asking for a reassignment. Contextualism may be more helpful if she objects to abortion in some contexts but not others. Rural Indians abort female pregnancies partly to avoid paying a dowry, and partly because only boys can inherit the family name and property, and bear the responsibility of supporting their parents. Marvin Harris suggests, however, that their behavior may have deeper roots.[7] In his view, female abortion, infanticide, and neglect were key population-control mechanisms in some early human cultures. Reducing the female population reduces the birthrate, whereas reducing the male population, such as through warfare, does not; one male can impregnate arbitrarily many females. (Harris sees warfare as maintaining buffer zones between tribal lands where no one settled, and where natural resources could regenerate.) If this theory is correct, female population control may once have been a precondition of human survival. The European visitor must now determine whether it remains an essential element of survival in rural India. If so, then doing business in the rural market may commit her to honoring the practices that allow that market to exist. On the other hand, she may conclude that this ancient form of population control has nothing to do with today's reality. Even if it does, ultrasound machines are manifestly unnecessary, as rural India has survived for ages without them, and they may actually upset and undermine traditional ways. If so, it is unethical for her to sell them in this market. The issue is difficult because it requires a clear understanding of the underlying worldviews as well as an anthropologist's grasp of the local culture.

The Muslim's struggle with contemporary American values goes equally to fundamentals. She may determine that some aspects of a woman's role in her home country exist for the smooth functioning of Middle Eastern society, in which case she might shed them in a radically different society, as some Muslim women shed the veil or head cover when living in the West. Other aspects of her role may flow directly out of an Islamic conception of human nature, in which case they are not subject to compromise. She must determine which analysis applies to her advertising job. Like many of us who encounter an alien culture, she will find herself developing a deeper understanding of her own culture.

Notes for Chapter 14

1. Hans Küng, *A Global Ethic for Global Politics and Economics*, Oxford University Press (New York, 1998).

2. Boye Lafayette De Mente, *Korean Etiquette and Ethics in Business*, 2nd ed., NTC Business Books (Lincolnwoord, Ill., 1994), 30.

3. John Rawls, *A Theory of Justice,* Harvard University Press (Cambridge, Mass., 1971).

4. Transparency International, *Transparency International Bribe Payer's Index 2002* (Berlin, 14 May 2002), table 1.

5. *Taiwan Economic News,* July 10, 2002.

6. Transparency International, table 1.

7. Marvin Harris, *Our Kind,* HarperCollins (New York, 1990).

15 *The United States and Multiculturalism*

The United States is monochronic, low context, rule based, individualist, masculine, and predominately Apollonian. It is characterized by low power distance and high uncertainty tolerance, and it is deeply committed to universalizing rationality. Its most clearly distinguishing trait, however, is its struggle with multiculturalism.

This nation of immigrants is by no means the world's only multiethnic country, as one immediately thinks of Brazil, Indonesia, and a host of others. Yet it is the only country that has set itself up consciously to assimilate diverse cultures. After long periods of struggle and failure, it has actually achieved some success in doing so. Hindus and Muslims, Protestants and Catholics, Jews and Palestinians, and any number of immigrant groups who were at each other's throats for centuries in the old country find themselves living peacefully next door to each other in their adopted country. Harmonious coexistence has occurred elsewhere, as between Moors and Christians in Spain, but never on the scale or with the regularity as in the United States. This is a major achievement by any measure. In an age characterized by cultural mixing and ethnic conflict around the globe, it is an achievement that begs to be understood.

The two popular models for cultural mixing in the United States are the melting pot and the salad bowl. The classical melting pot theory views the society as cheese fondue. The different cheeses influence the overall flavor, but the result is homogeneous: a single American culture. The salad bowl theory, currently in fashion, sees coexistence rather than merger, as ethnicities mix but retain their identity. A piece of lettuce remains lettuce no matter how thoroughly it is tossed with tomato and cucumber slices, and Hispanics remain Hispanics even while rubbing shoulders with Serbs, Haitians, and African Americans in their multicultural workplace.

The melting pot model is admittedly simplistic, but the salad bowl theory should raise eyebrows for anyone who has read the foregoing fourteen chapters. A culture works because the people in it share deep and often unacknowledged assumptions about who they are and how they should relate to one another. Even if there are many personalities and subcultures, they cannot coexist in the same society without some essential elements of commonality. The metaphor of the salad bowl suggests otherwise.

In this chapter I analyze the melting pot and salad bowl theories and ultimately conclude that the United States, like any functional society, has an overarching culture, which in its case happens to be a modified northern European culture. The melting pot is a better model of reality than the salad bowl, although much must be said about how and in what sense the meltdown occurs. I also conclude that the U.S. experience in cultural assimilation is not necessarily a fit model for other states that struggle with multiethnic populations. Before conducting this analysis, however, I attempt to describe what makes U.S. culture work, an exercise that will provide an opportunity to pass along some practical information to newcomers. After all, the United States is one of the world's chief destinations for visitors and emigrants.

A word of caution before I proceed. Although the United States is as open and information-rich a society as ever existed, two factors tend to block an adequate understanding of the country: its staggering diversity and Hollywood. Visitors or immigrants to the United States may assume that their limited exposure to the country presents them with a representative slice of life. Yet no slice is representative. Any given individual sees but a square centimeter in a gigantic patchwork quilt of ethnic groups, religions, socioeconomic strata, work-related subcultures, and regional variations. Fortunately, one can flourish in the United States while knowing relatively little about the country, a fact that helps ease the task of adjustment. A second barrier to understanding is the flood of popular entertainment with which the United States inundates the world. Americans[1] unconsciously adjust for the unreality of this highly stylized depiction of their lifestyle, but outsiders can be misled. Even longtime residents of the United States may base their impression of the country more on Hollywood fare than on reality, perhaps because it is easier to watch TV than to break out of one's niche and explore the cultural landscape. Although movies and TV serve awkwardly as a kind of mythological literature and, as such, contain a modicum of truth about the society that produced them, they say as much about everyday life as the misadventures of Olympic gods tell us about everyday life in ancient Greece.

A Rule-Based Culture

The disparate peoples of the United States are bound together, not by a common cultural heritage, but by a shared rulebook. The culture is low context to an extreme found nowhere else. A pizza box instructs the purchaser to remove the pizza before heating it. Lawn mowers bear a warning not to insert one's foot beneath the machine. Organizations are run according to voluminous policy manuals and codes of ethics posted on their Web sites. Hospitals ask patients to present "living wills" that specify when and whether the doctors should let them die. Disputes are resolved by reference to the precise wording of a lengthy contract or insurance policy. The multiyear backlog at family courts provides dramatic evidence of the extent to which implicit cultural norms no longer regulate life. Families call upon beleaguered judges to regulate the minutest details of their divorce settlements, child custody, visitation rights, and the disposition of inherited property. My wife, an attorney, told me of an incident in which three highly paid lawyers sat around a conference table arguing over which heir was entitled to a few cheap plastic toys. In another incident, a divorcée hauled her ex-husband into court for taking their son to get a haircut during his weekend for visitation. She asked the judge to exact punishment and forbid such behavior in the future.

A low-context society suits a nation of immigrants. Since norms tend to be transmitted explicitly rather than by cultural tradition, newcomers can get by with only minimal knowledge of the culture. Adding to the ease of adjustment is the country's long tradition of receiving immigrants, even if the Immigration and Naturalization Service is one of its worst-run bureaucracies. The atmosphere of freedom and a generally unobtrusive government (except during wartime) allow new residents to retain many of their customs. Adapting to a strange culture is always a challenge, but if one speaks English, the United States probably offers the world's mildest case of culture shock.

Although newcomers find no authoritarian government to oppress them, they must submit to the reign of universalizing rationality. Efficiency, objectivity, and the bottom line are in charge. Persuasion is based on logic and facts, although it is perfectly acceptable to combine them with an aggressive sales pitch. Disagreement and controversy are normal, although one should criticize with tact and take care to attack the issue, not the person. Negotiation is most successful when the parties appeal to principles of fairness and efficiency. Relationships can play a role, but most decisions in the professional world are ultimately based on objective criteria. People may hire their friends but also employ total strangers on the basis of resumes and interviews. Universalizing rationality governs the United States more completely than Europe because it is a binding force as well as a stress-management mechanism. It provides a means of resolving differences that people of all cultural persuasions can accept.

The extreme individualism of the United States gives its rule-based society a special flavor. Since there is no higher priority than the individual, there can be no justification for favoring one individual over another. Rules in the United States therefore tend to regulate by ensuring fair and equal treatment. Equality is understood as equality of opportunity, due to the country's emphasis on individual responsibility; whence the distrust of social welfare systems and the willingness to tolerate inequality of outcome if it can be explained by differences in effort or ability. Some newcomers to the United States may conclude that talk of justice and equality is a sham, due to manifest inequality of opportunity across socioeconomic sectors. This would be a serious mistake. However inept Americans may be in their implementation of a just society, they see fairness as an overriding value and try to achieve it in everyday life.

In Confucian cultures one should never act without considering the effect on face. In the United States one should never act without considering whether justice and equality are compromised. So simple a matter as "breaking line" is a serious offense and can evoke a sharp reprimand. To break line is to step ahead of someone who joined the queue earlier. One may question why a first-come, first-served priority would be considered self-evidently more just than some other queuing discipline. Why not allow those with more urgent business, or those who can finish their business more quickly, to go first? (It is not uncommon in the supermarket or at the copy machine to wave ahead someone with a small job, but such gestures are generally seen as optional rather than obligatory.) It is difficult to escape the fact that American perceptions of justice are based on cultural conditioning as much as universal logic. It is nonetheless crucial to learn what sort of conduct they regard as transparently just.

It is equally important to observe traffic laws to the letter. Such infractions as pulling ahead of another at the wrong time are strongly resented and can even trigger a violent response (e.g., road rage). The traffic laws are presumably "fair" because they depend only on the situation, not who is driving.

A "self-evident" principle of particular significance is the idea that the majority should rule. American political culture recognizes that the majority view can be unjust, and it developed a doctrine of human rights that overrides the popular will when necessary. Yet groups commonly make decisions on the basis of majority vote, a procedure that everyone seems to accept without question. Americans project this assumption into foreign policy with their oft-stated preference for elected governments (even if economic interests often override this preference). It is characteristic of Westerners to view their own cultural conventions as universal, because their acceptance of these conventions requires that they be seen as logically self-evident and therefore possessing the universality of logic.

Justice is a key element of dissent as well as conformity. One of the best ways to effect change in the United States is to cry "unfair!" Most complaints brought to an employer or government speak of injustice of some kind. In much of the world, grievances are based ultimately on a claim that those in authority are not taking proper care of their subordinates. This sort of appeal is regarded as whining or special pleading in the United States. Bosses are generally not expected to "care" about their subordinates, but they are most definitely expected to treat them equally.

Rules sometimes promote equality by legally requiring it. During the Civil War era, the Thirteenth Amendment to the U.S. Constitution prohibited slavery, and the famous "due process" language of the Fourteenth Amendment (1868) helped protect the rights of freed slaves. Nearly a century later in 1954, the Supreme Court declared that segregated public schools violated the Fourteenth Amendment and initiated a desegregation process that became the largest social-engineering effort in the nation's history. In the meantime, the Fifteenth and Nineteenth Amendments (1870, 1920) extended to all races and to women the right to vote. The civil rights activism of the 1960s brought a number of reforms. The landmark Civil Rights Act of 1964 barred racial segregation in situations connected with interstate commerce, including such public venues as bars, hotels, theaters, and the workplace. In particular it prohibited hiring that discriminates on the basis of race. A 1963 law mandated equal pay for men and women who do similar work, and a 1965 executive order first used affirmative action as a tool for promoting equality. The Fair Housing Act of 1968 strengthened provisions of the original Civil Rights Act of 1866 to prevent discrimination in the sale or rental of housing on the basis of race and other characteristics. This is particularly significant in a cultural sense if it helps to break up ethnic neighborhoods, since territoriality has long been associated with ethnic conflict. Legislative remedies continued into the 1990s, with the Americans with Disabilities Act (1990) and the 1991 amendment to the Civil Rights Act. Today almost any action that discriminates on the basis of such politically sensitive categories as race, sex, religion, national origin, disability, or sexual orientation is likely to be illegal. These laws are not just window dressing. In a rule-based society, well-timed and carefully drafted legislation can bring about genuine cultural change.

Politically correct speech can be seen as another rule-based mechanism for promoting equality. The phenomenon became important in the United States only in the last three or four decades, but it is scarcely a new idea. George Orwell's 1949 novel *1984* ridiculed the politically correct "newspeak" of totalitarian regimes. Nor is it exclusively a Western phenomenon, inasmuch as Thailand, for example, forbids lese-Majeste (speaking ill of the king) and banned the popular 1956 movie *The King and I* on the grounds that it portrayed the king of Siam as foolish. Yet Americans have carried political correctness to new extremes. The intent of politically correct speech is to avoid using derogatory terms for politically sensitive categories of people. In particular it discourages the use of "code language." It is politically incorrect, for example, to say that African Americans are good athletes, because this is code language for the claim that they are good at little else. Racial or ethnic stereotyping in general is frowned upon, because it may make it more difficult for members of these groups to obtain equal opportunity based on their individual talents and achievements. It is politically incorrect to discuss political correctness itself, as I am doing now, since to do so can function as code language for disapproval of the idea.

Political correctness is ridiculed for its excesses, as for example when one is expected to refer to short people as "vertically challenged," or when one stumbles over pronouns to avoid using the masculine gender too often. In a more serious vein, political correctness is faulted for restricting the free exchange of ideas, one of the pillars of a low-context society. Yet newcomers to the United States should not infer from these countercurrents that political correctness is anything less than mandatory in professional life. Careers have been destroyed by a single inappropriate remark. Political correctness is a crude instrument, but it attempts to address something deadly serious: the absolute necessity of living together peaceably in the world's most diverse society. The rules of politically correct speech are too complicated to present here, but one can imitate what others say in professional or public life—albeit *not* what they say in locker rooms or on radio talk shows. If one prefers a reference book, there is at least one dictionary of politically correct speech.[2] It is a bit difficult to use as a serious guide, however, because in typical American fashion, it pokes fun at the subject.

This brings me to the matter of humor. In this land of logic, efficiency, and political correctness, some relief is needed, and humor comes to the rescue (see Chapter 7). Stand-up comedians are a cultural institution, and the telling of carefully timed jokes is a folk tradition. Mark Twain, perhaps the nation's finest writer, was a humorist of the first rank. I just received a mail order catalog that features a Joke Master, which is a handheld computer that offers up a joke for any occasion. Americans also have a wacky sense of fun. I have a book cover photo of a barn in the rural United States with a gigantic painting of a cow on one wall. A cartoon-style balloon points to the cow's mouth and says, "Moo." It is hard to imagine such a sight in any other country.

Equality implies low power distance, and in most contexts the United States is a textbook example. There is little respect for authority. In many middle-class homes parents *suggest* to their children that they clean up their mess, a suggestion that needless to say tends to be ignored. As the children grow older, they may demand exclusive access to their bedroom, since anything else would be an invasion of their privacy. Presumably exceptions are made to allow the parents to change the sheets and throw out the hamburger wrappers. The same disrespect for authority extends to public figures. While in Guangzhou I met a journalist for *China Daily* who told me about her furlough in the United States the previous year. She had eagerly looked forward to experiencing the freedom of the American press, a sharp contrast with the censorship that characterizes Chinese media. However, she found reporters to be so gratuitously disrespectful to government officials that it was a relief to come home to a more civil environment.

One may ask how military discipline is possible in so antiauthoritarian a culture. It is possible because, as noted in Chapter 6, leadership rotates. The general of the army is in command because it is his turn to take charge. His authority derives wholly from the office he occupies at the moment, rather than his personal station. In civilian life, he waits in line at McDonald's like everyone else. The principle was illustrated early on at the 1780 Battle of Kings Mountain in North Carolina, a significant event in the American war for independence from Britain. Fiercely independent Scotch-Irish mountaineers who would take orders from no one less than the Almighty (and at times not even from Him) gathered and placed themselves under the command of Colonels John Sevier and Isaac Shelby long enough to defeat the British. This done, they instantly became their equals.

An interesting exception is the U.S. business corporation, which can be little less than totalitarian for its middle managers. It not only dictates what suit and suspenders one must wear, but it imposes something akin to thought control, disallowing any remark that might question the legitimacy of the company's value system. It demands total devotion that leaves little time for family or community. Naturally managers conform in order to succeed, and there is a selection effect in that the corporate environment tends to attract personalities who can tolerate it. There is no threat to egalitarianism in general, because employees can always quit the company and start their own businesses. Yet one must ask why such an authoritarian environment would develop in a radically egalitarian society. The readiest explanation is the Weberian thesis (see Chapter 11) that a corporation assumes a life of its own in a rationalistic culture that is based on tasks rather than persons. Loyalty and other relationships are not present to moderate the achievement of corporate goals, and the organization increasingly aligns itself toward accomplishing its task to the exclusion of all else. One might also speculate that since most managers come from the mainstream low-context culture, rather than ethnic subcultures that provide more support and guidance, they are receptive to an environment that structures their lives and gives them a purpose.

The de-emphasis of relationships is a recurrent theme in the United States. Long-term relationships can be helpful in professional life, but they are generally unnecessary, and Americans are notorious for avoiding them. There is a whole subculture of retired persons who live on the road, traveling from one RV park to another in their motor homes and recreational vehicles (RVs). The lure of freedom accounts for some of this, but the nomads themselves cite the fact that by moving from one trailer park to another, they can escape the long-term relationships associated with living at a fixed address.[3] There is a tacit understanding in the United States that displays of friendship imply nothing beyond the present moment. Total strangers interact on a first-name basis, even if they know they will never see each other again. Young American women commonly get into trouble when traveling abroad, where men take seriously the smiles and momentary attention to strangers that American men know are meaningless.

A rule-based culture is not necessarily egalitarian. Ancient Roman law, the precursor of the Western legal tradition, distinguished plebes from patricians. The egalitarianism of the United States derives from individualism as well as its rule-based culture. The ultimate source of individualism is a secular heritage that sees human beings as islands of consciousness in a disenchanted world (see Chapter 11). Yet this does not explain why individualism keeps growing stronger and families weaker. Some blame technology and its tendency to break up the extended family, which seems in fact to be part of the story. I am old enough to remember my relatives getting together to play folk music on their banjos, guitars, fiddles, and harmonicas, a tradition that TV soon replaced with individual entertainment. The automobile allowed us to relocate at will, and now we are hundreds of miles apart, even if the Internet is beginning to reconnect us. The deeper reason for the disintegration of the family, however, is simply that Western culture can tolerate it. Family loyalty requires energy, particularly in our mobile age, and cultures tend to drift away from energy expenditures that are inessential to their survival. Strong families are inessential because the West can replace them with other coping mechanisms, such as technology-based structuring of the physical and social environment.

Time Consciousness

The United States is the world's most time conscious society. Practically everything is scheduled. Even negotiations may begin with a set agenda to be covered in a fixed order. Punctuality is mandatory. Deadlines are taken seriously, and penalties may be written into contracts for their violation (a practice that, interestingly, also occurs in polychronic India). It has become popular to ask higher prices for shorter lead times, a scheme long practiced by airlines that charge more for tomorrow's flight than next week's. As suggested in Chapter 2, the monochronicity of the West is part of a stress-management system that organizes one's environment, including one's time. Time consciousness gets out of hand in the United States and often contributes to stress, perhaps due to the central role of the work ethic. Yet the country's relatively stable environment allows it to absorb time-related stress for the sake of the larger goal of achieving salvation through work (see Chapter 11).

Americans are known for their optimism and future-oriented outlook, which may stem from their frontier experience, unique in world history. The settling of a seemingly limitless wilderness, abounding in natural resources, may also account for the country's rugged individualism and wasteful habits. Some deplore Americans' disregard for history, but it allows them to forget old grudges that preoccupy so much of the world. No one cares that British troops once invaded Washington, D.C., and burned the Capitol. The American Civil War, in which brother fought brother, inspires fascination but little resentment. The view into the future is myopic, however. Many organizations seem to look little beyond the next annual report, or in some cases the next quarterly statement. There are exceptions: in the early twentieth century, engineers built aqueducts from the Catskill Mountains with enough capacity to supply pure water to a growing New York City for a century or more. As a result today's New Yorkers enjoy what is generally acknowledged to be the best tap water in the country. Such a farsighted venture is quite out of character.

Studying in the United States

Since many students travel to the United States to enroll in a school or college, a word about educational practices is in order. U.S. teachers immediately notice that most international students are reluctant to speak up in class. This is partly because the students are accustomed to a different style of instruction back home, where the professor hands down knowledge while students listen quietly and take notes. There is a deeper reason, however, since children of immigrants, particularly East Asian immigrants, exhibit a similar reticence even though they grew up in the United States. International students tend to have a strong respect for elders and often for teachers in particular, and speaking out in class could be interpreted as disrespectful. They may be reluctant to ask questions, which indicate lack of knowledge and therefore cause loss of face. They may also be self-conscious about their accents.

International students should bear in mind, however, that American teachers generally want them to participate in class discussion. Questions are welcome. Since teachers may view reticent students as uninterested or unintelligent, it is wise to make oneself heard. Students can tactfully question the ideas discussed in class while still respecting the teacher as an individual. As noted earlier, Americans distinguish the issue from the person, since a rule-based culture is impossible without such a distinction. It is always safe to say, "I don't understand why such and such is true," unless of course the instructor is from a culture that expects students to remain quiet, which is always possible given the multiethnic character of U.S. faculties. As for accents, Americans are accustomed to them.

Despite the advantages of speaking up in class, I have found that many international students, indeed most with Confucian backgrounds, can never bring themselves to do so. Respect for age and authority is embedded too deeply in their ancestral culture. It would be no less difficult for Americans abroad to forget about their rights as individuals. International students can nonetheless rest assured that American teachers find their courtesy and industry a pleasant contrast with the habits of some domestic students. They should never feel obliged to learn rudeness or neglect their studies in order to fit in.

Visiting students should also be aware that American instructors readily admit mistakes in class. This brings loss of face in much of the world but is expected in the United States. These conflicting expectations pose a dilemma for American teachers in multicultural classrooms. My policy, when I teach in the United States, is to follow the American custom and absorb my losses with the foreign students. When teaching abroad, however, I may try to slip out of mistakes without admitting them. My American colleagues will disapprove of this behavior, but Kantian consistency (as explained in the previous chapter) requires me to support the system that makes my teaching possible. Students in relationship-based, high–power distance cultures take their lessons seriously, and therefore learn, because they respect their teachers. As discussed in Chapter 7, it is difficult in such a culture for fallible human beings to command respect unless culture provides mechanisms to conceal their fallibility.

American teachers often find international students very diligent about following specific instructions but uncomfortable with taking the initiative or thinking creatively. It is not difficult to speculate about why "thinking out of the box" would be encouraged in the dominant Western societies. Since technology is the West's primary coping mechanism, innovation confers a selective advantage by upgrading technology with clever new ideas. Western societies that have not encouraged their Edisons are not likely to be dominant, and still less likely to attract students from abroad. Creativity and initiative play a less important structural role in some non-Western cultures, but many individuals nonetheless possess these traits and should feel free to develop them while studying in the United States.

Students in U.S. schools can be severely penalized or even expelled for plagiarism, a concept that scarcely exists in much of the world. It is true that domestic students commonly use material from the Internet without attribution, but this behavior is nonetheless unethical, and some schools are cracking down with sophisticated software that detects plagiarized passages. International students are at greater risk because they may see nothing wrong with pasting in downloaded material. They may consider themselves unworthy to write their own words on a topic when respected experts have spoken. (In fact, a kind of reverse plagiarism is traditionally practiced, and at one time even in the West, in which obscure writers attach a famous person's name to their own work.) The duty of students in much of the world is to demonstrate they have absorbed their culture's lessons, rather than to contribute their own ideas. As explained in Chapter 8, however, U.S. culture rests heavily on individual accountability. Students are therefore held personally accountable (and are personally rewarded) for the content of the essay they submit to the professor, which makes no sense unless they wrote it themselves. Moreover, they are expected to express their unique personalities by using their own words, in keeping with the American imperative to show individual initiative and creativity.

Students from abroad soon realize that most American students choose their own careers. They might be tempted to envy this kind of freedom, but it has its cost. Young adults in America are typically pushed from the nest and expected to fly on their own. They generally cannot rely on family networking to find them a job, and yet they may feel as pressured to succeed as Asian youth. Reality is complicated, and there are naturally many exceptions to the pattern. Yet few deny that adolescence in the United States, for all its freedom, is a wrenching experience that propels too many youth into unsuccessful careers, broken marriages, drug use, and lawlessness. The family discipline that visiting students find so oppressive is a form of support that many American students, in retrospect, might wish they had.

Stress Management

The major stress-management tools of the United States have all been introduced in the foregoing pages at one point or another, and so it remains only to collect them. Most perform a dual role by helping to knit society together as well. They are outlined in table 15.1.

The most visible mechanism is technology-based control of the environment (see Chapters 2, 6, and 11). This is what makes life so comfortable and convenient in the United States. It reduces everyday stress by providing predictability, and it allows Americans the luxury of generating new stress

TABLE 15.1

Stress-Management Mechanisms in the United States, and Their
Contributions to Social Cohesion

Mechanism	Contribution to Stress Management	Contribution to Social Cohesion
Technology-based structuring of the environment	Provides predictability and control in everyday life	Generates surplus wealth, some of which "trickles down" to all classes (but an unjust distribution can cause discontent)
Universalizing rationality	Supports science and technology	Supports "self-evident" rules of conduct that all subcultures can accept
Individual responsibility and the work ethic	Provide a sense of control over one's fate	Provide a wealth-distribution mechanism that can be seen as consistent with equality of opportunity
Primarily Apollonian lifestyle	Supports a well-ordered, structured environment	Promotes social stability
Masculine, competitive culture	Supports individual responsibility and the work ethic	Supports individual responsibility and the work ethic
Puritanism	Provides a sense of control through avoidance of impure acts, substances, and language	Enforces politically correct speech
Religion	Provides meaning that is absent in a skeletal, low-context culture	Teaches norms of conduct

through their frenetic lifestyle and work ethic. In the meantime it contributes to social cohesion through a "trickle down" process. The technology-based economy and infrastructure, in combination with a ruled-based, high-trust society (see Chapter 3), generate so much wealth that even people near the bottom of the economic ladder do well by comparison with the rest of the world, where half the population lives on less than $2 (U.S.) a day. However, even this high overall standard of living is consistent with social unrest if wealth is unjustly distributed. This could become a problem for the United States as the income gap widens, due in part to the conversion to a service economy in which relatively few information workers ("symbolic analysts" in Robert Reich's phrase) make most of the money.

The most fundamental mechanism, however, is universalizing rationality (see Chapters 1, 4, 11, and 14), which likewise plays twin roles. It is the foundation of the science and technology by which Americans structure their environment. It holds society together by providing "universally valid" and "self-evident" rules that all subcultures can acknowledge. Due in part to individualism, the rules enforce fairness above all else. Individualism goes hand in hand with individual responsibility and the work ethic (see Chapter 11). Both encourage the belief that one can control one's fate through individual effort and initiative, and they provide a principle for wealth distribution that people across subcultures can accept as fair.

The preference for rationally ordered surroundings makes the United States a predominately Apollonian culture, although as in all Western cultures there is a dialectic between Apollonian and Dionysian (see Chapter 7). The Dionysian appears in widespread drug use, binge drinking, and a weakened sense of reality. Theme parks that sanitize reality are irresistible. As computer, TV, and movie screens increasingly replace actual experience, truth and fantasy become figments of the same electronic world and blend indistinguishably. People become skeptical of everything except their own government conspiracy theories, a trend exploited by such wildly popular shows as *The X-Files*. Active imaginations make a positive contribution, however, by inspiring innovations that range from electric lights to personal computers. It is possible to dream as a Dionysian and realize one's dreams as an Apollonian. Dionysian subcultures energize the arts, as for example when African music combined with the rationality of the West to create rock and roll, blues, and jazz, all new idioms that attract audiences worldwide.

The belief in individual initiative makes the United States a masculine society, not so much in the sense that men dominate (even if they have historically) as in the sense that competition is encouraged. Learning to spell means competing in a spelling bee. Getting into shape means running in a marathon race. It is difficult for me to recall attending a public exhibition or conference in the United States that did not award a prize for the best hog or the best presentation. Competition is extolled as the driving force of the economy, although it can inspire enormous waste and destruction through duplication of effort and bankruptcies. As the ideal of equal opportunity becomes more nearly realized, competition increasingly replaces connections and social status as a mechanism for wealth distribution. The pressure on children to excel on grades and college entrance exams, for example, has become nearly as intense as in Japan, the world's most thoroughly masculine culture. Competitiveness and individualism are associated with the high uncertainty tolerance of the United States (see Chapter 7), which encourages entrepreneurship and risk taking. The American fascination with violence and guns might also be associated with its masculine culture. It is difficult to see a functional role for violence, although guns symbolize security for much of the population (see Chapter 8).

Religion in the United States operates on both the secular and overtly religious levels. Its main contribution to secular culture was to introduce Puritanism (see Chapter 12) through the Congregationalist settlers of New England. Europeans like to snicker at the Puritanical prudery of the United States, even if they were historically its source. Yet Puritanism is a much broader concept than prudery. It is Protestant Christianity's version of ancient purification rituals and teaches that one can escape ruination by avoiding unclean acts, substances, and language. American sex morals are actually liberal by world standards. The Puritanical focus has shifted from fornication and swearing to smoking, poor diets, insufficient exercise, and politically incorrect language. At my workplace, smokers are not only banished to the cold and wet Pittsburgh outdoors to pursue their habit, but they are technically forbidden even to stand near a doorway, a ruling worthy of Cotton Mather himself. Smokers from abroad would do well to heed the rules, since it is probably easier to get away with murder than with lighting up in the no-smoking section of a restaurant.

Religion is also important in its overt form (see Chapter 11). The commonly quoted statistic is that about half of Americans attend religious gatherings regularly, far more than in Europe and Japan. Organized religion covers a vast gamut: mainline Protestant denominations (which are shrinking); evangelical Protestant groups (growing); Roman Catholic, Orthodox, and Byzantine churches; such Asian faiths as Hinduism, Buddhism, Islam, Taoism, Jainism, Bahai, Zoroastrianism, and Sikhism; Santaría from the Caribbean; and such homegrown followings as Mormonism (the largest), Christian Science, Unitarianism, Seventh-Day Adventism, Scientology, Kwanzaa, the Unification Church, New Age philosophy, and cults too numerous to mention.

Religion presumably flourishes in the United States because the mainstream low-context culture is minimalist, saying much about work and justice but little about ultimate meanings. If the task of religion is to reconnect, then it has much to do in the cultural hodgepodge of the United States. Traditional cultures make sense of the world in a mythical story that is literary, explanatory, and moral all at once. Yet myth in America, as in other Western countries, has splintered into its literary, explanatory, and moral fragments, none of which has the power to integrate. Literary myth takes the form of movies and TV. These are entertaining, an important function of myth because it must hold one's attention. Yet since the overriding objective is profitability, they rarely provide a moral or cosmic dimension. In traditional cultures parents and other family members shape the literary world of their children in order to pass on their core values. Commercial entertainment in the United States has transferred this role from parents to corporate executives who have little choice but to serve narrow business interests.

The explanatory component of modern myth is science, which is by far the most successful. To satisfy its drive for a unified theory (a thoroughly religious impulse), science explains a vast array of phenomena on the basis of a few precise laws that permit one to predict and manipulate nature. This extraordinary achievement allows science to bear much of the weight carried by myths in traditional cultures. It is nonetheless incomplete, because it cannot address values explicitly. As the physical universe encompasses ever greater realms of time and space, the significance of human beings tends to zero as a limit.

The moral component of myth does little to brighten this depressing picture. It is negative in character, deriving minimal conditions for justice and human rights from the logic of moral discourse (see Chapter 14). It provides little positive guidance as to what people should do with their lives while being just and respectful of rights.

Overt religion may play a larger role in the United States than in other affluent countries, because Americans need it more. Europe and Japan inculcate a strong sense of ethnic identification and therefore tell people something about who they are and how they should behave. This is not possible in multiethnic America, and many people turn to religion for a place in the universe. The less affluent may join evangelical sects to resist a power structure based on rationalized institutions, as suggested in Chapter 8. The more affluent may prefer New Age philosophies or "California" editions of Eastern religions. Ethnic groups tend to retain their traditional faith. All this religious activity results in the plethora of religions already mentioned and presupposes, of course, that they can coexist peaceably in a way they often do not elsewhere.

The Melting Pot

The discussion has come around to multiculturalism, as all discussions of U.S. society must. It is a good point at which to consider the melting pot and salad bowl models introduced earlier. The melting pot deals with multiculturalism by denying its possibility. It allows for a multiethnic population but not a multicultural one. It insists that all groups must assimilate to a single overarching culture, at least within a generation or two. It acknowledges the tragic failure of this scheme at various points in history but sees steady progress.

The meltdown occurs in several ways. Two mechanisms have already been mentioned. The low-context culture is immigrant friendly, and universalizing rationality serves up "self-evident" rules to live by. A third factor is that national identity is based on patriotism and allegiance to the political system rather than membership in an ethnic group. The very procedure for becoming a citizen involves a civics lesson. The spontaneous and exuberant displays of flags and patriotism following the September 11 attacks show how Americans compensate for the lack of ethnic solidarity. Immigrants may initially see this as clubby behavior that excludes them, but it is an invitation to join in. When Arab Americans hang flags in their storefronts to demonstrate their loyalty to the United States, people approve.

It is true that most if not all ethnic groups have at some time been unwelcome and discriminated against. Even Scotch-Irish settlers, of thoroughly Anglo-Saxon background, were excluded from much of New England due to their Presbyterianism. Yet this very sort of discrimination triggers a mechanism for assimilation. Immigrants soon learn that they can improve their lot by using the rhetoric of human rights and participating in the political process. Latinos, for example, have propelled many of their number into elected office and thereby positioned their interests high on the public agenda. Both major candidates in the last Presidential election took care to demonstrate their (rudimentary) knowledge of Spanish. Even ethnic conflict can lead to political involvement that, in the long run, works against intolerance. In recent months Arab Americans have vigorously petitioned their Congressional representatives to favor the Palestinian cause in its conflict with Israel. One might wish that their political interests were less narrow, but this is a first step toward civic responsibility that is so vital to the success of the melting pot.

Civic involvement alone is probably insufficient to break down the ancient enmities that immigrants bring with them. Another factor may be that the classical conditions for ethnic conflict normally do not obtain. Such conflict usually takes place between similar peoples who occupy neighboring territories, since this is presumably the setting in which it once served the ecological purpose of preserving uninhabited land along the border (see Chapter 4). There have long been ethnic neighborhoods in the United States, and they have been associated with ethnic intolerance. But they are gradually disappearing, due in part to fair housing laws. Rather than adjacent territories peopled by similar ethnicities, in the manner of Protestants and Catholics in Ulster, we see mixed neighborhoods whose inhabitants have vastly different backgrounds. The mere fact that there are so many ethnicities, mingling inseparably at shopping malls and ball games, makes it rather awkward to maintain organized hatred against a particular one. Intolerance is also discouraged by the media, an instance in which the ersatz mythological literature of the United States finally lives up to its role.

We may have stumbled upon the most satisfactory explanation for the gradual dissolution of ethnic divisions: they are no longer worth the effort. Although it is apparently easy to learn ethnic hatred, its practice requires some effort. As mentioned earlier, cultures tend to invest substantial energy in a behavioral pattern only when it serves a cultural function. Ethnic identity serves such a function in much of the world, where it is a necessary binding force (see Chapter 1), and it may rely psychologically on hatred of the other. Yet U.S. society is explicitly set up to rest on mechanisms other than ethnic identification. Intolerance therefore serves no clear cultural purpose, and its energy cost keeps going up. People increasingly find other ways to spend their time.

American universalism facilitates the melting pot in another way that I, however, believe is becoming obsolete. If culture is merely language and cuisine, if everyone is basically the same inside, then newcomers can assimilate because they differ only superficially. The language barrier is overcome within a generation, and their cuisines only give Americans a chance to prove how multiethnic they are. Some of my colleagues can rattle off Italian dishes that most Italians have never heard of. This American trivialization of culture might be seen as integrative, because it allows Americans to view the assimilation of diverse cultures as an innocuous process of teaching them English and cultivating a taste for their food.

The ugly fly in the ointment is the Western conception of race, since the very universalism that unites cultures segregates races. As noted in Chapter 4, universalism attributes persistent and fundamental traits to biology, because it cannot accept that they are purely cultural. The association of culture and race cements rather than dissolves ethnic barriers, since racial characteristics are much slower to blend into the cheese fondue than cultural ones. One may cite the mixed parentage of many young people in the United States today as evidence of racial homogenization, but experience in Latin America suggests that even when most of the population has evolved to a broad mestizo race, elites continue to be racially distinguishable.

U.S. history confirms the special problems of integrating ethnic groups that look very different from the mainstream. In 1619 a ship flying the Dutch flag brought twenty Africans to Jamestown, Virginia, and unloaded the first shipment of slaves in what is now the United States.[4] This minor incident metastasized into a malignant social cancer that brought untold suffering, inspired a bloody civil war, and remains to be completely excised even today. Enslavement of human beings is intolerable under the Western worldview, but racism made it possible to believe that Africans were somehow less than fully human. The United States Supreme Court ruled in 1857 that Dred Scott, a fugitive slave, must be returned to his owners because he was property, not a human being. Although opposition to slavery was already brewing by the time of the American Revolution, the American political process was painfully slow to eradicate racist practices that presented the clearest imaginable violation of its fundamental principles.

Political and legal failure was equally evident in the case of the continent's native inhabitants. Europeans quickly discovered that Native Americans were familiar with the concept of a treaty, since covenants governed relations between native tribes. This provided a cultural bridge by which the natives and newcomers might work through the difficult process of resolving land claims. The process broke down, however, because the Europeans (not the native "savages") invariably violated the treaties, sometimes within days of signing them—presumably because the natives did not fully qualify for a type of moral agency that confers rights. The European Americans brought the violation of their own norms to a climax in 1832, when Samuel Worcester appealed a case to the U.S. Supreme Court, *Worcester v. the State of Georgia*. The facts of the case dealt narrowly with the right of Georgia to prevent Worcester from settling on Cherokee land.[5] But a larger principle was at stake. By this point, the U.S. government had arrived at a policy of resettling the native population on "reservations," a concept similar to the South African "homelands." Two years earlier President Andrew Jackson had convinced the U.S. Congress to pass the Indian Resettlement Act, which required native people to move to Indian Territory west of the Mississippi. The government had no such authority, however, if the Cherokee and other Indian nations were sovereign states. Chief Justice John Marshall ruled in the *Worcester* case that indeed they were, the implication being that the State of Georgia had no jurisdiction over Cherokee land, and the U.S. government could relocate the Cherokee only by negotiating a treaty for their removal. When Jackson was informed of the ruling, he was reported to have said, "John Marshall has rendered his decision; now let him enforce it."[6] This defiance of the Supreme Court represented a fundamental breakdown of the rule of law in the United States.

The result of this breakdown was a mass migration, known by the Cherokee as the Trail of Tears. Federal troops forcibly removed Cherokee, Chickasaw, Choctaw, Creek, and Seminole families from their homes and marched them hundreds of miles under conditions of extreme deprivation. Thousands perished. A small band of Cherokee survived by hiding in the mountains of Tennessee and North Carolina. Otherwise this book would not exist, since at least one of them numbers among my ancestors.

Advocates of the melting pot must deal with this ugly history. They must explain how universalism can knit peoples together if it is repeatedly overcome by a racism that denies moral agency to oppressed groups. Actually there is reason for cautious optimism. In recent decades, African Americans and Native Americans have made effective use of a legal system that once abrogated its own basic principles in order to deny them rights. A more fundamental dynamic concerns the origin of Western-style racism.

In Chapter 4 I described racist beliefs as the logical outcome of a universalism that cannot otherwise explain persistent and fundamental cultural difference. In this view, racism is not sui generis but a consequence of a state of affairs. If the state of affairs changes, racism may lose its cultural function in much the way that ethnic intolerance has. If a significant number of people in racial minorities become culturally compatible with the mainstream—if the cultural difference is no longer persistent and fundamental—then a racial explanation is no longer needed. This may in fact explain what is happening in the United States. It may be an unfortunate way to defeat racism, because it does so by partially homogenizing the cultures that are associated with race. I will deal with this objection shortly.

The Salad Bowl

The salad bowl model for U.S. culture attempts to address several weaknesses of the melting pot. The most evident is that the melting pot works best for a Western cultural mix. For most of U.S. history, ethnic groups in the United States have been primarily of European origin. Africans and Native Americans are obvious exceptions, but they were initially excluded from the melting pot. The West Coast received many Asian immigrants in the nineteenth century, but they fared only slightly better than other minority races. Presumably the melting pot could work in old times, to the extent that it did, because most people were of a Western persuasion and could resonate with the universalizing rule-based culture into which they assimilated. The U.S. population has become much more diverse in the last few decades, however. Demographers predict that within a few years European Americans will be in the minority. It is no longer possible to pretend everyone is the same inside. Only a salad bowl is possible now, or so it is said.

A second weakness of the melting pot scheme is less often remarked: the marginalization of political and civic institutions that historically made it possible. The immigrant's goal is frequently to obtain the coveted "green card" rather than citizenship. Those who are already citizens neglect to vote in most elections. As an excuse they cite the trivialization of political contests, which have become media entertainment with little substantive discussion of issues. The candidates parrot lines carefully vetted by media experts for maximum effect rather than express a coherent political philosophy. Recently I spent several hours in the Allegheny County courthouse waiting for jury duty. I studied several mural paintings that contained the symbols and texts of the American political system, such as the Bill of Rights and the Preamble to the Constitution. I was troubled by the fact that such displays strike us as dated or trite today. The builders of the century-old courthouse obviously took them very seriously.

The fundamental objection to the melting pot, however, springs from an ethic of multiculturalism. Assimilation fails to respect minority cultures. The story of the Native Americans, to which I have already alluded, makes the point well enough. Encroachment on another people's land is nearly as old as humanity, and Native Americans had a habit of doing it themselves. Yet there was something different about European expansionism. As universalists, they assumed that a single culture, theirs, was destined to occupy the entire continent. Minority peoples would simply convert to the mainstream civilization. This universalism became official policy when European Americans began to crave the last remaining land onto which they had relocated the native people. In 1879 the Carlisle Indian School was established in Pennsylvania to "civilize" native children by cutting their hair, making them wear Western clothes, and forbidding them to speak their native tongues. In 1887 the Dawes Act furthered assimilation by dividing tribal land into tracts, some of which went to individual native families, and the rest sold to whites. The aim was to destroy the tradition of communal land ownership, a bedrock principle of native cultures. At about this time the Paiute prophet Wovoka popularized the famous Ghost Dance religion, a revitalization cult (the first to be identified as such) that represented a last-gasp attempt of native peoples to save their cultures from extinction.[7] Its ability to unify tribes alarmed whites. On December 29, 1890, at Wounded Knee Creek, South Dakota, a contingent of U.S. soldiers massacred some three hundred men, women, and children of the Sioux tribe who participated in the Ghost Dance cult. It was the saddest day in the history of North America, as it symbolized the final destruction of the continent's native cultures.

I am as concerned about cultural extinction as anyone. Yet it is another thing to advocate multiculturalism within a single society. It is simply not possible. The mechanisms that allow subcultures in the United States to coexist are hallmarks of an overarching northern European culture: rule-governed behavior, a low-context social environment, and a hefty dose of universalizing rationality. The society is and can only be multi-subcultural, not multicultural. The illusion of multiculturalism springs from the very overarching culture whose existence is denied. American universalism trivializes cultural difference and therefore gives the impression that different cultures exist in the United States. A neighborhood in which people speak Spanish and eat tortillas is seen as an enclave of Mexican culture. Yet it may be only a collection of Mexican cultural fragments that have mingled with the mainstream culture around it. This may explain why "multicultural" America knows so little about world cultures. It sees only fragments that are like pottery shards. It is difficult to know how the pieces fit together unless one has seen the whole.

Multiculturalism's own diversity-training movement illustrates the need for an overarching culture. The movement began in the 1980s, when most new workers in the United States belonged to ethnic minorities.[8] Employers had little choice but to embrace multi-ethnicity and resolve its problems as best they could, for the sake of productivity. The first wave of diversity workshops was thoroughly Western in its approach. It took advantage of a guilt-based culture by "guilt tripping" participants, in particular by convincing white employees that they were racists. For a time white males were not allowed to run the workshops, since they were seen as part of the problem. There was a strong focus on politically correct speech, sensitivity training, and role-playing, reflecting the mainstream Puritan culture. A third technique was to bring racial attitudes to the surface through encounter groups and other forms of psychological manipulation. It was argued that racial attitudes were not acquired by logic and could not be eliminated by logic. This approach reflects the Western reliance on technology-based manipulation of nature to solve its problems.

A second wave of workshops characterized the 1990s. The primary motivation had evolved from productivity to a desire to avoid legal consequences. Federal law already held a company responsible for the discriminatory practices of its employees, but the new federal sentencing guidelines of 1987 prescribed lighter punishments for firms that had preventive programs in place. There was a rush to create codes of ethics, confidential hot lines on which employees could report violations, and new diversity-training programs. Firms also found the early programs to be ineffective, since they treated intolerance as a streak of evil that must be purged from individuals rather than reflections of the cultural system in which they live.[9]

The new style of workshop replaced guilt mongering with a different set of techniques that nonetheless remained thoroughly Western in spirit. Workers who struggled with discrimination were encouraged to "talk about it" in order to bring their feelings into the open, a natural tactic in a low-context culture. Conflict-resolution techniques became an important component of many workshops. Employees were provided with self-help methods based on "emotional intelligence" and "mind talk" techniques, reflecting a self-help movement that has become a major phenomenon of individualistic U.S. mainstream culture. A final maneuver was to enforce total equality in work teams, reflecting the ethic of egalitarianism. The lesson to be drawn from all this is that the new age of "multiculturalism" in the United States continues to presuppose an underlying rule-based culture.

A second lesson is that the U.S. approach to uniting a multiethnic society, based as it is on the American version of northern European culture, may not be suitable for such non-Western societies as India or Brazil. In India, for example, everyone has a social "place" based on caste or *jati*. Brazil is characterized by well-defined social strata that define the rights and privileges of their constituents. Malaysia, by contrast, has achieved some success with a Western technique. It uses affirmative action policies to promote greater equality between financially successful ethnic Chinese and the *Bumiputera* (indigenous) people. Yet Malaysian culture as a whole remains light-years from the American system.

E Pluribus Unum

The United States is a melting pot, but the cheese fondue metaphor is not quite right. It implies an undifferentiated mixture, while the United States is a kind of cultural federation in which distinct subcultures pay common allegiance to a national culture. Perhaps one should speak of a Mulligan stew in which potatoes and beef chunks float in a uniform broth representing the mainstream culture.

This model implies partial homogenization, since every morsel partakes of the broth. Latinos and African Americans can generally flourish in the mainstream only if they accept the rule-based orientation, low-context character, and universalism of the mainstream culture. This may be less than ideal, but it is necessary. It is consistent with the ethic of multiculturalism because it rules out multiculturalism only within a single society, where it is impossible anyway. The parent cultures can and should flourish in their home countries.

The case of Native American cultures is different, since their existence was at stake. Perhaps some reasonable partition of land might have been negotiated, allowing them to evolve and adapt to a changing world on their own terms. Unfortunately we cannot turn back the clock and do it right. Many Native Americans today work to resuscitate their customs and language, and pass them on through their children, but they are unlikely to rid themselves of the mainstream culture in which they are immersed. Perhaps they do not wish to do so. Yet there is every possibility that they can build distinctive subcultures that further enrich a society that is slowly learning tolerance.

The continued success of a Mulligan stew with ever more diverse ingredients depends on several factors. Immigrants and natives alike must honor their citizenship and participate in political and civic affairs. Racial and ethnic intolerance must continue to fade due to irrelevance. An alternative to overburdened legal and social welfare systems must be found for matters traditionally regulated by cultural norms. A new synthesis of literary, scientific, and moral myth must be forged to add substance to an increasingly skeletal, low-context culture that regulates but provides no meaning.

I believe an additional sort of change is necessary and already underway. Americans must stop trivializing culture. If they are to integrate the non-Western subcultures that are beginning to outnumber Western ones, Americans must face up to their vastly different origins. A trend of acknowledging cultural difference is already visible in the multicultural workplace, where ethnicities are beginning to be seen as bringing complementary strengths.[10] It was politically incorrect to mention cultural difference, but it is beginning to be celebrated—none too soon, since the United States's overbearing role in the world is incompatible with its specious assumption that everyone is basically the same inside.

A recognition of cultural difference need not undermine the universalizing rationality that is so fundamental to American unity. Intellectuals have already paved the way with the postmodern recognition that reality is amenable to alternate, equally valid interpretations (see Chapters 4 and 14). A Western worldview can coexist, without compromise of its universality, with radically alien worldviews. Americans are already tolerant and respectful of alternative lifestyles. I predict that as postmodernism seeps into the culture at large, Americans will accept the radical otherness of other cultures without abandoning their own unifying principles.

As an example I cite one of my favorite ethnographies, Elizabeth Warnock Fernea's *Guests of the Sheik*. Fernea had no training in anthropology but accompanied her anthropologist husband during this two-year field study of a Shiite village in southern Iraq. She brought the cultural innocence of middle-class America to an environment of almost inconceivable strangeness, where she nonetheless learned Arabic and determined to associate with her female neighbors as she might with neighbors back home. Her book is an honest, apolitical, and respectful account of a fascinating culture few Westerners experience. She writes that after a year or so of culture shock, she finally began to feel accepted and reasonably comfortable with her surroundings. One day, however, she took a female friend on an excursion that seemed perfectly innocent but, for complicated reasons, seriously compromised her friend's honor. From this incident she learned culture's central lesson, a lesson that I believe other Americans are ready to absorb as well. Her account echoes the beginning of this book and is a fitting note on which to end it.

How little I knew about the society in which I was living! During the year I had made friends, I had listened and talked and learned, I thought, a great deal, but the pattern of custom and tradition which governed the lives of my friends was far more subtle and complex than I had imagined. It was like the old image of the iceberg, the small, easily recognizable face on the surface of the water giving no idea of the size or shape or texture of what lies beneath.[11]

Notes for Chapter 15

1. In this chapter, the term *Americans* refers to residents of the United States in particular rather than North and South America in general.

2. Henry Beard and Christopher Cerf, *The Official Politically Correct Dictionary and Handbook,* Villard Books (New York, 1993).

3. Dorothy Counts and David Counts, "Home Is Where They Park It," *Anthropology Newsletter* 39 (no. 8, 1998): 9–10.

4. Howard Zinn, *A People's History of the United States,* Harper & Row (New York, 1980).

5. Charles Hudson, *The Southeastern Indians,* University of Tennessee Press (Knoxville, 1976).

6. Ibid., 463.

7. James Mooney, *The Ghost-Dance Religion and the Sioux Outbreak of 1890,* University of Nebraska Press (Lincoln, Neb., 1991, orig. published by U.S. Government Printing Office, 1896).

8. George Henderson, *Cultural Diversity in the Workplace,* Quorum Books (Westport, Conn., 1994).

9. Hellen Hemphill and Ray Haines, *Discrimination, Harassment and the Failure of Diversity Training: What to Do Now,* Quorum Books (Westport, Conn., 1997).

10. William Sonnenschein, *The Practical Executive and Workforce Diversity,* McGraw-Hill (New York, 1997).

11. Elizabeth Warnock Fernea, *Guests of the Sheik: An Ethnography of an Iraqi Village,* Anchor Books (New York, 1969), 266.

Further Reading

The aim of this book is to provide conceptual tools for understanding what makes a culture hang together. It shows how to apply these tools in seven specific countries, but no attempt is made to cover the full range of world cultures. Readers who anticipate a visit abroad should begin studying the host country before they depart. The following reading list may help. It is organized by country and lists useful sources for each.

Even after extensive research, however, one should be prepared for a surprise on arrival. Most of the books listed view cultures through a Western lens and may overlook or distort their most important characteristics. The best approach is to construct one's own theory, little by little, of what makes the culture tick, beginning with information culled from reading and continuing as one interacts with the culture.

The sources are selected for their immediate usefulness to travelers who wish to understand the host culture. The list generally omits specialized anthropological studies as well as purely historical treatments, since these may be less accessible or only indirectly relevant. It also omits travel guides, photo albums, and business publications that offer limited cultural insight of value to persons who intend to work in the country. Books dealing primarily with politics, war, and international relations are avoided. The list restricts itself to work published in English, generally after 1990. These criteria are relaxed somewhat if sources are scarce for a given country. Although a wealth of cultural material is available for some countries, there is little or nothing in print for some others. Potential authors, take note.

The citations for each country are arranged alphabetically by author. Some books contain chapters or sections on several countries; these books are listed under each relevant country. Many of the citations are annotated; comments in quotation marks are taken from the publisher's promotional material, while other comments are my own. A number of the books belong to the following series:

- *Comparative Societies* series, published by McGraw-Hill. These present sociological analyses of some major countries, including the status of the economy, the family, religion, and so forth.

- *Culture and Customs* series, published by Greenwood Publishing Group. These books generally cover history, religion, customs, media, and the arts.

- *Culture Shock* series, published by Graphics Arts Center Publishing Company. This is a broad and excellent collection of books generally (but not always) written by expatriates who have lived or worked in the country and have had to come to terms with the culture.

- *How to* series (entitled *Living and Working in . . .*), published by How to Books, Limited. These emphasize practical advice for expatriates but generally contain a chapter on cultural matters.

- *In Focus* series, published by Interlink Publishing Group. These books cover history, economics, society, and the arts in Caribbean and Latin American countries.

• *In the Know* series, published by Living Language. These provide advice on etiquette and culture as well as a CD that teaches some common phrases.

• *Interact* series, published by Intercultural Press. These interesting books compare various cultures with U.S. culture.

• *McGraw-Hill* series. These small books go by the titles *The French Way, The Italian Way,* and so on. They list cultural traits alphabetically.

• *NTC business* series, published by NTC Passport Books. These are more pamphlets than books, but they draw an interesting contrast with U.S. practices.

• *Oxfam Country Profiles* series, published by Oxfam Publications. These deal mainly with economic development.

• *Passport Pocket* series, published by World Trade Press. These small books contain a summary of etiquette and cultural traits.

• *Peoples of South-East Asia and the Pacific* series, published by Blackwell Publishers. These are anthropological treatises but are nonetheless sufficiently accessible to a lay audience and are useful.

• *Postcommunist States and Nations* series, published by Routledge. This series is primarily focused on political history, economics, and international relations, but social and cultural factors are usually mentioned.

• *Simple Guide* series, published by Global Books Limited. These cover etiquette and some basic cultural traits. They are used by the U.S. State Department.

• *Succeed in Business* series. This is the business version of the Culture Shock series.

• *Success Secrets* series. This is an updated version of the Succeed in Business series.

• *Survival Handbook* series, published by Survival Books. These books contain mainly practical advice for expatriates, but one can infer something about the culture from practical matters.

• *Teach Yourself* series, published by McGraw-Hill. These briefly summarize history, language, politics, the arts, religion, and some other cultural characteristics.

An expanded reading list is available online at http://ba.gsia.cmu.edu/culture. Click on a country to see all relevant citations. If a country is absent or inadequately covered, consult the following reference volume:

Carol R. Ember (Ed.), *Cultures of the World,* Macmillan (1999) ISBN 002865367X. An encyclopedia of world cultures. An unabridged version is available in ten volumes.

AFGHANISTAN

David Fleishhacker, *Lessons from Afghanistan,* DF Publications (2002) ISBN 0971717605. "Conventions about the use of time and space, attitudes about life stemming from thousand-year old traditions, and the practical necessities of living in a country fragmented by geography and history are the underlying facts of life in Afghanistan."

Chris Johnson, *Afghanistan,* Stylus Publications (1998) ISBN 085598385X. Oxfam Country Profiles series.

ALBANIA

Neil Olsen, *Albania,* Oxfam Publications (2000) ISBN 0855984325. Oxfam Country Profiles series.

Miranda Vickers and James Pettifer, *Albania: From Anarchy to Balkan Identity,* New York University Press (2000) ISBN 081478805X. Recent history (since 1985).

ALGERIA

Mohammed Saad, *Development through Technology Transfer: Creating New Cultural Understanding,* Intellect (2000) ISBN 1841500283. "Focusing on the experience of companies in Algeria, this book describes technology transfer as more than the hand-over of new technology hardware."

ARGENTINA

Fiona Adams, *Culture Shock: Argentina,* Graphic Arts Center Publishing Company (2000) ISBN 1558685294. Culture Shock series.

Andrea Campbell, *Passport Argentina,* World Trade Press (2000) ISBN 1885073216. Passport Pocket series.

William David Foster, Melissa Fitch Lockhart, and Darrell B. Lockhart, *Culture and Customs of Argentina,* Greenwood Publishing Group (1998) ISBN 0313303193. Culture and Customs series.

ARMENIA

Joseph R. Masih and Robert O. Krikorian, *Armenia: At the Crossroads,* Routledge (1999) ISBN 9057023458. Postcommunist States and Nations series.

AUSTRALIA

John Glynn, Martin O'Shannessy, and Rob Goodfellow, *Investing in Australia: A Cultural and Practical Guide,* Allan & Unwin, Australia (2000) ISBN 1865084611. Final chapter: "Australians Talk about Business Networking and Values."

David Hampshire, *Living and Working in Australia: A Survival Handbook,* Survival Books (1998) ISBN 1901130002. Survival Handbook series.

Philip R. Harris and Robert T. Moran, *Managing Cultural Differences: Leadership Strategies for a New World of Business,* 5th ed., Gulf Professional Publishing Company (2000) ISBN 0877193452. Updated edition of one of the earliest books in the field.

Fiona McGregor and Charlotte Denny, *Live & Work in Australia and New Zealand,* Vacation-Work (1997) ISBN 1854581155. Practical advice.

Angela Milligan, *Simple Guide to Australia: Customs and Etiquette,* Global Books Ltd. (2000) ISBN 186034061X. Simple Guide series.

Anthony Milner (Ed.), *Australia in Asia: Comparing Cultures,* Oxford University Press (1997) ISBN 019553672X. Includes discussion of business ethics.

Peter North and Bea Toews, *Success Secrets to Maximize Business in Australia,* Graphic Arts Center Publishing Company (2000) ISBN 1558685391. Success Secrets series.

George W. Renwick, *A Fair Go for All: Australian/American Interactions,* Intercultural Press (1991) ISBN 0933662963. Interact series.

Ilsa Sharp, *Culture Shock: Australia,* Graphic Arts Center Publishing Company (2001) ISBN 1558686134. Culture Shock series.

Laura Veltman, *Living & Working in Australia: Everything You Need to Know for Building a New Life,* How to Books Ltd. (2000) ISBN 1857032578. How to series.

AUSTRIA

Susan Roraff and Julie Krejei, *Culture Shock: Austria,* Graphic Arts Center Publishing Company (2001) ISBN 155868591X. Culture Shock series.

AZERBAIJAN

Charles Van Der Leeuw, *Azerbaijan: A Quest for Identity,* Palgrave Macmillan (2000) ISBN 0312219032. Mainly historical with one chapter on the recent situation.

BAHRAIN

Bruce Ingham and J. Fayadh, *Simple Guide to Arabia and the Gulf States: Customs & Etiquette,* Global Books Ltd. (2001) ISBN 1860340814. Simple Guide series.

Fred H. Lawson, *Bahrain: The Modernization of Autocracy,* Westview Press (1989) ISBN 0813301238.

BANGLADESH

Jim Monan, *Bangladesh,* Stylus Publications (1995) ISBN 0855983280. Oxfam Country Profiles series.

BELARUS

David R. Marples, *Belarus: A Denationalized Nation,* Routledge (1999) ISBN 9057023431. Postcommunist States and Nations series.

Jan Zaprudnik, *Belarus: At a Crossroads in History,* Westview Press (1993) ISBN 0813317940. "A native Belarusan paints a vivid picture of his country's complex past, paving the way for his analysis of the challenges now facing the republic in the wake of a disintegrating Soviet Union."

BELGIUM

Mark Elliott, *Culture Shock Belgium,* Graphic Arts Center Publishing Company (2002) ISBN 1558686061. Culture Shock series.

Renee C. Fox, *In the Belgian Chateau: The Spirit and Culture of a European Society in an Age of Change,* Ivan R. Dee, Inc. (1994) ISBN 1566630576. "A remarkable intellectual discourse and a rare glimpse of European culture."

Beverly Laflamme, *Living and Working in Belgium, Holland and Luxembourg,* Survival Books Ltd. (2001) ISBN 1901130266. Survival Handbook series.

Angela Milligan, *Simple Guide to Belgium: Customs and Etiquette,* Global Books Ltd. (2003) ISBN 1860340911. Simple Guide series.

BELIZE

Ian Peedle, *In Focus Belize: A Guide to the People, Politics and Culture,* Interlink Publishing Group (1999) ISBN 1566562848. In Focus series.

BOLIVIA

Mark Cramer, *Culture Shock: Bolivia,* Graphic Arts Center Publishing Company (1996) ISBN 1558682988. Culture Shock series.

Marcela Lopez Levy, *Bolivia,* Oxfam Publications (2001) ISBN 0855984554. Oxfam Country Profiles series.

Neil MacDonald (Ed.), *The Andes,* Stylus Publications (1993) ISBN 0855982004. Oxfam Country Profiles series.

Waltraud Queiser Morales, *Bolivia: Land of Struggle,* Westview Press (1992) ISBN 0813301971. "Considers the vibrant Indian culture, the mismanaged resources, and the foreign political and economic intervention as a microcosm of the third world."

Paul Van Lindert and Otto Verkoren, *Bolivia in Focus: A Guide to the People, Politics and Culture,* Interlink Publishing Group (2002) ISBN 1566562996. In Focus series.

BOSNIA AND HERZEGOVINA

Francine Friedman, *Bosnia: A Polity on the Brink,* Routledge (2002) ISBN 0415274354. Postcommunist States and Nations series.

Noel Malcolm, *Bosnia: A Short History,* New York University Press (1996) ISBN 0814755615. "An accessible account for general readers of the political and cultural history of Bosnia, exploding some myths about the origins and contin-uation of the present terrible strife."

BOTSWANA

Yousef Dadoo, Valmond Ghyoot, Dan Lephoko, and Gerrie Lubbe, *Multicultural Sensitivity for Managers,* Tsebanang Group, Rant en Dal, South Africa (1997) ISBN 0620212586. Particularly strong on African cultures.

BRAZIL

Marshall C. Eakin, *Brazil: The Once and Future Country,* Griffin Trade Paperback (1998) ISBN 0312214456. "[The book] reveals Brazil's many facets, including its racial melting pot (which often startles foreign visitors), economic challenges ('Brazil remains a rich country full of poor people'), and (in the book's most entertaining chapter) its carnival culture."

Elizabeth Ann Herrington, *Passport Brazil,* World Trade Press (forthcoming) ISBN 1885073186. Passport Pocket series.

George C. Lodge and Ezra F. Vogel (Eds.), *Ideology and National Competitiveness: An Analysis of Nine Countries,* Harvard Business School Press (1987) ISBN 0875841473.

Kevin Leon Neuhouser, *Modern Brazil,* McGraw-Hill (1998) ISBN 007289122X. Comparative Societies series.

Joseph A. Page, *The Brazilians,* Addison-Wesley (1995) ISBN 021441918. Perhaps the best available book on Brazilian culture. The author is intimately familiar with Brazil but writes from a U.S. perspective.

Voelker Poelzl, *Culture Shock: Brazil,* Graphic Arts Center Publishing Company (1997) ISBN 1558686371. Culture Shock series.

Jan Rocha, *Brazil,* Oxfam Publications (2000) ISBN 0855984333. Oxfam Country Profiles series.

Jan Rocha, *In Focus Brazil: A Guide to the People, Politics and Culture,* Interlink Publishing Group (2000) ISBN 1566563844. In Focus series.

Ronald M. Schneider, *Brazil: Culture and Politics in a New Industrial Powerhouse,* Westview Press (1996) ISBN 081332436X. Contains chapter on Brazilian culture.

BRUNEI (LOCATED ON THE ISLAND OF BORNEO)

Victor T. King, *The Peoples of Borneo,* Blackwell Publishers (1995) ISBN 0631172211. Peoples of South-East Asia and the Pacific series.

Heidi Munan, *Culture Shock Borneo,* Graphic Arts Center Publishing Company (1991) ISBN 1558680756. Culture Shock series.

BULGARIA

Vesselin Dimitrov, *Bulgaria: The Uneven Transition,* Routledge (2002) ISBN 0415267293. Postcommunist States and Nations series.

Emile Giatzidis, *An Introduction to Postcommunist Bulgaria,* Manchester University Press (2002) ISBN 0719060958. Table of Contents: Historical Background, Political Landscape, Economic Transformation, The "Re-birth" of Civil Society, Bulgaria's International Relations in the Postcommunist Era.

BURMA. SEE MYANMAR.

CAMBODIA

Ian Brown, *Cambodia,* Oxfam Publications (2000) ISBN 0855984309. Oxfam Country Profiles series.

James Fallows, *Looking at the Sun: The Rise of the New East Asian Economic and Political System,* Pantheon Books (1994) ISBN 067942251X. Describes new versions of capitalism that East Asian nations have developed to suit their social milieux.

I. W. Mabbett and David P. Chandler, *The Khmers,* Blackwell Publishers (1995) ISBN 0631175822. Peoples of South-East Asia and the Pacific series.

CANADA

Pang Guek Cheng and Robert Barlas, *Culture Shock: Canada,* Graphic Arts Center Publishing Company (2000) ISBN 155868087X. Culture Shock series.

Ken Coates, *Success Secrets to Maximize Business in Canada,* Graphic Arts Center Publishing Company (2001) ISBN 1558685421. Success Secrets series.

Philip R. Harris and Robert T. Moran, *Managing Cultural Differences: Leadership Strategies for a New World of Business,* 5th ed., Gulf Professional Publishing Company (2000) ISBN 0877193452. Updated edition of one of the earliest books in the field.

Benjamin A. Kranc and Karina Roman, *Living & Working in Canada: A New Life in Canada—All You Need to Know,* How to Books Ltd. (2000) ISBN 1857035534. How to series.

Janet MacDonald, *Living and Working in Canada,* Survival Books (1999) ISBN 1901130207. Survival Handbook series.

David M. Thomas (Ed.), *Canada and the United States: Differences that Count,* 2d ed., Broadview Press (2000) ISBN 1551112523. Contains a section titled "Social and Cultural Foundations."

Guang Tian, *Chinese-Canadians, Canadian-Chinese: Coping and Adapting in North America,* Edwin Mellen Press (1999) ISBN 0773422536. An ethnography about a key component of Canadian culture.

CHILE

Nick Caistor, *Chile In Focus: A Guide to the People, Politics and Culture,* Interlink Publishing Group (1998) ISBN 1566562317. In Focus series.

Guillermo I. Castillo-Feliu, *Culture and Customs of Chile,* Greenwood Publishing Group (2000) ISBN 0313307830. Culture and Customs series.

Susan Roraff and Laura Camacho, *Culture Shock: Chile,* Graphic Arts Center Publishing Company (2002) ISBN 1558686142. Culture Shock series.

CHINA

Tim Ambler, Morgen Witzel, *Doing Business in China,* Routledge (2000) ISBN 0415223296. "[The book] emphasizes the importance of *guanxi* (relationships) as the underpinning of virtually all businesses in China."

Richard E. Barrett and Fang Li, *Modern China,* McGraw-Hill (1998) ISBN 0072928263. Comparative Societies series.

Carolyn Blackman, *Negotiating China: Case Studies & Strategies,* Allen & Unwin (1998) ISBN 186448070X. "Carolyn Blackman draws on intensive case studies and her clear cultural understanding to reveal the tactics (conscious or unconscious) used by the Chinese."

Kevin Barry Bucknall, *Chinese Business Etiquette and Culture,* Boson Books (1999) ISBN 1886420556. "[The author] has negotiated in and published extensively about China, including two books and over twenty articles."

Pang Guek Cheng and Robert Barlas, *Culture Shock: Hong Kong,* Graphic Arts Center Publishing Company (2000) ISBN 1558681671. Culture Shock series.

Paulson Ching, *Doing Business in East Asia: A Practical Guide to China, Indonesia, Malaysia and Thailand,* Pelanduk Publications (1999) ISBN 9679784924.

Boye Lafayette De Mente, *Chinese Etiquette and Ethics in Business,* NTC Publishing Group (1994) ISBN 0844285242. De Mente knows China thoroughly, and the book is packed with details.

Boye Lafayette De Mente, *The Chinese Have a Word for It: The Complete Guide to Chinese Thought and Culture,* McGraw-Hill/Contemporary Books (2000) ISBN 0658010786. "[The book] sheds light on the character and personality of the Chinese by examining the meaning, historical significance, and use of more than 300 Chinese expressions."

Francis Fukuyama, *Trust: The Social Virtues and the Creation of Prosperity,* Free Press (1995) ISBN 0029109760. Prosperity depends on cultural factors. Descriptions of particular countries are well done (i.e., China, France, Germany, Southern Italy, Japan, Korea, Taiwan, U.S.A.).

Andrew Grzeskowiak, *Passport Hong Kong,* World Trade Press (1996) ISBN 1885073313. Passport Pocket series.

Richard Gunde, *Culture and Customs of China,* Greenwood Publishing Group (2001) ISBN 0313308764. Culture and Customs series.

Philip R. Harris and Robert T. Moran, *Managing Cultural Differences: Leadership Strategies for a New World of Business,* 5th ed., Gulf Professional Publishing Company (2000) ISBN 0877193452. Updated edition of one of the earliest books in the field.

Quanyu Huang, Joseph W. Leonard, and Chen Tong, *Business Decision Making in China,* Haworth Press (1997) ISBN 078900190X. "Of importance are the nuances of conducting business or political negotiations. Comparisons are made to corresponding Western thought processes."

Daniel R. Joseph, *Wen and the Art of Doing Business in China,* Cultural Dragon (2001) ISBN 0971334315. "Mr. Joseph learned that people grossly underestimate the influence culture has in business, as well as in economic and political development."

Peggy Kenna and Sondra Lacy, *Business China: A Practical Guide to Understanding Chinese Business Culture,* Passport Books, NTC Publishing Group (1994) ISBN 0844235563. NTC business series.

Josephine M. T. Khu (Ed.), *Cultural Curiosity: Thirteen Stories about the Search for Chinese Roots,* University of California Press (2001) ISBN 0520223411. Written for persons of Chinese ancestry who grew up elsewhere and are curious about their roots.

Jenny Li, *Passport China,* World Trade Press (1996) ISBN 188507316X. Passport Pocket series.

Larry T. L. Luah, *Success Secrets to Maximize Business in China,* Graphic Arts Center Publishing Company (2001) ISBN 1558685944. Success Secrets series.

Caroline Mason, *Simple Guide to China: Customs and Etiquette,* Paul Norbury (1999) ISBN 186034030X. Simple Guide series.

Anthony Pan, *Culture Shock: Beijing at Your Door,* Graphic Arts Center Publishing Company (2002) ISBN 1558686916. Culture Shock series.

Peregrine Media Group, *Smart Business: China,* Peregrine Media Group (1995) ISBN 1881487032. The basics, on cassette tape.

Jennifer Phillips, *In the Know in China: An Indispensable Cross-Cultural Guide to Working and Living Abroad,* Living Language (2001) ISBN 0609608150. In the Know series.

Sterling Seagrave, *Lords of the Rim: The Invisible Empire of the Overseas Chinese,* G. P. Putnam's Sons (1995) ISBN 0399140115. Readable account of economic role of expatriate Chinese, with historical depth.

Scott D. Seligman and Edward J. Trenn, *Chinese Business Etiquette: A Guide to Protocol, Manners, and Culture in the People's Republic of China,* Warner Books (1999) ISBN 0446673870. "Scott D. Seligman brings his considerable experience working and living in China to this revised and updated edition of his classic guide."

Kevin Sinclair and Iris Wong Po-yee, *Culture Shock: China,* Graphic Arts Center Publishing Company (2002) ISBN 1558686150. Culture Shock series.

Harvey Tripp, *Success Secrets to Maximize Business in Hong Kong,* Graphic Arts Center Publishing Company (2000) ISBN 1558685340. Success Secrets series.

Yuan Wang, Xin Sheng Zhang, and Rob Goodfellow, *Business Culture in China: An Insider's Guide,* Butterworth-Heinemann Asia (1998) ISBN 9810089775. Chapters cover Chinese business values, negotiation, management style, and consumer psychology.

Hu Wenzhong and Cornelius Grove, *Encountering the Chinese: A Guide for Americans,* Intercultural Press (1999) ISBN 1877864587. Interact series.

Tracey Wilen and Patricia Wilen, *Asia for Women on Business: Hong Kong, Taiwan, Singapore, and South Korea,* Stone Bridge Press (1995) ISBN 1880656175.

Kenneth Wilkinson, *Teach Yourself Chinese Language, Life, and Culture,* McGraw-Hill (2002) ISBN 0071407138. Teach Yourself series.

COLOMBIA

Raymond L. Gordon, *Living in Latin America,* NTC Publishing Group (1995) ISBN 0844293415. Interesting treatment of how to be a long-term houseguest in Colombia. Much general insight into Latin American culture.

Harvey F. Kline, *Colombia: Democracy Under Assault,* Westview Press (1995) ISBN 0813310717. "A comprehensive, current country profile . . ."

Neil MacDonald (Ed.), *The Andes,* Stylus Publications (1993) ISBN 0855982004. Oxfam Country Profiles series.

Raymond L. Williams and Kevin G. Guerrieri, *Culture and Customs of Colombia,* Greenwood Publishing Group (1999) ISBN 031330405X. Culture and Customs series.

CONGO, DEMOCRATIC REPUBLIC OF (FORMERLY ZAIRE)

Tshilemalema Mukenge, *Culture and Customs of the Congo,* Greenwood Publishing Group (2001) ISBN 0313314853. Culture and Customs series.

COSTA RICA

Mavis Hiltunen Biesanz, Richard Biesanz, and Karen Zubris Biesanz, *The Ticos: Culture and Social Change in Costa Rica,* Lynne Rienner Publishers (1998) ISBN 1555877370. Written with anthropological expertise for expatriates.

Tjabel Daling, *Costa Rica in Focus: A Guide to the People, Politics and Culture,* Interlink Publishing Group (2001) ISBN 1566563976. In Focus series.

Chalene Helmuth, *Culture and Customs of Costa Rica,* Greenwood Publishing Group (2000) ISBN 0313304920. Culture and Customs series.

Claire Wallerstein, *Culture Shock: Costa Rica,* Graphic Arts Center Publishing Company (2002) ISBN 1558686924. Culture Shock series.

CROATIA

William Bartlett, *Croatia: A Crossroads Between East and West,* Routledge (2002) ISBN 041527432X. "This work provides an in-depth study of the creation and development of Croatia as an independent state along with a discussion of recent changes and future prospects."

Milford Bateman (Ed.), *Business Cultures in Central and Eastern Europe,* Butterworth-Heinemann (1996) ISBN 0750624809.

CUBA

Mark Cramer, *Culture Shock: Cuba,* Graphic Arts Center Publishing Company (1998) ISBN 1558684115. Culture Shock series.

Mark Cramer, *Culture Shock: Havana at Your Door,* Graphic Arts Center Publishing Company (2000) ISBN 1558685316. Culture Shock series.

Emily Hatchwell and Simon Calder, *In Focus Cuba: A Guide to the People, Politics and Culture,* Interlink Publishing Group (1999) ISBN 1566562414. In Focus series.

William Luis, *Culture and Customs of Cuba,* Greenwood Publishing Group (2000) ISBN 0313304335. Culture and Customs series.

Stephen Williams, *Cuba: The Land, the History, the People, the Culture,* Running Press (1994) ISBN 1561381888. "[The book] traces Cuba's turbulent history from the time of Columbus to the present, touching on such areas as the tragedies of slavery, violent conquests, numerous dictatorships, and the beauty and spirit of the land."

CZECH REPUBLIC

Milford Bateman (Ed.), *Business Cultures in Central and Eastern Europe,*
Butterworth-Heinemann (1996) ISBN 0750624809.

Clarke Canfield, *Now Hiring! Jobs in Eastern Europe: The Insider's Guide to
Working and Living in the Czech Republic, Hungary, Poland, and Slovakia,*
Perpetual Press (1996) ISBN 1881199622. "[This book] provides the most
current information about life and work in the Eastern European countries."

Tim Nollen, *Culture Shock: Czech Republic,* Graphic Arts Center Publishing
Company (2002) ISBN 1558686169. Culture Shock series.

David Short, *Simple Guide to Customs and Etiquette in the Czech Republic,* Paul
Norbury (1996) ISBN 186034075X. Simple Guide series.

DENMARK

Judith Friedman Hansen, *We Are a Little Land: Cultural Assumptions in Danish
Everyday Life,* Ayer Company Publishers (1980) ISBN 040513424X. Chapters
on *festlighed* (festivity), *hygge* (cosiness), egalitarianism, nationalism, and
so forth.

Morten Strange, *Culture Shock: Denmark,* Graphic Arts Center Publishing
Company (2000) ISBN 1558682546. Culture Shock series.

F. Richard Thomas (Ed.), *Americans in Denmark: Comparisons of the Two
Cultures by Writers, Artists, and Teachers,* Southern Illinois University Press
(1990) ISBN 080931536X. Reflections by American expatriates in Denmark.

DOMINICAN REPUBLIC

Isabel Zakrzewski Brown, *Culture and Customs of the Dominican Republic,*
Greenwood Publishing Group (1999) ISBN 0313303142. Culture and
Customs series.

David Howard, *Dominican Republic: A Guide to the People, Politics and Culture,*
Interlink Publishing Group (1999) ISBN 1566562430. In Focus series.

ECUADOR

Nicholas B. Crowder, *Culture Shock: Ecuador,* Graphic Arts Center Publishing
Company (2002) ISBN 1558686053. Culture Shock series.

Michael Handelsman, *Culture and Customs of Ecuador,* Greenwood Publishing
Group (2000) ISBN 0313302448. Culture and Customs series.

Wilma Roos and Omer Van Renterghem, *In Focus Ecuador: A Guide to the
People, Politics and Culture,* Interlink Publishing Group (2000) ISBN
1566563852. In Focus series.

EGYPT

Molefi Kete Asante, *Culture and Customs of Egypt,* Greenwood Publishing Group
(2002) ISBN 0313317402. Culture and Customs series.

Philip R. Harris and Robert T. Moran, *Managing Cultural Differences: Leadership Strategies for a New World of Business,* 5th ed., Gulf Professional Publishing Company (2000) ISBN 0877193452. Updated edition of one of the earliest books in the field.

Susan L. Wilson, *Culture Shock: Egypt,* Graphic Arts Center Publishing Company (2002) ISBN 1558686363. Culture Shock series.

EL SALVADOR

Roy C. Boland, *Culture and Customs of El Salvador,* Greenwood Publishing Group (2000) ISBN 0313306206. Culture and Customs series.

Kevin Murray, *El Salvador: Peace on Trial,* Oxfam Publications (1997) ISBN 0855983612. Oxfam Country Profiles series.

ESTONIA

David J. Smith, *Estonia: Independence and European Integration,* Routledge (2002) ISBN 0415267285. Postcommunist States and Nations series.

David J. Smith, Artis Pabriks, Aldis Purs, and Thomas Lane, *The Baltic States: Estonia, Latvia and Lithuania,* Routledge (2002) ISBN 0415285801. Postcommunist States and Nations series.

ETHIOPIA

Ben Parker, *Ethiopia: Breaking New Ground,* Oxfam Publications (1995) ISBN 0855982705. Oxfam Country Profiles series.

FINLAND

Deborah Swallow, *Culture Shock: Finland,* Graphic Arts Center Publishing Company (2001) ISBN 1558685928. Culture Shock series.

FRANCE

Gilles Asselin and Ruth Mastron, *Au Contraire! Figuring Out the French,* Intercultural Press (2001) ISBN 187786482X. "[This book offers] a whole-picture view of French and American cultures . . . for all managers confronted with the management of cross-cultural issues."

Raymonde Carroll, *Cultural Misunderstandings: The French-American Experience,* University of Chicago Press (1990) ISBN 0226094987. Comparison of French and American culture, translated from the French.

Celia Dixie, *Teach Yourself French Language, Life, & Culture,* McGraw-Hill/ Contemporary Books (2000) ISBN 0658009079. Teach Yourself series.

Francis Fukuyama, *Trust: The Social Virtues and the Creation of Prosperity,* Free Press (1995) ISBN 0029109760. This book identifies cultural factors that influence prosperity. Descriptions of particular countries are well done (i.e., China, France, Germany, Southern Italy, Japan, Korea, Taiwan, U.S.A.).

Frances Gendlin, *Culture Shock: Paris at Your Door,* Graphic Arts Center Publishing Company (1999) ISBN 1558684050. Culture Shock series.

Charles Hampden-Turner and Alfons Trompenaars, *The Seven Cultures of Capitalism: Value Systems for Creating Wealth,* Doubleday (1993) ISBN 038542101X. Excellent sociological study of national characters of France, Germany, Japan, Netherlands, Sweden, United Kingdom, and U.S.A.

David Hampshire, *Living and Working in France: A Survival Handbook,* Survival Books (1999) ISBN 190113055X. Survival Handbook series.

Philip R. Harris and Robert T. Moran, *Managing Cultural Differences: Leadership Strategies for a New World of Business,* 5th ed., Gulf Professional Publishing Company (2000) ISBN 0877193452. Updated edition of one of the earliest books in the field.

Nadine Joseph, *Passport France,* World Trade Press (1996) ISBN 1885073291. Passport Pocket series.

George C. Lodge and Ezra F. Vogel (Eds.), *Ideology and National Competitiveness: An Analysis of Nine Countries,* Harvard Business School Press (1987) ISBN 0875841473.

Collin Randlesome, *Business Cultures in Europe,* 2d ed., Butterworth-Heinemann (1993) ISBN 0750608722.

Danielle Robinson, *Simple Guide to France: Customs & Etiquette,* Global Books Ltd. (2001) ISBN 1860340768. Simple Guide series.

Ross Steele, *The French Way: Aspects of Behavior, Attitudes, and Customs of the French,* McGraw-Hill–NTC (1995) ISBN 0844214957. McGraw-Hill series.

Sally Adamson Taylor, *Culture Shock: France,* Graphic Arts Center Publishing Company (2000) ISBN 155868056X. Culture Shock series.

GEORGIA

R. G. Gachechiladze and R. Anthony French (Ed.), *The New Georgia: Space, Society, Politics,* Texas A&M University Press (1996) ISBN 0890967032. Examines ". . . the shift to a market economy, regional variations in welfare, variations in levels of crime and drug use, and religious and ethnic tensions."

GERMANY

John Ardagh and Katharina Ardagh, *Germany and the Germans: The United Germany in the Mid-1990s,* Penguin USA (1996) ISBN 014025266. Critical discussion of some contemporary German behaviors.

Waltraud Coles and Uwe Koreik, *Simple Guide to Germany: Customs & Etiquette,* Paul Norbury (1998) ISBN 1860340318. Simple Guide series.

Nick Daws, *Living and Working in Germany,* Survival Books Ltd. (2000) ISBN 1901130355. Survival Handbook series.

Roland Flamini and Barbara Szerlip, *Passport Germany,* World Trade Press (1997) ISBN 1885073208. Passport Pocket series.

Hyde Flippo, *The German Way: Aspects of Behavior, Attitudes, and Customs in the German-Speaking World,* McGraw-Hill/Contemporary Books (1996) ISBN 0844225134. McGraw-Hill series.

Hyde Flippo, *When in Germany, Do as the Germans Do,* McGraw-Hill/ Contemporary Books (2001) ISBN 0844225533. Featuring "120 intriguing multiple-choice questions that are cross-referenced to fascinating articles on pop culture, customs, behavior, history, consumer trends, literature, tourist sights, business, language, and more."

Francis Fukuyama, *Trust: The Social Virtues and the Creation of Prosperity,* Free Press (1995) ISBN 0029109760. This book identifies cultural factors that influence prosperity. Descriptions of particular countries are well done (i.e., China, France, Germany, Southern Italy, Japan, Korea, Taiwan, U.S.A.).

Charles Hampden-Turner and Alfons Trompenaars, *The Seven Cultures of Capitalism: Value Systems for Creating Wealth,* Doubleday (1993) ISBN 038542101X. Excellent sociological study of national characters of France, Germany, Japan, Netherlands, Sweden, United Kingdom, and U.S.A.

Philip R. Harris and Robert T. Moran, *Managing Cultural Differences: Leadership Strategies for a New World of Business,* 5th ed., Gulf Professional Publishing Company (2000) ISBN 0877193452. Updated edition of one of the earliest books in the field.

Peggy Kenna and Sondra Lacy, *Business Germany: A Practical Guide to Understanding German Business Culture,* Passport Books, NTC Publishing Group (1994) ISBN 0844235555. NTC business series.

Harold R. Kerbo and Hermann Strasser, *Modern Germany,* McGraw-Hill (1999) ISBN 0072928190. Comparative Societies series.

George C. Lodge and Ezra F. Vogel (Eds.), *Ideology and National Competitiveness: An Analysis of Nine Countries,* Harvard Business School Press (1987) ISBN 0875841473.

Richard Lord, *Succeed in Business Germany,* Graphic Arts Center Publishing Company (1998) ISBN 1558683542. Succeed in Business series.

Peregrine Media Group, *Made in Germany,* Peregrine Media Group (1992) ISBN 1881487008. The basics, on cassette tape.

Jennifer Phillips, *In the Know in Germany: An Indispensable Cross-Cultural Guide to Working and Living Abroad,* Living Language (2001) ISBN 0609608177. In the Know series.

Patrick L. Schmidt, *Understanding American and German Business Cultures: A Manager's Guide to the Cultural Context in Which American and German Companies Operate,* Meridian World Press (2001) ISBN 0968529305. Begins with specifically cultural issues.

GHANA

John E. Kuada, *Ghana: Understanding the People and Their Culture,* Woeli Publishing Services (1999) ISBN 996497860X.

Rachel Naylor, *Ghana,* Oxfam Publications (2000) ISBN 0855984317. Oxfam Country Profiles series.

Steven J. Salm and Toyin Falola, *Culture and Customs of Ghana,* Greenwood Publishing Group (2002) ISBN 0313320500. Culture and Customs series.

GREECE

Benjamin J. Broome, *Exploring the Greek Mosaic: A Guide to Intercultural Communication in Greece,* Intercultural Press (1996) ISBN 1877864390. Interact series.

Alex Martin, *The Simple Guide to Customs and Etiquette in Greece,* Paul Norbury (1995) ISBN 1860340105. Simple Guide series.

Clive L. Rawlins, *Culture Shock: Greece,* Graphic Arts Center Publishing Company (2002) ISBN 1558686185. Culture Shock series.

GUATEMALA

Trish O'Kane, *In Focus Guatemala: A Guide to the People, Politics and Culture,* Interlink Publishing Group (1999) ISBN 1566562422. In Focus series.

Maureen E. Shea, *Culture and Customs of Guatemala,* Greenwood Publishing Group (2000) ISBN 031330596X. Culture and Customs series.

GUYANA

Ovid Abrams, *Metegee: The History and Culture of Guyana,* ElDorado Publications (1998) ISBN 0966070747. Metegee is an African dish that is popular in Guyana and a metaphor for the culture.

HAITI

Charles Arthur, *Haiti in Focus: A Guide to the People, Politics and Culture,* Interlink Publishing Group (2002) ISBN 1566563593. In Focus series.

J. Michael Dash, *Culture and Customs of Haiti,* Greenwood Publishing Group (2000) ISBN 031330498X. Culture and Customs series.

HUNGARY

Zsuzsanna Ardó, *Culture Shock: Hungary,* Graphic Arts Center Publishing Company (2000) ISBN 1558685308. Culture Shock series.

Milford Bateman (Ed.), *Business Cultures in Central and Eastern Europe,* Butterworth-Heinemann (1996) ISBN 0750624809.

Clarke Canfield, *Now Hiring! Jobs in Eastern Europe: The Insider's Guide to Working and Living in the Czech Republic, Hungary, Poland, and Slovakia,* Perpetual Press (1996) ISBN 1881199622. "[The book] provides the most current information about life and work in the Eastern European countries."

Philip R. Harris and Robert T. Moran, *Managing Cultural Differences: Leadership Strategies for a New World of Business,* 5th ed., Gulf Professional Publishing Company (2000) ISBN 0877193452. Updated edition of one of the earliest books in the field.

Laszlo Jotischky, *Simple Guide to Customs and Etiquette in Hungary,* Paul Norbury (1995) ISBN 1860340350. Simple Guide series.

ICELAND

Terry G. Lacy, *Ring of Seasons: Iceland—Its Culture and History,* University of Michigan Press (2001) ISBN 0472086618. Discusses some current cultural practices in a historical context.

INDIA

Robert Arnett, *India Unveiled,* Atman Press (1999) ISBN 0965290034. Arranged by state, this book is "perfect for browsing through by the armchair traveler, yet informative and engaging for any serious student of the culture of the subcontinent."

Sri Aurobindo, *Foundation of Indian Culture,* rev. ed., Lotus Press (1998) ISBN 8170585457. Written partly in response to Western coverage of India.

Hiru Bijlani, *Succeed in Business India,* Graphic Arts Center Publishing Company (1999) ISBN 0558683194. Succeed in Business series.

Rajiv Desai, *Indian Business Culture,* Butterworth-Heinemann (1999) ISBN 9810093276. Chapters include Indian Business: Weak Partner, Formidable Foe; Indian Government: Socialist Legacy; Indian Political Establishment: Emergent Trends; Indian Media: The Jewel in India's Democratic Crown; The Indian Academy: A Paradox; Key Issues.

Carol Henderson Garcia, *Culture and Customs of India,* Greenwood Publishing Group (2002) ISBN 0313305137. Culture and Customs series.

Philip R. Harris and Robert T. Moran, *Managing Cultural Differences: Leadership Strategies for a New World of Business,* 5th ed., Gulf Professional Publishing Company (2000) ISBN 0877193452. Updated edition of one of the earliest books in the field.

Manoj Joshi, *Passport India,* World Trade Press (1997) ISBN 1885073232. Passport Pocket series.

Venika Kingsland, Irene Slatter, and Arene Sanderson, *Simple Guide to India: Customs & Etiquette,* Paul Norbury (1999) ISBN 1860340466. Simple Guide series.

Gitanjali Kolanad, *Culture Shock: India,* Graphic Arts Center Publishing Company (2000) ISBN 1558681450. Culture Shock series.

Julia Cleves Mosse, *India,* Stylus Publications (1993) ISBN 0855982241. Oxfam Country Profiles series.

Joti Sekhon, *Modern India,* McGraw-Hill (1999) ISBN 0072928247. Comparative Societies series.

M. N. Srinivas (Ed.), *Caste: Its Twentieth Century Avatar,* Penguin Books India (1996). The best available book on the subject. The editor is India's leading anthropologist.

INDONESIA

Derek Bacon, *Culture Shock: Jakarta at Your Door,* Graphic Arts Center Publishing Company (1999) ISBN 1558684190. Culture Shock series.

Paulson Ching, *Doing Business in East Asia: A Practical Guide to China, Indonesia, Malaysia and Thailand,* Pelanduk Publications (1999) ISBN 9679784924.

Gergory J. Cole and Barbara Szerlip, *Passport Indonesia,* World Trade Press (1997) ISBN 1885073372. Passport Pocket series.

Cathie Draine and Barbara Hall, *Culture Shock: Indonesia,* Graphic Arts Center Publishing Company (1991) ISBN 1558680578. Culture Shock series.

Farid Elashmawi and Philip R. Harris, *Multicultural Management 2000,* Gulf Publishing Company (1998) ISBN 0884154947. Practical approach with useful exercises. Charts compare norms across Arab countries, Indonesia, Japan, Malaysia, and U.S.A.

James Fallows, *Looking at the Sun: The Rise of the New East Asian Economic and Political System,* Pantheon Books (1994) ISBN 067942251X. Describes new versions of capitalism that East Asian nations have developed to suit their social milieux.

Nicola Frost, *Indonesia,* Oxfam Publications (2003) ISBN 0855984813. Oxfam Country Profiles series.

Rob Goodfellow (Ed.), *Indonesian Business Culture,* Reed Academic Publishing Asia (1997) ISBN 981008420X. Covers Suharto's government, culture and language, role of Islam, ethnic Chinese, corporate culture, Westerners in Indonesia.

Philip R. Harris and Robert T. Moran, *Managing Cultural Differences: Leadership Strategies for a New World of Business,* 5th ed., Gulf Professional Publishing Company (2000) ISBN 0877193452. Updated edition of one of the earliest books in the field.

Angela Hobart, Urs Ramseyer, and Albert Leemann, *The Peoples of Bali,* Blackwell Publishers (2001) ISBN 0631227415. Peoples of South-East Asia and the Pacific series.

Victor T. King, *The Peoples of Borneo,* Blackwell Publishers (1995) ISBN 0631172211. Peoples of South-East Asia and the Pacific series.

Graham Saunders and Arene Sanderson, *Simple Guide to Indonesia: Customs & Etiquette,* Global Books Ltd. (2001) ISBN 1860340164. Simple Guide series.

Sterling Seagrave, *Lords of the Rim: The Invisible Empire of the Overseas Chinese,* G. P. Putnam's Sons (1995) ISBN 0399140115. Readable account of economic role of expatriate Chinese in Indonesia, with historical depth.

Michael Sinjorgo, *Succeed in Business Indonesia,* Graphic Arts Center Publishing Company (1997) ISBN 0558683550. Succeed in Business Series.

IRAN

Christiane Bird, *Neither East Nor West: One Woman's Journey Through the Islamic Republic of Iran,* McGraw-Hill (2001) ISBN 0072928190. A personal narrative but provides a close-up look at some customs and cultural traits.

Maria O'Shea, *Culture Shock: Iran,* Graphic Arts Center Publishing Company (1999) ISBN 1558684034. Culture Shock series.

IRAQ

Elizabeth Warnock Fernea, *Guests of the Sheik: An Ethnography of an Iraqi Village,* Anchor Books (1965, 1989) ISBN 0385014856. An honest but sympathetic portrait of everyday life in a Shiite village.

Freya Stark, *Baghdad Sketches,* Marlboro Press (1996) ISBN 0810160234. Iraqi culture in mid–twentieth century.

Charles Tripp, *A History of Iraq,* Cambridge University Press (2002) ISBN 052152900X. "In response to current events, Charles Tripp has updated his incisive book . . . to include developments as recent as mid-2002."

IRELAND

John Ardagh, *Ireland and the Irish: Portrait of a Changing Society,* Penguin USA (1997) ISBN 0140171606. "He has conducted dozens of interviews in all the provinces of the island . . . to create . . . [his] impressionistic portrait."

Patricia Levy, *Culture Shock: Ireland,* Graphic Arts Center Publishing Company (2000) ISBN 1558682473. Culture Shock series.

Aidan McNamara, *Simple Guide to Ireland: Customs and Etiquette,* Bravo Ltd. (2000) ISBN 1860340660. Simple Guide series.

ISRAEL

Nava Bloch, *Culture Shock: Jerusalem at Your Door,* Graphic Arts Center Publishing Company (2002) ISBN 155868638X. Culture Shock series.

Donna Rosenthal, *Passport Israel,* World Trade Press (1996) ISBN 1885073224. Passport Pocket series.

Lucy Shahar and David Kurz, *Border Crossings: American Interactions With Israelis,* Intercultural Press (1995) ISBN 1877864315. Interact series.

David Starr-Glass, *Simple Guide to Customs and Etiquette in Israel,* Paul Norbury (1996) ISBN 1860340555. Simple Guide series.

Dick Winter, *Culture Shock: Israel,* Graphic Arts Center Publishing Company (2000) ISBN 1558680888. Culture Shock series.

ITALY

Derek Aust and Mike Zollo, *Teach Yourself Italian Language, Life & Culture,* McGraw-Hill/Contemporary Books (2000) ISBN 0658008978. Teach Yourself series.

Mario Costantino and Lawrence R. Gambella, *The Italian Way: Aspects of Behavior, Attitudes and Customs of the Italians,* McGraw-Hill/Contemporary Books (1996) ISBN 0844280720. McGraw-Hill series.

Nick Daws, *Living and Working in Italy,* Survival Books Ltd. (2001) ISBN 1901130258. Survival Handbook series.

Francis Fukuyama, *Trust: The Social Virtues and the Creation of Prosperity,* Free Press (1995) ISBN 0029109760. This book identifies cultural factors that influence prosperity. Descriptions of particular countries are well done (i.e., China, France, Germany, Southern Italy, Japan, Korea, Taiwan, U.S.A.).

Frances Gendlin, *Culture Shock: Rome at Your Door,* Graphic Arts Center Publishing Company (1997) ISBN 1558683062. Culture Shock series.

Claudia Giosetti, *Passport Italy,* World Trade Press (1997) ISBN 1885073348. Passport Pocket series.

Amanda Hinton, *Living and Working in Italy: Staying in Italy—All You Need to Know,* How to Books Ltd. (2000) ISBN 1857035003. How to series.

Travis Neighbor and Monica Larner, *Living, Studying and Working in Italy: Everything You Need to Know to Fulfill Your Dreams of Living Abroad,* Henry Holt (1998) ISBN 0805051023. Practical information.

Victoria Pybus, *Live & Work in Italy,* Vacation-Work (1999) ISBN 1854581821. Practical information.

Collin Randlesome, *Business Cultures in Europe,* 2d ed., Butterworth-Heinemann (1993) ISBN 0750608722.

Hugh Shankland, *Simple Guide to Italy: Customs & Etiquette,* 3d ed., Global Books Ltd. (2001) ISBN 1860340865. Simple Guides series.

JAMAICA

Peter Mason, *In Focus Jamaica: A Guide to the People, Politics and Culture,* Interlink Publishing Group (2000) ISBN 1566562856. In Focus series.

Martin Mordecai and Pamela Mordecai, *Culture and Customs of Jamaica,* Greenwood Publishing Group (2000) ISBN 031330534X. Culture and Customs series.

JAPAN

Boye Lafayette De Mente, *Japanese Etiquette & Ethics in Business,* McGraw-Hill/ Contemporary Books (1994) ISBN 0844285307. Honest and first-rate analysis.

Boye Lafayette De Mente, *The Japanese Have a Word for It: The Complete Guide to Japanese Thought and Culture,* McGraw-Hill/Contemporary Books (1997) ISBN 0844283169. A dictionary of significant Japanese concepts, with an insightful mini-essay for each.

Dean Engel, *Passport Japan,* World Trade Press (1996) ISBN 1885073178. Passport Pocket series.

James Fallows, *Looking at the Sun: The Rise of the New East Asian Economic and Political System,* Pantheon Books (1994) ISBN 067942251X. Describes new versions of capitalism that East Asian nations have developed to suit their social milieux.

Charles Hampden-Turner and Alfons Trompenaars, *The Seven Cultures of Capitalism: Value Systems for Creating Wealth,* Doubleday (1993) ISBN 038542101X. Excellent sociological study of national characters of France, Germany, Japan, Netherlands, Sweden, United Kingdom, and U.S.A.

Philip R. Harris and Robert T. Moran, *Managing Cultural Differences: Leadership Strategies for a New World of Business,* 5th ed., Gulf Professional Publishing Company (2000) ISBN 0877193452. Updated edition of one of the earliest books in the field.

Carin Holroyd and Ken Coates, *Success Secrets to Maximize Business in Japan,* Graphic Arts Center Publishing Company (2000) ISBN 1558684808. Success Secrets series.

Osamu Ikeno and Roger J. Davies (Eds.), *The Japanese Mind: Understanding Contemporary Culture,* Charles E. Tuttle (2002) ISBN 0804832951.

Noriko Kamachi, *Culture and Customs of Japan,* Greenwood Publishing Group (1999) ISBN 0313301972. Culture and Customs series.

Peggy Kenna and Sondra Lacy, *Business Japan: A Practical Guide to Understanding Japanese Business Culture,* Passport Books, NTC Publishing Group (1994) ISBN 0844235520. NTC business series.

Harold R. Kerbo and John A. McKinstry, *Modern Japan,* McGraw-Hill (1997) ISBN 0070344264. Comparative Societies series.

George C. Lodge and Ezra F. Vogel (Eds.), *Ideology and National Competitiveness: An Analysis of Nine Countries,* Harvard Business School Press (1987) ISBN 0875841473.

Helmut Morsbach, *Simple Guide to Customs and Etiquette in Japan,* 2d ed., Paul Norbury (1995) ISBN 1860340008. Simple Guide series.

Peregrine Media Group, *Made in Japan,* Peregrine Media Group (1992) ISBN 1881487016. Basic business culture on cassette tape.

Jennifer Phillips, *In the Know in Japan: An Indispensable Cross-Cultural Guide to Working and Living Abroad,* Living Language (2003) ISBN 0609611143. In the Know series.

Rex Shelley, *Culture Shock: Japan,* Graphic Arts Center Publishing Company (1992) ISBN 1558680713. Culture Shock series.

Noriko Takada and Rita L. Lampkin, *The Japanese Way: Aspects of Behavior, Attitudes, and Customs of the Japanese,* McGraw-Hill/Contemporary Books (1996) ISBN 0844283770. McGraw-Hill series.

Noboru Yoshimura and Philip Anderson, *Inside the Kaisha: Demystifying Japanese Business Behavior,* Harvard Business School Press (1997) ISBN 0875844154. "Yoshimura and Anderson provide a healthy antidote to much of the mumbo jumbo about Japanese business practices perpetrated by journalists, businesspeople, and management consultants."

JORDAN

Peter Gubser, *Jordan: Crossroads of Middle Eastern Events,* Westview Press (1986) ISBN 0813300223.

Kamal Salibi, *The Modern History of Jordan,* St. Martin's Press (1999) ISBN 1860643310. Apparently the only history of Jordan written in English.

KAZAKHSTAN

Milford Bateman (Ed.), *Business Cultures in Central and Eastern Europe,* Butterworth-Heinemann (1996) ISBN 0750624809.

KENYA

Yousef Dadoo, Valmond Ghyoot, Dan Lephoko, and Gerrie Lubbe, *Multicultural Sensitivity for Managers,* Tsebanang Group, Rant en Dal, South Africa (1997) ISBN 0620212586. Particularly strong on African cultures.

Geoff Sayer, *Kenya,* Stylus Publications (1998) ISBN 0855983825. Oxfam Country Profiles series.

KOREA

Michael Breen, *The Koreans: Who They Are, What They Want, Where Their Future Lies,* St. Martin's Press (1999) ISBN 0312242115. "A veteran British journalist examines the history, culture, and economy of North and (principally) South Korea, where he lives for half of each year."

Donald N. Clark, *Culture and Customs of Korea,* Greenwood Publishing Group (2000) ISBN 0313304564. Culture and Customs series.

Boye Lafayette De Mente, *Korean Etiquette and Ethics in Business,* 2d ed., NTC Business Books (1994) ISBN 0844285234. Honest and insightful.

Boye Lafayette De Mente, *NTC's Dictionary of Korea's Business and Cultural Code Words: The Complete Guide to Key Words That Express How the Koreans Think, Communicate, and Behave,* McGraw-Hill/Contemporary Books (1998) ISBN 0844283622. A dictionary of cultural concepts, with a mini-essay for each.

James E. Hoare and Susan Pares, *Simple Guide to Korea: Customs & Etiquette,* Global Books Ltd. (2000) ISBN 1860340717. Simple Guide series.

Helen-Louise Hunter and Stephen J. Solarz, *Kim Il-song's North Korea,* Praeger Publications (1999) ISBN 0275962962. Portrait of life in North Korea.

Sonja Vegdahl Hur and Ben Seunghwa Hur, *Culture Shock: Korea,* Graphic Arts Center Publishing Company (1992) ISBN 1558681078. Culture Shock series.

Kevin Keating, *Passport Korea,* World Trade Press (1997) ISBN 1885073399. Passport Pocket series.

Peggy Kenna and Sondra Lacy, *Business Korea: A Practical Guide to Understanding Korean Business Culture,* Passport Books, NTC Publishing Group (1995) ISBN 0844235598. NTC business series.

Eun Young Kim and Un-Yong Kim, *A Cross-Cultural Reference of Business Practices in a New Korea,* Quorum Books (1996) ISBN 1567200192. "This is a reference to understanding changing cultures and business practices in Korea for scholars, and a comprehensive guide to Korean business practice, protocol, and communications styles for professionals."

L. Robert Kohls, *Learning to Think Korean: A Guide to Living and Working in Korea,* Intercultural Press (2001) ISBN 1877864870. Interact series.

John H. Koo and Andrew C. Nahm (Eds.), *An Introduction to Korean Culture,* Hollym International Corporation (2000) ISBN 1565910869. A reference work with much material on history, religions, the arts, and the Confucian character of the culture.

Paul A. Leppert, *Doing Business With Korea,* Jain Publishing (1997) ISBN 0875730434.

George C. Lodge and Ezra F. Vogel (Eds.), *Ideology and National Competitiveness: An Analysis of Nine Countries,* Harvard Business School Press (1987) ISBN 0875841473.

Chris Rowley, Tae-Won Sohn, and Johngseok Bae (Eds.), *Managing Korean Business: Organization, Culture, Human Resources and Change,* Frank Cass & Co. (2002) ISBN 0714682225.

Richard Saccone, *The Business of Korean Culture,* Weatherhill (1995) ISBN 1565910338. Korean business customs. Some general cultural information.

Richard M. Steers, Yoo Keun Shin, and Gerardo R. Ungson, *Chaebol: Korea's New Industrial Might,* HarperCollins (1989) ISBN 0887304915. *Chaebol* is Korea's version of a Japanese *keiretsu.*

Tracey Wilen and Patricia Wilen, *Asia for Women on Business: Hong Kong, Taiwan, Singapore, and South Korea,* Stone Bridge Press (1995) ISBN 1880656175.

KOSOVO

Noel Malcolm, *Kosovo: A Short History,* HarperCollins (1999) ISBN 0060977752.

KUWAIT

Jill Crystal, *Kuwait: The Transformation of an Oil State,* Westview Press (1992) ISBN 0813308887.

Bruce Ingham and J. Fayadh, *Simple Guide to Arabia and the Gulf States: Customs & Etiquette,* Global Books Ltd. (2001) ISBN 1860340814. Simple Guide series.

KYRGYZSTAN

John Anderson, *Kyrgyzstan: Central Asia's Island of Democracy?* Routledge (1999) ISBN 9057023903. Postcommunist States and Nations series.

LAOS

James Fallows, *Looking at the Sun: The Rise of the New East Asian Economic and Political System,* Pantheon Books (1994) ISBN 067942251X. Describes new versions of capitalism that East Asian nations have developed to suit their social milieux.

Grant Evans (Ed.), *Laos: Culture and Society,* University of Washington Press (2000) ISBN 9748709043. Anthology of anthropological essays.

Stephen Mansfield, *Culture Shock: Laos,* Graphic Arts Center Publishing Company (1997) ISBN 1558683011. Culture Shock series.

LATVIA

Artis Pabriks and Aldis Purs, *Latvia: The Challenge of Change,* Harwood Academic Publishing (2002) ISBN 9058231151. Academic treatment.

David J. Smith, Artis Pabriks, Aldis Purs, and Thomas Lane, *The Baltic States: Estonia, Latvia and Lithuania,* Routledge (2002) ISBN 0415285801. Postcommunist States and Nations series.

LEBANON

Thomas L. Friedman, *From Beirut to Jerusalem,* Doubleday (1989) ISBN 0385413726. A reporter's tale with a number of insights into the culture of the region.

Kamal Salibi, *A House of Many Mansions: The History of Lebanon Reconsidered,* University of California Press (1990) ISBN 0520071964. Objective history of the country.

LITHUANIA

David J. Smith, Artis Pabriks, Aldis Purs, and Thomas Lane, *The Baltic States: Estonia, Latvia and Lithuania,* Routledge (2002) ISBN 0415285801. Postcommunist States and Nations series.

Saulius Zukas (Ed.), *Lithuania: Past, Culture, Present,* Baltos Lankos (1999) ISBN 9986861500. Covers "Lithuania's historical, cultural, and economic development and situation on the eve of the 21st century."

LUXEMBOURG

Beverly Laflamme, *Living and Working in Belgium, Holland and Luxembourg,* Survival Books Ltd. (2001) ISBN 1901130266. Survival Handbook series.

MACEDONIA

Hugh Poulton, *Who Are the Macedonians?* Indiana University Press (2000) ISBN 0253213592. Ethnic history leading up to the present.

MALAYSIA

Paulson Ching, *Doing Business in East Asia: A Practical Guide to China, Indonesia, Malaysia and Thailand,* Pelanduk Publications (1999) ISBN 9679784924.

Farid Elashmawi and Philip R. Harris, *Multicultural Management 2000,* Gulf Publishing Company (1998) ISBN 0884154947. Practical approach with useful exercises. Charts compare norms across Arab countries, Indonesia, Japan, Malaysia, and U.S.A.

James Fallows, *Looking at the Sun: The Rise of the New East Asian Economic and Political System,* Pantheon Books (1994) ISBN 067942251X. Describes new versions of capitalism that East Asian nations have developed to suit their social milieux.

Philip R. Harris and Robert T. Moran, *Managing Cultural Differences: Leadership Strategies for a New World of Business,* 5th ed., Gulf Professional Publishing Company (2000) ISBN 0877193452. Updated edition of one of the earliest books in the field.

Victor King, *The Simple Guide to Malaysia: Customs & Etiquette,* Paul Norbury (2001) ISBN 1860340113. Simple Guide series.

Heidi Munan, *Culture Shock: Borneo,* Graphic Arts Center Publishing Company (1991) ISBN 1558680756. Culture Shock series.

Heidi Munan, *Culture Shock: Malaysia,* Graphic Arts Center Publishing Company
(2000) ISBN 1558680705. Culture Shock series.

Sterling Seagrave, *Lords of the Rim: The Invisible Empire of the Overseas
Chinese,* G. P. Putnam's Sons (1995) ISBN 0399140115. Readable account of
economic role of expatriate Chinese, with historical depth.

Lynn Witham, *Culture Shock: Kuala Lampur at Your Door,* Graphic Arts Center
Publishing Company (2000) ISBN 1558685367. Culture Shock series.

MAURITIUS ISLAND

Roseline NgCheong-Lum, *Culture Shock: Mauritius,* Graphic Arts Center Publishing Company (2000) ISBN 1558683054. Culture Shock series.

MELANESIA

Michael Kwaioloa and Ben Burt, *Living Tradition: A Changing Life in Solomon
Islands,* University of Hawaii Press (1997) ISBN 0824819608. Autobiographi-
cal, but reveals present culture of the Solomons.

Matthew Spriggs, *The Island Melanesians,* Blackwell Publishers (1997) ISBN
0631167277. Peoples of South-East Asia and the Pacific series.

MEXICO

William L. Canak and Laura Swanson, *Modern Mexico,* McGraw-Hill (1997)
ISBN 0070344310. Comparative Societies series.

John C. Condon, *Good Neighbors: Communicating With the Mexicans,* Intercultural Press (1997) ISBN 1877864536. Interact series.

Mark Cramer, *Culture Shock: Mexico,* Graphic Arts Center Publishing Company
(2002) ISBN 155868624X. Culture Shock series.

Boye Lafayette De Mente, *Mexican Etiquette and Ethics,* Phoenix Books (1997)
ISBN 0914778706. Honest and insightful.

Boye Lafayette De Mente, *There's a Word for It in Mexico: The Complete Guide
to Mexican Thought and Culture,* McGraw-Hill/Contemporary Books (1998)
ISBN 0844272515. Dictionary of cultural concepts, with a mini-essay for each.

Gus Gordon and Thurmon Williams, *Doing Business in Mexico: A Practical
Guide,* Haworth Press (2002) ISBN 0789012138.

Philip R. Harris and Robert T. Moran, *Managing Cultural Differences: Leadership
Strategies for a New World of Business,* 5th ed., Gulf Professional Publishing
Company (2000) ISBN 0877193452. Updated edition of one of the earliest
books in the field.

George C. Lodge and Ezra F. Vogel (Eds.), *Ideology and National Competitiveness:
An Analysis of Nine Countries,* Harvard Business School Press (1987)
ISBN 0875841473.

Randy Malat, *Passport Mexico,* World Trade Press (1996) ISBN 1885073305.
Passport Pocket series.

Peregrine Media Group, *Made in Mexico,* Peregrine Media Group (1994) ISBN
1881487024. Basics of business culture on cassette tape.

Arthur A. Natella (Ed.), *Business in Mexico: Managerial Behavior, Protocol, and Etiquette,* Haworth Press (1994) ISBN 1560244062. "[This book is] a guide to effective cross-cultural business dealings, addressing both culture and behavior as they relate to US-Mexican business protocol and relationships."

Jennifer Phillips, *In the Know in Mexico and Central America: An Indispensable Cross-Cultural Guide to Working and Living Abroad,* Living Language (2001) ISBN 0609608177. In the Know series.

John Ross, *Mexico In Focus: A Guide to the People, Politics and Culture,* Interlink Publishing Group (2002) ISBN 1566564212. In Focus series.

MICRONESIA

Francis X. Hezel, *The New Shape of Old Island Cultures: A Half Century of Social Change in Micronesia,* University of Hawaii Press (2001) ISBN 0824823931.

P. F. Kluge, *The Edge of Paradise: America in Micronesia,* University of Hawaii Press (1993) ISBN 082481567X. A realistic slice of life from Micronesia.

MOLDOVA

Charles King, *The Moldovans: Romania, Russia, and the Politics of Culture,* Hoover Institute Press (2000) ISBN 081799792X.

MOROCCO

Orin Hargraves, *Culture Shock: Morocco,* Graphic Arts Center Publishing Company (2001) ISBN 1558686258. Culture Shock series.

Peregrine Media Group, *Smart Business: Morocco,* Peregrine Media Group (1997) ISBN 1881487040. The basics, on cassette tape.

MOZAMBIQUE

Rachel Waterhouse, *Mozambique: Rising from the Ashes,* Oxfam Publications (1996) ISBN 0855983418. Oxfam Country Profiles series.

MYANMAR (BURMA)

H. C. Matthew Sim, *Myanmar on My Mind: A Guide to Living and Doing Business in Myanmar,* Times Books International (2001) ISBN 9812321381.

Saw Myat Yin, *Culture Shock: Burma,* Graphic Arts Center Publishing Company (1993) ISBN 1558681485. Culture Shock series.

NEPAL

Jon Burbank (Ed.), *Culture Shock: Nepal,* Graphic Arts Center Publishing Company (1992) ISBN 1558680764. Culture Shock series.

Sushil K. Naidu, *Nepal: Society and Culture,* South Asia Books (1999) ISBN 8185163936.

Omar Sattaur, *Nepal: New Horizons?* Oxfam Publications (1996) ISBN
    085598290X. Oxfam Country Profiles series.

NETHERLANDS

Charles Hampden-Turner and Alfons Trompenaars, *The Seven Cultures of
    Capitalism: Value Systems for Creating Wealth,* Doubleday (1993) ISBN
    038542101X. Excellent sociological study of national characters of France,
    Germany, Japan, Netherlands, Sweden, United Kingdom, and U.S.A.
Mark T. Hooker, *Simple Guide to Holland: Customs and Etiquette,* Paul Norbury
    (1997) ISBN 1860340857. Simple Guide series.
Hunt Janin, *Culture Shock: Netherlands,* Graphic Arts Center Publishing
    Company (1998) ISBN 155868400X. Culture Shock series.
Beverly Laflamme, *Living and Working in Belgium, Holland and Luxembourg,*
    Survival Books Ltd. (2001) ISBN 1901130266. Survival Handbook series.
Collin Randlesome, *Business Cultures in Europe,* 2d ed., Butterworth-Heinemann
    (1993) ISBN 0750608722.
Pat Rush, *Living & Working in the Netherlands: All You Need to Know for a
    Long or Short-Term Stay,* How to Books Ltd. (2001) ISBN 1857036077. How
    to series.
Jacob Vossestein, *Dealing With the Dutch: The Cultural Context of Business and
    Work in the Netherlands in the Early 21st Century,* rev. ed., Koninklijk
    Instituut voor de Tropen (Netherlands, 2001) ISBN 9068325639. "This new
    edition both follows the first in covering Dutch values and norms, and
    presents an up-dated picture of the latest economic, social and cultural
    changes in the country."
Colin White and Laurie Boucke, *The Undutchables: An Observation of the
    Netherlands, Its Culture and Its Inhabitants,* White Boucke Pub (2001) ISBN
    1888580224. "The Dutch are like the Scottish with the generosity beaten out
    of them."

NEW ZEALAND

Fiona McGregor and Charlotte Denny, *Live & Work in Australia and New
    Zealand,* Vacation-Work (1997) ISBN 1854581155. Practical advice.

NICARAGUA

Hazel Plunkett and Nick Caistor, *Nicaragua in Focus: A Guide to the People,
    Politics and Culture,* Interlink Publishing Group (2002) ISBN 1566564387. In
    Focus series.

NIGERIA

Yousef Dadoo, Valmond Ghyoot, Dan Lephoko, and Gerrie Lubbe, *Multicultural
    Sensitivity for Managers,* Tsebanang Group, Rant en Dal, South Africa (1997)
    ISBN 0620212586. Particularly strong on African cultures.

Toyin Falola, *Culture and Customs of Nigeria,* Greenwood Publishing Group (2000) ISBN 0313313385. Culture and Customs series.

Philip R. Harris and Robert T. Moran, *Managing Cultural Differences: Leadership Strategies for a New World of Business,* 5th ed., Gulf Professional Publishing Company (2000) ISBN 0877193452. Updated edition of one of the earliest books in the field.

NORTH KOREA. SEE KOREA.

NORWAY

Elizabeth Su-Dale, *Culture Shock: Norway,* Graphic Arts Center Publishing Company (1994) ISBN 1558681663. Culture Shock series.

OMAN

Abdulrahman Bin Ali Alhinai, *Ceremonies and Celebrations of Oman,* Garnet Publishing Ltd. (2000) ISBN 185964130X.

Calvin H. Allen, *Oman: The Modernization of the Sultanate,* Westview Press (1986) ISBN 0813301254.

Bruce Ingham and J. Fayadh, *Simple Guide to Arabia and the Gulf States: Customs & Etiquette,* Global Books Ltd. (2001) ISBN 1860340814. Simple Guide series.

PAKISTAN

Karen Mittman and Zafar Ihsam, *Culture Shock: Pakistan,* Graphic Arts Center Publishing Company (1991) ISBN 1558680594. Culture Shock series.

Khawar Mumtaz and Yameema Mitha, *Pakistan: Tradition and Change,* Oxfam Publications (1996) ISBN 0855983361. Oxfam Country Profiles series.

PALESTINE

Nava Bloch, *Culture Shock: Jerusalem at Your Door,* Graphic Arts Center Publishing Company (2002) ISBN 155868638X. Culture Shock series.

Samih K. Farsoun, *Palestine and the Palestinians,* Westview Press (1998) ISBN 0813327733. Offering "a sweeping social, economic, ideological, and political history of the Palestinian people from antiquity to the present."

PANAMA

Christopher Howard, *Living and Investing in the New Panama: A Guide to Living and Investing in the Panama of the New Millennium,* Costa Rica Books (2003) ISBN 188123312X.

Kenneth J. Jones, *Panama Now,* Focus Publications (2000) ISBN 9962551412. "The book is now in its fourth edition and has become a standard reference work, a top seller at bookstores and news stands throughout the Republic and sought-after by investors, scholars and travelers."

PAPUA NEW GUINEA

Laura Zimmer-Tamakoshi (Ed.), *Modern Papua New Guinea,* Truman State
University Press (1998) ISBN 0943549574. Academic treatment. "This
collection offers perspective and understanding into Papua New Guinea's
varied social scene and the challenging and economic realities of a recently
independent country."

PARAGUAY

Riordan Roett and Richard Scott Sacks, *Paraguay,* Westview Press (1991) ISBN
0865312729.

PERU

John Crabtree, *Peru,* Oxfam Publications (2003) ISBN 0855984821. Oxfam
Country Profiles series.
Henry F. Dobyns and Paul L. Doughty, *Peru: A Cultural History,* Oxford
University Press (1985) ISBN 0195020898.
Jane Holligan De Diaz-Limaco, *Peru in Focus: A Guide to the People, Politics
and Culture,* Interlink Publishing Group (1998) ISBN 1566562325. In Focus
series.
Cesar Ferreira and Eduardo Dargent Chamot, *Culture and Customs of Peru,*
Greenwood Publishing Group (2002) ISBN 0313303185. Culture and
Customs series.
Neil MacDonald (Ed.), *The Andes,* Stylus Publications (1993) ISBN 0855982004.
Oxfam Country Profiles series.

PHILIPPINES

James Fallows, *Looking at the Sun: The Rise of the New East Asian Economic
and Political System,* Pantheon Books (1994) ISBN 067942251X. Describes
new versions of capitalism that East Asian nations have developed to suit their
social milieux.
Luis Francia, *Passport Philippines,* World Trade Press (1997) ISBN 1885073402.
Passport Pocket series.
Joaquin L. Gonzales and Luis R. Calingo, *Success Secrets to Maximize Business in
the Philippines,* Graphic Arts Center Publishing Company (2000) ISBN
1558685405. Success Secrets series.
Charlie Pye-Smith, *The Philippines: In Search of Justice,* Oxfam Publications
(1997) ISBN 0855983671. Oxfam Country Profiles series.
Alfredo Roces, Grace Roces, and Shirley Eu, *Culture Shock: Philippines,* Graphic
Arts Center Publishing Company (1999) ISBN 1558686274. Culture Shock
series.
Paul A. Rodell, *Culture and Customs of the Philippines,* Greenwood Publishing
Group (2001) ISBN 0313304157. Culture and Customs series.

POLAND

Milford Bateman (Ed.), *Business Cultures in Central and Eastern Europe,* Butterworth-Heinemann (1996) ISBN 0750624809.

Clarke Canfield, *Now Hiring! Jobs in Eastern Europe: The Insider's Guide to Working and Living in the Czech Republic, Hungary, Poland, and Slovakia,* Perpetual Press (1996) ISBN 1881199622.

Philip R. Harris and Robert T. Moran, *Managing Cultural Differences: Leadership Strategies for a New World of Business,* 5th ed., Gulf Professional Publishing Company (2000) ISBN 0877193452. Updated edition of one of the earliest books in the field.

Natalie Kissel, *Passport Poland,* World Trade Press (1999) ISBN 188507333X. Passport Pocket series.

George Sanford, *Poland: The Conquest of History,* Routledge (1999) ISBN 9057023474. Postcommunist States and Nations series.

PORTUGAL

Sue Tyson-Ward, *Living and Working in Portugal: Staying in Portugal—All You Need to Know,* Trans-Atlantic Publications (2000) ISBN 1857035461. Practical information.

Sue Tyson-Ward, *Teach Yourself Portuguese Language, Life and Culture,* McGraw-Hill/Contemporary Books (2002) ISBN 0071396802. Teach Yourself series.

QATAR

Bruce Ingham and J. Fayadh, *Simple Guide to Arabia and the Gulf States: Customs & Etiquette,* Global Books Ltd. (2001) ISBN 1860340814. Simple Guide series.

Klaus Ferdinand, *Bedouins of Qatar,* Thames & Hudson (1993) ISBN 0813301254. A study of the Bedouin culture.

Stacey International, *Qatar,* Stacey International (2000) ISBN 0813301254. A country profile.

ROMANIA

Duncan Light and David Phinnemore (Eds.), *Post-Communist Romania: Coming to Terms With Transition,* Palgrave Macmillan (2001) ISBN 0333791878.

Steven D. Roper, *Romania: The Unfinished Revolution,* Routledge (2000) ISBN 9058230279. Postcommunist States and Nations series.

RUSSIA

Matthew Brzezinski, *Casino Moscow: A Tale of Greed and Adventure on Capitalism's Wildest Frontier,* Free Press (2001) ISBN 0684869764. Written by the nephew of Zbigniew Brzezinski.

Zita Dabars and Lilia Vokhmina, *The Russian Way,* NTC Publishing Group
(1995) ISBN 0844242969. NTC business series.

Sue Davis, *The Russian Far East: The Last Frontier,* Routledge (2002) ISBN
0415274257. Postcommunist States and Nations series.

Philip R. Harris and Robert T. Moran, *Managing Cultural Differences: Leadership
Strategies for a New World of Business,* 5th ed., Gulf Professional Publishing
Company (2000) ISBN 0877193452. Updated edition of one of the earliest
books in the field.

David E. Hoffman, *The Oligarchs: Wealth & Power in the New Russia,* Public
Affairs (2002) ISBN 1586480014. Offers a "descriptive volume that illumi-
nates current Russian politics and finance."

Nigel Holden, Cary L. Cooper, Jennifer Carr, and George Wright, *Dealing with
the New Russia: Management Cultures in Collision,* John Wiley & Sons
(1998) ISBN 0471964565.

Charles Mitchell and Barbara Szerlip, *Passport Russia,* World Trade Press (date
unknown) ISBN 1885073321. Passport Pocket series.

Yale Richmond, *From Nyet to Da: Understanding the Russians,* Intercultural
Press (1996) ISBN 1877864412. Interact series.

Neil Robinson, *Russia: A State of Uncertainty,* Routledge (2001) ISBN
0415271134. Postcommunist States and Nations series.

Sydney Schultze, *Culture and Customs of Russia,* Greenwood Publishing Group
(2000) ISBN 0313311013. Culture and Customs series.

Irene Slatter, *Simple Guide to Russia: Customs & Etiquette,* Paul Norbury (2000)
ISBN 1860340415. Simple Guide series.

Mikk Titma, Nancy Brandon Tuma, *Modern Russia,* McGraw-Hill (2000) ISBN
0072928239. Comparative Societies series.

Paul Wayne and Maria Wayne, *Culture Shock: Moscow at Your Door,* Graphic Arts
Center Publishing Company (2002) ISBN 1558686274. Culture Shock series.

Tatyana Webber and Stephen L. Webber, *Teach Yourself Russian Language, Life
and Culture,* 2d ed., McGraw-Hill/Contemporary Books (1999) ISBN
1877864587. Teach Yourself series.

Drew Wilson and Lloyd Donaldson, *Russian Etiquette and Ethics in Business,*
NTC Publishing Group (1996) ISBN 0844242160.

RWANDA

David Waller, *Rwanda: Which Way Now?* Oxfam Publications (1993) ISBN
0855982179. Oxfam Country Profiles series.

SAUDI ARABIA

Jeri Elliott, *Your Door to Arabia,* Kenneth Jolly (1992) ISBN 0473015463.
Lifestyle and etiquette.

Philip R. Harris and Robert T. Moran, *Managing Cultural Differences: Leadership
Strategies for a New World of Business,* 5th ed., Gulf Professional Publishing
Company (2000) ISBN 0877193452. Updated edition of one of the earliest
books in the field.

Bruce Ingham and J. Fayadh, *Simple Guide to Arabia and the Gulf States: Customs & Etiquette,* Global Books Ltd. (2001) ISBN 1860340814. Simple Guide series.

Sandra MacKey, *The Saudis: Inside the Desert Kingdom,* reprint, W. W. Norton & Company (2002) ISBN 0393324176. "A rare first-hand glimpse into the hidden realm of Saudi social and public life . . . Reprint of the 1987 hardcover edition . . ."

Andrew Mead, *Saudi Arabia: Business Travellers' Handbook,* Stacey International (2002) ISBN 1903185033.

Rosalie Rayburn and Kathleen Bush, *Living & Working in Saudi Arabia: How to Prepare for a Successful Short or Longterm Stay,* How to Books Ltd. (1997) ISBN 1857031520. How to series.

Hani A. Z. Yamani, *To Be a Saudi,* Paul & Company Publishing Consortium (1998) ISBN 1857563034. Sympathetic but critical look at Saudi society, covering history, Islam, the royal family, and oil.

SENEGAL

Robin Sharp, *Senegal: A State of Change,* Oxfam Publications (1994) ISBN 0855982837. Oxfam Country Profiles series.

SERBIA (FORMERLY YUGOSLAVIA)

Tim Judah, *The Serbs: History, Myth and the Destruction of Yugoslavia,* Yale University Press (2000) ISBN 0300085079. "Judah convincingly argues that Serbian nationalism is an outgrowth of the Serbs' own sufferings as victims of ethnic cleansing in past conflicts."

SINGAPORE

JoAnn Meriwether Craig, *Culture Shock: Singapore,* Graphic Arts Center Publishing Company (2002) ISBN 1558686282. Culture Shock series.

James Fallows, *Looking at the Sun: The Rise of the New East Asian Economic and Political System,* Pantheon Books (1994) ISBN 067942251X. Describes new versions of capitalism that East Asian nations have developed to suit their social milieux.

Alexandra Kett, *Passport Singapore,* World Trade Press (date unknown) ISBN 1885073380. Passport Pocket series.

Paul A. Leppert, *Doing Business With Singapore,* Jain Publishing (1997) ISBN 0875730426.

Audrey Perera, *Simple Guide to Customs & Etiquette in Singapore,* Paul Norbury (1998) ISBN 1860340407. Simple Guide series.

Sterling Seagrave, *Lords of the Rim: The Invisible Empire of the Overseas Chinese,* G. P. Putnam's Sons (1995) ISBN 0399140115. Readable account of economic role of expatriate Chinese, with historical depth.

Tracey Wilen and Patricia Wilen, *Asia for Women on Business: Hong Kong, Taiwan, Singapore, and South Korea,* Stone Bridge Press (1995) ISBN 1880656175.

SLOVAKIA

Clarke Canfield, *Now Hiring! Jobs in Eastern Europe: The Insider's Guide to Working and Living in the Czech Republic, Hungary, Poland, and Slovakia,* Perpetual Press (1996) ISBN 1881199622. "[This book] provides the most current information about life and work in the Eastern European countries."

Karen Henderson, *Slovakia,* Routledge (2002) ISBN 0415274362. Postcommunist States and Nations series.

SLOVENIA

Milford Bateman (Ed.), *Business Cultures in Central and Eastern Europe,* Butterworth-Heinemann (1996) ISBN 0750624809.

Bogomil Ferfila and Paul Arthur Phillips, *Slovenia: On the Edge of the European Union,* University Press of America (2000) ISBN 0761816623. The book discusses "Slovenia's transition from a socialist self-managed economy to a social market economy, its approach to Europe, and consequent transformation of its economic institutions."

SOMALIA

Mohamed Diriye Abdullahi, *Culture and Customs of Somalia,* Greenwood Publishing Group (2001) ASIN 0313313334. Culture and Customs series.

SOUTH AFRICA

Yousef Dadoo, Valmond Ghyoot, Dan Lephoko, and Gerrie Lubbe, *Multicultural Sensitivity for Managers,* Tsebanang Group, Rant en Dal, South Africa (1997) ISBN 0620212586. Particularly strong on African cultures.

Phillip T. Gay, *Modern South Africa,* McGraw-Hill (2001) ISBN 0072352116. Comparative Societies series.

Philip R. Harris and Robert T. Moran, *Managing Cultural Differences: Leadership Strategies for a New World of Business,* 5th ed., Gulf Professional Publishing Company (2000) ISBN 0877193452. Updated edition of one of the earliest books in the field.

Charles Mitchell and Barbara Szerlip, *Passport South Africa,* World Trade Press (1998) ISBN 1885073194. Passport Pocket series.

Dee Rissik, *Culture Shock: South Africa,* Graphic Arts Center Publishing Company (1993) ISBN 1558681493. Culture Shock series.

Matthew Seal, *Living & Working in South Africa: Survive and Thrive in the New South Africa,* How to Books Ltd. (date unknown) ISBN 1857035550. How to series.

SOUTH KOREA. SEE KOREA.

SPAIN

Helen Wattley Ames, *Spain Is Different,* Intercultural Press (1999) ISBN 1877864714. Interact series.

Kevin Bruton, *The Business Culture in Spain,* Butterworth-Heinemann (1994) ISBN 0750618310. "Understanding the beliefs, attitudes, and values that underpin commercial activities . . . may be more important for doing business there than understanding the language."

Mark Cramer, *Culture Shock: Barcelona at Your Door,* Graphic Arts Center Publishing Company (2002) ISBN 1558686126. Culture Shock series.

Marie Louise Graff, *Culture Shock: Spain,* Graphic Arts Center Publishing Company (1992) ISBN 1558686304. Culture Shock series.

David Hampshire, *Living and Working in Spain: A Survival Handbook,* Survival Books (2000) ISBN 1901130509. Survival Handbook series.

Peggy Kenna and Sondra Lacy, *Business Spain: A Practical Guide to Understanding Spanish Business Culture,* Passport Books, NTC Publishing Group (1995) ISBN 0844235636. NTC business series.

Judith Noble and Jaime Lacasa, *The Hispanic Way,* McGraw-Hill/Contemporary Books (1990) ISBN 0844273899. McGraw-Hill series. Also applies to Hispanic regions of Latin America.

Himilce Novas, *Passport Spain,* World Trade Press (1997) ISBN 1885073356. Passport Pocket series.

Collin Randlesome, *Business Cultures in Europe,* 2d ed., Butterworth-Heinemann (1993) ISBN 0750608722.

Edward F. Stanton, *Culture and Customs of Spain,* Greenwood Publishing Group (2002) ISBN 0313314632. Culture and Customs series.

Mike Zollo and Phil Turk, *Teach Yourself Spanish Language, Life, & Culture,* McGraw-Hill/Contemporary Books (2000) ISBN 0658008986. Teach Yourself series.

SRI LANKA

Robert Barlas and Nanda Wanasundera, *Culture Shock: Sri Lanka,* Graphic Arts Center Publishing Company (1991) ISBN 1558685022. Culture Shock series. The factional violence has subsided since the publication of this volume.

Douglas Bullis, *Succeed in Business Sri Lanka,* Graphic Arts Center Publishing Company (1997) ISBN 1558683208. Succeed in Business series.

SUDAN

Chris Peters, *Sudan: A Nation in the Balance,* Oxfam Publications (1996) ISBN 0855983167. Oxfam Country Profiles series.

SWEDEN

Ake Daun, *Swedish Mentality,* Pennsylvania State University Press (1996) ISBN 0271015020. "Covering everything from child-rearing to academia, [the author] sheds considerable insight into Swedish culture. . . ."

Christina Johansson Robinowitz and Lisa Werner Carr, *Modern-Day Vikings: A Practical Guide to Interacting with the Swedes,* Intercultural Press (2001) ISBN 1877864889. Interact series.

Charlotte Rosen Svensson, *Culture Shock Sweden,* Graphic Arts Center Publishing Company (1997) ISBN 1558682996. Culture Shock series.

SWITZERLAND

Aldo Albert Benini, *Modern Switzerland,* McGraw-Hill (1998) ISBN 0070344272. Comparative Societies series.

Shirley Eu-Wong, *Culture Shock: Switzerland,* Graphic Arts Center Publishing Company (1995) ISBN 1558682481. Culture Shock series.

Michael Wells Glueck, *Living Among the Swiss,* Author's Choice Press (2002) ISBN 0595241719. Combination of travel guide and lightweight cultural commentary.

David Hampshire, *Living and Working in Switzerland: A Survival Handbook,* Survival Books (2000) ISBN 1901130169. Survival Handbook series.

Francois Micheloud, *Passport Switzerland,* World Trade Press (2001) ISBN 1885073887. Passport Pocket series.

Jonathan Steinberg, *Why Switzerland?* Cambridge University Press (1996) ISBN 0521484537. Offering "a unique analysis of the structures that make Switzerland work and provides a short, concise 'working model' for the visitor or student."

SYRIA

Coleman South, *Culture Shock: Syria,* Graphic Arts Center Publishing Company (2001) ISBN 1558686118. Culture Shock series.

TAIWAN

Christopher Bates, *Culture Shock: Taiwan,* Graphic Arts Center Publishing Company (1995) ISBN 1558681752. Culture Shock series.

Kevin Chambers, *Succeed in Business Taiwan,* Graphic Arts Center Publishing Company (1999) ISBN 1558684212. Succeed in Business series.

Jeffrey E. Curry and Barbara Szerlip, *Passport Taiwan,* World Trade Press (1997) ISBN 1885073275. Passport Pocket series.

Gary Marvin Davison and Barbara E. Reed, *Culture and Customs of Taiwan,* Greenwood Publishing Group (1998) ISBN 0313302987. Culture and Customs series.

James Fallows, *Looking at the Sun: The Rise of the New East Asian Economic and Political System,* Pantheon Books (1994) ISBN 067942251X. Describes new versions of capitalism that East Asian nations have developed to suit their social milieux.

Francis Fukuyama, *Trust: The Social Virtues and the Creation of Prosperity,* Free Press (1995) ISBN 0029109760. This book identifies cultural factors that influence prosperity. Descriptions of particular countries are well done (i.e., China, France, Germany, Southern Italy, Japan, Korea, Taiwan, U.S.A.).

Peggy Kenna and Sondra Lacy, *Business Taiwan: A Practical Guide to Understanding Taiwan's Business Culture,* Passport Books, NTC Publishing Group (1994) ISBN 0844235539. NTC business series.

George C. Lodge and Ezra F. Vogel (Eds.), *Ideology and National Competitiveness: An Analysis of Nine Countries,* Harvard Business School Press (1987) ISBN 0875841473.

Tracey Wilen and Patricia Wilen, *Asia for Women on Business: Hong Kong, Taiwan, Singapore, and South Korea,* Stone Bridge Press (1995) ISBN 1880656175.

THAILAND

Paulson Ching, *Doing Business in East Asia: A Practical Guide to China, Indonesia, Malaysia and Thailand,* Pelanduk Publications (1999) ISBN 9679784924.

Robert Cooper and Nanthapa Cooper, *Culture Shock: Thailand,* Graphic Arts Center Publishing Company (1991) ISBN 1558680586. Culture Shock series.

James Fallows, *Looking at the Sun: The Rise of the New East Asian Economic and Political System,* Pantheon Books (1994) ISBN 067942251X. Describes new versions of capitalism that East Asian nations have developed to suit their social milieux.

John P. Fieg, *A Common Core: Thais and Americans,* Intercultural Press (1989) ISBN 0933662807. Interact series.

Visnu Kongsiri, Derek Tonkin and Arene Sanderson, *The Simple Guide to Thailand: Customs & Etiquette,* Paul Norbury (1998) ISBN 1860340261. Simple Guide series.

Paul Leppert, *Doing Business with Thailand,* Jain Publishing (1992) ISBN 0875730442. Provides some information on customs and culture at the beginning of the book.

Robert Slagter and Harold R. Kerbo, *Modern Thailand,* McGraw-Hill (1999) ISBN 0070344280. Comparative Societies series.

Bea Toews and Robert McGregor, *Success Secrets to Maximize Business in Thailand,* Graphic Arts Center Publishing Company (2000) ISBN 1558685413. Success Secrets series.

Naomi Wise, *Passport Thailand,* World Trade Press (1998) ISBN 1885073194. Passport Pocket series.

TURKEY

Arin Bayraktroglu, *Culture Shock: Turkey,* Graphic Arts Center Publishing Company (2002) ISBN 1558686126. Culture Shock series.

UGANDA

Ian Leggett, *Uganda,* Oxfam Publications (2001) ISBN 0855984546. Oxfam Country Profiles series.

UKRAINE

Meredith Dalton, *Culture Shock: Ukraine,* Graphic Arts Center Publishing (2001)
    ISBN 1558686320. Culture Shock series.
Marta Dyczok, *Ukraine: Movement without Change, Change without Movement,*
    Routledge (2000) ISBN 9058230252. Postcommunist States and Nations
    series.
Andrew Wilson, *The Ukrainians: Unexpected Nation,* Yale University Press
    (2000) ISBN 0300083556. Current cultural and political situation in historical
    context.

UNITED ARAB EMIRATES

Gina L. Crocetti, *Culture Shock: United Arab Emirates,* Graphic Arts Center
    Publishing Company (2002) ISBN 1558686339. Culture Shock series.
Bruce Ingham and J. Fayadh, *Simple Guide to Arabia and the Gulf States:
    Customs & Etiquette,* Global Books Ltd. (2001) ISBN 1860340814. Simple
    Guide series.
Peggy Kenna and Sondra Lacy, *Business U.K.: A Practical Guide to Understand-
    ing British Business Culture,* Passport Books, NTC Publishing Group (1995)
    ISBN 0844235601. NTC business series.
Malcolm C. Peck, *The United Arab Emirates: A Venture in Unity,* Westview Press
    (1986) ISBN 0865311889.

UNITED KINGDOM

Julie Brake and Christine Jones, *Teach Yourself Welsh Language, Life, and
    Culture,* McGraw-Hill/Contemporary Books (2002) ISBN 0071407227.
    Teach Yourself series.
Anne Fraenkel, Richard Haill, and Seamus ORiordan, *Teach Yourself English
    Language, Life, and Culture,* McGraw-Hill/Contemporary Books (2002)
    ISBN 0071407146. Teach Yourself series.
James Grant, *Culture Shock: Scotland,* Graphic Arts Center Publishing Company
    (2002) ISBN 155868607X. Culture Shock series.
Charles Hampden-Turner and Alfons Trompenaars, *The Seven Cultures of
    Capitalism: Value Systems for Creating Wealth,* Doubleday (1993) ISBN
    038542101X. Excellent sociological study of national characters of France,
    Germany, Japan, Netherlands, Sweden, United Kingdom, and U.S.A.
David Hampshire, *Living and Working in Britain: A Survival Handbook,* Survival
    Books (1999) ISBN 1901130509. Survival Handbook series.
Orin Hargraves, *Culture Shock: London at Your Door,* Graphic Arts Center
    Publishing Company (2001) ISBN 1558686231. Culture Shock series.
Timothy Harper, *Passport United Kingdom,* World Trade Press (1996) ISBN
    1885073283. Passport Pocket series.
Philip R. Harris and Robert T. Moran, *Managing Cultural Differences: Leadership
    Strategies for a New World of Business,* 5th ed., Gulf Professional Publishing
    Company (2000) ISBN 0877193452. Updated edition of one of the earliest
    books in the field.

Peter Hobday, *Simple Guide to England: Customs & Etiquette*, Paul Norbury (1999) ISBN 1860340369. Simple Guides series.

Ewart James, *NTC's Dictionary of the United Kingdom: The Most Practical Guide to British Language and Culture*, McGraw-Hill–NTC (1997) ISBN 0844258563. Defines cultural concepts.

George C. Lodge and Ezra F. Vogel (Eds.), *Ideology and National Competitiveness: An Analysis of Nine Countries*, Harvard Business School Press (1987) ISBN 0875841473.

Janet MacDonald, *Living and Working in London*, Survival Books (2000) ISBN 1901130118. Survival Handbook series.

Peter North, *Success Secrets to Maximize Business in Britain*, Graphic Arts Center Publishing Company (2000) ISBN 1558684816. Success Secrets series.

Terry Tan, *Culture Shock: Britain*, Graphic Arts Center Publishing Company (2000) ISBN 1558680616. Culture Shock series.

UNITED STATES OF AMERICA

Robert N. Bellah, Richard Madsen, William M. Sullivan, Ann Swidler, and Steven M. Tipton, *Habits of the Heart: Individualism and Commitment in American Life*, Harper & Row (1985) ISBN 0060970278. Role of individualism versus community in the U.S.A. Title is a phrase of Alexis de Tocqueville.

Mark Cramer, *Culture Shock: California*, Graphic Arts Center Publishing Company (1997) ISBN 1558683615. Culture Shock series.

Mark Cramer, *Culture Shock: New York at Your Door*, Graphic Arts Center Publishing Company (1999) ISBN 1558685022. Culture Shock series.

Dean W. Engel, *Passport USA*, World Trade Press (1996) ISBN 1885073151. Passport Pocket series.

Francis Fukuyama, *Trust: The Social Virtues and the Creation of Prosperity*, Free Press (1995) ISBN 0029109760. Prosperity depends on cultural factors. Descriptions of particular countries are well done (i.e., China, France, Germany, Southern Italy, Japan, Korea, Taiwan, U.S.A.).

Charles Hampden-Turner and Alfons Trompenaars, *The Seven Cultures of Capitalism: Value Systems for Creating Wealth*, Doubleday (1993) ISBN 038542101X. Excellent sociological study of national characters of France, Germany, Japan, Netherlands, Sweden, United Kingdom, and U.S.A.

David Hampshire, *Living and Working in America: A Survival Handbook*, Survival Books (1998) ISBN 1901130452. Survival Handbook series.

Orin Hargraves, *Culture Shock: Chicago at Your Door*, Graphic Arts Center Publishing Company (1999) ISBN 1558684247. Culture Shock series.

Philip R. Harris and Robert T. Moran, *Managing Cultural Differences: Leadership Strategies for a New World of Business*, 5th ed., Gulf Professional Publishing Company (2000) ISBN 0877193452. Updated edition of one of the earliest books in the field.

Jennifer Phillips, *In the Know in the USA: An Indispensable Cross-Cultural Guide to Working and Living Abroad*, Living Language (2003) ISBN 0609611135. In the Know series.

David M. Thomas (Ed.), *Canada and the United States: Differences that Count,* 2d ed., Broadview Press (2000) ISBN 1551112523. Contains section titled "Social and Cultural Foundations."

Alexis de Tocqueville, *Democracy in America,* ed. Harvey C. Mansfield, trans. Delba Winthrop, University of Chicago Press (2000) ISBN 0226805328. Originally published in 1835, but remains the definitive study of U.S. culture.

Esther Wanning, *Culture Shock: USA,* Graphic Arts Center Publishing Company (1991) ISBN 1558680551. Culture Shock series.

Jane Koen Winter, *Culture Shock USA—The South,* Graphic Arts Center Publishing Company (1996) ISBN 1558682465. Culture Shock series.

URUGUAY

Martin Weinstein, *Uruguay: Democracy at the Crossroads,* Westview Press (1988) ISBN 0865312907.

VENEZUELA

Kitt Baguley, *Culture Shock: Venezuela,* Graphic Arts Center Publishing Company (2000) ISBN 1558685014. Culture Shock series.

Mark Dinneen, *Culture and Customs of Venezuela,* Greenwood Publishing Group (2001) ISBN 0313306397. Culture and Customs series.

Daniel Charles Hellinger, *Venezuela: Tarnished Democracy,* Westview Press (1991) ISBN 0813307007.

VIETNAM

Kevin Chambers, *Succeed in Business Vietnam,* Graphic Arts Center Publishing Company (1997) ISBN 0558683577. Succeed in Business series.

Jeffrey Curry and "Jim" Chinh Nguyen, *Passport Vietnam,* World Trade Press (1997) ISBN 1885073259. Passport Pocket series.

Claire Ellis, *Culture Shock: Vietnam,* Graphic Arts Center Publishing Company (1995) ISBN 1558682422. Culture Shock series.

Christopher Engholm, *Doing Business in the New Vietnam: For Investors, Marketers, and Entrepreneurs,* Prentice Hall Trade (1995) ISBN 013325853X. Includes communication, negotiation, and etiquette.

James Fallows, *Looking at the Sun: The Rise of the New East Asian Economic and Political System,* Pantheon Books (1994) ISBN 067942251X. Describes new versions of capitalism that East Asian nations have developed to suit their social milieux.

Mark W. McLeod and Nguyen Thi Dieu, *Culture and Customs of Vietnam,* Greenwood Publishing Group (2001) ISBN 0313304858. Culture and Customs series.

Geoffrey Murray, *The Simple Guide to Vietnam Customs & Etiquette,* Paul Norbury (1997) ISBN 1860340903. Simple Guide series.

James W. Robinson, *Doing Business in Vietnam,* Prima Publishing (1994) ISBN 1559585919. Offers some cultural advice and tips on etiquette.

YEMEN

Paul Dresch, *A History of Modern Yemen,* Cambridge University Press (2001) ISBN 052179482X. Focuses on recent history, since the founding of the state in 1990.

Bruce Ingham and J. Fayadh, *Simple Guide to Arabia and the Gulf States: Customs & Etiquette,* Global Books Ltd. (2001) ISBN 1860340814. Simple Guide series.

Manfred W. Wenner, The *Yemen Arab Republic: Development and Change in an Ancient Land,* Westview Press (1991) ISBN 0891587748.

ZIMBABWE

Oyekan Owomoyela, *Culture and Customs of Zimbabwe,* Greenwood Publishing Group (2002) ISBN 0313315833. Culture and Customs series.

Robin Palmer and Isobel Birch, *Zimbabwe: A Land Divided,* Oxfam Publications (1992) ISBN 0855981784. Oxfam Country Profiles series.

Index